The Althouse Press
Faculty of Education, The University of Western Ontario
*Singleton and Varpalotai*, STONES IN THE SNEAKER:
ACTIVE THEORY FOR SECONDARY SCHOOL
PHYSICAL AND HEALTH EDUCATORS

# STONES IN THE SNEAKER

## ACTIVE THEORY FOR SECONDARY SCHOOL PHYSICAL AND HEALTH EDUCATORS

Edited by
Ellen Singleton and Aniko Varpalotai

**THE ALTHOUSE PRESS**

First published in Canada in 2006 by
THE ALTHOUSE PRESS
Dean: *Allen Pearson*
Director of Publications: *Greg Dickinson*
Faculty of Education, The University of Western Ontario
1137 Western Road, London, Ontario, Canada  N6G 1G7

Editors: *Greg Dickinson, Staci Rae, and Geoffrey Milburn*
Editorial Assistant: *Katherine Butson*
Cover Design: *Lois Armstrong*

Library and Archives Canada Cataloguing in Publication

Stones in the sneaker : active theory for secondary school physical and health educators / edited by Ellen Singleton and Aniko T. Varpalotai.

Includes bibliographical references.
ISBN 0-920354-56-4

1. Physical education and training—Study and teaching (Secondary) 2. Inclusive education. I. Singleton, Ellen, 1948- II. Varpalotai, Aniko Theresa, 1958-

GV361.S86 2006          613.7'071'2          C2005-907280-6

Printed and bound in Canada by Hignell Book Printing Ltd., 488 Burnell Street, Winnipeg, Manitoba, Canada  R3G 2B4

# Contents

Acknowledgements                                                                 i

Foreword                                                                        iii
    *Nancy Melnychuk*

Preface                                                                         ix
    *Ellen Singleton and Aniko Varpalotai*

Chapter One                                                                      1
    "Listening for a Change": Understanding the Experiences
    of Students in Physical Education
    *M. Louise Humbert*

Chapter Two                                                                     27
    Health Literacy
    *Andy Anderson and David Booth*

Chapter Three                                                                   43
    "This Is the Kind of Experience I Plan to Encourage":
    Competition and Fair Play in High School Physical Education
    *Ellen Singleton*

Chapter Four                                                                    71
    Eastern and Western Approaches to Physical
    and Health Education
    *Chunlei Lu*

Chapter Five                                                                    87
    "Dancing Is for Sissies!"
    *Marnie Rutledge*

Chapter Six                                                                    101
    The Role of Family Studies in Comprehensive School Health
    *Laura Tryssenaar*

Chapter Seven                                                                  119
    Researching Perceptions of Physical Education Classes
    *Joanne Y. Pelletier*

Chapter Eight                                                                  139
    "Look at That Cow Over There": Sexual Harassment
    and Shaming of Adolescent Girls in High School
    Physical Education
    *Helen Jefferson Lenskyj and Cheryl van Daalen*

Chapter Nine                                                       155
    Developing a White Race-Consciousness: A Foundation for
    Culturally Relevant Physical Education for Aboriginal Youth
    *Joannie Halas*

Chapter Ten                                                        183
    Through Another Looking Glass: Gender, Social Issues,
    and the Media Impact on Body Image
    *Jennifer D. Irwin and Patricia Tucker*

Chapter Eleven                                                     203
    Rural Schools/Rural Communities: Partnerships Between
    Physical and Health Educators and Public Health Nurses
    *Aniko Varpalotai and Beverly D. Leipert*

Chapter Twelve                                                     223
    The Experience of Disability in Physical Education
    *Donna L. Goodwin, Paul Gustafson, and Brianne N. Hamilton*

Chapter Thirteen                                                   255
    Masculinity in Physical Education: Socialization of
    New Recruits
    *Tim Hopper and Kathy Sanford*

Chapter Fourteen                                                   277
    Teaching Within the Law: Liability for Physical Harm and
    the Need for Proper Risk Management
    *Gregory M. Dickinson*

Chapter Fifteen                                                    303
    Teaching Within the Law: The Human Rights Context
    of Physical and Health Education
    *Gregory M. Dickinson*

# *Acknowledgements*

It has been through the contributions of a small army of people that this book has been produced. We would like to acknowledge and thank the following people for helping to make this dream of ours a reality: The Althouse Press Publications Committee; the diligent editorial team of Dr. Greg Dickinson, Dr. Geoff Milburn, Katherine Butson, Staci Rae, and Dianne Nemcek; Lois Armstrong, Supervisor of the Media Centre at the Faculty of Education at The University of Western Ontario, who created the cover art for this book; our knowledgeable, critical, and very helpful external reviewers; all of our scholarly chapter contributors, many of whom are recognized as international experts in their fields of study in health and physical education. We are indeed fortunate to be able to gather these authors together in this book. We gratefully acknowledge the support of our colleagues within the Council of University Professors and Researchers (CUPR), the University Affairs section of the Canadian Association for Health, Physical Education, Recreation and Dance (CAHPERD), who continue to advocate for high-quality physical and health education at all levels of education and research. Finally, we acknowledge the contribution of our students, whose inquiring minds and enthusiasm to get on with the job make our teaching experiences so challenging and enjoyable.

Ellen Singleton and Aniko Varpalotai

# *Foreword*

I invite you to approach this book with an open mind, as you listen to the voices of students, student teachers, professionals, and teacher educators who examine and question the status of physical education and health education today. The fifteen chapters present thought-provoking and sometimes disturbing insights into controversial issues challenging individuals, schools, and communities. An underlying theme of inclusion and social justice permeates every chapter, as issues of ethnicity, culture, gender, class, sexuality, and (dis)ability are addressed in relation to physical (in)activity, physical education, and health education. These common threads inconspicuously weave the chapters together as the authors discuss social constructs and constraints, inequities, empowerment, traditional sport, competition and male dominance, marginalization, stereotyping, the objectified body, body image, and body-mind relationships. They explore the relationships between teachers and students, schools and communities, teachers and other professionals, health and physical education, health and family studies, literacy and movement, dance and physical education, and physical and health education as they relate to the law. The experts voice a need for holistic approaches that incorporate and integrate, not separate and isolate, and for partnerships within physical education and health programs in schools and the community, and within teacher preparation programs.

You will be mindfully engaged as you consider how these problematic topics are integral to becoming a physical education or health education teacher. You will find yourself reflecting upon your own life history, your experiences as a student in physical education classes, as an athlete or non-athlete in the school and community, as a preservice teacher, an in-service teacher, a coach, and perhaps also as a teacher educator. Knowledge gained from each chapter will prompt you to revisit your beliefs and practices and to ponder ways in which to contribute to a renewed vision of physical and health education that meets the demands and expectations of today's youth. Each author will enhance your understanding of pertinent issues and alternative solutions, and will, either subtly or overtly, engender a passion within you to confront the challenges and to make a difference.

Chapter One alerts us to the concerns of students in a physical education learning environment, many of which are reiterated in subsequent chapters. Humbert reminds us of the importance of listening to students who suggest that "fun"—being physically active in an inclusive environment—is the most important thing in physical education class. She challenges physical educators to "make waves" because students' health depends on our commitment to making a difference. "School physical education classes offer the best opportunities to positively influence the patterns of children and youth," she advises.

In Chapter Two, Anderson and Booth ask that you consider health literacy, among other things, as heuristic inquiry, enabling you to search internally and to actively/reflectively engage your total self in contemplating the issues that emerge in the rest of the chapters. From the understanding the authors provide concerning the experience of health literacy "as a form of mindfulness," you will become more conscious of health as a way of looking at the world, and of seeing it in terms of your own life. As you come to better understand what it means to be healthy, you will be better enabled to assist youth in "living up to their full potential as human beings." Health is a critical and necessary literacy for full participation as a human being in society.

Although competition has traditionally been an integral component of high school physical education, Singleton urges you in Chapter Three to question its presence in, and relationship to, fair play. She states that the place and role of competition have been "ignored" and left "unexamined"; but, in this chapter she prods you to think about its place and influence in both male and female physical education classes as a gendered, socially constructed concept.

In Chapter Four, Lu presents an insightful contribution to cross-cultural dialogue at both a practical and theoretical level as he discusses the differences between Eastern and Western approaches to physical and health education, the causes of these differences, a rationale for integrating Eastern approaches into Western physical and health education, and ways to implement this integration. He asks that you question, from both the Eastern and Western perspectives, the body-mind relationship prevalent in physical and health education.

In Chapter Five, Rutledge stresses the importance of "the somatic, moving sense experience" of dance, with its potential to develop feeling, expressive bodies in contrast to the learning of functional movement, which traditionally dominates physical education programs. She asks where the "experience of dance" does and should fit within the discipline of physical education.

Tryssenaar explains in Chapter Six how family studies and health and physical education are complementary, sharing similar challenges and sensitive issues in improving students' health and well-being. A detailed comparison between family studies and health and physical education curricula in relation to comprehensive school health issues presents a strong case for the inclusion of family studies in physical and health education and collaboration among those teaching in the two areas.

Pelletier and her student teachers provide insights into planning appropriate units by listening to one's students. In Chapter Seven, they present factors that affect female students' negative perceptions of the physical education learning environment and suggest that these are also typical of many less-skilled males. Their findings reinforce other authors' discussions of inequities and the ways in which students are marginalized in physical education. The student teachers' experience as researchers positively contributed to their interest and confidence in undertaking further research and pursuing lifelong professional development.

Lenskyj and Van Daalen, in Chapter Eight, claim that the emphasis on competition and the unwelcoming climate in many physical education programs lead to high drop-out rates for female students from physical education programs. According to adolescent girls, the struggle for gender equality and equity remains a concern, as prejudices toward body size, shape, and weight, skill level, and sexual orientation still prevail.

In Chapter Nine, Halas advocates a need for culturally sensitive and relevant curricula in light of an ever-increasingly diverse cultural student body in physical education classes. She examines the challenges and inequities of racism, with its negative impact on aboriginal students' experiences of physical education. She urges educators to develop relationships with aboriginal youth so they will "fit in" and want to actively participate in physical activity programs in the community and physical education programs at school. Otherwise, these students will not lead active, healthy lifestyles, now or in the future.

In Chapter Ten, Irwin and Tucker explore the concept of body image, the differential experiences of males and females, the influence of the media and social groups on body image, and provide an overview of disordered eating, and suggestions for promoting positive body image among young adults. They explain how the media endorses images and standards that are impossible to achieve and claim that the "idealized physical appearance in the media is taking its toll on young people." They recommend that we invest time and energy into how we ought to treat ourselves rather than focusing on how we ought to look.

Varpalotai and Leipert explore in Chapter Eleven "the mutual challenges and benefits for both educators and public health nurses in rural schools and communities." They discuss numerous insightful possibilities in extending the community school model to incorporate health care, and describe ways in which teachers and public health nurses can work together to effectively promote appropriate health care.

In Chapter Twelve, Goodwin, Gustafson, and Hamilton discuss the importance of teacher-student relationships in defining inclusive physical education. They suggest that the needs of teachers, as well as those of students, be placed in the equation of inclusive education; "rather than the child [with a disability] getting ready for the class, the regular class gets ready for the student with a disability." The teacher's perceived competence equates to a positive attitude which, in turn, tends to result in a more inclusive environment. The authors argue the importance of developing this competence within a teacher education program so that preservice teachers come to know that an ecological approach to instruction that incorporates individualized instruction, student choice, collaborative decision making, and adaptive devices—and not the curriculum or activities—will accommodate diverse student needs.

Issues of hegemonic masculinity, which have pervaded generations of physical education discourse and practice, are highlighted by Hopper and Sanford in Chapter Thirteen. The authors examine the impact of the dominance of male role models and the gendered valuing of coach/teacher characteristics on the professional development of preservice teachers and "effective" teaching. They question the socialization of physical education teachers who "draw dominantly from an exclusive coaching orientation rather [than] from a more inclusive teaching orientation," which has far-reaching implications for teaching and learning.

The final two chapters address legal issues related to teaching physical education. In Chapter Fourteen, Dickinson examines "tort, and even criminal, liability for accidents and the need for appropriate risk management that mirrors the legal principles of negligence." By citing particular cases, he highlights the physical and legal dimensions of risk that can be controlled through proper risk-management strategies to help reduce or eliminate risk and the potential loss of life or serious injury. Dickinson considers several human rights dimensions of teaching physical and health education in Chapter Fifteen. He discusses, for example, accommodation of students with disabilities, of those whose beliefs and practices may collide with curricular content, and of those who may be experiencing harassment within the learning environment, as well as accommodation of the teacher's right to speak about his or her sexual orientation.

In closing, I would like to thank the editors, Ellen Singleton and Aniko Varpalotai, for their foresight in recognizing a need for a book focused on critical issues facing physical and health education teachers and teacher educators in Canada today. No doubt you will recognize differences between *Stones in the Sneaker* and a typical curriculum and instruction text—you will experience an authentic connectedness as you read this book. Your inspiration, understanding, and commitment will lead to improved physical and health education programs in schools, and teacher education programs in universities which, in turn, will assist youth to lead more physically active and healthier lives.

Nancy Melnychuk

# *Preface*

Stones in the Sneaker is the product of years of teaching and reflecting on physical and health education in secondary schools and post-secondary institutions across Canada. Collectively, the authors have a vast and diverse range of teaching and research experiences and share a common concern for the health and well-being of adolescent students of all backgrounds and abilities. This book is written primarily for preservice teacher education students, and physical and health educators in the secondary school system. However, it will also be of interest to those teaching in related grades and subject areas such as family studies (see Tryssenaar), working in allied fields such as public health nursing (see Varpalotai and Leipert) and in areas of health promotion. As a collection, these essays respond to a frequently voiced need for a Canadian resource that addresses not so much the "how-to" methods of teaching physical and health education—there are outstanding books on this topic already—but rather the social and cultural issues underpinning our subject areas. Each chapter represents one of the many "stones" that trouble us in our day-to-day teaching and interactions with our students. Health and physical education teachers are no longer able (if they ever were) to walk into a classroom or gym holding exactly the same expectations for all of their students. Neither can teachers expect to teach all of their students in exactly the same way, nor can they evaluate students using a single set of criteria. Although some readers may remember their school experiences to the contrary, it should come as no surprise that the "one-size-fits-all" model of teaching is defunct. But, if you were to take a general poll of the public, you may be startled to find that many people retain impressions of high school health and physical education classes that resonate more strongly with this approach than with any other. Many adult Canadians do not have positive memories of their school health and physical education experiences. Some tend to confuse physical education with interschool sport, and conversations with non-teaching

friends about teaching issues and concerns often end in an impassioned discussion about competitive sports that, in fact, have little or no connection
with classes conducted in the gymnasium (see Singleton and Rutledge).

Similarly, health education evokes memories of irrelevant and dry
classroom sessions, squeezed in between the more appealing physical activity
periods held in the gym or outdoors. Although there are many opportunities
and "teachable moments" throughout the school program for health education in the less-formal sense, the actual marriage between physical and health
education in most curriculum documents is, at best, an uneasy fit and an in-
equitable partnership. The same holds true for teacher education programs
across the country. Although physical education specialists at the secondary
school level are required to take a preservice course in this subject, health is
often offered as an elective, open to all and not necessarily required of the
physical educators. There are at least two consequences to consider. First, if
physical education students do not choose this elective, they may not be well
prepared to teach health as a part of their teaching assignments. Second, and
perhaps more positively, an open health elective enables *all* teachers to become qualified in a subject that is important in the secondary school not only
as a formal subject, but one that emerges daily in classroom discussions, and
in extracurricular settings. Health, in a sense, is both marginalized and uni-
versalized through its treatment within pre-service education and curriculum policies. In the broadest sense, the health education of students is everyone's responsibility. The emerging idea of "comprehensive school health" is a
broad umbrella that encompasses the formal curricula of both physical education and health, but also goes well beyond these subjects to include related
subject areas as well as informal, extracurricular, and community connections. There are implications here for teacher educators, as well as school administrators. As stated in a recent article in the *Physical and Health Education
Journal*, "Good health is a prerequisite for learning" (CAHPERD 2003, 11).

Although much has been written about sports issues in this country, physical and health education has remained in the shadows, within provincial ministry of education curriculum policies, where it is frequently an
optional subject area, suffering from a lack of teaching resources. This book
was born out of our own growing frustrations in trying to locate appropriate
readings for our preservice education and kinesiology students. Through
conversations with colleagues facilitated by the Canadian Association for
Health, Physical Education, Recreation and Dance (CAHPERD) and the
affiliated Council of University Professors and Researchers (CUPR) net-
works, the idea for this book was conceived. By all accounts, physical edu-

cation and health in the secondary schools have never been more necessary. Medical experts, politicians, youth workers, parents, teachers, and the media all express concerns about obesity, poor fitness levels, substance abuse, nutrition and body image, sexuality, violence, and a myriad of other issues, all of which are addressed in the physical and health education curriculum. Furthermore, with escalating health care costs and an aging population, there is renewed interest in disease prevention, and in developing lifelong health and fitness habits which we now know will pay dividends many years ahead.

Unfortunately, many high school students are choosing not to continue in physical and health education when participation is no longer compulsory. When asked why, they will tell you that they do not like the competitive atmosphere of the class, or the repetitive nature of the activities, or the tensions they experience between genders in coeducational classes (Humbert and Blacklock 1997). When asked what would help them to choose to stay in these courses, students indicate that they want their health and physical education classes to be more inviting, personally and physically safe, welcoming for all, and fun. Students also want their classes to be interesting, informative, and useful, and to serve as an introduction to activities they can pursue throughout their lives. They want to learn more about the physical capacities of their growing bodies, about their social responsibilities, and how to get along with each other in positive and productive ways. Curriculum documents in every province in Canada endeavour to accomplish these aims; however, there are ongoing policy and practice debates in which we must participate. This book is intended to be both a catalyst and a participant in such discussions—hence the reference to "Active Theory."

Critics have long argued that physical education has persisted in nurturing associations with health in order to maintain a sort of spurious "scientific" credibility for its presence in school curricula—particularly at the secondary-school level. Although this claim is arguable, the inclusion of physical education and health in school curricula across Canada has a much more varied and interesting history. Physical education gained entrance into the elementary-school system near the turn of the twentieth century when educators began to focus on theories of play as a means of engaging young students in the learning process. That is, theories that emphasized the necessity of enabling children to learn "naturally" through play-oriented activities enabled physical educators to introduce movement-based activities into school programs. At the secondary-school level,

the inclusion of physical education as a school subject was shaped by intentionally gendered purposes that viewed physical education as both masculine entertainment and a means of improving and maintaining feminine
health and beauty in the unfamiliar and potentially damaging world of
scholastics. Thus, when school authorities in the early 1900s decided, for
reasons of safety and morality, to include competitive athletics as an extracurricular school activity, it was an easy step for physical educators to justify
the introduction of competitive games and drill as desirable "character
builders" for boys. At the same time, in an effort to promote credibility and
acceptance for their courses in movement-based gymnastics, female physical education instructors allied themselves closely with medical practitioners who were willing to extol the benefits of moderate and highly controlled physical activity for young women (Cahn 1994; Cassidy and Kozman
1943; Carr 1998; Green 1986; Gurney 1979; Howell and Howell 1969;
Lenskyj 1986; Lockhart 2002; Nixon and Cozens 1935; Sharman 1934;
Skillen 1998; Smith and Cestaro 1998; Vertinsky 1990).

Health also has a long and varied history as a subject in school programs. An examination of health textbooks over the last 150 years or so indicates that "health" as a school subject has veered from didactic lessons
strictly focused on human physiology to paternalistic lectures on how to
maintain personal hygiene, preserve food, or properly prepare for a first date
with someone of the opposite sex. The content of school health courses,
and of the textbooks developed to teach this material, has traditionally
been (and perhaps still is) strongly influenced by cultural conventions dic-
tated by conservative, middle-class values. These texts present a fascinat-
ing window into the social and cultural attitudes and expectations of the
era in which they were written, and there is no reason to think that they do
not continue to do so today. Within the past fifty years we have become
much more concerned and open about issues relating to previously taboo
subjects. These include sexuality in all its forms, mental health and mental
illnesses, and violence in relationships ranging from bullying to sexual harassment, and sexual abuse to domestic violence, usually against girls and
women.

"Health" and "physical education," when viewed together, focus
on the whole human being. As such, there are many benefits to be found in
examining the associations these courses have maintained over time. In
combination these two fields provide a rich and complementary study into
the scientific, cultural, and pedagogical meanings of the human body's development, function, and movement over time (Andress et al. 1949;

Baruch, Montgomery and Bauer c.1950; Chittick 1956; Cutter 1850; Donatelle et al. 2004; Fraser and Porter 1923; Halpenny and Ireland 1911; Macfadden and Oswald c.1900; Nattress 1893; Provincial Board of Health 1886; Richmond, Pounds, and Corbin, 1987; Swartout 1938).

During their practice teaching experiences, preservice students will encounter a variety of health and physical education teachers who are knowledgeable, experienced, conscientious, and caring professionals doing their best to develop habits of healthy, active living in all of their students. Student teachers and seasoned professionals, alike, need to continually reflect on their practice, critically assess the needs of their students, and be open to new and different ways of approaching their pedagogy. Familiarity with the social and cultural contexts of the school and community is an important place to start. Rural and urban communities may be quite different in their needs and resources—the social, cultural, and religious backgrounds of students must be taken into account. Although the actual content of the curriculum may not be all that different from one community or school to the next, curricular approaches and delivery modes may need to accommodate and adapt to parental concerns, community traditions, and accessibility of resources.

Chapters within this book examining partnerships within rural communities (Varpalotai and Leipert), the needs of aboriginal students (Halas), and the inclusion of those with disabilities (Goodwin et al.) all point to various ways in which teachers must take into account the diversities within their classrooms. Planning for an inclusive curriculum (Pelletier) that is respectful of students' human rights (Dickinson) is an essential foundation in the teaching of health and physical education.

The purpose of this book is to give student teachers a head start in developing, and experienced teachers the opportunity to reflect on, their teaching philosophies. Graduate students may wish to consider how things have changed since their own teacher education programs, and during the time they have been teaching. As seemingly new issues come to the forefront, they challenge our assumptions about a subject area that is very much confronted by changing values and understandings about physical and mental health issues, leisure time pursuits, and the inclusion of those previously sidelined or left out altogether. The following chapters offer discussions on social and cultural issues present in school health and physical education today. Some topics may be very familiar to you, while others may not be so familiar. Educators from across Canada who are noted for their research in these areas have contributed their expertise to this book. You may agree with what they have to say, and then again, you may not. The book's intent is not to convince you that there is a single best way of understanding the issues. Each of the chapters in this book invites the reader to ask difficult questions about the purposes of physical and health education, about the context within which they are teaching, and about the outcomes they wish for each of their students. Teachers are encouraged to interrogate the existing curriculum policies and practices within their jurisdictions, even as they are required to teach to achieve certain "expectations," "standards," and "outcomes" by the end of each course. Regardless of how rigid or flexible curriculum guidelines may appear to be, all teachers have the opportunity to develop courses of study that will best meet the needs and situations of their unique groups of students. Taking into account gender, culture, abilities, and the availability of resources within the school and the community enables teachers to create courses that will be relevant, appealing, and sensitive to the needs of their particular students.

Of all curriculum areas, the subjects of health and physical education together have the greatest potential for effecting lifelong, positive lifestyle habits among students. We have the option of reproducing the exclusive world of competitive sport, where the winner takes all, or ensuring that all of our students, regardless of background, have the tools, skills, and knowledge necessary for a lifelong pursuit of health and wellbeing in all of the ways in which we define these terms. As Anderson and Booth explain, these forms of "literacy" are as fundamentally important as any of the others that have been heralded as the "basics" within our education system.

Each generation of physical and health educators has before it the opportunity to critically assess the pedagogical foundations of its subject areas. Theory and practice in education are indeed active and dynamic—awaiting creative and thoughtful educators to reflect on what has gone before, and to question the assumptions and beliefs of these domains. Often it is the voices from the margins that call our attention to areas that have been neglected and overlooked. Those who have not been privileged by traditional norms and expectations are often the clearest proponents of change. Many of us engaged in the teaching of physical and health education have been blessed with good health, athletic ability, and opportunities since childhood to pursue sport and physical activities in many forms. We will encounter students in our classes who mirror our own positive experiences, and it is tempting to teach to those we understand the best. However, these students are in the minority. Most of our students are those who have not enjoyed the positive experiences of physical activities. They are also most at risk for health concerns. It is our duty as educators to ensure that our pedagogy and our interactions with our students are inclusive and take into account the vast array of diversities found in every classroom in this country.

Among the unique contributions this book makes is bringing forward the voices of those who have been marginalized in physical and health education classes in the past. By listening to those who are not altogether comfortable in our existing programs, by focusing on the "lived experience" of our students, we are asked to rethink what physical and health education ought to be about. In this textbook we intend to address some of the existing tensions within the curriculum, such as the uneasy alliance between physical education and health; the privileging of traditional, competitive sports at the expense of other activities such as dance or tai chi (see Lu); and the ways in which those new to the profession are socialized to replicate and reproduce the ways of their predecessors (Hopper and Sanford). All of these tensions beg to be unpacked, challenged, and reconsidered. The opportunity for renewal within this subject domain is here and now.

We have chosen not to organize the chapters into specific sections, or even group them into distinct health and physical education topics. It is the eclectic nature of the issues interwoven throughout both health and physical education that we hope you will focus on in this book. Regardless of whether a chapter concentrates on health or on physical education, we believe that issues of race, class, gender, culture, and ability permeate every text and contribute to its constructed meaning and significance. But we cannot effectively examine these issues unless we are clear about the context in which they appear, that is, in secondary schools located in every corner of Canada. Secondary schools in Canada come in every conceivable size and with every conceivable timetable configuration. Some schools have every piece of athletic equipment imaginable, and some schools have little or none. Some schools are single-sex; most are coeducational. Although most classes are taught in English, or French, some are taught in Inuktitut, or Cantonese. Some schools are located in the heart of our largest cities, and a few are in the most remote reaches of our immense and varied country. Just as Canada is a land of contrasts, so, too, are its schools and we must understand, acknowledge, and celebrate this diversity before we can begin to appreciate fully the points that are made in the chapters in this book.

On the other hand, there is some method in the order in which we have placed the chapters. Humbert's chapter on "Listening for change," and Anderson and Booths' on "Health literacy" both provides excellent grounding for readers to approach subsequent chapters with a firm sense of the fundamental issues facing secondary-level health and physical educators in contemporary schools. Students and their instructors are invited to roam throughout the book, investigating topics as they arise in their classes and practicum experiences.

The final two chapters in the book, both by Dickinson, provide practical and ethical dimensions that are critical to professional practice. Risk management and safety are basic imperatives for physical educators. We owe a duty of care to our students, and we must always be vigilant that all of our activities—from the most basic to the most adventurous—are as safe as they reasonably can be. Human rights, too, are just as crucial for all educators—but again, there are issues which are more apparent in physical and health education than they might be in some other areas of the school curriculum. It is each teacher's responsibility to be aware of these concerns, to attend actively to them in each class, and to model appropriate legal and ethical behaviour for their students.

Our intent is that you, the reader and practitioner, understand that there are indeed critical pedagogical issues accompanying the teaching of health and physical education, and that your approach will have a profound effect on your students. Not long before this book went to press, Chantal Petitclerc was named "Canadian of the Year" by *Maclean's*, Canada's national newsmagazine (Gillis 2004). The winner of five gold medals in wheelchair racing at the 2004 Paralympics in Athens, credited her high school physical education teacher with introducing her to swimming following the accident in which she broke her spine and lost the use of her legs. Soon after, she was competing in wheelchair athletics—and the rest, as they say, is history. Physical and health educators have the potential to make a difference in the lives of every one of their students.

This book is intended to help you enter a professional dialogue around some of the most controversial social and cultural topics that resonate through health and physical education classes across Canada. Do not ignore those "stones in the sneaker"—they are there to remind us that teaching is dynamic, that it engages with the social and cultural context, and that it needs to be continually re-examined. It is hoped that this book will inspire a critical reflection about one's teaching philosophies and practices, together with ongoing dialogue with one's colleagues and students. These issues will continue to evolve, and new ones will emerge, particularly as the media and other channels of information bring them to our attention. By keeping abreast of emerging issues we will develop keener perceptions and become more attuned to the needs of our students. We may forge new alliances and create new opportunities within our schools and communities; physical and health education is not limited by time and space. There is ample room for creating learning and activity opportunities beyond the required curriculum through mounting extracurricular programs, engaging parents and school councils, and working with local recreation and health care providers. Beyond the basic foundations of our subjects, we need to advance the core notions of integration and inclusion, for all the possibilities they bring. Thinking more broadly and deeply about the scope and variety of our subjects is a habit, like daily physical activity and healthful living, that we hope you will practise for your entire teaching career.

Ellen Singleton and Aniko Varpalotai

## References

Andress, J. M., I. H. Goldberger, M. Dolch, and G. T. Hallock. 1949. *Growing big and strong*. Boston: Ginn and Company.

Baruch, D., E. Montgomery, and W. W. Bauer. c1950. *You*. Toronto: W. J. Gage and Company.

Cahn, S. K. c1994. *Coming on strong: Gender and sexuality in twentieth-century women's sport*. Toronto: Maxwell Macmillan Canada.

CAHPERD/ACSEPLD. 2003. Voices and Choices: A Resource for Comprehensive School Health. *Physical & Health Education Journal*, Autumn, 11–16. Available at: www.healthcanada.ca/voicesandchoices

Cassidy, R., and H. C. Kozman. 1943. *Physical fitness for girls: A textbook for teacher education and a guide to teachers in curriculum revision*. New York: A. S. Barnes and Company Inc.

Carr, D. 1998. What moral educational significance has physical education? A question in need of disambiguation. In *Ethics & Sport*, ed. M. J. McNamee and S. J. Parry, 119–33. London: E&FNSPON.

Chittick, R. 1956. *Health for Canadians*. Toronto: Macmillan.

Cutter, C. 1850. *First book on anatomy, physiology, and hygiene, for grammar schools and families*. Boston: Benjamin B. Mussey and Company.

Donatelle, R. J., L. G. Davis, A. J. Munroe, A. Munroe, and M. Casselman. 2004. *Health: The basics, Third Canadian Edition*. Toronto: Pearson Education Canada.

Fraser, D. T., and G. D. Porter. 1923. *Canadian Health Book*. Toronto: Copp Clark.

Gillis, C. 2004. 2004 in Review—Canadian of the Year: Chantal Petitclerc. *Maclean's*, 27 December, 26–28.

Green, H. c1986. *Fit for America: Health, fitness, sport and American society*. New York: Pantheon Books.

Gurney, H. 1982. Major influences on the development of high school girls' sports in Ontario. In *Her story in sport: A historical anthology of women in sports*, ed. R. Howell, 472-93. West Point, NY: Leisure Press.

Halpenny, M. A., and L. B. Ireland. 1911. *How to be healthy*. Toronto: W. J. Gage and Company.

Howell, N., and M. L. Howell. 1969. *Sport and games in Canadian life*. Toronto: Macmillan.

Humbert, M. L. and Blacklock, F. (1998). *Girls in Action: Speaking Out*. Video. Ottawa: CAHPERD.

Lenskyj, H. 1986. *Out of bounds: Women, sport and sexuality*. Toronto: The Women's Press.

Lockhart, B. 2002. Exercise for life. Keeping teenage women in PE classes. Available at: http://communications.uvic.ca/edge/gibbons.pdf

MacFadden, B., and F. Oswald. c1900. *Fasting, hydropathy and exercise*. London: Bernarr MacFadden.

Nattress, W. (1893). *Public school physiology and temperance*. Toronto: William Briggs.

Nixon, E. W., and F. W. Cozens. 1935. *An introduction to physical education*. Philadelphia: W. B. Saunders.

Provincial Board of Health. 1886. *Manual of hygiene for Schools and Colleges*. Toronto: William Briggs.

Richmond, J. B., E. T. Pounds, and C. B. Corbin. 1987. *Health for life*. Sunnyvale, CA: Scott, Foresman and Company.

Sharman, J. R. 1934. *Introduction to physical education*. New York: A. S. Barnes and Company.

Skillen, A. 1998. Sport is for losers. In *Ethics and Sport*, ed. M. J. McNamee and S. J. Parry, 169–81. London: E&FNSPON.

Smith, T. K., and N. G. Cestaro. 1998. *Student-centered physical education*. Champaign, IL: Human Kinetics.

Swartout, H. O. 1938. *Home guide to health*. Oshawa, ON: Canadian Watchman Press.

Vertinsky, P. 1990. *The eternally wounded woman*. Manchester, UK: Manchester University Press.

Chapter One

# *"Listening for a Change"*:

## Understanding the Experiences of Students in Physical Education

## M. Louise Humbert

The vital role that physical activity plays in enhancing the health and wellbeing of children and youth has been well documented (Bailey 2000; MacKelvie, Khan, and McKay 2002; Pate et al. 2002). However, in Canada, less than half of youth aged twelve to seventeen are considered active enough to obtain those benefits (Canadian Fitness and Lifestyle Research Institute 2004). We know that as children age they become less physically active, and girls and young women are less active than boys and young men at all ages (Stone et al. 1997).

These low levels of physical activity predispose children and youth to a variety of diseases and conditions. For example, Tremblay and Wilms (2000) determined that in the past fifteen years, the prevalence of obesity has tripled in Canadian children aged seven to thirteen. One of the major causes of this alarming increase in childhood obesity is low levels of physical activity (Tremblay and Wilms 2000). The health consequences of an inactive, progressively obese society are well documented. In fact, the inevitable and predictable increase in the prevalence of type 2 diabetes mellitus is being seen across North America as physical activity levels decline and rates of obesity soar (Hansen, Fulop, and Hunter 2000; Harris, Perkins, and Whalen-Brough 1996).

Apart from physical inactivity's being a major cause of obesity and diabetes, a sedentary lifestyle is linked to numerous other chronic diseases, such as heart disease, osteoporosis, and certain cancers. Although the onsets of these chronic conditions are reported during the second and third decades of life, their incidence can be reduced by regular physical activity during childhood and youth (Leslie, Sparling, and Owen 2001). Unfortunately, current research suggests that the development of regular physical activity habits in most youth has not yet been accomplished (Wharf Higgins et al. 2003). When these findings are coupled with evidence that suggests that quality of life in one's later years can be influenced by physical activity patterns that are established in youth and persist into adulthood (Bailey 2000; Malina 1996; Pate et al. 2002), the importance of physical activity adoption and maintenance in childhood and youth cannot be understated.

What can be done? How can the activity levels of children and youth be increased? How can their health be enhanced today and in the future? Numerous authors have emphasized the integral role schools play in offering children and youth the necessary knowledge, skills, and opportunities for being physically active (McGraw et al. 2000; Mendelein, Baranowski, and Pratt 2000; Sallis and McKenzie 1991; Tremblay 1998). In fact, it has been suggested that schools may be the only major institutions that can address the physical activity needs of children and youth (Sallis and McKenzie 1991).

Physical education programs are an integral component of any school-based initiative designed to increase the physical activity levels of children and youth (Prochaska et al. 2003; Sallis and McKenzie 1991; Tremblay 1998). Physical education classes are frequently cited as offering some of the best opportunities to positively influence the physical activity patterns of children and youth (American College of Sports Medicine 1988).

Now, more than ever, opportunity knocks on the door of physical educators. The call to increase the physical activity levels of all Canadians, in particular children and youth, has never been louder. Teachers of physical education are well positioned to answer this call. They have a unique opportunity to share their love of movement, and to open wide the door of physical activity to children and youth of all ages and abilities.

How are physical educators responding to this opportunity? Are current physical education programs meeting the needs of students? Are physical education classes designed and taught in ways that will positively influence the activity levels of youth today and in the future? The following letter was written by a young woman in response to an article in a national magazine that suggested daily physical education was needed to address the rising rates of obesity among young people in Canada (DeMont 2002):

> As a student going into grade 10, I know first hand that having more physical education classes will not solve the problem. All I ever did was the same sports over and over—basketball soccer and hockey etc. Not all kids enjoy being pushed around, demeaned and shamed because they are not good at competitive sports, me included. Why not create alternative phys-ed classes that offer programs such as outdoor education, hiking, bike riding and jogging? (Macdonald 2002, 6).

These are sobering words for physical educators at all levels. It would be easy to dismiss the comments as isolated; however, research indicates that students often report that they are dissatisfied with several aspects of their physical education classes (Corbin 2002; Gibbons et al. 1999; Humbert 1995a, 1995b; Humbert et al. 2003; Humbert, Goddard, and Avery 1998; Olafson 2002; Reed and Bertelsen 2003; Tannehill, Romar, and O'Sullivan 1994). The gap that exists between the needs and desires of students and their experiences in physical education classes may be one of the reasons that the majority of high school students in Canada choose not to take physical education classes when they are no longer compulsory.

If physical educators are to make the best use of the opportunities provided, time must be made to listen to the experiences of their students. This idea was reinforced for me a few years ago in a conversation with a friend who taught physical education at a local high school. He told me that the biggest challenge he faced in his teaching was to offer a physical education program that met the needs of the vast majority of his students, who were not at all like him! I was intrigued by this concept and asked him to explain. He commented that most of his students were not the gifted athletes that he and many other physical education teachers were. The majority of his students did not view movement as an integral part of their lives and they certainly did not share his love of physical activity.

During the last decade, I have had the privilege of listening to hundreds of students discuss their experiences in physical education classes and physical activity programs. Listening to these young people has opened my eyes and my heart to a world of which I was previously unaware. From the ten years that I taught physical education to high school students, I have few recollections of listening to my students. In fact, I have only one memory of sitting down with my students to ask for their input on any aspect of their physical education program. I have learned that this was a serious mistake, one that I would suggest not be repeated by anyone who is truly committed to fostering a love of physical activity in students. My experiences listening to students have shown me that it is only when we truly listen that we can begin to meet the needs of our students. Van Manen (1991) identified this need to listen and understand as "pedagogical understanding." He explained, "Pedagogical understanding is sensitive listening and understanding....What could be more important than to have a sense of what things are like for a particular child...?" (83).

If physical educators take the time to listen and to try to understand the experiences of students, it may indeed be possible to achieve pedagogical understanding. Such an understanding may give them the courage to question the taken-for-granted notions that permeate many of the components of physical education programs. If they begin to see physical education through the eyes of their students, they may be able to look critically at the activities and the environment that exist in physical education programs.

The following comment was shared with me by a young woman who participated in a study focused on understanding the experiences of young women in physical education classes:

> This is a once in a lifetime opportunity. I mean, how often do you ever have anyone coming to your school to ask you what you think? You know, it is usually them telling you what you should do and what you should be thinking...they never ask you. (Humbert 1995a, 165)

These comments were made at the end of the study and I recall that, as I left her on that day, I was both elated and troubled by her words: Elated because I was so pleased that she felt that the time we had spent together had been worthwhile; troubled in that the opportunity to share her feelings and thoughts was something she had not previously experienced.

In the years since this study, there has been increased interest in giving students opportunities to discuss their experiences in physical education classes. The majority of this work has been with girls and young women (Fenton, Frisby, and Luke 1999; Gibbons et al. 1999). It is unfortunate that little is known about the thoughts, feelings, and attitudes of boys and young men regarding their physical education experiences. More attention must be paid to listening to and understanding the experiences of boys in physical education classes.

Over the years, I have learned that most young people want to be physically active, and they look to their physical education classes as a chance to move, to learn new skills, and to be with their friends. Similar to the experiences of Corbin (2002), I have also learned that "most high school students have positive feelings about physical activity, but negative feelings about physical education" (135). If physical educators are to play a significant role in addressing the challenge of increasing the physical activity levels of youth, if they are going to seize the opportunity presented to them, I would suggest that their first step should be to listen—to listen, and to try to understand the experiences of their students, many of whom are nothing like them!

This chapter will focus on two of the areas that are most frequently discussed when I speak with young people: the environment in physical education classes, and the important role that having fun plays in their physical education experiences. All of the words that you will read are from students in grades 7 to 12, who have participated in several studies focused on their experiences in physical education classes. All of the names used are pseudonyms.

## The Dream

I wish that everyone could go to phys-ed, do the best they can, and have fun and feel comfortable. I know that sounds like a dream, but I think that feeling comfortable is so important. If you don't feel comfortable, you can't be yourself, you can't do as well. It is almost like you need to feel like you belong in phys-ed, like it is OK for you to be there. It seems like most of the time only the good people get that feeling. (Humbert 1995a, 122)

These are the words of Eva, a young woman who stopped taking physical education immediately after it was no longer compulsory. I vividly remember Eva telling me, "I got out of there as soon as I could." When I first heard her discuss her dream for physical education, I was surprised to learn that a young woman who so eagerly chose to stop taking physical education would have any thoughts of a dream for physical education classes. Eva's comments about her dream caused me to reflect on my own hopes and dreams for physical education programs. I recall thinking that because of my experiences in physical education, my dream may be quite different from Eva's. Feeling comfortable in physical education classes had always come easily for me. It seemed like I always had fun, I felt like I belonged. Thinking back, I guess you could say I was comfortable there—so comfortable that I chose to pursue a career that would allow me to spend most of my day in a physical activity setting!

What about the students in our physical education classes? Do they feel comfortable? Or are they like Eva, waiting to get out as soon as they can? If our main goal as physical educators is to promote lifelong physical activity, it is essential that we work to create the environment that Eva described. For many students, this feeling of belonging and feeling comfortable is pivotal to their enjoyment and satisfaction in physical education classes (Lirgg 1994; Ennis et al. 1997; Treanor et al. 1998). Feeling comfortable in a physical education class will mean different things to different students. However, there are several common factors that physical educators can address to improve the experiences of students.

### *It Starts With the Teacher*

Both girls and boys desire a physical education teacher who is approachable and understanding. Greg, a student in grade 9, explained:

> You know I think a phys-ed teacher that you can approach and talk to, is so important. You know, some phys-ed teachers are so arrogant that [they] think they run the world. They just tell everyone to run and do this and do that. This year was different, we had a teacher who ran with us when he could, and treated us with respect. It did not matter if you were on one of his teams or not, he still seemed to care about you. I wish they could all be like that. (Humbert 2003)

Carly, a grade 11 student, explained her wish for a relationship with her physical education teacher like the one experienced by the girls on the school teams:

> I wish our teacher could get personal with us, like she does with the girls on her teams. It seems like she talks to them all the time. I wish she would talk to the rest of us. That way I think I could talk to her more, about all kinds of stuff, not just phys-ed. I mean if you have a problem you should be able to have someone you can talk to. It must be nice to know that you have someone to talk to at school other than your friends. (Humbert, Goddard, and Avery 1998, 21)

The importance of "feeling connected" with physical education teachers was also reported in the work of Ennis et al. (1997). These authors determined that high school students valued a teacher who treated them with respect and expressed concern for and interest in them.

Students often tell me that they want their physical education teacher to try to understand what it is like not to be "good at everything."

> *Bonnie:*  I think that they should be more understanding. I mean you could be trying your hardest and they will say that you are not even trying. They don't understand because they are the people that can do everything.

> *Yvonne:*  Yeah, it just comes natural to them. (Humbert and Chad 1997)

In a discussion about the difference between elementary and high school physical education classes, Robert suggested that, for the first time, he was enjoying physical education in high school because he had a teacher who supported his efforts:

> Like I am not the best, but our teacher this year, he really encourages us to do our best. That is all he wants, it doesn't matter to him if you are the best. He seems to know that everyone can't be good at everything, he kind of just understands us. I really like that, it makes me want to try even harder. (Humbert 2003)

The importance of offering encouragement and being approachable to students was evident in the work of Chalmers (1992), who determined that students greatly valued a teacher who understood them:

> Encouragement, praise and help from their teachers improved the respondents' self-concepts and increased their motivation to participate, thereby increasing their levels of participation and performance. Each teacher had particular ways of encouraging students. What was important for the students was that they felt understood which provided reassurance. The respondents appreciated the interest their teachers showed in them and valued individual attention and time taken just to talk to them. (4–5)

## *I Belong Here*

Students frequently report that an essential ingredient to feeling comfortable in a physical education class is the establishment of an atmosphere that is free from harassment and that supports the efforts of the individual. Issues such as changing clothes in locker rooms, compulsory uniforms, and disparaging comments from other students are frequently raised as sources of discomfort in physical education classes. These feelings are particularly evident in discussions with girls who report that the pressure to have the "ideal" body is frequently magnified in physical education settings. It is apparent that feelings of body image dissatisfaction and anxiety are increased when young women enter a physical education setting. Eva recalled her experiences in grade 9:

> I remember I had algebra in first class and that whole class the only thing I could think of was, "Oh no, I have gym next." I worried about it so much, like I was just tormented. I made myself sick just thinking about it, I hated it so much. I just did not want to do it. I felt so awkward wearing that uniform and having to change in front of everyone, and then we had to shower, it was so awful. All during algebra I could not concentrate, I was just thinking of having gym next. (Humbert 1995a, 74)

In addition to the difficulty of changing in front of others, young women often report receiving demeaning and harassing comments in physical education classes. Most often these comments come from their male classmates: "If there is a bigger girl running around the gym and they are running a little bit slow and the guys are dashing by thinking they are so good, then they say something like 'thump, thump, thump, there must be an earthquake'" (Canadian Association for Health Physical Education Recreation and Dance 1997). Beyond comments about their bodies, young women often report being sexually harassed in physical education classes (Scraton 1992). Such harassment is evident in the recollections of Celeste, a grade 10 student:

> Well I was dancing with a guy in physical education in grade 9, and he started looking me up and down and saying "hmmmm" and then he did a lizard mouth. The guys are really bold, they would take your shirt and like touch it right here (on the breast) and say "oh is this cotton or something like that?" and they are touching you. (Humbert 1996, 151)

Discussions around harassment and anxiety in locker rooms are noticeably absent when boys come together to discuss their experiences in physical education. Their comments tend to centre on the opportunity physical education classes provide to "stay in shape." Adam, a grade 10 student, suggested that his primary reason for taking physical education was to keep fit: "keeping fit is important because I don't want to get fat." Tom agreed and commented, "the girls like boys with six-packs, and I just don't want to get fat" (Humbert 2003).

An issue frequently debated in the literature is the instruction of physical education in single-sex or coeducational (coed) classes (Browne 1992; Gibbons et al. 1999; Griffin 1989; Scraton 1992; Treanor et al.1998). When given an opportunity to comment on their preference between single-sex and coed classes, the majority of the young people with whom I have spoken state that they prefer single-sex classes. The following comments of two grade 9 boys illustrate the importance of the environment that is established in same-sex classes:

Mason:     I like grade 9 phys-ed 'cause there are no girls. All the girls in grade 8 did not want to do anything. They just kind of got in the way; no one wanted them on the teams.

Ernie:     I like it better too. We can play harder and lots of guys will try new stuff if the girls aren't there. When the girls are there, no guy wants to foul up. There is a lot less pressure without the girls. (Humbert 2003)

Numerous studies (Derry and Phillips 2004; Humbert 1995a; Humbert, Goddard, and Avery 1998; Lirgg 1994; Ryan, Fleming, and Maina, 2003; Treanor et al. 1998) have determined that many girls and young women prefer single-sex physical education classes. Girls and young women frequently comment that they feel "safe" and more comfortable in same-sex classes. April, a grade 11 student, explained:

I like all-girls classes 'cause girls can just relate to each other better and there is nobody cutting anyone down, it is just all girls and you can be yourself and you don't have to worry about what the guys are thinking or saying. (Humbert, Goddard, and Avery 1998, 25)

Emily, a grade 9 student, offered an example of how boys' behaviour limited the participation of girls in her coed physical education class:

> It got so bad last year that most of the girls in my class would not even change for phys-ed anymore. There were only two of us left who ever took part in phys-ed. One day some of the girls in the class told me "I just feel like an idiot in phys-ed." So, I really tried to encourage them and I really tried to pass the ball to them, but they got intimidated when the boys would groan or roll their eyes if they missed a pass or a basket. After that they did not want to play anymore. (Humbert 1995b, 67)

These feelings support the work of Griffin (1989), who determined that in coeducational physical education classes

> boys often tend to dominate games, ignore female teammates and complain about participating with girls. Girls may hang back, intimidated by boys' harassment and aggressiveness or eventually lose interest and drop out, bored and discouraged. (25)

Although students seem to prefer that physical education classes be taught in a single-sex environment, it is important to note that regardless of the organizational structure, students want their physical education teachers to establish an environment that supports and accepts the efforts of all students. Abusive and demeaning comments should not be tolerated and every effort should be made to model acceptance of all students, regardless of their physiques or physical abilities. Policies and practices that put students in situations in which they do not feel comfortable must be reviewed and changed so that all students can feel welcome, comfortable, and accepted in their physical education classes. This was Eva's dream; it is one worth pursuing.

### Fun is the Most Important Thing

> If I was the one in charge of phys-ed, you know the one who makes all the decisions, I would tell the teachers to make phys-ed fun. The best thing we could promise someone that took phys-ed was that they would have fun. Fun is the most important thing. (Humbert 1995a, 90)

When I ask students to discuss their experiences in physical education classes, the importance of having fun is always emphasized. I have learned that, for most young people, having fun truly is the most important thing. When I first heard students talk about having fun in physical education classes I became very nervous, because I had read numerous articles warning of the danger of including fun as an objective in physical education programs. Bean and Kinnear (1989) stressed that "[i]f this concern with fun becomes an obsession, there is a danger of jeopardizing the educational content of physical education programs..." (19). Whitehead (1988) reported that students in physical education classes "may on occasion have fun, but physical education is not centrally a vehicle for such diversionary occupation" (155). Williams (1994) warned physical education teachers that an overemphasis on students having fun would land them in the "Physical Education Hall of Shame" (17).

Concerns about the inclusion of fun in physical education classes are not limited to academic papers or practitioner journals; a review of the goals and aims of physical education curricula in Canada revealed that few, if any, provinces state that fun is part of physical education. Yet, for most students, it is apparent that having fun is central to a positive physical education experience. "Having fun" in physical education is not the trivial, meaningless concept that I had initially feared. Students often tell me that their idea of fun centres on being physically active with their friends in a supportive and inclusive environment.

## I Want to Move

> Sometimes there is just way too much sitting around or we just listen or watch other people do things. If I wanted to learn that way, I would watch it on TV. I want to do the stuff, not watch someone else. If you don't get to play, it is not much fun. (Humbert 2003)

Students frequently tell me that they want to be active in their physical education classes. The chance to get out of a desk and move is often seen as one of the best things about physical education. Jack, a grade 10 student, explained:

> Well, in school we sit most of the time, it is so nice to have one period where we actually get to do something instead of just sit and listen all day. Phys-ed is great because we get to move and you feel so much better after. (Humbert 2003)

Davis believed that having an opportunity to move was the main reason he had fun in his physical education classes:

I just basically have fun in phys-ed because I get to move. I mean you don't have to sit at a desk and work, we spend so much time sitting, you just want to get out there and play and move and have fun because...before you know it, you are back to sitting in a desk. (Humbert 2003)

Becky and Angie, two grade-ten students, reported that they disliked physical education classes that did not provide them with opportunities to be active:

Angie:      I didn't like tennis; there were not enough courts so people had to sit out.

Becky:      Cricket was fun, but there were too many players and half the time I did not get to play, it really wasn't much fun. (Humbert 1995a, 93)

### *It Is Fun if I Am Good at It*

As well as desiring opportunities to be active in their physical education classes, students frequently report that their enjoyment of an activity is dependent upon having the skills needed to participate in the activities offered in a physical education program. Participants in a study conducted by Portman (2003) reported that they enjoyed physical education classes if they felt that they were successful at an activity. Fairclough (2003) determined that "High School students' enjoyment in physical education was consistently related to their level of perceived competence" (15).

When asked to describe a situation in physical education class that was fun, Ernie, a grade 9 boy, offered the following example:

I remember having a lot of fun when we played football because I was the quarterback and I had a pretty good game. I started out weak but then I fought back. And you know the last time we played softball I hit pretty good, despite getting thrown out at home. I don't know, I just...I think my happiest times in grade 9 phys ed have been when I feel like I am good enough, like I can fit in. That is when I have the most fun. (Humbert 2003)

Like Ernie, Sarah, a student in grade 7, explained that her "best times" in physical education occurred when she felt she had the skills to participate:

I am not very good at most of the stuff we do, but I really like to dance. When we do dance in phys-ed I feel like I finally fit in because do you know what? I can do it; I am not the one who is the worst. On those days I have so much fun, it is just the best when I feel like I can be good enough to be part of everything. (Humbert et al. 2003)

Such feelings may be an indication of what Csikszentmihalyi (1975) termed the concept of "flow." A feeling of flow occurs when there is a balance between the challenges of an activity and the skills of the participant (Singer 1996). Chalip et al. (1984) noted that "in gym classes the more students feel skilled, the more they wish to be doing whatever they are doing" (14). Mandigo and Thompson (1998) suggested that fun and flow are similar constructs. They emphasized the importance of offering students in physical education opportunities to experience flow and suggested that physical education teachers provide opportunities for students to have fun, by offering activities that achieve a "balance between an individual's skill level and the challenges of an activity" (154). Martens (1996) encouraged physical educators to provide opportunities for students to experience flow, because he believed that they would keep students involved in physical activity:

The flow experience is so pleasing, it is intrinsically rewarding. We will engage in activities for no other reason than to experience flow, because it is fun. There are many ways to disrupt flow, to take the fun out of activity. If we take the fun out of physical activities we take the kids out of them. They turn their interests elsewhere. (307)

When offered an opportunity to discuss why his friends would not want to be physically active, Dennis, a student in grade 8, suggested:

People won't do stuff if they feel like they are not good at it. If someone is athletic, you know a sporty person; they are usually ready to try anything. If another person is not very athletic, they are not likely to try stuff, they don't try, they never get better and then they never do anything. I bet it stays like that their whole life. (Humbert 2003)

## Choosing to Compete

Students in all grades continually emphasize the importance of having both the competence and confidence necessary to participate in the activities offered in a physical education program. In most cases these comments were made in discussions that focused on the level of competition in their physical education classes. Joseph, a grade 8 student, posed an excellent question:

> A lot of what we do in phys-ed is too competitive. Sometimes it is so serious that it is no fun. I mean it is OK if you are good at it, but if you are not good at it who wants to play like that? (Humbert et al. 2003).

To alleviate differences in skill levels, a group of grade 10 boys suggested that two levels of physical education were needed and that, if this could be accomplished, students would have a lot more fun. Nick explained:

> There are guys who are not really into sports and they don't have much confidence or anything, they are really quiet. It can't be much fun for them. And then there are the people who are really good at sports, they have a lot of confidence; they are the ones that have all the fun. I think we should change things so that everyone can have fun. Maybe have two types of phys-ed, one that is really serious and competitive for the people who are really good and one for the people who are not that good. Everyone needs to have the chance to play and have fun or they won't want to come to phys-ed. (Humbert 2003)

When asked what he would change about physical education, Liam suggested that he would offer two types of classes:

> I guess I'd change, the competition part. I mean I like the seriousness of being good at sports, but other guys, the ones that are not that good at stuff, they don't like it. And the other guys, they make fun of them and then they feel stupid. I think they should have a serious class and a not so serious class. That way the kids that are not so good, will have a chance to play and then they would probably get better and for sure they would have more fun. (Humbert 2003)

An emphasis on competition is often offered as one of the main reasons girls and young women are dissatisfied with their physical education classes. Comments such as, "I hated phys-ed because it was too competitive" and "When people start to get competitive, it takes all the fun out of phys-ed" are frequently heard when young women discuss their physical education experiences. Like those of the grade 10 boys, the following comments from two grade 11 girls support the importance of recognizing and accommodating different levels of ability and interest.

> *Lauren:* I think you should be able to pick your skill level and then play with people like you. I am sure I would improve and then people like me would have a chance. Then everyone would have fun. Some people are just way too competitive.
>
> *Nina:* Ya, that would be way better, they could have one level for the super sports people. You know the ones who are always running and grabbing the ball, and one for the people like me who aren't so good. (Humbert 1995a, 115)

Gilligan (1982) suggested that because girls and young women place a great deal of importance on relationships, they frequently find competitive activities and the disputes that often surround them problematic. The feelings of Deserai, a grade 9 student, are a good example of this:

> I am not really much for trying out for teams and competing, I just want to do stuff for the fun of it. I don't really like competing against other people because they get angry if you beat them or you get discouraged if they beat you. Or if you are really into a game and someone on your team misses, you might get angry with them, and I really don't want people to be mad at me. (Humbert 1995a)

Later in our conversation, Deserai told me that she had the most fun when she worked with people, not against them: "I remember when Connie and I tried to beat our goal, like we tried to get forty passes in a row. That was so much fun because we were working together."

The preference of many girls and young women to work with a partner rather than against an opponent is problematic if they are participating in physical education classes that are focused on winning and losing. Knoppers (1988) suggested that

> [t]he emphasis on competition may also be problematic for those who value an ethic of care, an ethic rooted in the sensitivity of others. They may hesitate to endorse activities which emphasize the "I win, you lose" ethic as it may damage their connections and relationships with others (Gilligan 1982; Shakeshaft 1986). Instead, those who value the ethics of care may respond more to activities, which emphasize cooperation. Since more girls than boys tend to endorse an ethics (*sic*) of care (Gilligan 1982), the domination of competitive activities in the curriculum would have more of an impact on them than it would boys. (55)

The problematic nature of competition is evident in the words of Eva, who, while offering a solution to the "problem" of competition, lamented that all the girls in the class could not get along:

> I think the only way you could get the competition out of there is to have the people that can play really well play their own game and the people who can't just go and play their own game. But when you do that sort of thing, it kind of means that the class can't work together and I think they should be able to, it is just too bad that they can't. (Humbert 1995a, 116)

Unlike girls, for many boys, having an opportunity to compete and win is often cited as an important factor in their enjoyment of physical education (Fairclough 2003). Boys frequently suggest that the teacher should pick the teams, so that everyone has a chance to win. Kenny suggested that he had fun when there was a challenge and he was on a team that had a chance to respond to the challenge:

> I like it when the teacher picks the teams 'cause then one is not stacked. It is all about having the chance to win, not simply just winning each time we play. When I think I have a chance to win, I try harder, and it is a lot more fun. (Humbert 2003)

However, the hazards of not being skilled enough to compete are evident in Brian's thoughts:

> If the captains pick the teams they get stacked or the people who are not very good, or don't know what they are doing, don't get picked. I guess they kind of get left behind and they feel bad, so they won't want to play the game at all 'cause they know they

just aren't good enough to compete, you know to be part of the game. (Humbert 2003)

Because it is apparent that skill level is an important determinant of physical activity, physical education teachers should be encouraged to modify games and activities whenever possible so that more students can participate. Williams (1994) suggested that a primary goal of all physical educators should be to increase the level of participation of all students in their classes.

The benefit of modifying traditional games and activities is evident in the comments of Sarah, a grade 10 student:

> I like playing volleyball, but not real volleyball. Last year we sat on the floor and played, that was so much fun. I like beach volleyball too, when we played we could hit it as many times as we wanted, and we could serve from the attack line. It was way better, I felt like I could do it. (Humbert et al. 2003)

By suggesting that the restrictions imposed by rules and regulations be eased, students are asking for more opportunities to participate in physical activity. The following conversation with a group of grade 9 girls illustrates this conclusion:

Ali: I can't throw or catch or bat or anything. I tried to avoid going up to bat. The best time was in grade eight...they let the people that did not want to play baseball, and well that was pretty much all of the nonathletic people, play kickball. That was great.

Melissa: Yeah I remember that...kickball was the best.

Josie: For sure, 'cause you don't need much coordination, you just boot the ball and run, that was so much fun.

Ali: I mean, I know I am not very good, why would I want to play a game like baseball and everyone see how bad I am? (Humbert et al. 1998, 99)

## The Same Stuff Over and Over

For many students, the repetition of activities from one year to the next is a source of great dissatisfaction. Elizabeth, a student in grade eleven, commented, "Yuck, we do volleyball and basketball every year. It is nice to learn something new for a change." These feelings were echoed by Tasha, a grade 10 student: "A lot of the team sports we do every year, you know volleyball, basketball, soccer and track. We do the same stuff year after year. It is just so boring" (Humbert, Goddard, and Avery 1997). Chalip et al. (1984) determined that if a balance between the skills of the participant and the challenges of the activity are not present, then one of two states will occur: anxiety or boredom. A group of grade 10 girls offered the following thoughts while reflecting on their past year in physical education:

*Kelly:*   We should do more interesting things, instead of the same things over and over.

*Barb:*   Like this year was just a repeat of last year's activities.

*Tanya:*   It was like the same thing over and over again, the same units and everything.

*Marie:*   It is kind of a waste of time. (Humbert and Chad 1997)

Students often view physical education class positively if new activities are taught. Isabel, a student in grade 11, reported that she was enjoying physical education much more because she was learning new things: "This year they taught us First Aid and CPR—it was so cool. We are learning how to do step aerobics and Pilates. Everything is so much better because it is all new stuff" (Humbert, Goddard, and Avery 1997).

Phillip, also in grade eleven, commented that he felt that physical education in grades nine and ten should be changed so that it is more like grade eleven:

They should do more fun stuff in grade nine and ten, things like rock climbing, karate, cricket, you know stuff we have not done before. They do that kind of stuff in grade 11 but by then it is too late. Most of the kids have stopped taking physical education. (Humbert 2003)

Like Phillip, Sam suggested that he was looking forward to physical education in grade 11, because he would have the opportunity to participate in new activities: "I would really like to learn new things like they do in grade eleven. They get to go golfing, swimming, and roller blading" (Humbert 2003). Jeff explained that he, too, was looking forward to grade 11 physical education because he felt that he would be able to learn activities that he could do outside of school hours:

I signed up for grade eleven phys-ed because you get to do new stuff, like scuba diving and kayaking. Things you could do on a summer vacation. I mean in the summer I can't find a bunch of guys to do sports with but I could rent a tank and go scuba diving or I could find a friend and play tennis. (Humbert 2003)

It is interesting to note that girls often view the chance to learn new activities as an opportunity to learn in a more equitable and comfortable environment. Colleen, a student in grade 12, explained that learning a new sport was fun because "then no one can look down at you, they are no good either, they can't talk about you and say she is no good" (Humbert 1995a). Aerin, a student in grade 10, explained that she was looking forward to physical education in grade 11:

You get to learn different sports, like golf, cross country and down hill skiing. So now there will be guys who aren't as good as the girls in some stuff. That would be so great for a change, everything will be more even. (Humbert et al. 1998, 106)

## It Is Fun if I Am with My Friends

Students rarely discuss the idea of having fun in physical education classes without also mentioning the importance of being with their friends. This was the case with a group of grade 9 girls who were asked how they would ensure that girls had fun in physical education classes:

Susan:      We would tell them that they could be with their friends.

Iris:       Like when people play badminton, they could go in groups with their friends.

Camille:    That is right, that is all it would take, we would tell them that they would have lots of chances to be with their friends. (Humbert 1995a, 108)

When given an opportunity to suggest what she would have changed about her grade 12 physical education class, Rhonda explained that she wished that there had been more of her friends in her class: "It is really hard if you don't have any friends in the class, or if you have one friend, and then one day she is not there" (Humbert and Chad 1997). Barb, a grade 10 student, not only emphasized the importance of friends, she also discussed how she was concerned about people who did not seem to have many friends in her physical education class: "I mean we all try to be friends, but some people in the class, they feel left out and I just feel so bad for them. Physical education is not fun if your friends are not there too" (Humbert 1995a, 109).

Conversations with boys indicate that they, too, value the presence of friends. Sam, a grade 8 boy, suggested:

> I think if we want to get kids more active we should make sure they know that they can bring their friends or that they would meet new friends by participating. It is always better to do stuff with your friends. (Humbert 2003)

Jacob, a student in grade 11, commented on the role that his friends play in helping him stay active: "My friends help me to get out and do stuff. I think friends play a huge role in if you are active or not" (Humbert 2003).

The presence of friends can also offer students the motivation and security to try new activities, as this group of grade 9 students confirmed:

> Bob:      If we could give more kids the chance to be active with their friends, I think things would be a lot better.
>
> Christy:  Like get them to be active with a group and they will feel more motivated.
>
> Bob:      Yeah, get them to go and do things with people that they like.
>
> Christy:  Right, I don't do stuff by myself, I mean I would never join something alone, but if my friends went, I would try it, if they liked it then I would probably keep going. (Humbert et al. 2003)

If physical educators are going to encourage more young people to be physically active, the importance that students place on having fun in their physical education classes must be addressed. Students often report that they want to learn new skills, have opportunities to participate with students of similar abilities, and be with their friends. If students have fun in their physical education classes, they may have positive feelings about physical education, and about physical activity in general. Thus, it is vital that physical educators recognize that, for their students, fun truly is the most important thing!

## Conclusion

I hope that the words of these young people inspire all physical educators to reflect critically on their programs, and whenever possible, to listen to their students. The years I have spent listening to my own students have had a profound impact on me. I now read and listen differently, and I frequently find myself wondering whether individuals who write and speak with authority regarding physical education classes have involved students in their work. I hope that, for the readers of this chapter, this is just the beginning of a journey of listening to students. Perhaps van Manen's words (1991) can become a reality for us all: "If only the adult would really listen, it might make the adult more thoughtful and understanding about the child's world" (84).

A word of caution: By listening to students, responding to their concerns, and involving them in efforts to encourage them to pursue a lifetime of physical activity, teachers risk being viewed as "uncertain," "soft," or "too student-centred." I have been called all of these things, and more. When I hear physical education teachers lamenting that their students do not want to do anything, or that they are simply lazy, I find myself wondering whether they have taken the time to listen to their concerns and desires. I believe that if we listen to students and respond with programs that meet their needs and desires, we can help young people lead healthier, more physically active lifestyles.

Corbin (2002) commented that, too often, enthusiastic young teachers enter schools, try to make changes, and are told by experienced teachers to leave things the way they are. "Some of these teachers become socialized to not make waves and thus to not make a difference" (141). I believe that one of the major challenges facing all physical educators is to make a difference in the lives of youth, and this often means making waves. The health of young people depends on physical education teachers making a difference. Opportunity truly does knock on the door of all physical education teachers. Will you open the door and listen...for a change?

### References

American College of Sports Medicine. 1988. Physical fitness in children and youth. *Medicine and Science in Sports and Exercise* 20:422–23.

Bailey, D. 2000. Is anyone out there listening? *Quest* 52:344–50.

Bean, D. and Kinnear, G. 1989. An obsession with fun? *Runner* 28(4):19–20.

Browne, J. 1992. Coed or not coed? That is the question. *ACHPER National Journal*, (winter):20–23.

Canadian Fitness and Lifestyle Research Institute. 2004. *Socio-demographic and lifestyle correlates of obesity.* Ottawa: Canadian Institute for Health Information.

Chalip, L., M. Csikszentmihalyi, D. Kleiber, and R. Larson. 1984. Variations of experience in formal and informal sport. *Research Quarterly for Exercise and Sport* 55(2):109–16.

Chalmers, S. 1992. The influence of teachers on young women's experiences of physical education. *New Zealand Journal of Health Physical Education and Recreation* 25(4):3–6.

Corbin, C. B. 2002. Physical activity for everyone: What every physical educator should know about promoting lifelong physical activity. *Journal of Teaching Physical Education* 21:128–44.

Csikszentmihalyi, M. 1975. *Beyond boredom and anxiety.* San Francisco, CA: Jossey-Bass Publishers.

DeMont, J. 2002. Growing up large. *Maclean's* 5 August, 20–26.

Derry, J. A., and J. A. Phillips. 2004. Comparisons of selected student and teacher variables in all-girls and coeducational physical education environments. *Physical Educator* 61(1):23–35.

Ennis, C. D., D. J. Cothran, K. S. Davidson, S. J. Loftus, L. Owens, L. Swanson, and P. Hopsicker. 1997. Implementing a curriculum within a context of fear and disengagement. *Journal of Teaching in Physical Education* 17:52–71.

Fairclough, S. 2003. Physical activity, perceived competence and enjoyment during high school physical education. *European Journal of Physical Education* 8:5–18.

Fenton, J., W. Frisby, and M. Luke. 1999. Multiple perspectives of organizational culture: A case study of physical education for girls in a low-income multiracial school. *AVANTE* 5(1):1–22.

Gibbons, S., J. Wharf Higgins, C. Gaul, and G. Van Gyn. 1999. Listening to female students in high school physical education. *AVANTE* 5 (2):1-20.

Gilligan, C. 1982. *In a different voice.* Cambridge: Harvard University Press.

Griffin, L. 1989. Assessment of equitable instructional practices in the gym. *Canadian Association of Physical Education and Recreation Journal* 55(2):19–22.

Hansen, J. R., M. J. Fulop, and M. K. Hunter. 2000. Type 2 diabetes mellitus in youth: A growing challenge. *Clinical Diabetes* 18 (2):52–56.

Harris, S. B., B. A. Perkins, and E. Whalen-Brough. 1996. Non-insulin dependent diabetes mellitus among First Nations children. *Canadian Family Physician* 42:869–76.

Humbert, M. L. 1995a. The experiences of young women in physical education classes. Ph.D. diss., University of Alberta.

———. 1995b. On the sidelines: The experiences of young women in physical education classes. *AVANTE* 1(2):58–77.

————. 1996. Nowhere to hide. The experiences of girls in physical education classes. *Women's Education des femmes* 14:2.

————. 2003. What do the boys have to say? Unpublished data.

Humbert, M. L. and Blacklock, F. (1998). *Girls in Action: Speaking Out.* Video. Ottawa: CAHPERD.

Humbert, M. L., and K. E. Chad. 1997. Physical activity and the health of young women: An innovative approach. Unpublished paper presented at the International Congress on Women's Health Issues, Saskatoon, Saskatchewan.

Humbert, M. L., K. E. Chad, K. Spink, N. Muharjine, and T. Girolami. 2003. If you could be the one in charge.... Unpublished paper presented at the annual conference of the Canadian Association of Health, Physical Education, Recreation and Dance, Winnipeg, Manitoba.

Humbert, M. L., T. Goddard, and P. Avery. 1997. An opportunity to close the gap. Paper presented at the Learning from Practice seminar of the Dr. Stirling McDowell Foundation for Research into Teaching, Saskatoon, Saskatchewan.

————. 1998. Closing the gap: Addressing the experiences of young women in high school physical education classes. Report submitted to the Dr. Stirling McDowell Foundation for Research into Teaching, Saskatoon, Saskatchewan.

Knoppers, A. 1988. Equity for excellence in physical education. *Journal of Physical Education, Recreation & Dance* 59(6):54–58.

Leslie, E., P. B. Sparling, and N. Owen. 2001. University campus settings and the promotion of physical activity in young adults: Lessons from research in Australia and the USA. *Health Education* 101:116–25.

Lirgg, C. D. 1994. Environmental perceptions of students in same-sex and coeducational physical education classes. *Journal of Educational Psychology* 86(2):183–92.

Macdonald, A. 2002. Letter to the editor. *Maclean's* 19 August, 6.

MacKelvie, K. J., K. M. Khan, and H. A. McKay. 2002. Is there a critical period for bone response to weight bearing exercise in children and adolescents? A systematic review. *British Journal of Sports Medicine* 36:250–57.

Malina, R. M. 1996. Tracking of physical activity and physical fitness across the lifespan. *Research Quarterly for Exercise and Sport* 67(3):548–55 (special issue).

Mandigo, J. L., and L. P. Thompson. 1998. Go with the flow: How flow theory can help practitioners to intrinsically motivate children to be physically active. *Physical Educator* 55(3):145–59.

Martens, R. 1996. Turning kids on to a physical activity for a lifetime. *Quest* 48:303–10.

McGraw, S. A., D. Sellers, E. Stone, K. A. Resnicow, S. Kuester, F. Fridinger, and H. Wechsler. 2000. Measuring implementation of school programs and policies to promote healthy eating and physical activity among youth. *Preventive Medicine* 31:86–97.

Mendlein, J. M., T. Baranowski, and M. Pratt. 2000. Physical activity and nutrition in children and youth: Opportunities for performing assessments and conducting interventions. *Preventive Medicine* 31(2):S150–S153.

Olafson, Lori, 2002. I hate phys. ed.: Adolescent girls talk about physical education. *The Physical Educator* 59(2):67–74.

Pate, R. R., P. S. Freedson, J. F. Sallis, W. C. Taylor, J. Sirard, S. G. Trost, and M. Dowda. 2002. Compliance with physical activity guidelines: Prevalence in a population of children and youth. *Annals of Epidemiology* 12:303–08.

Portman, P. A. 2003. Are physical education classes encouraging students to be physically active? Experiences of ninth graders in their last semester of required physical education. *Physical Educator* 60(3):150–61.

Prochaska, J. J., J. F. Sallis, D. J. Slymen, and T. L. McKenzie. 2003. A longitudinal study of children's enjoyment of physical education. *Pediatric Exercise Science* 15(2):170.

Reed, J. A., and S. L. Bertelsen. 2003. The relationship between the perceptions of students and instructors of the importance of their objectives in physical education activity classes. *Physical Educator* 60(1):19–27.

Ryan, S., D. Fleming, and M. Maina. 2003. Attitudes of middle school students toward their physical education teachers and classes. *Physical Educator* 60(2):28–42.

Sallis, J. F., and T. L. McKenzie. 1991. Physical education's role in public health. *Research Quarterly for Exercise and Sport* 62(2):124–37.

Scraton, S. 1992. *Shaping up to womanhood: Gender and girls' physical education.* Buckingham: Open University Press.

Shakeshaft, C. 1986. A gender at risk. *Phi Delta Kappan* 67:499–503.

Singer, R. N. 1996. Moving toward the quality of life. *Quest* 48:246–52.

Stone, E. J., T. L. McKenzie, G. K. Welk, and M. L. Booth. 1998. Effects of physical activity interventions in youth: Review and synthesis. *American Journal of Preventive Medicine* 15(4):298–315.

Tannehill, D., J. E. Romar, and M. O'Sullivan. 1994. Attitudes towards physical education: Their impact on how physical education teachers make sense of their work. *Journal of Teaching in Physical Education* 13:406–20.

Treanor, L., K. Graber, L. Housner, and R. Weingand. 1998. Middle school students' perceptions of coeducational and same sex physical education classes. *Journal of Teaching Physical Education* 18:43–56.

Tremblay, M. Autumn 1998. The preservation of physical education: Our children's lives depend on it! *Canadian Association for Health, Physical Education, Recreation and Dance Journal* 64(3):34–36.

Tremblay, M., and J. D. Wilms. 2000. Secular trends in the body mass index of Canadian children. *Canadian Medical Association Journal* 163(11):1429–33.

van Manen, M. 1991. *The tact of teaching: The meaning of pedagogical thoughtfulness.* London, ON: The Althouse Press.

Wharf Higgins, J., C. Gaul, S. Gibbons, and G. Van Gyn. 2003. Factors influencing physical activity levels among Canadian youth. *Canadian Journal of Public Health* 94(1):45–51.

Whitehead, M. 1988. The danger of fun. *The British Journal of Physical Education* 19(4):155.

Williams, N. F. 1994. The physical education hall of shame: Part II. *Journal of Physical Education, Recreation & Dance* 65(2):17–20.

# Chapter Two

# *Health Literacy*

## Andy Anderson and David Booth

In this chapter we examine several meanings of literacy and its conceptual roots to develop a definition and criteria for *health literacy*. Generally, we assert that education for health literacy is an important area of study in schools, not only because of the implications health has for quality of life but also because the study of health is about human interaction with the world around us. Health can be an important context for studying not only health issues but also the nature of how we learn—processes such as critical thinking, problem-posing and problem-solving, and practical reasoning can be better understood and strategically employed.

The study of various health texts relevant to elementary and secondary school students offers robust opportunities to explore diverse issues that deeply concern all people and their communities, for example, family relationships, racism, substance abuse, poverty, violence, pollution, and human sexuality. These issues often evoke emotion, interest, controversy, and expressions of concern for social justice, democracy, and empowerment. Through a closer examination of health issues such as body image, nutrition habits, and the effects of poverty, students can critically examine how they have constructed knowledge in relation to prior knowledge and beliefs. Working from these perspectives, they are able to reconstruct and represent ideas in new and imaginative ways. In this way students begin to realize they can *author* choice and create alternatives in relation to their life challenges and ambitions (Anderson 1999). In short, the rationale for students' studying health is comparable to the rationale for their studying science and history: it is a part of human understanding and experience.

Those who lack an understanding of what it means to live a healthy life lack a full understanding of the nature of our relationships with each other, our environments (geographical and cultural), and ourselves.

The study of health represents a preservation and accumulation of discursive information that explores a wide variety of topics and relationships—from disease pathology to spiritual healing; from poverty to active engagement in civic and social affairs; from obesity to access to recreational facilities. We relate our arguments about the importance of health to critical thinking, autonomy, empowerment, and action competency. At the end of the chapter, we theorize about health as a form of intelligence or mindfulness that activates and integrates a wide array of intellectual, factual, and experiential knowledge important for making decisions in almost every facet of life.

Throughout this chapter we refer to a constructive engagement with various "texts": an assortment of ways, formats, or genres that hold meaning, including print, films, television, storytelling, drama, dance, students' writing, conversations, neighbourhood environments, graffiti, music, modelled behaviour, and Internet web pages. Students are exposed continually to these various texts and to ignore their impact would be missed opportunities for educators. More important, we consider these texts not simply as other ways of expressing or receiving ideas, but also as other ways of experiencing knowledge and developing wisdom.

We are concerned primarily with health literacy from the perspective of educators. We want to encourage and enable discussion within the education community about the value of literacy for health in terms of the learner's development. We challenged ourselves to address this central question: What are the various texts—written, oral, social, cultural, and political—that students must "read" to be successful in diverse and complex settings that have an impact on their health—mentally, physically, socially, spiritually, and in terms of their living conditions and life chances? Being conversant with one text form does not always afford access to another. For example, the text of tagging and other forms of graffiti can be read by adolescent gang members but not likely by Shakespearean scholars. In other words, literacy is content- and context-specific. We present literacy, therefore, as a way to explore a variety of worlds of experience and understanding. Health literacy is, therefore, a way in which to present a consciousness and a concern about self and the world in which we live.

## Literacy Defined

According to Friere and Macedo (1987), literacy is about "conscientization," the process of becoming critically conscious of the sociohistorical, political, and media-saturated world in which people live and learn. They write that

> literacy cannot be reduced to the treatment of letters and words as purely mechanical domain. We need to go beyond this rigid comprehension of literacy and begin to view it as the relationship of learners to the world, mediated by the transforming practice of this world taking place in the very general milieu in which learners travel. (viii)

Much of the dialogue about literacy is grounded in certain beliefs about the learning process and the sense of agency one can expect to gain and expend in the process of becoming literate. To us, learning is a sense-making process. In relation to prior knowledge and beliefs, new knowledge is constructed *by the learner*. We are not, however, totally free to construct meaning. The making of experience is influenced by "others" and "otherness," in the social contexts in which we live—families, friends, media, neighbourhoods, and cultures. For example, how we define beauty is a function of time and place. Definitions of beauty that have their origins in the fashion industry have an enormous impact on body image, body acceptance, self-worth, and social behaviour. Health literacy is therefore concerned with meaning, motivation, and morality, tied in with all the texts of our lives.

If we look deeply into this notion of constructed knowledge, however, we see that there is also inherently a sense of agency. Given a chance to examine more critically the myth of beauty, we begin to realize that there are alternative perspectives. Our choices have been influenced by our texts, but we can also begin to realize that knowledge is not fixed, finite, and complete, but rather that it is subject to continuous change and interpretation. Knowledge construction is the result of mental efforts by each person to reason, understand, and come closer to what Parker Palmer (1998) refers to as the *great thing* about the subject matter, having a deeper sense of what the text *author* intended and, perhaps more importantly, what it means to the *reader*. To the notion of literacy as self determination, self reliance, and autonomy, we add the insights of Jerome Bruner who referred to literacy as "the technology for the empowerment of the mind" (Wells and Chang-Wells 1992, 138).

We join Bruner in promoting the notion that *becoming* literate means being thoughtful not only about what has been "said," but also about what it means to the reader, listener, or viewer. Being literate is an interactive process which results in the generation, not simply the consumption, of ideas, understanding, and insight. It means being aware of how what one has learned fits into one's life experiences. It means understanding that knowledge shapes, and is shaped by, human interaction. Literacy is best understood, therefore, as a tool that enables people to interact with the world around them in ways that promote deeper and ongoing learning.

A heuristic is a tool that enables us to inquire more deeply into the nature of human experience—our own and others'. The root meaning of "heuristic" comes from the Greek word *heuriskein*, meaning to discover or to find. It refers to a process of internal search through which one discovers the nature and meaning of experience and develops methods and procedures for further investigation and analysis. As a heuristic, health literacy equips learners to access information and services, and to develop the skills that enable a person to relate and connect the new knowledge or ideas to day-to-day living. Complex levels of literacy prepare individuals and groups to critically examine the conditions or circumstances in their lives that interact with opportunities to be healthy. To these distinct qualities we add the capacity to engage in ongoing learning about one's own health. A health-literate person would also be alert and insightful about the change process, its influences and inhibitors, the effects of broader issues such as race, gender, and socio-economic status, as well as power and politics. Health literacy is heuristic inquiry. All heuristic inquiry begins with the internal search to discover, a passionate desire to know, and a devotion and commitment to pursue a question that is strongly connected to one's own identity and selfhood. The *self* of the researcher is present throughout the process, and while understanding the phenomenon in increasing depth, the researcher also experiences growing self-awareness and self-knowledge. Health literacy, therefore, is best understood as a form of consciousness and conscience; a way of knowing about the world, not just as others would have us see it, but as we understand it in terms of our own lives.

The real voyage of discovery is not the seeing of new landscapes but the seeing with new eyes. Health literacy enriches our sense of connectedness with "what is out there" and with "what is within me" in reflective thought, feeling, and awareness. As a heuristic process, health literacy requires a return to self, a recognition of self-awareness and a valuing of one's own experience. Connectedness is autobiographical.

## An Example of Health Literacy in Action

Before we examine the various modes of literacy, we offer a topic for consideration in the classroom to show the various ways in which literacy might be experienced by students. Physical activity is an important way to achieve good health; however, the way students experience physical activity can have an important impact on their feelings about movement and its benefits and risks, their beliefs about their movement competencies, and their decisions about whether to be active in the future. Teachers can prepare a series of lessons, each designed with particular outcomes in mind. For example, in one session students participate in a sport-oriented approach to physical activity. The official game of basketball is broken into discrete elements, in which students are drilled for skill mastery. Next, students participate in modified versions of basketball. Last, students create their own version of the game, using other pieces of equipment, such as, a frisbee, a bean bag, and a rubber chicken in place of the traditional basketball. They debrief after each episode, identifying the focus of each session and the pros and cons of each approach. More important, students relate the structure of the game to opportunities for participation. Furthermore, they can be challenged to think about how parks and community play areas can be designed to maximize opportunities for physical activity that capitalize on people's abilities to be creative and inclusive.

Other activities include inviting students to examine the meanings of health that are promoted in the media. Groups can scan popular magazines and newspaper advertisements to compile a list of indicators of "good" health. They are then encouraged to determine whether the health promoted in the media is for public good (people are entitled to enjoy good health) or private good (businesses profit from the sale of their products). Closer to home, students observe playground play and tally the number and kinds of activities that students enjoy during recess and lunch breaks. Activity records, which include the kind and duration of activities performed both during and outside of school, can be analyzed in relation to parental support, after-school employment, cost of participation (equipment, travel), and gender. Interviewing others to determine what interests they would like to pursue to become more involved in physical activity might reveal that the school curriculum is out-of-touch with the realities of students' lives. In one school, for example, students were surveyed to determine why so many were hanging around the smoking area before school. Their response was simply, "We aren't allowed into the school before

classes and no one will supervise us if we want to workout or play basketball."

The health literacy-focused educator is portrayed here as one who
avoids being indifferent. The educator's role is to prepare learners to get involved in planning their education, helping them create the critical capacity to consider and participate in the direction and dreams of that education
rather than merely following blindly. Within the modes of literacy, we en-
vision students' progress towards active citizenry as well as personal fulfillment.

## Modes of Health Literacy

Different modes of literacy involve engagement with a text in different ways, which in turn results in different relationships and differences
in the way learners connect. In this section we provide a brief overview of
Wells and Chang-Wells's (1992) five modes of engagement for literacy. To
these five modes we add a sixth that we have drawn from recent discussions
in the health-promotion literature about health literacy, as well as a seventh that we have identified from our discussion of heuristic inquiry. Each
mode should not be considered in isolation from the others; rather, we encourage a holistic view of literacy. In other words, modes of literacy for
health interconnect as they do in other areas of the school curriculum—language arts, music, drama, science, sociology, biology, and anthro-
pology. We separate them here to show several dimensions of health
literacy and to provide suggestions that help to organize our thinking about
what activities and classroom experiences might encourage an understanding of health literacy that transcends the accumulation of preselected
knowledge and skills.

Wells and Chang-Wells (1992) write,

> Every written text has a physical form—marks inscribed on a
> surface that represent the writer's meanings according to the
> conventions of a linguistic code. When the use of a text focus-
> ses on the code—on the encoding/decoding relationship be-
> tween meaning and its physical representation, and the
> conventions that govern it—I [sic] shall talk about this as en-
> gaging with the text in the *performative* mode. This is the mode
> we adopt, for example, when we are proofreading something we
> have written or when we are skimming through a telephone di-

rectory, looking for a particular entry. Of necessity, beginning readers and writers have to devote a considerable amount of their attention to learning how to use the code. However, even for them, a concern with form is rarely the primary purpose. Competence in the performative mode is therefore best seen as a means to engaging with the text in other modes.... (138)

For health literacy, the first mode, *performative competence*, might entail the ability to encode or decode certain road signs; recognize symbols that indicate harmful or hazardous materials found in the home; identify emergency phone numbers (911, fire department, police, poison help-line); read a map to locate hospitals in the area; recognize certain dangers in play areas, such as needles, broken glass, or weapons; or interpret body language—threatening gestures, shame, grief, worry, or joy.          *added to smith*

The second mode is *functional*. Text is treated as an adjunct, or a means to the achievement of some other purpose, for example, using the appropriate form to pay money at the bank, leaving instructions for another member of the family to prepare dinner, or finding out from the instructional manual how to use a recently acquired machine (Wells and Chang-Wells 1992). The text functions instrumentally as a means to an end. In health literacy functional competence would entail: reading a poster about fire prevention in the home to prompt the adoption of fire safety measures (such as installing smoke detectors, recording emergency numbers by the phone, identifying emergency exit procedures); using a web site to learn more about the benefits of nutritious eating or food preparation and preservation techniques; or, listening to a speaker's advice about sun protection practices—*slip* on a shirt, *slap* on a hat, and *slop* on sunscreen.

In the third mode, called the *informational* mode, text is treated

as a channel by means of which information is communicated from one person to another. Validity or significance of the information is not important; the focus is on accuracy of comprehension or on clarity and conciseness of expression. Consulting a reference book to find the facts on a question or to identify an unknown flower or bird would be examples of this mode of engagement, as would writing a routine report or completing a questionnaire. (Wells and Chang-Wells 1992, 139)

To promote health literacy in this mode, students might examine reliable and current information in brochures about sexually transmitted infections; participate in a survey about youth health issues, such as tobacco use,

*① having or serving a utilitarian purpose.*
*significance is np for achievement*

*② functional mode - use text for a purpose to achieve something*
*validity & significance*

*③ informational mode - accuracy of comprehension or on clarity & conciseness (brief but comprehensive) of expression.*

alcohol abuse, teen pregnancy, and physical inactivity; prepare a portfolio of newspaper clippings that could be characterized as "good news" stories; collect information about the incidence of injury during particular sporting events held at school; or, determine the implied meaning of prescription medication instructions—"one tablet three times daily" really means "take one pill every eight hours," but if you miss taking the pill, when are you supposed to take it? Do you double up the next time?

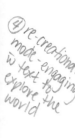

*④ re-creational mode - engaging w text to explore the world*

Wells and Chang-Wells's fourth mode is engagement with text as a verbal artifact. In calling this mode *re-creational,* they attempt to capture the sense of engagement with text as an end in itself undertaken for the pleasure of constructing and exploring a world through words, whether one's own or those of another. Examples of this mode include expressions of ideas presented in letters to friends or entries in a personal journal (Wells and Chang-Wells 1992, 139). In terms of health literacy, recreational activities might include preparing a radio commercial to promote healthy eating; mounting a student photographic exhibition to show the anguish of alienation; dramatizing an abusive relationship; or, reading a biography about a resilient person.

The fifth mode, according to Wells and Chang-Wells, is important throughout the other modes of engagement. It is the *epistemic* mode—its name being derived from *episteme,* the Greek word for knowledge. In this mode, the text is treated not as representation of meaning that is already decided, given, and self-evident, but as a tentative and provisional attempt on the part of the writer to capture his or her current understanding in an external form so that it may provoke further attempts at understanding as the writer or a reader dialogues with the text to interpret its meaning (Lotman 1988 cited in Wells and Chang-Wells 1992). Engagement with the text involves critically examining its meanings and implications. In the midst of epistemic involvement a fruitful dialectic evolves, what Scardamalia and Bereiter (1985) refer to as "the content space and the rhetorical space" (quoted in Wells and Chang-Wells 1992, 140). The transaction between the representation on the page and the representation in the brain advances one's intellectual, moral, or affective understanding to an extent that would otherwise be difficult to achieve. "To be *fully* [italics added] literate, therefore, is to have both the ability and the disposition to engage with texts epistemically when the occasion demands" (Wells and Chang-Wells 1992, 141). Epistemic engagement for health literacy involves examining text critically. Learners are encouraged to question the messages, to ask important questions, such as, "Whose interests are being

*state of mind involving knowledge*

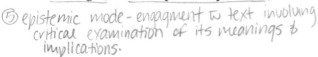

*⑤ epistemic mode - engagement w text involving critical examination of its meanings & implications.*

served?"; "Whose voice is spoken, whose voice is silent?"; and, "What does the phrase *nothing about us without us* mean to you?" Person, place, and purpose are emphasized in the epistemic mode.

As we stated above, it is "important to emphasize that any text can be engaged with in any of the five modes, and that during a complete literacy event, one may move between modes, with each mode supporting and facilitating the others" (Wells and Chang-Wells 1992, 141). This relationship is depicted in Figure 1.

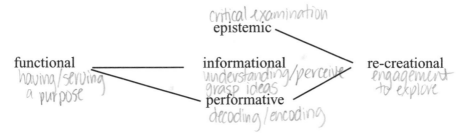

critical examination
epistemic

functional

having/serving
a purpose

informational

understanding/perceive
grasp ideas

performative

decoding/encoding

re-creational

engagement
to explore

*Figure 1:* Modes of Literacy

If we apply this model to the modes presented above we can imagine how important health questions might arise. In finding out information, what are considered reliable sources? What happens when recommended health practices conflict with traditional beliefs about health? For example, for many people, a health checkup involves a visit to the doctor and supplying a sample of body fluids, usually urine and blood, for laboratory analysis. In some cultures, checking up on health occurs at sunrise, while bathing in cool mountain waters and meditating to position oneself spiritually, emotionally, mentally, and physically closer to the creator or nature.

Literacy, broadly construed, relates not only to the ability to interpret and construct texts, but also to the ability to think about them critically. There is growing recognition in the critical thinking movement that critical thinking involves the ability to participate in ongoing conversations (through a wide variety of texts) about important issues (Applebee 1996; Paul and Elder 1999). Furthermore, proponents of critical literacy contend that one important goal of literacy instruction should be to apply critical thinking to achieve deeper understanding of existing social conditions and power relations, on the premise that such understanding, in combination with the ability to engage in critical discourse, can be a vehicle for change.

The National Health Education Standards Committee defined health literacy as the ability to access, interpret, and apply health knowledge and services to decisions about health (Joint Committee on National Health Education Standards 1995). They and the practitioners and curriculum planners who follow these standards characterize health literacy as the life skills of health promotion. Four key components comprise education for health literacy: critical thinking; effective communication; self-directed learning; and, responsible citizenry. More recently, Nutbeam's (2001) discussion of literacy for health focused on three areas of literacy designed to

(a) prepare students to obtain relevant health information— *functional* literacy;
(b) relate knowledge of health and interpersonal skills to personal and social situations—*interactive* literacy; and,
(c) reflect on the underlying issues and environmental factors, for example, racial and ethnic concerns, economic and social status, as well as other political and cultural factors that have an impact on opportunities to be healthy—*critical* literacy.

Fundamental fairness and equity are cited as quintessential in closing the gap in health between "have" and "have-not" people, countries, and races. The gap, we are learning, consists of differences not just in services, but also in the conditions that lead to wellbeing. Despite this orientation, Healthy People 2010[1] (USDHHS 2000) does not include the forward-looking notion of "potential" in the health literacy definition. However, the broad definition of health literacy proposed in the World Health Organization (WHO) health promotion glossary does include this concept:

> Health literacy represents the cognitive and social skills which determine the motivation and ability of individuals to gain access to, understand and use information in ways which promote and maintain good health. (WHO 1998)

This definition was discussed at a Health Literacy Workshop at the 5th WHO Global Conference on Health Promotion (PAHO/Yale/Pfizer workshop on Health Literacy, Mexico City, June 2000). The workshop resolved to widen the glossary definition to include the dimensions of community development and health-related skills beyond health promotion; the aim is to understand health literacy not only as a personal characteristic, but also as a key determinant of population health.

Employment stability, educational opportunities, and community involvement, for example, make a big difference in the conditions which contribute to engagement in society and the feelings of belonging and acceptance that accompany participation. The educational activities associated with understanding and addressing the gap through literacy are endless. Student discussions may concentrate on health factors, such as, social bonding, friendships, civic involvement, employment stability, and education. Teachers can challenge students to relate feelings of shame and vulnerability, worries about debts, job security, and housing, and social alienation and bullying, to self-esteem, self-confidence, alcohol and drug abuse, violence, and crime. They can be asked: "Explain this statement—Poverty makes you sick"; "Defend this statement—Education is health"; "Describe ways that members of the school community can promote social cohesion and work together to reach valued and shared goals, promote equity of opportunity and involvement, and to further the idea that 'we're all in this together.'"

The language of health can become an important area of analysis as part of discussions about functional, performative, and critical literacy. Medical terminology is often difficult to understand and unrelated to other dimensions of health such as the spiritual, emotional, and social. The language of body systems typically gathers and communicates very little about the person. This rather cold and distant stance toward health can be threatening and intimidating. Health is often reduced to medical measurements (e.g., heart rate, blood pressure, body temperature). Treatment and recovery are geared more often toward practices that expect passive and compliant patients to wait for someone else to tell them what to do. This can create risks. Furthermore, there is increasing evidence to show that active involvement in the decision-making process, i.e., the person's participation in the construction and administration of his or her pathway to wellness, yields better results and a faster recovery from traumatic illness. Biomedical information seldom takes into account the person, ignoring his or her beliefs about self, family and friendships, goals, passions, and ambitions. Language can be a strong indicator of "who knows," "who is involved," and "who is left out." Language can be an indicator of privilege, power structures, and participation.

Health behaviours can tell us a good deal about human nature. In an effort to make sense of the strange goings-on inside our bodies we develop our own forms of reasoning and explanations. Home remedies, medicinal folklore, and traditional healing practices are attempts to assume greater control over the factors and forces that affect our quality of life, and to enhance our resistance against and recovery from whatever disease we face. Educators can explore folk wisdom and add a dimension to their literary repertoires at the same time.

Understanding health from the students' perspective can help teachers customize their designs for curriculum and instruction. Imagine a health class where students reach beyond organic functioning and engage in a discussion of terms, such as valve, chambers, and blood pressure, and metaphors for the heart and its work (such as pump), along with everyday expressions, such as, "take heart," "have a heart," "put your heart into it," and "express heartfelt thanks." In a mathematics class, what might be learned about the heart from a comparison of heart rates of children at different ages, of boys and girls, of cats and dogs and other species? In a grade 11 language arts class, learning about "messages from the heart" might involve reading and composing love letters, greeting cards, or love stories. What is the "language of love"? When our feelings "come from the heart," what emotions and instincts do we call on? The language of health is clearly linked to social practices. The contexts in which health is discussed affect how we communicate.

Health literacy is about recognizing that there are many ways of knowing and showing what you know; it is about exploring alternative and multiple realities, viewing problems from beyond the messages of lived experience, making proactive and adaptive choices in relation to external and internal forces; it involves knowing that the choices a person makes have the potential to transform reality; it is about understanding the "community" in which we live, think, and feel, and about how we are affected by those around us; it is also about understanding that we can be activists, reformers, and agents of change. When we realize the potential of health literacy to make things better and to make better things, we can start the change process. As part of a nationwide study, groups of health enthusiasts in schools gathered to tell their stories about health promotion. Each forum generated over 100 different activities in schools they characterized as working for health. In all instances, more than 25 percent of the programs were aimed at helping or caring for others in the school or the community (for example, a hat and mittens campaign, peer helpers, the Terry Fox Walk/Run for Cancer). Activism for health in schools appears to be as much about building a sense of belonging, affiliation, and caring as it is about fighting cancer and heart disease. Students want to make changes that reflect their values and beliefs about what makes life good at school.

At some schools, student turnover is extremely high. To help combat the stress and confusion this can generate, schools can set up a committee to welcome new students and their families. The committee can help the families to get established and feel at home in the school and in the community, by helping them locate the resources they need to settle in—doctors, libraries, hockey and swimming programs, bus schedules, homework helpers, babysitting services, and laundromat locations. Every new student begins a scrapbook, portfolio, or diary that showcases school life, from year to year, or in many cases, school to school. Activism for health in schools is aimed at social inclusion through care for others.

Health literacy is not an easy concept to categorize. It is perhaps better not to define it too rigidly but rather to focus interpretation on the experience of health literacy. We propose, therefore, the concept of health literacy as a form of mindfulness. Langer (1997) uses the idea of mindfulness to situate her arguments about learning outcomes. She reasons that intelligence is a means of achieving desired outcomes. That is, it is a linear process moving from problem to resolution as rapidly as possible. It is developed from an observing expert's perspective by focusing on stable categories and dependency on remembered facts and learned skills in contexts that are sometimes perceived as novel.

Mindfulness, she argues, is concerned with reality identified through several possible perspectives. Mindfulness should be considered a process of stepping back from both perceived problems and perceived solutions to view situations as novel, a process through which meaning is given to outcomes developed from an actor's ability to experience personal control by shifting perspectives (110). Intelligence is focused on the attainment of learning outcomes, whereas mindfulness is concerned with what was the outcome or sense made by the learner as a result of the learning process. Similarly, health is an interpretive, subjective experience gained in relation to the purpose for which it exists, the people for whom it exists, and the places in which it occurs.

## Literacy is Health

Literacy is linked to health in a number of ways. In developing countries, improvements in levels of literacy related to reading, writing, and numeracy, especially for women, result not only in better-paying and stable jobs, but often also in delays in marriage and pregnancy, fewer children, reductions in the rate of infant mortality, and an overall improved respon-

siveness to the heath care needs of the entire family (Kickbusch 2001;
World Bank c2000). According to Health Canada (1999), educational attainment appears to prepare people to pursue careers that are fulfilling, to
enjoy relationships at home, at work, and in the community that are rewarding and meaningful, and to engage in a variety of recreation and leisure
pursuits that further protect individuals and families from health risks.
Higher levels of education, for example, are linked to smoke-free living,
greater frequency of exercise, and a lower incidence of alcohol and drug
abuse. Literacy is a determinant of health because it enables people to work
toward goals and aspirations, and to make better choices—about housing,
occupations, family care, and participation in community, social, and civic
affairs. It contributes to the development of human and social capital and,
according to Filmer (1999), overall economic growth. As an intellectual
resource, literacy enhances the overall functional capacity of the individual
to reason practically, think critically, make discerning choices, and engage
in reasoned action.

Questions about which students might inquire further include:

◈ What is healthy about the experiences of spending time with
friends, attending a ceremony as a member of a faith community, working together to establish a neighbourhood vegetable
garden, helping others with reading difficulties?
◈ What is the experience of feeling connected with nature?
◈ What is healthful about the experience of exercise?

Methods of inquiry might entail the deployment of a number of modes of
literacy—reading, writing, interviewing, listening to stories, creating a
poster, or mounting a photographic display.

## Health as a Way of Looking at the World

How might being mindful of health change the way we name and
frame problems, and explore cause and effect relationships? We propose
that health-minded educators seek to create a learning environment that
fosters a sense of belonging, encourages students to assume active roles in
the learning process, and uses health promotion concepts, such as equity
and empowerment, to guide practice. Health-minded administrators insti-
tutionalize norms of egalitarianism and value the involvement of those
most affected by the way schools operate. Health-minded parents ensure
that their children are ready to learn and actively build connections within

their communities to ensure that they have the resources needed to live in dignity. Health-minded students recognize their importance as *difference makers*.

## Conclusion

In this chapter, we explored definitions of literacy and then applied the key components of literacy to health education. We then argued that health is a critical addition to the growing list of literacies needed for full participation in society. We argue this for three reasons: (a) without literacy for health, young people are at risk—not just at risk of life-threatening diseases but also at risk of not fully living up to their potential as human beings; (b) education for health offers students opportunities to engage in the consideration of issues and problems that have worldwide significance and impact; and, (c) education for health literacy can be an important opportunity for students to understand the influence of education, social-economic circumstances, cultural and historical contexts, and political policy on the choices and chances people have to live healthy lives. As literate beings, we *read* ourselves into an awareness of what it means to be healthy.

### Note
1. Healthy People 2010 is a set of health objectives for the United States to achieve over the first decade of the new century. It can be used by many different people, communities, professional organizations, and others to develop programs to improve health. Its goals are to increase the quality and years of healthy life and the conditions that enable all persons to attain this outcome.

### References
Anderson, A. 1999. Using health education to develop literacy. *Research for Educational Reform* 4:21–33.

Applebee, A. N. 1996. *Curriculum as conversation*. Chicago: University of Chicago Press.

Filmer, D. 1999. The structure of social disparities in education: Gender and wealth. *Policy Research Report on Gender and Development Working Paper No. 5*. Available at: www.worldbank.org/gender/prr. Washington, DC: World Bank.

Friere, P., and D. Macedo. 1987. *Literacy: Reading the word and the world*. South Hadley, MA: Bergin and Farvey Publishers.

Health Canada. 1999. *Toward a healthy future: Second report on the health of Canadians*. Available at: www.hc-sc.gcca/hppb/phdd/report/text_versions/english/index.html [This site is no longer active.]. Ottawa: Health Canada.

Joint Committee on National Health Education Standards. 1995. National health
    education standards: Achieving health literacy. Atlanta: American Cancer
    Society.
Kickbusch, I. 2001. Health literacy: Addressing the health education divide.
    *Health Promotion International*, 16(3):289–97.
Langer, E. 1997. *The power of mindful learning*. Reading, MA: Addison Wesley.
Nutbeam, D. 2001. Health literacy as a public health goal. *Health Promotion International* 15:259–67.
PAHO/Yale/Pfizer workshop on Health Literacy. A workshop presented at the 5th
    World Health Organization Conference on Health Promotion. Mexico City,
    June 2000.
Palmer, P. 1998. *The courage to teach: Exploring the inner landscape of a teacher's life.*
    San Francisco: Jossey-Bass Publishers.
Paul, R. W., and L. Elder. 1999. Critical thinking: Teaching students to seek the
    logic of things. *Journal of Developmental Education* 23:34–35.
Scardamalia, M., and C. Bereiter. 1985. Development of dialetical processes in
    composition. In *Literacy, language and learning: The nature and consequences of
    reading and writing*, ed. D. Olson, N. Torrence, and A. Hildyard. Cambridge:
    Cambridge University Press.
United States Department of Health and Human Services, Office of Disease Pre-
    vention and Health Promotion. 2000. Healthy people 2010. Available at:
    www.health.gov/healthy people
Wells, G., and Gen Ling Chang-Wells. 1992. *Constructing knowledge together:
    Classrooms as centers of inquiry and literacy*. Portsmouth, NH: Heinemann.
World Bank. c2000. *Entering the 21st century: World development report, 1999/
    2000*. New York: Oxford University Press.
World Health Organization. 1998. *Health Promotion Glossary*. Geneva: The
    Author.

Chapter Three

# *"This Is the Kind of Experience I Plan to Encourage":*

## *Competition and Fair Play in High School Physical Education*

## Ellen Singleton

*Would you describe yourself as competitive?*
*Do you think girls are more or less competitive than boys?*
*Would you encourage your students to be competitive in PE class?*
*How would you ensure 'fair play' happened in your classes?*

(Singleton 2004)

### Introduction

It may seem that a chapter examining competition in physical education class could not be anything other than brief. After all, what is there to talk about? In most parts of the world, people participate in sporting activities. Sports are generally considered to be competitive in various ways—winners and losers are designated, individuals attempt to better a previous personal best, team members strive to attain ever better group co-operation in order to attain a goal. In North America, as well as many other parts of the world, team sports and various dual and individual games and physical activities are taught in school physical education. Therefore, competition is an inescapable aspect of high school physical education. Or, is it?

Although I think competition has a role in secondary physical education classes, I have some questions about it, just the same. How big a part should competition play in physical education? What is its role? Should it be a star, or an extra? How should competition's role be played in physical education class? Should it be welcomed into the gymnasium as a motivator and a mediator, or tossed out as a troublemaker?

Competition can be a troublesome presence in high school physical education classes (Humbert and Blacklock 1999; Gibbons 1999; Wilson 2002), but it is rarely discussed (or even mentioned) in class. Further, there is no mention of competition in provincial curriculum guides, but "fair play" is emphasized. Why highlight "fair play" if competition is not an issue? Although physical educators readily acknowledge the presence of competition in their classes, they rarely consider the influence competition may have on their students' attitudes toward physical activity. The purpose of this chapter is to introduce a study that examines what physical education student teachers think about competition and fair play based on their practicum experiences.

Competition is connected to school physical education through ideological ties that are political, gendered, cultural, and moral in nature. For example, Canadian curricula are heavily weighted toward instruction in team and individual sports that are considered to be an indisputable part of the fabric of our western culture (Kohn 1995). Games such as basketball, hockey, football, baseball, badminton, and soccer—staples in any Canadian high school physical education curriculum—are, in the world outside of school, *necessarily* competitive for a variety of reasons. Professional and amateur sports reproduce in endless permutations and combinations the desirability of the competitive, capitalist economy under which we live (Kirk and Tinning 1990; Rail 1998; Fernandez-Balboa 1997). This is most effective when sport is provided as a form of entertainment. In the commercial world of sport, men who can play games well, that is, with skill, determination, and aggression, are rewarded with high status and often a great deal of money. Because some athletes rise to fame and fortune from very poor countries or impoverished personal backgrounds, sport serves to reinforce the traditional capitalist belief that all one really needs to succeed is a little talent and the willingness to work hard, regardless of other factors such as race, ethnicity, gender, or money. Furthermore, high-profile professional sport reproduces and reinforces very tenacious cultural assumptions about the nature of the competition in which females and males may engage.

Competition is assumed to be an essential aspect of professional sport, one that benefits spectators and players alike. For example, most spectators enjoy experiencing the tension and suspense inherent in watching an evenly matched and well-played game unfold. In addition, players may compete for a variety of intrinsic and extrinsic reasons, such as personal satisfaction, remuneration, or recognition from others (Butcher and Schneider 1998).

Because the incentives to cheat can be very high in professional sport, the personal conduct of athletes has long been associated with moral character. Notwithstanding the high-profile criminal activities of a minority of mostly male professional athletes, young people in our culture are encouraged to emulate the more desirable on- and off-the-field behaviour of famous male (and, to an ever greater extent, female) athletes.

Perhaps popular competitive team sports continue to be included in contemporary physical education curricula simply because "big box" gymnasiums and easily attainable equipment most readily lend themselves to the accommodation of large classes of students. A more compelling argument, however, for justifying the continued and deliberate inclusion of competitive team and individual sport instruction in the schools is found in philosophical considerations of character development and fair play.

## *"The Sand of the Desert is Sodden Red..."*

In fact, "character development" was one of the primary justifications for including team sports in the school curriculum in the first place, at least for the male half of the population in western European society (Carr 1998; Green 1986; McIntosh 1979; Nixon and Cozens 1935; Sharman 1935; Singleton 2003). Throughout the nineteenth century, before the emergence of free public schooling for the poor and working classes, upper echelons of British society routinely sent their male children away at an early age to one exclusive boarding school or another; in the language of the time, these were referred to as "public schools." These schools provided an education considered necessary for the preparation of a gentleman, a male who would be expected, at maturity, to take a leading role in business, the military, government, the church, academics, science, or medicine.

Because most boarding schools provided organized classes for only a relatively small portion of the day, it was not uncommon to have unrestrained groups of juvenile males vandalizing the towns and countrysides in which their schools were located. As early as 1816, English public schools, such as Rugby,[1] introduced competitive team sport into their daily routines as a means of keeping active young boys occupied during their time away from class. The popular notion of "muscular Christianity" quickly became associated with participation in rough-and-tumble competitive team sports at these schools. That is, a moral code focused on honour, fairness, responsibility, teamwork, loyalty, and courage was applied to participation in school sport as a means of justifying the inclusion of these games in the school curriculum. Enthusiastic participation in competitive sport became a necessary aspect of the character development of the young men who were expected to become leaders in England's ever-expanding imperialistic endeavours. A verse from Sir Henry Newbolt's (1862-1938) best-known poem, *Vitai Lampada* or *They Pass on the Torch of Life*, vividly illustrates this point of view:

> The sand of the desert is sodden red, —
> Red with the wreck of a square that broke; —
> The Gatling's jammed and the Colonel dead,
> And the regiment blind with dust and smoke.
> The river of death has brimmed his banks,
> And England's far, and Honour a name,
> But the voice of a schoolboy rallies the ranks:
> 'Play up! play up! and play the game!' (Chitty 1997, 110)

While young elite males were playing games for Queen and country, some privileged young females were quietly participating in their own team games at their own public schools (Hult 1994; McCrone 1987; Vertinsky 1994). English girls' boarding schools came into prominence somewhat nearer the end of the nineteenth century. Because most schools emulated the organization of existing boys' schools, team games were included as part of the extracurricular schedule (McCrone 1987; Fletcher 1987). And, although girls also played games for patriotic purposes, the elements of patriotism and character development on which they focused were quite different. It was considered the natural responsibility of these elite young women to produce and nurture healthy offspring who would be fit to maintain the Empire of the future. The vigorous physical activity found in organized competitive sport provided young women with a means of maintaining their health and reproductive strength. To further justify the inclusion of games in the curriculum, educators were quick to point out that a healthy, active female was also an attractive female, and that moderate, closely monitored participation in team games contributed greatly to a young woman's overall modest character, health, and beauty. Like their male counterparts, early female physical educators employed character development to justify the inclusion of female competitive team activities in school:

> Women should also recognize the need of perfect organization in all parts calling for teams, crews or champions. The ethical value of "athletics for women" may be placed side by side with the physical value. The necessary submission to strict discipline, the unquestioning obedience demanded by the officers, the perfect control of the temper and sensitiveness under coaching, together with the very fact she must be absolutely unselfish in order to become a loyal and valued member of her organization, develops a young woman's character while she develops her muscles. (Hill 1903, 13)

Regardless of whether they were female or male, proponents of vigorous competitive physical activity justified the inclusion of these activities in school curricula by weaving their benefits into the cultural expectations of the time for appropriate masculine and feminine behaviour (Sharman 1935). Thus, masculine competition resulted in team loyalty, individual courage under fire, and the ability to follow a game plan through to the end—necessary traits for success in the cutthroat world of business. It was no coincidence that, while team games for males were busy providing effective leaders for the public domain, competitive games played by females were intent on developing disciplined, obedient, and cooperative team players—in other words, ideal wives and mothers.

Once organized schooling became not only available, but also compulsory for the masses, competitive sport was gradually introduced into the curriculum for medical as well as moral reasons (Hill 1903; Hult 1994; Park 1987; Vertinsky 1994). In elementary schools in the United States and Canada, informal recess activities gradually gave way to organized classes of rhythmic activities, gymnastics, and military-style drills and marching designed to improve the posture and the health of both girls and boys (Cartu 1980). Team games, at first organized and played by older male students outside of school, were gradually taken over by educators, in an effort to curb "the competitiveness, commercialization and elitism" (Lenskyj 1986,

69) rampant in these sport programs. Female physical education instructors also strongly advocated institutional control of games and sports, in part to protect their students' reputations, and in part to protect their own.

> The initiative in the introduction of games should be taken by the school authorities, not by the pupils, as a part of the scheme of education; a playground, and, if possible, a playshed for use in bad weather provided, and an instructor of games appointed. Where this cannot be done, games of the severity of hockey and basket-ball should not be permitted to exist as school organizations, and inter-scholastic matches should be prohibited. (Hill 1903, 12)

Teachers of boys and girls justified the inclusion of competitive team games, first, in school extracurricular activities and, then, as a recognized school subject through an often passionate promotion of the character-building potential of sport participation:

> Games should be taught as a *subject*, so that those who play them may get lessons from them, may see their grand side, and may see how they develop whatever is best in a man, if only they are done rightly....What need is there to go to a dull statistic-book to get such ideas as Co-operation, Division of Labour, Independent Activity, and Originality, Honour, Discipline, and so on, into a boy's mind, when there is a special field of study in which a boy is *bound* to be interested, if he *is* a boy. (Schmidt and Miles 1901, 60–61) [italics in original]

## Curriculum, Competition, and Fair Play. Oh My!

Today, physical education is a common subject in all elementary and secondary schools across Canada; it is compulsory usually until the completion of the first year of high school. Senior-level classes in physical education are offered as electives. Although military drills and marching are rarely encountered anymore, fitness activities, dance, gymnastics, outdoor pursuits, and aquatics, as well as individual, dual, and team sports, make up a varied and challenging curriculum for many Canadian students (Ministries of Education). When it comes to team sport instruction, most physical education curriculum guides place an instructional focus on game concepts and skills acquisition, and many promote teaching perspectives that highlight developmental appropriateness, healthy living, safety, and cooperative learning approaches. Because every secondary-level physical education curriculum guide in Canada includes individual and team games and sports as integral parts of a complete physical education program for Canadian youth, it is interesting and, to my mind, significant that none mentions competition as an element of game participation that needs examination. It is as if those who devise curriculum guides visualize team games and sports strictly in terms of their concrete instructional potential for safe and healthy living. Although it may appear at first glance that physical education curriculum guides focus only on the technical aspects of instruction for any given topic, that is, the practical skills rather than the theoretical or philosophical foundations a second, more penetrating glance reveals that most guides call for attention to the principles and practices of fair play. This is an intriguing inconsistency that serves to further accent how competition in class is overlooked.

Sport philosophers and sociologists are fond of examining questions of fair play associated with competitive professional and elite amateur team sport located in the community (Butcher and Schneider 1998; Bergmann Drewe 1999, 2000). They are less interested in exploring questions concerning competition and fair play that arise within the institutional confines of school physical education, often because the pedagogical constraints under which competition and fair play take place put these elements into a "special class." That is, because physical education is a compulsory class for the majority of students, the choice of whether to participate—a fundamental aspect of philosophical thought—is removed. I have explored elsewhere the problems associated with trying to relate philosophical arguments concerning competition and fair play at elite levels with the modified or lead-up team games often offered in physical education (Singleton 2003). Although sport may have entered schools a century ago by riding on the ethically upright back of "character development," it is simply not clear whether we *can* or even *should* continue to use that argument to justify the presence of physical education in the schools today.

Peter Arnold (1997) is one sport philosopher who has examined competition and fair play, specifically in school physical education. Arnold contends that education must be viewed in terms of its initiation value to students, and its own intrinsic worth, "not for purposes, good or bad, that lie outside it" (9). He explains that "the initiation view of education is one that involves the young being initiated into those worthwhile aspects of human endeavour that are available to them" (8), and that education must have intrinsic as well as extrinsic worth. Arnold bases his argument on a theory formulated first by Peters (1966) and later by Hirst and Peters (1970), that a "worthwhile" subject or activity features both knowledge and understanding. Moreover, *how* a subject is taught is as important as *what* is being taught, and thus the methods adopted for instruction must be moral ones. Arnold points out that sport, when viewed as a valued human practice, "pursued for its own internal goals in the form of its skills, tactics, strategies and standards in a moral way for their own sake...is in and of itself educative" (8), and that it is improper to use sport to attempt to achieve specific extrinsic purposes such as character development or social improvement. Although these purposes are often given as reasons for including competitive sport activities in schools, he argues they should be viewed as beneficial, but not necessarily guaranteed outcomes, rather than as primary objectives for their inclusion.

Although Arnold's contention is compelling, the notion that sport participation and moral character development go hand in hand is well rooted in tradition and emotion. It is difficult to entirely dispel this argument, especially among groups who have a vested interest in keeping the association between character development and competition close and visible. For example, the International Fair Play Committee (IFPC) (2004) strongly supports the notion that "[t]he objectives of schools should include the fostering of an overall attitude of fairness and fair play" (April 2, 2004). According to the IFPC, students should participate in competitive team sport principally because of the moral benefits that accrue from experiencing and complying with the rule-bound nature of games. From this perspective, as players understand and voluntarily follow the rules of the game, they will learn, as a matter of course, the value of moral behaviours that may be applied in and out of specific sporting situations.

> Sport promotes values such as respect, tolerance, fairness and team spirit. Adhering to rules, demonstrating solidarity with other members of the team and the willingness to make an effort are not learned on command but in an emotional, 'incidental' way at school and in leisure-time activities. Sport enables individuals to learn more about their physical and psychological strengths and weaknesses. Children and young people learn to control themselves and to view their opponent as a partner, even in critical situations. Thus sport is a medium for transferring these values to other areas of life. (April 2, 2004)

The relationships among competition, fair play, and pedagogical sport experiences are complex, overlapping, and often slippery. Although curriculum guides tend to downplay or ignore competition as an aspect of instruction, they also recognize the need for students to experience and integrate such values as fairness, justice, responsibility, and care into their personal lives. Competition may be overlooked or even ignored, but it is clearly and undeniably present in class. Humbert and Blacklock (1998), Gibbons et al. (1999), and Wilson (2002) have vividly demonstrated that students are aware of competition in physical education classes regardless of whether the class is segregated or coeducational.

When the links among competition, fair play, and pedagogical practice in physical education are examined more closely, a number of questions arise. How do teachers view competition in class when competition is a highly valued aspect of their own lives? Upon what basis do teachers determine whether a student, a class, or even an entire gender is competitive? Given that competition is present, what value do teachers think competition has for their physical education classes? What do teachers think about fair play, and how do they establish fair play conduct in their gymnasiums? And finally, what connections do teachers make between competition and fair play? That is, what do teachers' thoughts about fair play tell us about how competition is managed in physical education? Students, teachers, school administrators, and parents may hold radically different opinions about the place, the value, and the purpose of competitive sport instruction in physical education class.

Education students who are majoring in physical education are very well positioned to respond to these questions. In fact, many may respond from up to three perspectives—student, competitor, and teacher. Student teachers are well placed to report on what it means to integrate personal beliefs and experiences with pedagogical challenges in the gymnasium, and to reflect upon some of the implications this may have for their future teaching practices. In the following sections, I describe and analyze a study designed to investigate how secondary-level physical education student teachers in Ontario plan to integrate personal beliefs about competition and fair play into future pedagogical situations.

## *"Your Answers Will Be Completely Anonymous."* *A Survey About Competition and Fair Play*

One hundred thirty-eight responses from seventy-two females and sixty-six males enrolled in intermediate/senior physical education classes were returned from six out of a possible nine Ontario universities offering the Bachelor of Education (B.Ed.) degree. The survey was sent to instructors of intermediate/senior[2] physical education classes in mid-March, and, because the B.Ed. degree program in Ontario is one year in duration, all students were either just beginning to teach or were currently engaged in teaching their final practicum when they completed the survey. Just two questions concerning demographic information were asked—the respondent's gender, and a brief description of his or her student teaching experiences in physical education as of the date of the completion of the survey (see Table 1). Only four females and three males indicated that they had not yet taught a physical education class. Of the remaining sixty-eight women, the majority (thirty-six) had taught only segregated girls' physical education, sixteen had taught both coeducational and segregated girls' physical education classes, nine had taught only coeducational physical education, three had taught segregated boys' and coed classes, two had taught a combination of segregated girls, segregated boys *and* coed physical education classes, and two had taught only segregated girls and segregated boys classes. Of the remaining men (sixty-three), the majority (twenty-eight) had taught a combination of coeducational and segregated boys' classes, while twelve had taught coeducational only, twelve had taught segregated boys' classes only, eight had taught segregated girls', segregated boys' *and* coeducational physical education classes, and one had taught either segregated girls only, or segregated girls and coeducational physical education classes.

Student Teaching Experience (N = 138)

Female: N72

| NO PE | SEGG ONLY | COED ONLY | SEGG/CO | SEGB/CO | SEGG/B/CO | SEGG/B |
|---|---|---|---|---|---|---|
| 4 | 36 | 9 | 16 | 3 | 2 | 2 |

Male: N66

| NO PE | SEGB ONLY | COED ONLY | SEGB/CO | SEGG/CO | SEGG/B/CO | SEGG ONLY |
|---|---|---|---|---|---|---|
| 3 | 12 | 13 | 28 | 1 | 8 | 1 |

*Table 1:* Student Teaching Experience

In Part Two of the survey, participants were asked about their opinions and observations concerning the influence and motivational possibilities (or hindrances) of competition from a *personal* perspective ("Would you describe yourself as competitive?"), a *gendered* perspective ("From your school experiences would you say girls are more or less competitive than boys?"), and a *pedagogical* perspective ("Would you encourage students to be competitive in your classes?"). Finally, respondents were asked to write what they thought "fair play" meant in physical education class, and how they would ensure that "fair play" happened in the classes they would be teaching in the future.

## "No One Really Likes Losing, Do They?" Personal Responses about Competition

It is perhaps not surprising that of the 138 student teachers who answered the question, "Would you describe yourself as competitive?", 122 responded "yes." It has been well documented (Brown 1999; Curtner-Smith 2001; Lawson 1988; Lortie 1975) that students, both women and men, who choose to enter teacher preparation programs in physical education often come from similar backgrounds that feature positive experiences in physical activity and competition. (See, for example, Chapter Thirteen by Hopper and Sanford in this text). More remarkable perhaps is that fifteen participants indicated that they did not believe they were competitive. Responses were fairly evenly distributed among men and women, with sixty-four female and fifty-eight male students responding "yes." The "no" responses were more or less equally divided—seven women and eight men responded negatively. An overview of written responses to this question indicated that participants generally considered competition to mean at least one of three things—a strong desire to win, motivation to help them make their best effort, and a means of judging personal improvement. As more than one respondent claimed, competition was important "in every way—sport, life, academics." Both males and females wrote that they "hate to lose," "hate failure," or "hate being last." Other respondents, both female and male, felt competition provided opportunities to exert their best effort, regardless of the actual outcome of the game: "I always try my best and am upset when I know I could have done better" (female respondent); and, "I enjoy the competition. If I lose, that's fine as long as I perform well and the level of the game is high" (male respondent). Finally, for some participants, competition served as a means of improving personal competency in a sport or game. The following comments from male respondents illustrate this point of view:

> "I try my hardest and strive to improve so I can be successful at a sport."

> "I compete with myself more than with other people."

> "[I]constantly want to improve."

Female respondents made similar observations about themselves:

> "[I'm] not so much competitive with others as I am with myself. [I] do everything possible to help [my] team win."

> "I challenge myself to improve in results."

> "[I'm] always trying to beat past performance, (not always wanting to win)."

Although it may seem to be an obvious assumption that physical education student teachers would tend to self-identify as competitive, the impact this perspective has on these beginning teachers' future practice is not as simple as it appears. An examination of the student teachers' observations about the competitive interests of their female and male students follows, as well as an exploration of the teaching strategies and approaches these beginning educators plan to take with their physical education classes. Finally, an examination of how the study participants' understand connections between fair play and competition will explore more thoroughly some deeply held assumptions maintained by physical educators about competition in their classes.

## *"Many Girls Are Less Motivated." Responses about Gender and Competition*

Girls' segregated or coeducational classes made up a significant portion of the total number of classes taught by the study respondents. Physical education classes in Ontario high schools are generally segregated for the compulsory grade 9 year, and often also for grade 10. Senior-level elective classes in grade 11 and grade 12 are usually coeducational. One survey question asked respondents whether they had observed female high school physical education students to be more or less competitive than boys, regardless of the level or composition of the class. The majority of participants (109 out of 138) indicated they had observed that girls were less competitive than boys. Sixteen indicated girls were generally more competitive, and twenty-six either were unable to say or believed girls were both more and less competitive than males, depending upon the circumstances. Reasons given by those who observed that girls were less competitive than boys in physical education focused on their students' preference for "socializing" and for fun, their reluctance to put any effort into the class, the lack of confidence some girls displayed in their skills, and girls' preference for cooperative group activities:

> "The girls in my classes were more interested in fun, not [in] winning/losing." (female respondent)

> "Girls pass the ball more, want to get others involved. Girls are more worried about having fun than winning." (male respondent)

> "They enjoy cooperative drills. They are usually hesitant because their skills are low." (female respondent)

> "In girls' PHE, there was much more positive reinforcement and support given to each other for passing and teamwork in the basketball unit I observed. (male respondent)

> "Floor hockey—girls less running/activity and more socializing...did not care about bettering themselves/skills." (female respondent)

> "Girls used modified rules in rugby that involved sharing, for instance. They have less animosity between teammates and opponents. More seem to care less who wins." (male respondent)

> "[Some] girls are less confident in their physical abilities and would be therefore more comfortable playing for fun, i.e., an increased emphasis on participation." (female respondent)

> "Overall the experiences showed they [girls] were not interested in the physical aspects of the activities." (male respondent)

Not one respondent thought to question the meaning of "competition," or more significantly, what competition might mean to their female students. As most of the preceding and following quotes indicate, competition was generally equated as much with attitude and confidence as it was with skill:

"Boys play—very intense and physical. Girls play—more relaxed and friendly trying to include everyone." (female respondent)

"In my practicum, girls enjoyed the social aspects [in general]. Boys played basketball games, while girls chatted and took shots at the basket." (male respondent)

"While I was teaching gr. 9 girls' floor hockey, I also had the chance to observe [a] gr. 9 boys' class playing floor hockey... What a difference! Boys argued more, were more aggressive and had to win." (female respondent)

"Through my observations I found boys' PE classes to be most intense and competitive. I've observed many girls' PE classes where the majority of the class seemed uninterested in what was taking place." (male respondent)

"During my first practicum I observed a boys' PE class on wrestling. Given that this is an activity that encourages competitiveness I found the class to be highly competitive with those both in and out of their weight class. During my most recent practicum I taught a class of grade 11 girls who were determined always to help each other to succeed. This sentiment prevailed through units on volleyball, basketball and wall climbing. This is the kind of experience I plan to encourage in my classrooms in the future." (female respondent)

Respondents also noted that the circumstances under which students were expected to compete had some effect on their students' attitudes and willingness to participate in the class. Although some respondents believed that girls and boys were equally competitive, they felt that coed class groupings could be particularly problematic for their female students, regardless of how competitive the girls may have seemed in segregated situations:

"Both are competitive depending on how you present the situation. Has to be something of interest to students." (male respondent)

"I think it totally depends on the class and its composition. Girls and boys can be equally competitive and it tends to vary according to the activity." (female respondent)

"Especially when girls are in a co-ed class, they tend to allow the boys to 'take over'. I had many instances where girls were less motivated to get changed into their gym clothes and challenge themselves physically." (male respondent)

"When we brought the girls' and boys' class together the girls were more intimidated by the boys." (female respondent)

"When teaching coed classes, the girls did not want to sweat and seemed more concerned with the social aspect of class." (male respondent)

"Less competitive especially when in coed classes, otherwise in segregated gender classes it's about even." (female respondent)

"More competitive if with only girls; if coed, they're more docile." (female respondent)

One female respondent felt that girls were more competitive when playing activities they were comfortable with, and less competitive if they did not feel challenged by the activity, if they did not have much skill, or if they did not feel they were having fun. Only one respondent commented that there was a possibility that some boys were not competitive in physical education class[3]: "Depends on the individual. Some girls are extremely competitive as are some boys, and some aren't."

So far, the results of this study indicate that female and male physical education student teachers tend to self-identify as competitive people who not only enjoy, but seek out competition in sporting situations and often in other aspects of their lives as well. Furthermore, these novice physical educators observed during their physical education student teaching experiences that not all students enjoy competition. They noted that some students may actively avoid situations they feel are too competitive. Female high school physical education students, in particular, were observed to have other motives for participating in physical activity. Fun, cooperative activities, and group support seem to override the experiences of winning (and losing), individual effort, and group success over a rival, which often seem to characterize male high school physical education classes. Coeducational classes were seen to present difficulties for female students. Even though many student teachers believed girls and boys could be equally competitive, the nature of the competition favoured by males in coeducational classes tended to override the interests of the girls. These observations lead to the following questions: Does competition have a positive or negative effect on students in high school physical education? What influence do the study respondents feel competition had on the students in their practicum physical education classes? These questions are examined in the following section.

## *"A Healthy Level of Competition that Suits the Students' Needs": Pedagogical Responses*

### *The Influence of Competition*

When respondents were asked whether they thought competition provided a positive or a negative influence on their students, 116 out of 138 answered, "both." Twenty felt competition was only positive, and two thought competition had a purely negative influence on students. The response of "both" may seem like an easy compromise to a tough question. However, from the perspective of self-identified "very competitive" individuals who were just completing their first experiences with teaching classes of students, some of whom obviously did not share their enthusiasm, the decision to answer "both," together with the accompanying comments, demonstrates a growing awareness among these student teachers concerning an enduring problem in school physical education. What *are* you supposed to think (and do!) when students refuse to participate in your class?

Of course, not all respondents felt that the presence of competition was necessarily the determining factor in a student's reluctance to participate. That is, although competition was "part of what sports are all about" (male respondent), the influence competition had on a student depended greatly on the nature of the personality that student brought to class. Thus, the influence competition had on students "[d]epends on the nature of the student. Some thrive on competition, others hate it" (female respondent). Although student personality certainly may have an effect on how that individual approaches activities in class, assuming that some students will just "naturally" love or hate the experience of competition is similar to assuming that some students will just "naturally" be more highly physically skilled and therefore "better" physical education students than others. From my perspective, this thinking does not allow much room for learning in physical education class. Why bother teaching when attitudes and skills are predetermined before the student even steps into the gymnasium?

Many respondents explained that they answered "both" because they felt competition offered both possibilities and pitfalls for their students. On the one hand, respondents felt competition offered benefits for their students that included increased motivation to participate and increased effort when participating; a fostering of cooperation between individuals and groups; encouragement for individuals and groups to set goals and work toward them; the provision of challenge; and the development or raising of standards for personal improvement. As one female respondent observed, "Students experience success and failure (and learn from both). [This includes] team work, team leadership, cohesiveness, dedication and determination."

On the other hand, respondents felt competition, if unchecked, could contribute to the development of a negative atmosphere in class, one where students' self-esteem was undermined, and less confident students were intimidated or discouraged from taking part. Fully 30 percent of those who included written responses to this question commented that they believed skill was the deciding factor in whether a student welcomed or rejected competition in class. More highly skilled students, such as varsity or community-level athletes, were more likely to seek out, encourage, and enjoy competitive experiences in class. As one respondent bluntly noted, "The students with the greater skills succeed and the students who are less skilled fail. In essence it [competition] promotes and highlights skill level differences in the class" (male respondent). As a result, competitively oriented classes could be "divide[d] between better players and not so great players in team sports. [Competition] can decrease playing time of the not so athletic players when a team (or certain players on a team) want to win" (female respondent).

For many of the study respondents, the trick to effectively managing competition in class depended on the judicious application of when and how much competition was "allowed" in class. Respondents commented:

"[Competition is] negative depending on how it's handled." (male respondent)

"A healthy level of competition that suits the students' needs is beneficial." (female respondent)

"If it is emphasized too much, some students may not feel able to participate (i.e., feel inadequate, others prevent full participation). If it is appropriately used, competition offers fun, incentive and motivation." (female respondent)

"It can both motivate students to participate and for those who are not so skilled serve to turn them off of PE. It depends on how it's allowed to manifest." (male respondent)

Knowing when to encourage competition, and when to rein it in, was considered the key to enhancing their students' class experiences.

Many respondents listed benefits of competition for their students, but in the same breath indicated that they understood not all high school students liked competition or did well in class if they were placed in competitive situations. Although this may seem somewhat contradictory, when the student teachers' responses concerning their own competitive nature, their observations about female and male attitudes to competition, and their own plans for future teaching approaches are factored in, the response of "both" to the question of whether competition has a positive or negative influence on high school physical education students begins to make more sense. The following section examines how respondents would go about organizing students' competitive experiences in light of their responses to the question, "Would you encourage your students to be competitive in class?"

### Encouraging and Discouraging Competition in Class

One hundred fourteen (fifty-nine women and fifty-five men) out of 138 respondents, (83 percent) indicated that they would encourage, or at least not discourage, their students from being competitive in physical education class. Just sixteen respondents (nine women and seven men), or 12 percent, answered they would not encourage their students, and seven (four women and three men) answered they would both encourage and discourage competitiveness in their students. Only four respondents, two female and two male, did not provide a written response to this question. Those who responded in the affirmative generally fell into one of two groups—those who suggested *concrete actions or practical suggestions* they would take to promote competition, and those who provided *reasons* for promoting competition. Interestingly, few responses included both practical suggestions *and* reasons. Some practical suggestions from the men included the following:

- ◈ give rewards
- ◈ give privileges to the winning team/individual
- ◈ set up a tournament
- ◈ keep score
- ◈ give winners lunch coupons for the cafeteria

- ❖ have losers clean up the gym
- ❖ give winners a trophy
- ❖ hold tournaments at the end of units
- ❖ have students strive to beat class bests (e.g., in fitness testing)
- ❖ pair students of like ability
- ❖ encourage peer teaching during class
- ❖ teach advanced techniques for a sport or activity
- ❖ allow all students access to advanced knowledge
- ❖ give verbal encouragement and compliments.

Female respondents suggested the following practical actions to promote competition in the physical education class:

- ❖ hold tournaments
- ❖ have winners play on (King's court)
- ❖ hand out prizes
- ❖ place students in teams with skill levels that are matched to each other
- ❖ motivate by playing the boys against the girls
- ❖ have those who are competitive and enjoy competition divide into two groups, competitive and non-competitive, during sport activities.

Even though the survey question asked, "In what ways would you encourage your students to be competitive?", most respondents who indicated they would encourage their students to be competitive chose to explain *why* they would encourage their students rather than *how* they would do so. Their reasons generally fell into one of three categories: the usefulness of competition for improving personal performance; the social and personal benefits of teamwork; or, the positive contribution of competition in raising motivation and generally improving participation and effort among students in the class. The answers from the majority of respondents who answered "yes" to this question, both female and male (thirty-three out of ninety-seven or 34 percent), fell into the first category—competition should be encouraged for personal improvement. That is, regardless of whether the activity was fitness testing or basketball, student teachers indicated they would encourage their high school students to use competition to concentrate solely on beating their own previous accomplishments, and to focus for the most part on enhancing personal improvement:

"Competitive against themselves. Challenge themselves to improve in a given activity." (male respondent)

"Striving to compete against themselves or a clock—not against one another." (female respondent)

"Individually competitive. To do better in individual performances. Compete against themselves." (male respondent)

"They should be competitive to the point where they are always striving to do their best and improve on previous performance. Self competition should be emphasized [versus] competition on the basis of comparison with others." (female respondent)

"Self improvement. The fact that improvement happens when we push ourselves. So competing with our own personal standards is essential." (male respondent)

"Focus on personal competitiveness that promotes student self-competition to push hard and improve since last time—'personal bests.' Promote an environment that encourages participation, energy and enthusiasm." (female respondent)

Fewer respondents indicated that competition presented their students with positive opportunities to experience cooperative team activities, and to experience the satisfaction of striving toward a group goal (nineteen of ninety-seven responses or 20 percent. Some respondents gave more than one reason for encouraging competition in class).

"Encourage team co-operation. Motivate teammates. Challenge each other." (female respondent)

"Encourage students to compete as a team and to have team work be a criteria [sic] for success/victory, i.e., everyone needs to touch the ball to score a point." (male respondent)

"Stress that competition between teams involves each team member having a role (some skilled players can act as coach, some as 'encourager'). A team's success depends on all players contributing in whatever way they can." (female respondent)

"By arranging students into groups/teams they are forced to work together in a competitive setting. This places the respon-

sibility on an entire group of students rather than individuals."
(male respondent)

"Sometimes healthy competition encourages team work, motivation and drive." (female respondent)

"Team effort. Everyone is a specialist." (male respondent)

The third reason given by student teachers for encouraging competition focused on the potential of carefully moderated competitive activities to increase individual participation and effort in the class (twenty-nine of ninety-seven responses or 30 percent. Some respondents provided more than one reason). The most succinct response came from a male respondent: "Effort = competition." Other responses on this theme included the following:

"Everyone to participate. Exposure to peers (new friends are made). Try *your best* at whatever you do. Have fun!" (female respondent)

"At times I would encourage them to play hard, and to play to win." (male respondent)

"Give effort—not necessarily to win but to try their hardest." (female respondent)

"Increase effort to try to maximize performance. Competitive while including everyone. Try to win while playing fair and including sportsmanship." (male respondent)

"Play hard. Do their best. Respect the rules and others." (female respondent)

Those few student teachers who indicated they intended to avoid incorporating competition into their classes, and those who indicated they would encourage only selected aspects of competition, wrote very similar responses to describe what they would do. That is, they would highlight cooperative games, designate no winners or losers in game situations, and emphasize skill acquisition.

Those who planned to encourage competition in their classes did so because they believed many aspects of competition led to positive physical and emotional experiences for their students, particularly if the competitive event was carefully monitored and controlled. Whether competition was purposely harnessed in class to motivate individuals to strive for their personal best, or used as a vehicle for attaining group goals or as a motivator to increase participation and effort, the presence of competition in class was welcomed, and even sought out, as a potentially enjoyable means to desirable ends.

Competitive sport is often assumed to bring moral benefits to participants. In school physical education, one of the ways in which morality (as it is related to participation in competitive activities) is addressed is through the implementation of standards of "fair play." Because fair play is based on philosophical principles directly affected by competitive play—do not cheat; do not be irresponsible; do not be exclusive—there is an inextricable link between the two concepts that is not often explored in class-based sport situations. In fact, I find it somewhat puzzling that competition is never directly addressed in Canadian physical education curriculum and program guides, despite the fact that almost every guide specifically directs that fair play principles should be taught and observed. The final two sections of this chapter present the study respondents' thoughts about fair play and offer several conclusions.

## *"Establish Clear Expectations":* *Fair Play in Physical Education Class*

The respondents were asked what they thought "fair play" should mean in physical education class. Sixty-nine females and sixty-two males chose to write responses which were grouped under four broad topics: "Rights" (equal opportunity to play, equal time to play, competitive play on and against teams of equal ability); "Rules" (consistent rules observation); "Relationships" (team effort, inclusion, and acceptance of all, respect for each other and the game); "Responsibilities" (honesty, good personal conduct, support for others, safety). Each time a respondent referred to an item under these topic headings, another point was added to the total.

FEMALE: N=69

| RIGHTS | RULES | RELATIONSHIPS | RESPONSIBILITIES |
|--------|-------|---------------|------------------|
| 36 | 33 | 55 | 30 |

MALE: N=62

| RIGHTS | RULES | RELATIONSHIPS | RESPONSIBILITIES |
|--------|-------|---------------|------------------|
| 24 | 30 | 43 | 30 |

*Table 2:* Meaning of Fair Play

Both men and women commented on the necessity of consistently enforcing game rules and ensuring students played in safe, supportive, and welcoming atmospheres. Female respondents were more empathic than their male counterparts about the need to provide equal opportunities for students to play on teams of equal ability, and to include all students.

Some responses were brief (e.g., "Don't cheat"), whereas others went into more detail:

"Everyone should have the opportunity to be active, participate, and play. Everyone should be given opportunities for success. Everyone should follow the rules and include others in what they are doing." (female respondent)

"Respect for teammates, co-competitors; respect rules; grace in defeat, as well as victory; respect referees, coaches; understand etiquette; understand teamwork and positive encouragement." (male respondent)

"Fair play means equal opportunity to participate; mutual respect and concern for each other; a safe environment physically and mentally." (female respondent)

Just as respondents were asked how they would encourage or discourage competition in class, they were asked how they would ensure fair play happened in their classes. A variety of suggested strategies emerged:

"Monitor closely; address, discuss issues; educate as to expectations re: fair play, etiquette, and equal time for participation." (male respondent)

"Establish equal teams; provide a variety of activities (i.e. something to meet each student's interests). Focus on improvement, not the end result." (female respondent)

"Teach it, the meaning of fair play. Mark students, give students good marks and feedback for fair play. Sit out fair play violators until they realize their mistakes." (male respondent)

"Establish clear expectations at the beginning of the year (and reinforce in a visual way, i.e., posters/handouts). Reward, praise positive student behaviour. Be a role model and set the example." (female respondent)

Study respondents consistently indicated they wanted their classes to be safe, inclusive, welcoming, and positive places for all of their students. And, although most student teachers personally subscribed to the "masculine model" of competition (the importance of winning, of individual effort, and of team cooperation for success over a rival), they also indicated that they had observed that many of their female students did not exert much effort, resisted full participation, and clearly preferred cooperative activities that featured group support. Although they were able to offer many *reasons* for utilizing competition in class, not many students chose to offer *strategies* for doing so. Most respondents indicated they believed fair play provides the guidelines for students' behaviour while they are competing in class. Furthermore, they believed that when they set out clear expectations for fair play, they are attempting to establish safe and equitable class conditions, thus alleviating some of the aspects of competition their (particularly female) students consider to be less desirable.

## Conclusion

In the introduction to this chapter I claimed that competition is a troublesome topic in high school physical education. Its presence and influence in high school physical education classes seem to be, with few exceptions, unexamined by teachers and their students. This does not mean that competition necessarily should be downplayed in or even eliminated from high school physical education. Neither does it mean that competition is not important in the lives of the people most closely associated with it—physical education teachers, and students who participate, enthusiastically or reluctantly, in class.

The survey responses illustrate that these particular respondents consider competition to be a fundamental aspect of pedagogical practice in physical education, although there is little agreement on just how it should be handled. Regardless of how student teachers intend to deal with competition in their classes, and regardless of the reasons they give for accommodating or minimizing competition, all claim that competition is a factor in their teaching.

In this chapter, I have attempted to illustrate the personal attitudes and beliefs about competition that a specific group of novice physical educators in Ontario brings to pedagogical practice, and some of the ways in which they plan to use competition to cope with the diverse interests and demands of their student populations. Detailed written responses to study questions provided further evidence confirming that these particular student teachers enter the profession sharing similar perspectives about competition. They believe it has been for them, and can be for their students, a beneficial influence. Tensions begin to emerge when the somewhat narrow beliefs shared about competition by these survey respondents collide with the negative experiences many students (particularly female) associate with physical education class. That is, student teachers learn quickly that their female high school physical education students appear to have other motives for participating in physical activity. Female students want fun, cooperative activities, and group support while they are participating in team sport activity. These aims are incongruent with winning (and losing), individual effort, and group success over a rival—elements which characterize both male high school physical education classes and the personal attitudes of the student teachers themselves.

All respondents were asked, in a related question, how they thought their own feelings about competition might affect the way they would teach their classes in the future. Responses tended to group according to gender. That is, male respondents were more likely to indicate that they intended to use their knowledge about and experience with competition to do one of three things. First, they would not let their competitive interests affect their teaching approach. In their opinion, physical education class is not supposed to be competitive, and they would not let their personal preference for competition affect their pedagogical practice. Second, they would purposely incorporate competition into classes. Because "life is competitive," it is necessary to introduce competition into classes to provide positive experiences for students—to help them learn to deal with competition in other aspects of their lives. Last, they would rely on their personal competitive experiences to tell them when to promote competition in class and when to downplay it. These teachers believed in the importance of providing positive role models for the appropriate and productive use of competition to improve student self-discipline as well as personal performance. Female respondents, on the other hand, commented that although they would include competition in their classes, they would emphasize fun, participation, and self-improvement, and avoid situations that produced winners and losers.

Curriculum guides never mention competition as a concept, an experience, or even as a point of view worth exploring more deeply or from different perspectives. Competition is rarely, if ever, examined in pedagogical circles as a gendered concept, or as a socially constructed concept that may mean different things to different people. Student teachers are also rarely introduced in their undergraduate programs to alternate approaches to competitive activities, and what these may look like for female and male students and teachers. The same holds true for professional preparation programs in teacher education.

At the beginning of this chapter I asked some questions. I am going to close by asking a few more. Could there be different ways of being competitive? Which is more important in fair play—following rules or encouraging relationships? Do the principles of fair play you promote in class affect the nature of the competition in which your students engage? And, finally, should you discuss competition and fair play with your students?

I am going to leave you to answer these questions in four ways. First, reflect upon your own competitive experience and consider how it may affect your current point of view. Second, pay attention to the responses your practicum students have to competitive situations. Third, observe your Associate (Cooperating) teacher, and how he or she deals with competition. Last, based on what you know now, what do you think your approach to competition and fair play will be in the future? What kind of experience do you *you* plan to encourage?

## Notes

1. Available at: www.rugbyschool.net/sub/history/SchoolHistory/rugbyschool.htm
2. Intermediate/Senior classes are focused on preparing teachers for grades 7 to 12 in Ontario schools.
3. Recent research (Davison 2000; Messner 1994; Sabo 1994) has demonstrated clearly, however, that not all male high school physical education students enjoy competitive experiences that highlight winning and losing, individual effort, and domination of a rival. None of the student teachers in this study indicated an awareness of such resistant attitudes on the part of their male students.

## References

Arnold, P. 1997. *Sport, ethics and education.* London: Cassell.

Bergmann Drewe, S. 1999. Acquiring practical knowledge: A justification for physical education. *Paideusis* 12(2):33–44.

———. 2000. The logical connection between moral education and physical education. *Journal of Curriculum Studies* 32(4):561–73.

Brown, D. 1999. Complicity and reproduction in teaching physical education. *Sport, Education and Society* 4(2):143–60.

Butcher, R., and A. Schneider. 1998. Fair play as respect for the game. *Journal of the Philosophy of Sport* 25:1–22.

Carr, D. 1998. What moral educational significance has physical education? A question in need of disambiguation. In *Ethics and Sport*, ed. M. J. McNamee and S. J. Parry, 119–33. London: E&FNSPON.

Cartu, L. P. 1980. *Social and political changes and the development of physical and health education within the Ontario public education system 1841- 1918*. Master's thesis, College of Education, Brock University, St. Catharines, Ontario.

Chitty, S. 1997. *Playing the game: A biography of Sir Henry Newbolt*. London: Quartet Books.

Curtner-Smith, M. 2001. The occupational socialization of a first-year physical education teacher with a teaching orientation. *Sport, Education and Society* 6(1):81–105.

Davison, K. G. 2000. Boys' bodies in school: Physical education. *The Journal of Men's Studies* 8(2):255–66.

Fernandez-Balboa, J-M., ed. 1997. *Critical postmodernism in human movement, physical education, and sport*. New York: State University of New York Press.

Fletcher, S. 1987. The making and breaking of a female tradition: Women's physical education in England, 1880-1980. In *From 'fair sex' to feminism: Sport and the socialization of women in the industrial and post-industrial eras*, ed. J. A. Mangan and R. J. Park, 145–60. Totowa, NJ: Frank Cass.

Gibbons, S., J. Wharf Higgins, C. Gaul, and G. Van Gyn. 1999. Listening to female students in high school physical education. *AVANTE* 5(2):1–20.

Green, H. 1986. *Fit for America: Health, fitness, sport and American society*. New York: Pantheon Books.

Hill, L. E. 1903. *Athletics and out-door sports for women*. New York: The Macmillan Company.

Hirst, P. H., and R. S. Peters. 1970. *The logic of education*. London: Routledge and Kegan Paul.

Hult, J. S. 1994. The story of women's athletics: Manipulating a dream 1890-1985. In *Women and sport: Interdisciplinary perspectives*, eds. D. M. Costa and S. R. Guthrie, 83–106. Champaign, IL: Human Kinetics.

Humbert, M. L., and F. Blacklock. 1998. *Girls in action: Speaking out*. Video. Ottawa, ON: CAHPERD.

International Fair Play Committee. 2004. *Topic of the month*. Available at: http://www.EYES.2004.info/6148.0.html [This site is no longer active.].

Kirk, D., and R. Tinning. 1990. *Physical education, curriculum and culture: Critical issues in the contemporary crisis*. London: The Falmer Press.

Kohn, A. 1995. *No contest: The case against competition*. Boston: Houghton Mifflin Company.

Lawson, H. 1988. Occupational socialization, cultural studies, and the physical education curriculum. *Journal of Teaching in Physical Education* 7:265–88.

Lenskyj, H. 1986. *Out of bounds: Women, sport and sexuality*. Toronto: The Women's Press.

Lockhart, B. 2002. Exercise for life. Keeping teenage women in PE classes. Available at: http://communications.uvic.ca/edge/gibbons.pdf

Lortie, D. 1975. *Schoolteacher: A sociological study.* Chicago: University of Chicago Press.

McCrone, K. E. 1987. Play up! Play up! And play the game! Sport at the late Victorian girls' public schools. In *From 'fair sex' to feminism: Sport and the socialization of women in the industrial and post-industrial eras,* ed. J. A. Mangan and R. J. Park, 97–129. Totowa, NJ: Frank Cass.

McIntosh, P. C. 1979. *Fair play: Ethics in sport and physical education.* London: Heinemann.

Messner, M. 1994. Boys and girls together: The promise and limits of equal opportunity in sports. In *Sex, violence and power in sports,* eds. M. A. Messner and D. F. Sabo, 197–201. Freedom, CA: The Crossing Press.

Ministries of Education. Available at: www.destineducation.ca/intstdnt/annex-c8_e.htm

Nixon, G. W., and F. W. Cozens. 1935. *An introduction to physical education.* Philadelphia: W. B. Saunders Company.

Park, R. J. 1987. Sport, gender and society in a transatlantic Victorian perspective. In *From 'fair sex' to feminism: Sport and the socialization of women in the industrial and post-industrial eras,* ed. J. A. Mangan and R. J. Park, 58–93. Totowa, NJ: Frank Cass.

Peters, R. S. 1966. *Ethics and education.* London: Allen and Unwin.

Rail, G. ed. 1998. *Sport and postmodern times.* New York: State University of New York Press.

Sabo, D. 1994. Different stakes: Men's pursuit of gender equity in sports. In *Sex, violence and power in sports,* ed. M. A. Messner and D. F. Sabo, 202–13. Freedom, CA: The Crossing Press.

Schmidt, F. A., and E. H. Miles. 1901. *The training of the body for games, athletics, and other forms of exercise.* London: Swan Sonnenschein and Company, Limited.

Sharman, J. R. 1935. *Introduction to physical education.* New York: A. S. Barnes and Company.

Singleton, E. 2003. Rules? Relationships?: A feminist analysis of competition and fair play in physical education. *Quest* 55:193–209.

———. 2004. Survey for Intermediate/Senior Physical Education Student Teachers in Ontario Universities. Unpublished manuscript. The University of Western Ontario.

Vertinsky, P. 1994. Women, sport, and exercise in the 19th century. In *Women and sport: Interdisciplinary perspectives,* ed. D. M. Costa and S. R. Guthrie, 63–83. Champaign, IL: Human Kinetics.

Wilson, B. 2002. The "anti-jock" movement: Reconsidering youth resistance, masculinity, and sport culture in the age of the Internet. *Sociology of Sport Journal* 19:206–33.

Chapter Four

# Eastern and Western Approaches to Physical and Health Education

## Chunlei Lu

Eastern[1] approaches to physical and health education have become increasingly popular in the West.[2] For example, Eastern movement disciplines (EMDs)[3] and Chinese medicine (e.g., acupuncture, herbs, natural healing) are becoming commonplace and it is not difficult at all to find an acupuncturist in a city or to locate an EMD studio in a town in the West.

This chapter will discuss the following questions: (a) What are the differences between Eastern and Western approaches to physical and health education? (b) What causes the differences? (c) Why should Eastern approaches be integrated into Western physical and health education? and (d) How can Eastern approaches be integrated into Western physical and health education? The following discussion is not merely a response to the rapid social acceptance of Eastern approaches in the West, but rather an active contribution in the cross-cultural dialogue at both the practical and theoretical levels.

## What Are the Differences Between Eastern and Western Approaches to Physical and Health Education?

The West's encounter with the East is one of the most significant world events of our time. On one hand, Western physical and health education has been predominant in the East since it was invaded by the West

71

about two hundred years ago. On the other hand, Eastern thought and practice, especially EMDs, were introduced to the West around the 1900s, but they were not accessible to the general population until the 1960s. As the result of the Western popularization of EMDs in the 1970s and 1980s, they are no longer foreign in North American society. New generations are growing up with the images and terminologies of EMDs. According to Yang (1996), EMDs have rapidly "become an integrated part of Western mainstream culture, in particular, of sport and physical culture" (1).

Despite the frequent interactions between both cultures in today's world, people can still have considerably different reactions to Eastern and Western approaches to physical and health education. Easterners are attracted to but also disoriented by Western approaches to health (e.g., Western medical concepts) and physical education (e.g., gymnastics, sports). Even translating "physical education" into Chinese is troublesome; it is difficult to find an equivalent, simply because there is no such notion as "physical" education or "physical" activity in the East. Therefore, "EMD" would be a complete misnomer for "physical" activity.

Similarly, many Westerners feel both confused and fascinated by Eastern approaches to health (e.g., holistic medicine) and physical education (e.g., tai chi, yoga). For instance, Westerners are perplexed when they notice EMD practitioners facing certain directions during practices, or when they observe traditional Chinese medicine (TCM) physicians putting acupuncture needles into the human body as a treatment for various diseases where there seems to be no connection between the positioning of the needles and the problem parts of the body. Nevertheless, both Easterners and Westerners have benefited from the cross-cultural exchanges.

Issues remain, however, regarding East-West interactions at both the practical and theoretical levels in the areas of physical education and health education. Substantial distinctions are visible as to how to stay healthy. For example, it would be normal to decrease the heart rate when practising Eastern meditation such as yoga and *qi gong*; this is, of course, just the opposite of the Western perception of active healthy living. Wearing a Walkman when jogging seems normal to Westerners, but, to many Easterners, this indicates that the body and mind are doing different things. Are both approaches to physical and health education valuable? What accounts for the differences between them?

## Why are There Differences Between Eastern and Western Approaches to Physical and Health Education?

The fundamental differences between Eastern and Western cultures result from their ontological understandings of the universe, nature, and humanity. *Dao* theory is one of the most influential ontological theories in the East (Chinese Philosophy Unit of Philosophy Department of Beijing University 2001; Xu 1996). As one of the most eminent intellectuals in the East and the primary founder of Daoist philosophy, Lao Zi (Lao Tzu or Lao Tse) explains that the *Dao* gives birth to *yin-yang* and eventually to everything in the universe. The *Dao* is independent of human will and fundamentally determines everything (Lao 1994).

Ontologically, ancient Chinese culture believes that the universe is an integral and inseparable whole (Li 2001; Zhu 1993). Everything in the universe originates from and is unified within the wholeness. This wholeness is also described as *Dao* (Martial Art Administration Center of State Department of Physical Activity, Sport, and Recreation 1998). Therefore, the Daoist ontology can be considered the epistemology of EMDs (Xu 1996). To Lao Zi, *Dao* is the "oneness" (Lao 1994).

Furthermore, *Dao* appears in the form of *qi*. Everything in the universe originates from *qi* (*yin-yang qi*) and is the product of the change of *qi*. Yet, *qi* itself never changes substantially. As explicitly explained in another ancient Chinese philosophy, the Five Element Theory, things in the universe are opposite and complementary to each other; each promotes and restrains the other, thus providing the harmony in the universe. Therefore, the view of anything including human life, health, and the body-mind relationship is placed within the large vision of the universe.

This "human-nature" unity indicates that (a) humanity and nature are fundamentally the same, which means that humanity is the miniature universe; and (b) humanity and nature are essentially connected, which suggests that humanity follows nature and does not go against it in order to survive and develop (Xu 1996). This unitary view also refers to the integral harmony between humanity and the surrounding environment, and between humanity and human society. Therefore, in TCM, professionals diagnose and provide treatment based on seasons, geographical location, and social characteristics of particular patients (Li 2001).

Ancient East Indian philosophy has a comparable vision. For example, "yoga" is derived from the Sanskrit root, "*yuj*," which means to bind, join, attach, yoke, direct and concentrate one's attention on, and to use and apply; it also means union or communion (Devi 2000; Whaley 1974). Similar to other EMDs, yoga is a theory and practice aimed at unifying or integrating self and the universe, the body, and the mind.

EMDs also employ this holistic view. People actively apply *qi* or *prana* (see table 1) in their EMD practice (Jiang 1995; Martial Art Administration Center of State Department of Physical Activity, Sport, and Recreation 1998). People can directly perceive or feel the existence of *Dao* when achieving a certain level in yoga or *qi gong* (Lao 1994). Many EMDs also adopt what is observed and learned from natural phenomena, such as, mountains, thunder, clouds, water, animals, and flowers as forms of practice and take seasons and locations (external settings) and human organs (internal settings) into consideration. Therefore, it is natural and unproblematic for people who learn EMDs to achieve a holistic view of things, including human being (body-mind), human society, health, life, nature, and eventually, the universe.

|  | Life force or energy | Energy centre | Energy channel | Exemplary practice form | Oppositional term |
|---|---|---|---|---|---|
| Chinese | *qi* | *dan tian* | *jing lou* | *qi gong* | *yang-yin* |
| Sanskrit | *prana* | *chakras* | *nadis* | *yoga* | *yo-ga* |

*Table 1:* Similar Terms with Respect to Human Body and Health in Chinese and Sanskrit

## Why Should Eastern Approaches Be Integrated into Western Physical and Health Education?

The proposal to integrate EMDs into Western physical and health education is based on the four core values of EMDs: philosophy (e.g., learning about the meaning of the universe, nature, and the self); health (e.g., keeping fit, healing disease); education (e.g., respect, self-control); and culture (e.g., heritage) (Xu 1996). I will discuss the need to integrate EMDs into Western physical and health education from the perspectives of philosophy, culture, health, and curriculum in relation to these core values.

## EMDs and Philosophy

It is apparent that many Westerners are becoming increasingly keen to learn Eastern philosophies such as Daoism and Buddhism. Yet, many of them experience frustration and confusion in their attempts to do so. Even those who gain a considerable knowledge of Eastern philosophy seem to have a limited comprehension because it requires "embodied understanding" rather than understanding that is solely theoretical. This is precisely what Eugen Herrigel, the German philosopher, experienced in learning Zen (Herrigel 1989). Therefore, it would be much easier and more natural for children and youth to approach Eastern philosophy and to obtain related benefits if EMDs were part of the school curriculum. As identified by Clarke (1997), the EMD experience of a new generation could ease the alien feelings and misconceptions about Eastern thought in Western society.

For centuries, the body-mind relationship has been an enigma that has caused substantial problems in the West (Mechikoff and Estes 2002). In contrast, it is of little concern to Easterners, who have two typical responses to "What is your mind?" or "What is the body-mind relationship?" First, they do not understand the question. Second, those who do understand the question do not know how to respond. For Easterners, it would be the same as answering a question such as, "What is the relationship between the left hand and the right hand?" Zhuang Zi, one of two primary Daoist gurus, tells a story about the head and tail of a snake. He indicates that although the head and tail are at opposite ends of the snake's body, they are an inseparable oneness (Chinese Philosophy Unit 2001), as are body and mind, left and right, *yin* and *yang*, and so forth.

Kauz (1977) discovered that Western students are unaware that the Eastern view of humans differs from their own: in general, Eastern thought does not divide humans into body and mind. Kauz suggests that students should not feel surprised when they notice their EMD instructors' concerns with more than students' physical development. In fact, the true understanding of the body-mind relationship is when we sincerely do not know how to respond adequately to the question, "What is the body-mind relationship?" When the question is no longer relevant to the person or when it vanishes in the person's "mind," he or she truly obtains the answer. This is also acknowledged by Western scholars such as Kennedy (1993), who states that to "know no self" means that all of nature becomes self, and Smith (1999), who declares, "The Self cannot understand itself until it loses itself in the work of great relinquishment" (24). EMDs are neither a type of physical activity nor a type of mental activity, but rather a path to approach the understanding of the self, life, and truth. That is why EMDs amaze many Western learners: EMDs can teach philosophy through physical movement.

For thousands of years, many Easterners have viewed mind-body as *yin-yang*, a non-dualistic but holistic unit in which one constantly influences the other. In practising EMDs, people regulate *qi*, freely crossing meridians (energy channels) in the body to achieve the balance of *yin qi* and *yang qi* to prevent or heal diseases. EMD professionals also acknowledge that the most important part in training is not the physical but the mental aspect. The ultimate goal of learning EMDs is to find *Dao* (truth), whereas health and other benefits are merely natural byproducts. That is why a real martial artist is usually a philosopher and a medical professional.

This mind-body reciprocal effect has been evident in both theory and practice in the East for thousands of years (Martial Arts Administration Center 1998). As Kauz (1977) suggests, the qualities of body and mind gained from a study of EMDs would stand an individual of any age in good stead. Aside from having elements that can enhance the quality of our lives, EMDs "can bring us to a sense of our wholeness" (141).

### EMDs and Culture

According to recent census reports, Asians are ranked as the largest group of immigrants in Canada, comprising 58 percent during 1991–2001. The 2001 census showed that persons of Chinese origin, who represent 3.5 percent of the population, have become the largest of more than 200 visible minority groups in Canada. There were nearly half a million Chinese people living in Toronto and almost 18 percent of the population in Vancouver was Chinese (McCarten 2003). This growing cultural diversity has trickled down to schools. For example, Chinese students comprise the largest population, up to over 90 percent, in many classrooms in the Greater Vancouver area.

Some practising teachers have started questioning whether it is appropriate to teach all immigrant students an exclusively Canadian or Western curriculum. Teacher educators suggest that multicultural approaches to teaching should be intentionally employed in Canadian schools. Integrating EMDs into the curriculum would broaden students' horizons, enhance their awareness, and enrich their experience of cultural diversity in schools. It would also encourage an understanding and appreciation of Eastern culture and the students who are part of it. A physical education teacher who participated in a recent research project on integrating EMDs into Western physical education curriculum warned, during an interview,

> EMDs have developed for thousands of year[s]. They do not just involve one group of people, for example, Chinese, Indian, Korean, or Japanese. Basically, billions of people have similar ways of thinking. In fact, if we do not start accepting more of this kind of thinking that is outside our box, we are getting into trouble. North America and Western Europe have a tremendous amount of economic and military power in the world. If they do not start recognizing and accommodating a lot of what is going on philosophically in the rest of the world, we get big problems because the rest of the world feels frustrated. (Lu 2004, 171)

This practising teacher's comments resonate with the work by scholars such as Bhabha (1994), Brown et al. (1997), Smith (2002), and Young (2001) in the areas of cross-cultural studies, globalization discourse, post-colonialism, and postmodernism. These theories unlock the door for the suppressed and marginalized cultures. Smith (1999) affirms that Western economic and political powers have relied upon the suppression and obliteration of other cultures since the Renaissance, and now others from eastern and southern continents are claiming their places within the new world order. One of the leading immigration psychologists, J. W. Berry (2001), also confirms that cultural accommodation and the fostering of intercultural relations are more important than mere cultural assimilation. Delpit (1997) suggests that cross-cultural dialogue not only requires open eyes and ears but also open hearts and minds. "It is not easy, but it is the only way to learn what it might feel like to be someone else and the only way to start the dialogue" (594). Teachers are in an ideal position to play a role in getting all of the issues on the table to initiate true dialogue (Delpit 1997).

## EMDs and a New Understanding of Health and Wellness

Many EMD practitioners address the general and specific health benefits of learning EMDs. They also realize that EMDs help them have a better understanding of health, well-being, and healing, and to see a different means of achieving a healthy lifestyle. Almost all identify physical, psychological, and social benefits of EMDs, such as relaxation, concentration, body control, and other health- and skill-related fitness practices.

Easterners have a fundamentally different outlook on the human body, illness, health, and wellness. Eastern health is based on Eastern philosophy while Western health is based on science. For example, Chinese movement disciplines, TCM, Chinese cookery, traditional Chinese arts, and traditional Chinese architecture are all based on Eastern philosophy. In other words, it would be unlikely that a person would understand EMDs without knowing the underlying Eastern philosophy. Learning EMDs, therefore, involves learning Eastern philosophy (Lu and Yuan 1991). Chinese and East Indians simultaneously developed a similar perspective of the human body and health (see Table 1) thousands of years ago (Devi 2000; Martial Art Administration Center 1998; Werner 1977), which differs significantly from that of Westerners.

As discussed earlier, philosophically, in TCM the cause of disease is the violation of the *Dao*. *Qi* is the means of the *Dao*. TCM has worked successfully for thousands of years. It is among the most influential medical systems in the East and is achieving increasing recognition in the Western world. According to TCM, one is inclined to suffer disease if any of the following conditions are in place.

1. *The person's good* qi *is not strong enough.* This implies that no one can guarantee the maintenance of strong, good *qi* unless he or she takes care of himself or herself constantly in terms of diet, lifestyle, etc.

2. The yin qi *and* yang qi *are not balanced as a result of excessive* yin qi *or* yang qi. This indicates that no one can have absolutely balanced *yin qi* and *yang qi*, only relatively balanced *yin-yang qi*. Such a balance requires that we look after ourselves.

3. *Qi does not flow freely along the energy channels.* *Qi* always moves in any live body; the termination of its motion indicates the end of life. This message encourages us to relax in our daily lives. When we are stressed, *qi* becomes stagnant—an eventual recipe for getting diseases.

4. *Qi is in disarray.* Many diseases result when *qi* is in disarray. An ill person would be healthy if *qi* were under control and in harmony (Jiang 1995; Li 2001).

The process of practising EMDs for the most benefit can be viewed as slowing down→being quiet→being with self→letting *qi* flow→balancing *yin qi* and *yang qi*→strengthening good *qi*→achieving and maintaining health.

The other Eastern approach toward health that is different from that of Westerners is that human emotion has a direct health impact on the human body. Western scientists and health professionals know that physical activities or treatments (e.g., medicines) can relieve the effects of some mental problems. But how the mind affects the body is far from understood. Only recently, having been prompted by alternative medical practices, are some Western professionals realizing that the linkage of body and mind is a "two-way street." For thousands of years, Chinese have believed that excessive anger hurts the liver; excessive joy, the heart; excessive sympathy, the spleen; excessive grief, the lungs; and, excessive fear, the kidneys (Xu 1991).

In contrast, Western culture tends to promote the idea of "the more, the better." For instance, the motto of the most influential sport ideology, the Olympics, is "*Citius* (faster), *Altius* (higher), *Fortius* (stronger)." Striving for "more" represents one of the core values in Western thought. From the perspective of traditional Chinese philosophy or medicine, excessiveness may result in health problems and diseases. It is also understood that people do not have to work to their extremes in order to be productive at the expense of hurting themselves. Cross-cultural philosophical thinking prompts some teachers to ask, Should we always encourage our students to be faster, higher, and stronger in comparison to others? Should we teach them how to slow down, or to be with self? How should teachers perceive waving arms around in tai chi or sitting motionless in yoga in terms of getting fit or healthy? How could we assess the internalized and individualized EMDs?

There is a palpable conflict between Eastern and Western views of health in both theory and practice. Yet, the integration of Eastern and Western thought would be not only a challenge but also an opportunity to learn and gain benefits for both teachers and students in the West.

## EMDs and Curriculum

Since the middle of the nineteenth century, when physical education was introduced as part of the school curriculum, its focus has evolved from physical training to enhancing performance-related fitness and competitive sports skills. Currently, the emphasis of physical education is on the health-related fitness, behavioural competencies, and motor skills needed for lifelong engagement in healthy and satisfying physical activity (Kirchner and Fishburne 1998; Rink 1997). Many countries have developed national standards or guidelines for physical education. Consequently, states (or provinces) and local school districts have adopted standards in their curriculum development (Rink 2002; Siedentop and Tannehill 2000).

In particular, many Western countries, including Canada (CAHPERD 2003), propose the inclusion of EMDs in national or provincial physical education programs. The following changes in the physical education curricula in a number of Canadian provinces represent a trend in physical education curriculum development, not only in Canada but in the West in general:

- ◈ The aim of the physical education curriculum is to enable individuals to develop the knowledge, skills, and attitudes necessary to lead an active and healthy lifestyle—EMDs can play a significant role in realizing this goal;
- ◈ There are more outcome-based rather than activity-based programs, which allow teachers to select a variety of activities—including EMDs—as a means of achieving the outcomes;
- ◈ More inclusive curricula have opened the door to non-traditional (in the West) Eastern activities;
- ◈ Competition and team sports are de-emphasized, whereas co-operation, enjoyment, participation, effort, and more individual lifetime activities—all of which are emphasized in EMDs—are promoted.

Integrating EMDs does not mean adding more issues in physical education curriculum development, but rather reconstructing or reconceptualizing the physical education curriculum through the lenses of the body-mind relationship, multiculturalism, and holistic health and wellness.

EMDs are not "a new kid on the block." They are not merely a new type of activity, a new health promoter, a new stimulus for cultural awareness, or a philosophical type of movement that is expected to enhance physical education for the simple sake of gaining equal status with cognitive education. The integration of EMDs into Western physical education curriculum wholeheartedly represents an urgent request from cross-cultural studies, post-colonialism, and globalization discourse. Ultimately, EMDs, with their focus on the true "self" rather than the activity, and their treatment of the "body" as a subject rather than an object, could facilitate the holistic development of all dimensions of a truly healthy human being—the unity of body, mind, and spirit. This re-conceptualization of Western physical education curriculum through the addition of EMDs would not only improve the curriculum itself but also enrich the understanding of curriculum theorizing and development.

## How Can EMDs Be Integrated into Physical and Health Education?

Research demonstrates that teachers are willing to integrate EMDs into their physical and health education curricula, especially at the secondary-school level (Lu 2004). EMDs are also deemed necessary in other subject curricula. Teachers who include EMDs may consider them as part of a warm-up, cool-down, or transition between activities or classes; some teachers, however, regard EMDs as a unit of activity to be taught.

A recent study (Lu 2004) identified a number of appropriate ways to integrate EMDs into physical education programs:

1. Teachers could attend EMD workshops offered at conferences and regular professional development seminars that are related to health and physical education.

2. Teachers could learn from appropriate EMD teaching videos or other EMD teaching materials and then practise prior to introducing these activities in class.

3. Conversely, teachers could learn EMDs in class by following videos with their students; by taking advantage of multiple classes taught this way, teachers would likely learn faster than their students, and could then provide additional instruction by applying general principles of motor learning and development in their classes. This type of learning may also give students the opportunity to perceive their teachers as open-minded, amicable, and approachable; they would learn EMDs in a friendly atmosphere.

4. Teachers could invite EMD instructors from the community into their classes to teach. Instructors will often visit without expecting an honorarium because they are anxious to promote EMDs. This partnering would strengthen the connections between the school and the community. In addition, the parents of some students practise and teach EMDs. In some cases they might be invited to teach in the school.

5.  Teachers could attend community EMD schools to learn for their own benefit, as well as for the purpose of integrating EMDs into their classes. However, financial and time issues may be involved. Nevertheless, this would be one of the best ways because teachers could systematically learn EMDs in a reasonable period of time.

It could be argued that students should learn EMDs in the community because the time allotted for physical education is limited and the curriculum already crowded. Yet, the reality is that any activity could be learned within the community. However, most children would not have an opportunity to experience EMDs in the community because of financial, time, and transportation constraints or other parental concerns. In addition, public schools should function as the place to provide education for all children and youth.

The integration of EMDs into school physical and health education requires that they be introduced into related university programs. In fact, many teachers believe that prospective teachers should have knowledge of and some experience with a variety of activities. Learning EMDs is a good means for student teachers to become open-minded and to break away from the traditional modes of teaching that they experienced during their own schooling. Often, only a few team sports are offered at the secondary level, corresponding to the extracurricular sport seasons. University students are often perceived as having the advantage of possessing unstructured minds, allowing them to easily accept new things. Student teachers can learn EMDs for personal and professional awareness, knowledge, skills, and other benefits, through regular physical activity courses, campus recreational programs, private sector classes, community programs, and professional development workshops and conferences.

In general, re-orienting to physical education curriculum by integrating EMDs involves three stages. It is first necessary to demonstrate the evidence of the multiple benefits of EMDs and get more teachers and school boards interested in and accepting of EMDs as a better way to achieve various curriculum outcomes. Second, one must transcend the superficial benefits of EMDs to attain body-mind harmony. Finally, physical education must be reconceptualized to assist students to develop a healthy body, mind, and spirit unity, and to be a truly holistic *one* person. This is not a purely Eastern or Western way, but rather a hybrid, a new ideology stemming from the benefits of both Eastern and Western thought and practice.

The process of integrating EMDs into Western physical and health education should be expected to generate challenges, such as, issues of teaching qualifications, potential violence from using martial arts, religious objections to the practising of Eastern meditation, and students' negative reactions resulting largely from Westerners' ignorance and misconceptions about EMDs.

## Conclusion

Integrating EMDs does not mean replacing the Western physical education curriculum, but rather helping Westerners to rediscover the lost body-mind relationship. Accepting EMDs does not mean giving up one's exterior "self" (the self that drives one to be productive or goal-oriented), but means that a person is assisted in finding the lost inner self (the true self) and maintaining a balanced life. Being with an outside self (e.g. being goal-oriented, living according to the imperatives of "go-go-go," "rush-rush-rush," and "higher-faster-stronger," and longing for self "identity") without a balanced inner "self" contributes to unhealthy living, and eventually to an impasse, in a human being, in a curriculum, and in a culture.

Eastern philosophies that EMDs bring into the West, such as oneness, can enhance both theory and practice in Western physical and health education programs, permitting a reinterpretation of health and wellness. The integration of EMDs into Western physical and health education programs can also enrich cultural awareness and foster multiculturalism.

In arguing for the integration of EMDs, I do not intend to favour Western physical and health education at the expense of losing the ancient core of values in EMDs. Rather, I encourage the integration of EMDs into Western epistemology and seek to generate a better understanding of physical education and health education in the context of cross-cultural interactions. In so doing, the education of a person *through*, not *of*, the "physical" can be fostered and multiculturalism cultivated. The "third space" of hybridity for peaceful dialogues can be created, cultural accommodation and appreciation (not assimilation) can be generated, and the horizons that different peoples view can be shared.

## Notes
1. The East refers to two of the most influential ancient civilizations in world history—Chinese and East Indian—and their surrounding cultures.
2. The West refers to North America and Europe.

3.  Eastern movement disciplines (EMDs) are a cluster of activities based on dominant Eastern philosophies and developed historically and geographically in Asian contexts. EMDs consist of Eastern martial arts (e.g., aikido, judo, karate, kung fu, tae kwon do, tai chi) and Eastern meditation practices (e.g., *qi gong* and yoga) that contain core values and other components of Eastern culture.

## References

Berry, J. W. 2001. A psychology of immigration. *Journal of Social Issues* 57(3):615–31.

Bhabha, H. 1994. *The location of culture*. London: Routledge.

Brown, P., A. H. Halsey, H. Lauder, and A. S. Wells. 1997. The transformation of education and society: An introduction. In *Education: Culture, economy, and society*, ed. A. H. Halsey, H. Lauder, P. Brown, and A. S. Wells, 1–44. Oxford: Oxford University Press.

CAHPERD. *Physical education 2000*. Available at: www.cahperd.ca/e/PDFs/PE2000.pdf

Chinese Philosophy Unit of Philosophy Department of Beijing University. 2001. *History of Chinese philosophy*. Beijing: Beijing University Press.

Clarke, J. J. 1997. *Oriental enlightenment*. London: Routledge.

Delpit, L. D. 1997. The silenced dialogue: Power and pedagogy in educating other people's children. In *Education: Culture, economy, and society*, ed. A. H. Halsey, H. Lauder, P. Brown, and A. S. Wells, 582–94. Oxford: Oxford University Press.

Devi, N. J. 2000. *The healing path of yoga: Time-honored wisdom and scientifically proven methods that alleviate stress, open your heart, and enrich your life*. New York: Three Rivers Press.

Herrigel, E. 1989. *Zen in the art of archery*. Trans. R. F. G. Hull. New York: Vintage Books.

Jiang, B. ed. 1995. *The theoretical foundations of Wu Shu*. Beijing: People's Press of Physical Activity, Sport, and Recreation.

Kauz, H. 1977. *The martial spirit: An introduction to the origin, philosophy and psychology of the martial arts*. New York: The Overlook Press.

Kennedy, D. 1993. Child and fool in the Western wisdom tradition. *The Journal of Philosophy for Children* 11(1):11–21.

Kirchner, G., and G. J. Fishburne. 1998. *Physical education for elementary school children*. Boston: WCB/McGraw-Hill.

Lao, Z. 1994. *Wisdom of Laotse*. Trans. Y. Lin. Taipei, Taiwan: Zhengzhong Book Press.

Li, D. ed. 2001. *Fundamental theory of traditional Chinese medicine*. Beijing: People's Health Press.

Lu, C. 2004. *East meets West: A cross-cultural inquiry into curriculum theorizing and development in physical education*. Ph.D. diss., University of Alberta, Edmonton, Canada.

Lu, C., and L. Yuan. 1991. The Eastern-Western cultural influence on physical education and sports. *Journal of Shandong Medical University* 5(4):64–67.

Martial Arts Administration Center of the State Department of Physical Activity, Sport, and Recreation. 1998. *Qi gong professional textbook.* Beijing: People's Press of Physical Activity, Sport, and Recreation.

McCarten, J. 2003, January 22. More immigrants, diversity, colour. *Edmonton Journal*, A2.

Mechikoff, R. A., and S. G. Estes. 2002. *A history and philosophy of sport and physical education.* Boston: McGraw-Hill.

Rink, J. 1997. *National standards for physical education.* ERIC Document Reproduction Service No. ED406361.

Rink, J. 2002. *Teaching physical education for learning.* Boston: McGraw-Hill.

Siedentop, D., and D. Tannehill. 2000. *Developing teaching skills in physical education.* Mountain View, CA: Mayfield Publishing Company.

Smith, D. G. 1999. Identity, self, and other in the conduct of pedagogical action: An East/West inquiry. In *Pedagon*, ed. D. G. Smith, 11–25. New York: Peter Lang.

Smith, D. G. 2002. Globalization and curriculum studies. In *Teaching in global times*, ed. D. G. Smith, 47–82. Edmonton, AB: Pedagon Press.

Werner, L. 1977. *Yoga and Indian philosophy.* Delhi, India: Motilal Anarsidass.

Whaley, P. 1974. *Yoga: A beginner's guide.* London: G. Bell and Sons, Ltd.

Xu, C. Z. 1991. *Hui Ming Qi Gong.* Beijing: Higher Education Press.

Xu, C. ed. 1996. *Introduction to the discipline of wu shu.* Beijing: People's Press of Physical Activity, Sport, and Recreation.

Yang, J. B. 1996. *American conceptualization of Asian martial arts: An interpretive analysis of the narrative of taekwondo participants.* Ph.D. diss., University of North Carolina at Greensboro, North Carolina.

Young, R. C. 2001. *Postcolonialism: An historical introduction.* Oxford: Blackwell Publishers Ltd.

Zhu, B. 1993. *A fundamental guide to yi study.* Guang Zhou, Guang Dong: Guang Zhou Press.

## Chapter Five

# *"Dancing Is for Sissies!"*

## Marnie Rutledge

---

*Dance is not taught as an art in any university. There it is still
in the gymnasium.*

Agnes de Mille, 1984

### Dance and Physical Education:
### An [Un]likely Partnership?

This chapter outlines the ways that we experience dance. Issues around dance and gender, objectifying the body, and expressive versus functional movement will be discussed. Examining these issues may provide insight, as well as provoke conversation, about the positioning of dance in physical education.

Dancing is the body's text—dance movement is expression. There is much variety and scope applied to the terms *dance* and *dancing*. Common elements of dance include both movement of the body—involving a heightened kinesthetic sensory awareness of the timing and response of the body to music—and expressive movement—a communication through movement of ideas, experiences, and feelings. Dance has been defined as those steps, gestures, forms, patterns, and styles done or made when one *intends* to dance—socially, recreationally, expressively, theatrically, or artistically in one's own cultural forms. At one level, we experience dance as spectators, at another, as participants.

When we participate in dancing, we either replicate preset movements, or we create our own movements. When replicating, we are often learning folk or social dances, while concentrating on the correct performance of the steps to the music. When we are creating, we are using our movement in an expressive and personal style to communicate. Both of these ways of experiencing dance are evident in education programs. When we watch dance, we are learning to appreciate the dancing of others—as part of an education about dance as an art form. Examples of these processes in dance education are evident in the statements of purpose for organizations such as the National Dance Association of AAHPERD (the American Alliance for Health, Physical Education, Recreation and Dance), daCi (dance and the Child international), and the dance special interest group of CAHPER (the Canadian Association for Health, Physical Education and Recreation) (see Wall and Murray 1990, 162–164). These documents emphasize that dance should be a part of one's general education. In addition, having learning experiences in expressive forms of movement is important. Common elements espoused in dance education include artistic, aesthetic, expressive, and cultural forms.

How dance is positioned in physical education programs often relates to particular ways of experiencing dance and dancing. Typically we see replication as a dominant process in physical education, whereas creative expression tends to dominate in separate dance programs, or dance programs affiliated with the fine arts. Aerobic dancing, line dancing, swing and jive dancing, and simple folk and novelty dancing are examples of the predominant dance forms taught in physical education programs. In these forms, the body is controlled and disciplined to conform to particular ways of knowing and moving. Dance is often justified solely as an activity that contributes to fitness. The experience of the expressive body is almost non-existent.

## Dance Education

In education, spoken and written languages are the dominant forms of expression, and we lose touch with our expressive bodies. In the study of physical education, the body becomes objectified—measured, for example, in terms of flexibility, endurance, and strength—and functional outcomes of movement become more important than the movement itself. The movement is a means to an end. This practice is reinforced by an emphasis on games and fitness. Movement is often separated from intrinsic bodily sensations. Knowledge becomes abstracted from somatic being. Creating or composing using bodily movement, rather than replicating or conforming movement patterns, has the potential for empowering and humanizing experiences in dance and physical education. Bergmann Drewe (1996) suggests that the concept of physical education needs to be expanded to include an aesthetic dimension, and that creative dance helps students give form to their ideas and feelings through movement.

Slattery (1995) acknowledges the importance of the fine arts in curriculum development and states that "knowledge is not logically ordered and waiting to be discovered, rather it is constructed on experiences of the whole body and being" (214). Aesthetic education can be transformational rather than technological, and learning is stimulated by a sense of future possibilities and a sense of what might be. Encouraging a more integrated aesthetic process in dance education requires that the movement is intentionally experienced as expressive and creative, and that there is a focus on the processes of improvisation and creation, as opposed to replication and assessment. As well, individuality and difference are supported and respected, and attention is given to the feeling of our bodies in action. I encourage a connection of the movement to the imaginative, unique, and unusual. It is also important that dance experiences are performed in a physically and emotionally safe environment.

What does it mean to learn and understand through our moving bodies? Shapiro (1998) offers an example of an embodied pedagogy: "one that taps into the emotional mapping of the lives we live within a social context...[providing] ways of understanding how this deeper reality of feeling can be used to develop a critical understanding of the relationships between self and culture...[and a] philosophy of education concerned with not simply understanding the world but changing it" (2). For example, dance can bring students back to a conscious sense of their own bodies, feelings, and thoughts. Shapiro advocates "development of a curriculum and pedagogy for dance education that incorporates concerns for issues of power, identity, gender, and cultural differences" (7). Central to this discussion are imagination, creativity, and attention to "body memories," which can lead to a more critical understanding of one's life. Shapiro envisions a form of dance education that reflects on "lived experiences," validates difference, denies universal claims to truth, and seeks to empower students with a renewed attention to the body. "The intent of the learning experience [in dance] moves from one of learning movement vocabulary for the sake of creating dance to gaining an understanding of the self, others, and the larger world for the possibility of change" (15).

Aesthetically significant dance education includes creating, performing, and appreciating dance. Simply learning steps and replicating actions do not provide a meaningful dance education. Aesthetic appreciation is not an automatic outcome of educational dance. A conscious intention to expression in movement is required. If physical educators are often uncomfortable with their own expressive bodies—how can they bring students to an appreciation of their expressive, aesthetic bodies? The situation in which dance finds itself "may in part be explained by a political and cultural reluctance to accept the value or even the existence, of the knowledge embodied in the dance experience" (Bannon and Sanderson 2000, 11). The arts have the capacity to encourage creative, empowering, and imaginative visions. Sport and functional movement is goal-directed and emphasizes a disembodied knowing of the body. This knowledge is privileged in institutions that study and train people in the fields of physical education and, to some degree, dance education. Education in white North American culture discounts intuitive, tacit knowledge in favour of measurable outcomes. Recent renovations to school physical education curricula (for example in Alberta) are primarily about outcome-based objectives.

## Dance in (Physical) Education: Dancing in the Dark

Rose Hill published an article in the *Canadian Journal for Health, Physical Education, and Recreation* in 1982 proposing that consideration be given to teaching sport and dance, rather than physical education. In this way, both functional bodily movement in sports and expressive bodily movement in dance could be included. Hill argued in favour of equal time for sport and dance. Dominant practices in physical education privilege sport and functional movement. Rudolf Laban's model (Wall and Murray 1990), which distinguishes between functional movement and expressive movement, forms the basis for many elementary physical education curricula in Canada. His analysis of movement includes space, effort, relationship, and the body, and provides a model for moving and understanding movement. My own experience in teaching movement education for children and youth in a teacher education program at a university supports the belief that Laban's model and dance education as expressive movement have been espoused in required courses for elementary education and secondary education students for the last thirty to forty years. This is likely true for most of the teacher education and physical education programs across Canada. However, students still come to university with limited or no dance experience from school programs in physical education—not much is changing in school programs. Is there something underneath the surface of curriculum and program that gets in the way of change? Is the dominant, often unspoken judgment that "dancing is for sissies" undermining dance in physical education? I realize that I am inclined to generalize here, and I am certainly aware of examples of extensive and exciting dance programs that are happening in isolated situations. However, I continue to see the majority of incoming education students express non-existent or minimal dance education.

## Dance and Gender

### Dance-Phobia in Physical Education

The film *Billy Elliot* (2000) offers a vivid example of the common perceptions about men in dance. In 1984 in a small mining town in England, a single father comes to grips with the fact that his youngest son, Billy, is choosing to take ballet lessons instead of boxing. The pivotal scene, when the father shows up at the ballet class and discovers Billy dancing rather than boxing, expresses the horror, anger, frustration, and humiliation his dad feels. The discussion that follows between Billy and his dad emphasizes the contrast between Billy's perceptions of dance and those of his father. I would venture to guess that this scene also represents the feelings and beliefs of some professionals in physical education—dancing is for sissies, boys don't dance unless they are gay, and so on. Billy assures his dad that he is not a "poof" (homosexual) just because he likes to dance.

Dance experiences in physical education reinforce traditional male and female roles in society. Ballroom and social dance provides a good example. In reviewing the most common dance forms taught in teacher education programs and in schools, we see an emphasis on social forms such as ballroom dancing and line dancing. Dance in schools attempts to fit dominant heterosexual male norms. Male and female students, usually separated for most of their physical education classes, are suddenly brought together for a short unit on social dance. Little wonder there are management challenges in these situations—much more is going on than learning how to dance! Here the traditional social practices of dance are reified. The boys choose partners and students learn waltz, foxtrot, swing or jive dances, along with mixers and round dances. The men practise leading and the women practise following. Girls are to be silent and to do as they are told, and the boys are in charge. If a female physical educator is the primary teacher of the dance unit, the belief that women teach dance, and men teach games, may get reinforced.

How can we examine the normative performance of gender and disrupt common practices? Girls and boys may have different movement expectations placed on them. Sport becomes problematic for conventionally feminine girls, and dance becomes problematic for conventionally masculine boys. The traditional performance that has men leading and women following is one example of a dominant practice in social dance classes. Having both men and women lead, or having same-gender couples in social dance, as well as teaching expressive forms of dance, encourages other possibilities in the dancing class. In addition, experiencing the dances of other cultures, wherein gender roles are expressed differently through social and folk dances, offers different perspectives. For example, the Greek dance, *Hasapiko*, was traditionally danced by men: "Until recently men and women seldom danced together, although chains of men and women danced at the same time" (Lawson 1980, 69). Also, for many young Ukrainian children—boys, as well as girls—dance training is a common experience outside of school.

According to Burt (1995), "[i]n dance there is no possibility of opting out entirely from dominant gender ideologies" (48). Dance emphasizes a feminine discourse, athletics a masculine discourse—this dualism both defines what can be expressed through dance and provides a position for resisting dominant cultural discourses. "An individual's femininity or masculinity is measured or examined against conventional standards, represented in popular media and reinforced by schools, families, religions, medicine, the law and other institutions" (Shogan 1999, 53). Physical education's connection to games, sport, and athletics emphasizes masculine performance. Dance is incompatible with physical education to the extent that physical education is primarily concerned with sport, which in turn engages conventionally masculine movement. The hidden curriculum—or what is said by what is *not* taught—is that "dancing is for sissies."

Our experience of the body is a social and psychological construction. "Because the body is marginal to verbal discourse, its expressiveness is one such potential site of opposition...the presentation of the male body in dance [has] the potential for undermining and threatening the maintenance of male power" (Burt 1995, 72). Ted Shawn, an important modern dance figure from the 1930s, argued that dance was not "pansy" or "sissy," seemingly attempting to fit dominant heterosexual male norms, rather than challenging them (Burt 1995). As Shogan (1999) argues in her book, *The Making of High Performance Athletes*, "a girl in sport must not only practise sport skills, she must practise 'masculine' skills" (55). I might argue, the boys in dance must not only practise dance skills, they must practise *feminine* skills. If, as Billy Elliot's father assumed, this implies that boys who dance are gay, then it is not surprising that discounting dance props up traditional beliefs about sport and masculine power—physical education is no place for dancing bodies!

### Dancing Bodies

Something happens when we objectify the body: the subjective body is silenced. Measuring, monitoring, and assessing bodies in physical education objectify the body. Our bodies are something outside of ourselves—we control and manipulate them and measure their performance against motor-skill, fitness or competitive standards. Our experiences of our bodies in motion diminish in relation to the results. We are uncomfortable with our sensuous, expressive, subjective bodies—we are out of touch with our bodies. We are much more comfortable with objective measures such as weight, height, strength, body fat, flexibility and attitude scales. The touchy-feely feminized movement is not acknowledged in physical education. Knowing in dance concerns body awareness and movement awareness—kinesthetic, synesthetic, and aesthetic. This integrated approach to movement allows students to respond individually to the stimuli, while being mindful of their bodies at all times. Dancing is more than just knowing how to do a movement, it involves an expressive intent. This expressive intent is also meant to be included in dance forms that emphasize replication. For example, when performing a tango or a waltz, the expression of the style of the dance is integral to the dancing. The sensual sneaking and darting of the tango is much different from the swing and lilt of the waltz. The vigorous prancing action in the *troika* folk dance is meant to express the beautiful, synchronized action of horses pulling a sleigh—a representation by peasants of the elite class who travelled around in three-horse sleighs, or *troikas*.

Learning dancing contributes to becoming bodily sensitive as Parviainen (2002) argues. Bodily knowledge is not about correctly performing a movement skill, but about being able to negotiate, modify, and adapt the skill for the purpose of expression. Articulated knowledge about dance cannot replace its felt counterpart of dancing.

> We experience the lived substance of dance through our own kinetic flow of being...dance cannot exist outside the body... my individuality (which is unique) and any human condition

(which is universal) are inescapably present in my dance.
(Fraleigh 1987, xv–xxiv)

How is dancing contingent upon our beliefs about the body? By examining dancing in various cultures, we can see how dance styles and customs reveal cultural notions about the body—for example, the held torso and intricate leg and footwork in Irish dance compared to the gyrating and moving torso in Hawaiian dance. Dancing is non-verbal representation of personal expression. Dance *dis*-putes and *dis*-rupts privileged notions of the body in physical education. In this way, dance is *dis*-regarded, *dis*-approved of, and *dis*-associated from the study of physical education *unless* it is *dis*-embodied. Dance is *diss-ed*! To conform to the privileged discourse of physical education, the body becomes objectified and is studied in its anatomy, physiology, psychology, or sociology. The expressive, personal, and sensual experience of the lived body, as it responds to the world, is neither acknowledged nor valued.

How then can we say that we are physically educated if we do not *know* our expressive subjective body? Felt body knowledge is often undervalued; instead, we have a dominant view that knowledge is minded. Dualisms privilege one over the other—mind over body, male over female. Motion may have its own meaning. Creative dance focuses on the lived experience of dancing, a dancing for self. "Dance can be taken as meaningful action which can be treated as text" (Blumenfeld-Jones 1995). Polanyi (1966) proposed two kinds of knowing, an intellectual kind (knowing what or knowing that) and a bodily kind (knowing how). Knowledge can be seen as both embodied (or procedural) and theoretical (or propositional). How does one's body know what it does through movement?

"Meaning is rooted in the sensory life of the body" (Abram 1997, 80). Merleau-Ponty's work suggests that "the world is not what I think but what I live through" (1962, xvi). The self cannot be separated from either the body or the world. The self is constituted as a lived body. This lived body is the way that one interacts in the world. Merleau-Ponty's work is committed to exploring aspects of our embodied existence that usually remain outside of theoretical language. This view contrasts with the mind-body binary and situates consciousness in the body. This requires an investigation of the body's non-verbal expression and its relationship to verbal expression. For Merleau-Ponty, we are not self-housed in predominantly passive bodies. Rather, who we are—including our bodies—is continually being created by the world (Albright 1997, 47). Exploring our subjective bodies through expressive movement recognizes the lived body experience.

　　　What kind of human and social vision underpins the research and writing in physical education? One that often emphasizes competition in athletics, objectified bodies in fitness, and healthy living models. What kind of human and social vision is reinforced in physical education programs of study and the pedagogy practised in them? One that emphasizes core experiences in anatomy, physiology, and sport psychology—a scientized body. This is the basis for many professional and university undergraduate programs. A joint degree program in physical education and education that stresses *sport* history, *sport* psychology, and sociology of *sport* is one such example. Imagine, as Shapiro (1998) states, "an education that is focused on human praxis—the thoughtful and conscious struggle to reshape our world into one that is more just and compassionate, and [to] understand through our *embodied knowledge* what it might mean to live freer and more empowered lives" (9). This vision seeks to empower people for social transformation through a "renewed attention to the body" (8).

　　　Is there a process that leads to an awareness of and attention to particulars in the moving body—body knowledge that enhances the learning and performing of physical skills and leads to an ability to project the body into the world in performance? To have body wisdom—to be physically educated—we need to be able to attend to this multiplicity of sensory experiences and be able to translate them into purposeful movements. Susan Stinson (1995) is influenced by this lived experience of dancing in her thinking and writing. She knows that artistic form is not only external but also internal. Dancers "know that *shape* is not only about what something looks like on the outside, but what it feels like on the inside" (43). We can develop ways in which body and mind breathe together and are fully coordinated—such as dance. Dance, sport, and other forms of physical activity have the potential to confront us with our embodied knowing. Dance education can provide activities that support and encourage the expressive aspects of individual bodies.

　　　Education, according to H'Doubler (1968), involves impression and expression. When we examine the notion of impressive bodies, expressive bodies, thinking bodies, and dancing bodies, we see the impact that high-quality dance experiences can have on students. Impressive bodies, or knowing bodies, experience an understanding of the subjective process whereby movers understand, create and use knowledge. Important to the experience of creative dance and dance composition are a focus on and commitment to the improvisational experience. When we are exploring ideas with our bodies, we are moving with a heightened personal sensitivity to the feelings in our bodies. We are working to be completely free of distracting thoughts and movement habits. This requires being present in the moment, trusting the body's response and action. It also requires an attitude of non-judgment—dismissing such thoughts as "how do I look?" This heightened attention to the body, to the present ongoing movement, is particularly important in activities such as dance, yoga, and many martial arts and artistic sports. The internal focus on the body is not often emphasized in other physical activities and sport. People who are skilled in sport and games may not have experience attending to the body in the moment, rather they are often focused on the result of the movement—to score the goal, make a defensive play, etc. As well, it is unusual for athletes to articulate subjective, aesthetic feelings that arise from their participation in sport. But, being with one's body, being comfortable with one's creative and expressive body, is an important element of being physically educated.

To be able to express, to inform, and to articulate is an important outcome of education. Students may be able to utilize movement as a form of expression. Dance and body explorations have the capacity to inform us about many things; not the least of which is how disciplined, normalized gestures are inscribed on our bodies through other means. Dance can provide active play with tactility. Motion is not unthinkable: "The body is capable of understanding more things at once than can be articulated in language" (Browning 1995, 46). Some of the most moving scenes from *Billy Elliot* are the intense, spontaneous dancing moments when Billy expresses his joy of movement, or his frustrations about how his family feels about his dancing. The way he uses movement to express his feelings illustrates the power of the body's expression. When he articulates what dancing means to him at the audition for the ballet school, he talks about his subjective feelings of the experience of dancing—a sense of disappearing, of being transformed, and of flying.

## The D-Word
### Marginalizing Dance in Physical Education

Looking at the history of the D-word in Canadian physical education, we can trace the change in the national organization, from CAHPER to CAHPERD in 1994. "Following the lead of the American Association which added 'D' for 'Dance' to its title (thus becoming AAHPERD) in February 1980, the Dance Committee of CAHPER named an 'ad hoc' committee to assess the benefits of adding the 'D' to CAHPER" (Gurney 1983,

138). However, action to add the "D" was postponed because of other pressing issues in CAHPER. At the national convention in Moncton in 1993, members of the Dance Committee "unanimously passed a motion to pursue the addition of the word 'Dance' to the title of CAHPER" (Murray 1994, 27). In 1994, at the Annual General Meeting of CAHPER in Victoria, two motions were passed and carried unanimously to approve the addition of "Dance" to the name of the association and to include the "D" for "Dance" in the name.

The work of the Dance Committee of CAHPER (1965–80) was significant. This committee included representatives from each province who met twice a year and were committed to raising the profile of dance in schools across the country. Financial support for these meetings and projects gradually disappeared and the work of the Dance Committee diminished. However, various projects, workshops, dance position statements, as well as input into the National Convention, were just some of the contributions that the Dance Committee made. After fifteen years of negotiating, dance was finally recognized as a distinct part of the National Association—CAHPER became CAHPERD. In "Quotes to support the addition of 'D' to CAHPER," Robbins (1994) said,

> As a professional association it is our responsibility to ensure that people are exposed to functional and expressive movement. Our name should reflect our commitment to dance as an important part of the movement continuum. (40)

Murray (1994) argues that "[d]ance plays a significant role within each of physical education, recreation and health and offers unique potential to all people for its expressive and artistic nature (27)." Jean Cunningham (1994), a former chair of the Dance Committee of CAHPER, supports this vision of dance in physical education:

> Dance can be an alternative to or an integral part of physical education. The latter instance offers a potentially powerful union, as the athleticism of sport infuses the intentionally symbolic and aesthetic world of dance. The "D" for dance in CAHPERD refers to, and celebrates this larger vision of physical education. Furthermore, it suggests new possibilities, an open mind and the energy of change. (40)

A debate within the dance community about the place of dance in education has been ongoing, however, as is evidenced by various position papers and articles in professional journals (Bannon and Sanderson 2000; Bergmann Drewe 1996; Hong 2001; and Shapiro 1998). Some models see dance as just another activity (like volleyball or gymnastics). Other models see dance as more appropriately connected to fine arts—the expressive, creative, performing, and appreciating aspects of an aesthetic education. Is dance more compatible with physical education than with fine arts education? Fine arts programs potentially allow us to connect with the aesthetic experience and the expressive subjective body. In New Zealand schools, dance has traditionally been included in the physical education program. Recent revisions to the national curriculum, however, placed dance in the fine arts program alongside drama, music, and the visual arts. Now all four disciplines in the fine arts are required from grades 1 to 8 (Hong 2001). In this model, physical education emphasizes the development of physical skills, whereas the fine arts program is broader in scope and includes aesthetic education. Students develop an appreciation for movement as an art form, the expressive and artistic or qualitative dimensions of the movement. In some curricula, dance stands alone as its own subject area on a par with physical education or music. Whatever its position, dance in CAHPERD has been acknowledged as an equal partner with physical education, recreation, and health within the Canadian Association—at least in name. The dominant discourse in this association that privileges objective bodies and functional movement, as well as culturally dominant masculine and feminine ideologies, may however limit the dance discourse, and reinforce the position that "dancing is for sissies."

The relevance of aesthetic awareness in education also informs this discussion. Proponents of art education believe that experiences in the arts help to keep our senses alive. Despite the evolving number of artistic sports, an understanding of the aesthetic experience is not espoused in physical education programs in schools or in teacher preparation programs. Dance can inform the artistic sports significantly, in both the elements of artistic impression and the training of an expressive body. It may also be possible to reach more students with curriculum models in physical education that include expressive activities.

The debate about the positioning of dance in school programs—in physical education (practical approach), in fine arts (artistic, expressive approach), or in dance as a separate subject area altogether (artistic, aesthetic, and cultural approach) is interesting. Educational systems privilege minded (cognitive) function over body (feeling) knowledge.

This position is reinforced in physical education. The pedagogy of physical education emphasizes a curriculum that defines physical, cognitive, social, and affective objectives. The feeling, expressive body is not developed through this model. In fact, the somatic, moving, sensing experience is not emphasized in physical education. In a system that already marginalizes non-academic subjects—fine arts and physical education, for example—support for a separate dance subject area may indeed limit dance experiences even more or, on the other hand, promote an elitist dance curriculum. The debate continues. When Billy Elliot attended his first ballet class, he said, "I feel like a right sissie." But he overcame the obstacles to follow his dream and become a world-class dancer—at the same time disrupting the notion that "dancing is for sissies."

## References

Abram, D. 1997. *The spell of the sensuous.* New York: Vintage Books.

Albright, A. C. 1997. *Choreographing difference: The body and identity in contemporary dance.* Hanover, NH: Wesleyan University Press.

Bannon, F., and P. Sanderson. 2000. Experience every moment: Aesthetically significant dance. *Research in Dance Education* 1(1):5–26.

Bergmann Drewe, S. 1996. *Creative dance: Enriching understanding.* Calgary, AB: Detselig Enterprises Ltd.

Blumenfeld-Jones, D. 1995. Dance as a mode of research representation. *Qualitative Inquiry* 1(4):391–401.

Brenman, G., and J. Finn. 2000. *Billy Elliot.* Ottawa, ON: Universal Studios Canada Inc. Motion Picture.

Browning, B. 1995. Samba: The body articulate. In *Bodies of the text, dance as theory, literature as dance,* ed. E. W. Goellner and J. S. Murphy, 39–56. New Brunswick, NJ: Rutgers University Press.

Burt, R. 1995. *The male dancer: Bodies, spectacle, sexualities.* New York: Routledge.

Cunningham, J. 1994, Summer. *CAHPER Journal* 60(2):40.

de Mille, A. 1984. *The dance notebook: An illustrated journal with quotes.* Philadelphia: Running Press Book Publishers.

Fraleigh, S. 1987. *Dance and the lived body: A descriptive aesthetics.* Pittsburgh: University of Pittsburgh Press.

Gurney, H. 1983. *The CAHPER story, 1933-1983.* Vanier, ON: The Canadian Association for Health, Physical Education and Recreation.

H'Doubler, M. 1968. *Dance: A creative art experience.* Madison: The University of Wisconsin Press.

Hill, R. 1982. Let's teach sport and dance. *CAHPER Journal* 48(4):13–16.

Hong, T. 2001. Getting cinders to the ball. *New Zealand Physical Educator* 3(1):4–6.

Lawson, J. 1980. *European folk dance.* New York: Books for Libraries, Arno Press Inc.

Merleau-Ponty, M. 1962. *Phenomenology of perception.* London: Routledge and Kegan Paul Ltd.

Murray, N. 1994, Spring. Should a capital "D" be added to CAHPER? *CAHPER Journal* 60(1):27.

Parviainen, J. 2002. Bodily Knowledge: Epistemological reflections on dance. *Dance Research Journal* 34(1):11–26.

Polanyi, M. 1966. *The tacit dimension.* New York: Doubleday and Company, Inc.

Robbins, S. 1994, Summer. Quotes to support the addition of 'D' to CAHPER. *CAHPER Journal* 60(2):40.

Shapiro, S. 1998. Toward transformative teachers: Critical and feminist perspectives in dance education. In *Dance, power, and difference: Critical and feminist perspectives on dance education,* ed. S. Shapiro, 7–21. Windsor, ON: Human Kinetics.

Shogan, D. 1999. *The making of high-performance athletes.* Toronto: University of Toronto Press.

Slattery, P. 1995. *Curriculum development in the postmodern era.* New York: Garland Publishing, Inc.

Stinson, S. W. 1995. Body of knowledge. *Education Theory* 45(1):43–54.

Wall, J., and Murray, N. 1990. *Children and movement: Physical education in the elementary school.* Madison, WI: WCB Brown and Benchmark Publishers.

Chapter Six

# The Role of Family Studies in Comprehensive School Health

## Laura Tryssenaar

Health Canada's recommendation for comprehensive school health begs the inclusion of family studies as part of an integrated approach to promoting healthy students in healthy schools. This chapter invites the reader to consider family studies and health and physical education as complementary rather than competing programs. A history of these school subjects clarifies their shared journeys. Family studies and health and physical education share similar challenges in improving student health and well-being. A better understanding of family studies and its relevance for health education is needed to appreciate its fundamental importance in comprehensive school health.

In their Consensus Statement on School Health, the Canadian Association for School Health (CASH) identifies two components of comprehensive school health—instruction and social programs. They make the following recommendations for health instruction in schools:

- ◈ a comprehensive K–12 health curriculum;
- ◈ a K–12 physical education curriculum;
- ◈ a K–12 family studies/home economics curriculum;
- ◈ the integration of health into subject areas; formal and informal learning, the development of awareness, knowledge, attitudinal change, decision making, skill building, behavioural change and social action;

◈ effective preservice and in-service training; adequate teaching/
   learning materials; and appropriate teaching methodologies.
   (Canadian Association for School Health 2003, 1)

This chapter will examine the relationship between family studies and
health education curricula.

The Canadian Association for Health and Physical Education,
Recreation and Dance (CAHPERD 2003) recognizes the difficulty of developing a national perspective for health education in Canada because
philosophies and approaches to health education differ across provinces.
The same is true for family studies or home economics education in Canada. In this chapter, I focus on Ontario education because of my involvement in teaching family studies in this province since 1976. Therefore, I
refer to the school subject as "family studies," which is the title that has
been used in this province for more than three decades (Tryssenaar 1993).
Although other provinces continue to name it home economics or human
ecology, all who teach family studies, home economics, or human ecology
share the Canadian Home Economics Association (CHEA) philosophy
that the "mission is to enhance the quality of life for individuals and families"(CHEA 2002, 56).

Family studies is closely aligned with Health Canada's definition of
health and its understanding of comprehensive school health (CSH).
Health Canada states that

> health is concerned with the quality of life of all Canadians. It
> encompasses social, mental, emotional, and physical health,
> and is influenced by a wide range of biological, social, eco-
> nomic, and cultural factors. (Health Canada 2002, 1)

Furthermore, "CSH views health as a resource for daily living" (ibid.). Similar themes are evident in The Ontario Ministry of Education definition of
family studies:

> Family studies is an interdisciplinary subject area integrating so-
> cial and physical sciences in the study of topics arising from
> daily life. It includes the study of individual and family develop-
> ment, relationships, parenting, decision-making, resource man-
> agement, food and nutrition, clothing and textiles, housing and
> health sciences. (Ontario Ministry of Education 2000b, 11)

Health has been integrated into family studies since its origin as domestic science. The family, in all of its physical, social, emotional, mental, and spiritual contexts, is a major determinant of the health of individuals and the nation.

## A History of Health and Family Studies

Family studies and health education share similar histories. Both were introduced into public education over 100 years ago as a response to the need for higher standards of sanitation and hygiene and to a call for educational reform at the beginning of the twentieth century. Historically, public health initiatives have followed a pattern as outlined in the United States by The Center for Health and Health Care in Schools (CHHCS):

> Key health care strategies began with quarantine and sanitary reform, followed by maternal and child health programs, antibiotics, and finally, screening and treatment progressing to managed care. Focus of health activities started with water systems and pasteurization, personal hygiene, the hospital as a center of care, to categorical health programs, to modern conceptualizations of healthy communities. (CHHCS 2004, 1)

Health, as a school subject, followed a similar development. At the end of the 1800s and into the early 1900s, schools were the vehicle for reaching the greatest number of people in a sparsely populated Canada. It was an era in which many Canadians did not have access to newspapers or magazines. Radio, television, and electronic media had not yet been invented. School was the place to inform the public about epidemics and communicable disease and to promote nutrition and healthful behaviours. Direct instruction in the elementary schools regarding sanitation, pasteurization, and hand-washing soon followed. Vaccinations for smallpox, and later for tuberculosis, were first carried out through the schools (CHHCS 2004). The belief was that school children would not only take the health message home to their families, but would model it themselves for the next generation.

The Victorian obsession with hygiene is central to the origins of family studies as a school subject. Family studies has its roots in domestic science, which was established in Ontario in the late 1880s and later became known as home economics. Family studies continues to be misunderstood because of vestiges from its earlier connections with "stitchery" and "cookery;" however, domestic science, home economics, and family studies have evolved in response to the changing health and associated needs of families.

## Hygiene and Domestic Science: 1897–1936

Domestic science was introduced into elementary schools in 1897 in response to the efforts of Adelaide Hoodless, who dedicated her life to the training of young women in domestic science following the death of her youngest child from drinking contaminated milk (Tryssenaar 1993). She saw the necessity for school-based training in a society where home was no longer a manufacturing centre, but a place where scientific knowledge of housing, sanitation, hygiene, home economics, and child care was essential.

A climate of educational reform at the turn of the century, influenced in part by the progressivism expressed in the writings of John Dewey (1897), helped to further the cause of domestic science in schools. Dewey advocated experiential, hands-on learning instead of the traditional teacher-directed, rote-learning canon of that era. Domestic science for girls and manual training for boys incorporated Dewey's ideals and allowed schools to schedule these subjects as parallel programs (Heyman, Lawson, and Stamp 1972). Although family studies no longer reflects the gender segregation of domestic science versus manual training, it has retained the experiential, hands-on pedagogy favoured by Dewey.

Literature on the history of home economics indicates that domestic science was concerned with far more than sewing and cooking instruction. It was concerned with the hygiene of domestic life, the science of right living, and the health of the home (Peterat and DeZwart 1995; Rowles 1964; Skrypnek 2002; Tryssenaar 1993). Science and sanitation were combined in teaching about food preservation, laundry techniques, scalding dishes, the thorough cooking of food, and the boiling of milk and water to prevent illness. Responsibility for the health of the family was squarely on the shoulders of women (Berry 1995) and public schools were the means for transferring such vital matters to the next generation of mothers.

Domestic science, which continued to be optional in elementary schools, achieved a place in secondary schooling through the growing acceptance of vocational or technical education. The growth of vocational education received its impetus in the 1920s from increasing enrolments in secondary schools and the thriving manufacturing economy, which led business leaders to call for the vocational training of students (Stamp

1982). Preparing students for their roles in society included training young women for their future vocation as homemakers. New facilities constructed for vocational education included high school classrooms equipped for instruction in dressmaking and cooking.

## Home Economics and Health: 1937–72

Cooking and sewing were also but a small part of what was becoming known as "home economics." In an article first published in 1922, entitled "Why is Home Economics a School Subject?", Elizabeth Berry (1995) noted that the teachers of these subjects "gradually came to realize that they had to deal with food, clothing, and shelter viewed from the standpoints of production, hygiene, economics, and art" and, further, that these subjects included what continues to be a central tenet of contemporary family studies courses—"a study of the relation of the members of the family to each other and to society" (Berry 1995, 36).

Between 1937 and 1972 in Ontario, the subject known as home economics was structured around science, economics, and art with an underlying ideal of perfection. The standards of home economics could be achieved by following the precise "how-to" kind of instruction that dominated the field (Tryssenaar 1993). Economics underscored the practical nature of the selection and management of food, clothing, and housing. In food courses, the science of nutrition—a growing field of study—was balanced with the art of food preparation and presentation. The economy of home sewing and housing was balanced with creativity and the art of gracious living. Courses in home management and child development were viewed from both a scientific and an economic perspective. Healthy eating and nutrition, cleanliness, safe home environments, and a concern for healthy growth and development of children were evidence of the continued connection between health and home economics. However, social changes affecting families, and women in particular, soon challenged the traditional ideal of home economics as training for the vocation of homemaker.

The social fabric of home and family changed dramatically throughout the 1960s with growth in the number of homemakers participating in the paid workforce. Divorce rates were on the rise, more children were being raised in single-parent and reconstituted families, and the roles of men and women in families and society were changing. Home economics curricula began to focus on the changing family in response to these so-cial trends.

## Health Perspectives in Family Studies: 1972–98

In 1972 in Ontario, not only did the curriculum change, but the name changed as well (Tryssenaar 1993). Courses became coeducational and were organized around themes developed cooperatively with students. Family as environment, quality of family relationships, building family rela-tionships, and decision making as it related to family relationships were ex-amined in all courses. The importance of meeting individual and family needs became central to the exploration of issues such as health and well-being, self-concept, sexuality, divorce, and daycare. Family studies evolved from training girls in hygiene and sanitation to engaging young men and women in a better understanding of family and human relationships in ev-eryday life.

Pedagogical changes were also spelled out in the family studies guidelines at the intermediate level by the Ontario Ministry of Education (1972). Teachers were encouraged to include group work, skits, role play, discussion, film, and interviews, and to involve students in community ac-tivities. Television, radio, and print media of all kinds were suggested as ways in which to bring the world into the classroom. The changes were pro-found and allowed family studies to align with the social sciences.

The family studies curriculum continued to respond to social change. The curriculum of the 1970s was revised in 1987, becoming more streamlined and truly elective in nature by eliminating prerequisites. It in-cluded guidelines for the grades 7 and 8 family studies courses, as well as secondary-level courses that could be delivered at three levels of diffi-culty—basic, general, or advanced. At the grade 9 or 10 level, family stud-ies focused on food and clothing. Grade 11 or 12 family studies courses encompassed parenting (a completely new course), housing, and econom-ics in the family. The Ontario Academic Course (OAC), Families in Cana-dian Society, became the capstone and prepared students for related courses at the postsecondary level. Although this curriculum retained some traditional-sounding titles, its aim was to give students the "self-con-fidence, interpersonal skills, and awareness they [would] need in order to function well in a family context and manage their own family life in a cli-mate of societal, cultural, technological, and scientific change" (Ontario

Ministry of Education 1987, 4). Family and human relationships continued to provide the context for all courses.

In 1987, family studies was clearly defined as *"the social science of people's relationships with each other in their primary social unit and their relationships in society"* [italics in original] (Ontario Ministry of Education 1987, 4). The family studies curriculum of the late 1980s and 1990s opened the door to teaching about some of the deepest concerns of society. Physical, social, and cultural factors affecting all aspects of family wellbeing were addressed. Topics of consequence for teachers and students of family studies included eating disorders, body image, physical and interpersonal safety, child abuse and neglect, parental disharmony, power issues in relationships, sexuality, dating violence, teen pregnancy, marital violence, cohabitation, custody, remarriage, aging, and death. Reflection and critical thinking underscored a transformation from the technical "how to" framework of home economics to the interpretive stance of family studies, which asks, "What does *this* mean for individuals and families?"

Given the new direction taken in family studies, it is not surprising that physical and health education was suggested as one of the ministry guidelines with similar content that could be combined with family studies for developing new courses. Healthy Active Living was one such collaboration between family studies and physical and health education in some boards. The family studies focus on human development, sexuality, and healthy relationships was combined with physical and health education concerns about fitness, daily activity, and substance use and abuse. For the first time, curriculum integration was recommended in the Ministry guidelines, blurring the boundaries of what before had been distinctly separate courses.

## The Ontario Curriculum:  1998–Present

A mere ten years later, the Conservative government in Ontario under the leadership of Premier Mike Harris brought in sweeping educational reforms in the guise of the "Common Sense Revolution" (Gidney 1999). In response to the government's pledge for a more rigorous and relevant curriculum, and to support the reduction of secondary schooling from five years to four, the entire K–12 school curriculum was rewritten, published, and implemented with unprecedented haste (Majhanovich 2002). Documents for school subjects from grades 1 to 8 were released in 1998, grades 9 and 10 documents were published in 1999, and those for grades 11 and 12 in 2000. The new curriculum policy, known as *The Ontario Curriculum*, was standardized in terms of layout and design for all subject disciplines at all grade levels.

Every course of study now begins with a course description that may be supplemented, but not otherwise changed, by course selection calendars. A clear listing of the overall and specific expectations that students must achieve by the end of the course follows. Assessment and evaluation procedures have also been standardized. All courses must be evaluated based on an achievement chart that specifies four categories—knowledge and understanding, thinking and/or inquiry, communication, and application. Although teachers find these categories "forced" in some courses, they facilitate the generation of computer comments under each of them for the Ontario Report Card that is common across all grade levels.

## Implications for Family Studies and Health Education

The new curriculum has had both positive and negative implications for family studies and health education. At the secondary-school level, family studies is now clearly situated as a social science. In fact, it dominates the social sciences and humanities curriculum guideline (Ontario Ministry of Education 1999b, 2000b), comprising thirteen of the nineteen courses governed by the guideline. In spite of achieving such a strong identity in secondary education, family studies courses remain optional.

A positive outcome for family studies was the government's promise of textbook dollars to support the new curriculum. Publishers moved to provide Canadian textbooks written by teachers of family studies to support the new guidelines, including *Individual and Family Living in Canada* (Holloway and Meriorg 2001), *Parenting in Canada: Human Growth and Development* (Cunningham, Meriorg, and Tryssenaar 2003), *Individuals and Families in a Diverse Society* (Holloway et al. 2003), and *Food for Today: First Canadian Edition* (Witte et al. 2003). Teacher resource guides developed for these textbooks have not only helped teachers implement the new courses, but have continued to promote the kinds of constructive, experiential, hands-on teaching strategies that are characteristic of the family studies subject area.

On the negative side, as a direct result of the Harris government's reforms, family studies no longer exists at the elementary-school level in Ontario. The family studies program for grades 7 and 8, so clearly evident in the 1987 curriculum, was expunged from *The Ontario Curriculum,*

*Grades 1–8*, and although there was great potential for integrating family studies into other school subjects, this integration did not occur. Compared with British Columbia, which has a K–12 home economics curriculum (British Columbia Ministry of Education 1998), Ontario lags behind in achieving the Canadian Association for School Health recommendation for a comprehensive K–12 family studies/home economics curriculum. Ironically, teacher education in family studies for the primary/junior division is available in Ontario (Dryden 2002) even though the curriculum does not exist. The challenge for such a preservice program is locating the places in the elementary curriculum where family studies can be integrated.

The Ontario Curriculum, however, includes a definitive health and physical education curriculum for grades 1–8 (Ontario Ministry of Education 1998) that includes three components—healthy living, movement, and active participation. These are introduced in grade 1 and continue to be addressed in age-appropriate increments in subsequent grades. Healthy Living, as the health component of the curriculum, is divided into four strands—healthy eating, growth and development, personal safety and injury prevention, and substance use and abuse. These strands are repeated with greater sophistication in every grade. A clear benefit for comprehensive school health is that health and physical education is compulsory at the elementary-school level, but whether adequate class time is provided for healthy living instruction remains questionable.

At the secondary-school level, family studies and health and physical education compete for student enrolment. Perhaps an unintended consequence of the new curriculum is how it polarizes family studies and health education. Although they are seen as totally unrelated, each subject area provides relevant and complementary health content that is important for students at all grade levels (Ontario Ministry of Education 1999a; 2000a). Both have an important role to play if the goal is to achieve comprehensive school health.

## Comprehensive School Health Issues

The Canadian Association for Comprehensive Health (Safe Healthy Schools 2003) identifies ten issues as critical in comprehensive school health: heart health, mental health, environmental health/allergies, tobacco, substance abuse, physical activity, nutrition/food safety, sexuality/STDs/HIV, safety/violence, and injury prevention. Figure 1 compares the family studies and health and physical education courses in *The Ontario Curriculum* that address these health issues.

| Family Studies Curriculum (Social Sciences) | | Comprehensive School Health Issues | Health & Physical Education Curriculum | |
|---|---|---|---|---|
| 9/10 | Food & Nutrition | *Heart Health* | 9/10 | Healthy Active Living |
| 12 | Food & Nutrition Sciences | | 11 | Health for Life |
| 9/10 | Individual & Family Living | | 11 | Health for Life |
| 11 | Managing Personal & Family Resources | *Mental Health* | 11/12 | Healthy Active Living |
| 12 | Individuals & Families in a Diverse Society | | | |
| 9/10 | Individual & Family Living | *Environmental Health/Allergies* | 11 | Health for Life |
| 11 | Parenting | | 12 | Recreation & Fitness Leadership |
| 11 | Living & Working with Children | | | |
| 11 | Parenting | *Tobacco* | 9-12 | Healthy Active Living |
| 11 | Living & Working with Children | | 11 | Health for Life |
| 9/10 | Individual & Family Living | *Substance Abuse* | 9-12 | Healthy Active Living |
| 11 | Parenting | | 11 | Health for Life |
| 11 | Living & Working with Children | | | |
| 9/10 | Food & Nutrition | *Physical Activity* | 9-12 | Healthy Active Living |
| 9/10 | Individual & Family Living | | 11 | Health for Life |
| 12 | Food & Nutrition Sciences | | 12 | Exercise Science |
| | | | 12 | Recreation & Fitness Leadership |
| 9/10 | Food & Nutrition | *Nutrition/Food Safety* | 10 | Healthy Active Living |
| 9/10 | Individual & Family Living | | 11 | Health for Life |
| 12 | Parenting & Human Development | | 12 | Recreation & Fitness Leadership |
| 12 | Food & Nutrition Sciences | | | |

| | | | | |
|---|---|---|---|---|
| 9/10 | Individual & Family Living | | 9-12 | Healthy Active Living |
| 11 | Parenting | | 11 | Health for Life |
| 12 | Issues in Human Growth & Development | Sexuality/ STD/HIV | | |
| 12 | Individuals & Families in a Diverse Society | | | |
| 9/10 | Individual & Family Living | | 9-12 | Healthy Active Living |
| 11 | Managing Personal & Family Resources | | 12 | Recreation & Fitness Leadership |
| 11 | Parenting | | | |
| 11 | Living & Working with Children | | | |
| 12 | Parenting & Human Development | Safety/Violence | | |
| 11 | Issues in Human Growth & Development | | | |
| 12 | Individuals & Families in a Diverse Society | | | |
| 9/10 | Individual & Family Living | | 9-12 | Healthy Active Living |
| 9/10 | Food & Nutrition | | 12 | Exercise Science |
| 11 | Managing Personal & Family Resources | Injury Prevention | 12 | Recreation & Fitness Leadership |
| 11 | Shelter & Living Spaces | | | |
| 11 | Parenting | | | |
| 11 | Living & Working with Children | | | |

Figure 1: Comparison of family studies and health curricula applications for critical issues in comprehensive school health.

Safety and violence prevention are addressed at length in family studies courses from the perspective of human relationships. Family violence (between spouses, parents and children, caregivers and the elderly, and other family members) and schoolyard violence (bullying) are of primary concern. Sexuality, on the other hand, particularly as it relates to sexually transmitted diseases, AIDS, and reproduction, is the domain of health and physical education, as are physical activity and injury prevention. What is common to both family studies and health education courses is their focus on decision-making, problem-solving, and conflict-resolution skills as the means of engaging students in a personal commitment to health and wellbeing.

The context in which the issues are addressed is what differentiates the programs. Parenting courses in family studies might examine the effects of tobacco, alcohol, or substance abuse on the fetus during pregnancy, whereas health and physical education courses focus on how tobacco affects student health. Likewise, the senior-level Healthy Active Living courses examine mental health as a specific construct of individual health, whereas family studies courses address it in the context of the family. In theory, family studies and health education are more complementary than competitive and together they offer a thorough, well-balanced approach to addressing the issues of comprehensive school health.

Ideally, given the recommendations for instruction to achieve comprehensive school health, all students would continue to take courses in family studies and health and physical education at each grade until the completion of high school. In Ontario, however, it is possible to complete four years of secondary education and take only one course in health and physical education and none in family studies. At the secondary level only one credit in health and physical education is compulsory—most often the grade 9 Healthy Active Living course, whereas family studies courses are optional. The existence of a high-quality curriculum does not guarantee the availability of that curriculum to all students.

To provide a more comprehensive delivery of health education to a wider student population, the combined resources of family studies and health and physical education should be considered. The following suggestions are possibilities for coordinating efforts between family studies and health classes to make the best use of resources and to reach the most students:

- ❖ have students in both family studies and health create displays for a "health fair" based on one or more of the Comprehensive Health Issues outlined in Figure 1 and invite all students, teachers, and administrators to attend;
- ❖ combine classes when exploring similar topics in family studies and health to make the best use of guest speakers, videos, or drama presentations;
- ❖ have students in health and family studies classes team up to provide "health challenges" for the rest of the student body;
- ❖ run a poster contest related to specific health issues in which family studies and health students compete, not only for prizes,

but also for the opportunity to display their posters in the best locations around the school;
◈ have students from both subject areas team up to create and present daily health messages for the school announcements;
◈ have students prepare a series of drama presentations relating to health or personal safety issues and showcase them for other classes in family studies and health or at a junior or senior assembly.

By combining their efforts, students may begin to see health as being both personal *and* relational.

The challenge of meeting the goal of comprehensive school health may require more drastic means than simply leaving it up to teachers to combine family studies and health education whenever it appears to be convenient to do so. It is time to rethink the traditional means of delivering health education. Rather than continue to combine health with physical education, the time may be right for formally requiring the combination of health and family studies.

## A Case for Delivering Health Education via Family Studies

The Canadian Association for Health, Physical Education, Recreation and Dance (CAHPERD) recognizes that "health education is increasingly becoming an add-on subject, with little-to-no structured curriculum time" (CAHPERD 2004, 1). Timetabling difficulties arise when health and physical education are combined into one school subject. Health instruction requires a classroom, whereas physical education calls for a gymnasium, and to provide two facilities for one subject is sometimes daunting. Timetabling, as well as the quality of the health program being delivered, is further complicated by segregated classes, a greater time allotment for physical activity than for health, and a demand for classrooms by other subject areas. Are health topics and issues given the same time and attention for males and females in gender-segregated health classes? Is there enough time in the health component of health and physical education courses to provide students with the depth of understanding required for sensitive issues? What message are we sending students about the importance of health education if the health component of the course is dropped altogether in favour of the physical education component or if it is taught in change rooms, hallways, cafeterias, or other marginal areas of the school? Family studies, in contrast, is scheduled in one classroom and integrates health-related issues into an entire course of study.

Some concerns regarding health education go beyond timetabling. CAHPERD also raises concerns regarding teacher education, claiming that

> many teachers teaching health are ill-prepared and ill-equipped to teach the subject. Teacher preparation courses and professional development opportunities in health education are often neither mandatory nor available; and sorting out the myriad of health education resources can be confusing. (CAHPERD 2003, 1)

A study of students' perceptions of their experiences in sexuality education also raises questions about teacher education:

> In addition to helping teachers acquire a breadth of knowledge about and comfort in teaching sexuality education, teacher education programs also need to ensure that teachers have and can use a wide repertoire of teaching methods that will be relevant to the learning needs of a diverse student population. Emphasis needs to be placed on understanding how students might experience a unit rather than on how to "teach the curriculum." (Noon and Arcus 2002, 15)

Teachers' relationships with curriculum begin to take shape during their preservice training and continue to evolve as they enact the curriculum with their students (Tryssenaar 2004). In family studies the sensitive nature of the curriculum is of vital importance from the beginning.

Teaching controversial topics requires a "vigilant subjectivity" (Deluca 2000). Teachers need to be attuned to issues of equity, nuances of fear or embarrassment, vestiges of cultural beliefs, gender differences in maturity and readiness to approach a topic, and individual student differences in acceptance and tolerance of self and others. Teachers of family studies work daily in this realm. Because they are concerned with the quality of everyday life of individuals and families, their teaching strategies intentionally personalize curriculum content. They understand that their subject area is deeply sensitive, highly personal, and often controversial. Family studies courses are intended to address the interconnectedness of wellbeing with human reality and to allow teachers the time needed to discuss controversial topics in detail and to explore sensitive issues in depth.

Family studies teachers continue to respond to the changing needs of individuals and families in society and are now concerned with the alarming increase in childhood and adult obesity facing society. Schools may well be advised to acknowledge the critical role of family studies in addressing this problem and to re-examine how health education is delivered. Daily physical activity is essential in combatting obesity and should be compulsory for all students. Health education, however, which does not receive the instructional time it deserves, could be integrated into a compulsory "health and family studies" course. Such a course might include the principles of healthy nutrition, the skills in selecting and preparing healthful food, and the role of individuals and families in ensuring healthy lifestyle choices. Furthermore, with thirteen family studies courses available at the secondary-school level in the social sciences and humanities curriculum guideline (Ontario Ministry of Education 1999b, 2000b), it would be possible to incorporate many, if not all, of the health expectations that are not being addressed in health and physical education because of time constraints or inadequate training.

The Director-General of the World Health Organization observed that "[a]n effective school health program...can be one of the most cost effective investments a nation can make to simultaneously improve education and health" (WHO Director-General, April 2000). The possibilities that family studies offers to an effective school health program should not be overlooked.

## Conclusion

How does Ontario fare in achieving the instructional recommendations for comprehensive school health? It does have a K–12 physical education curriculum that includes a healthy living component. It does not have a K–12 family studies/home economics curriculum—it is offered only as an optional program at the secondary-school level. Health is integral to family studies; therefore family studies offers a number of possibilities for sharing resources and approaches with health education classes.

Schools provide students with formal health education through family studies and health and physical education and informal health education through related school and community events outside of the classroom. Both family studies and health education are geared toward developing the awareness, knowledge, attitudinal changes, decision-making and other skills, behavioural changes, and social action required for optimal health. There are adequate teaching and learning materials available because of the growing number of Canadian textbooks being published. Family studies continues to develop and reinforce appropriate teaching strategies for addressing sensitive issues relating to healthy families and human relationships.

There is still more to be done with respect to preservice and in-service training of teachers for delivering health education in a comprehensive manner that is appropriate for all students. Family studies continues to provide opportunities for health instruction based on the concerns of everyday life. With its roots in hygiene and sanitation, and its heart in the wellbeing of individuals and families, family studies adds a crucial dimension to comprehensive school health.

## References

Berry, E. 1995. Why is home economics a school subject? In *An education for women: The founding of home economics education in Canadian public schools*, ed. L. Peterat and M. L. DeZwart, 33–39. Charlottetown, PEI: Home Economics Publishing Collective, University of Prince Edward Island.

British Columbia Ministry of Education. 1998. Home Economics K to 12 Overview. *Home Economics 11 and 12: Integrated Resource Package 1998*. Vancouver: Government of British Columbia. Available at: www.bced.gov.bc.ca/irp/he1112/curorg.htm#over

Canadian Association for Health, Physical Education, Recreation and Dance (CAHPERD). 2003. *Promoting quality school health: The Canadian situation*. Surrey, BC: Health and Physical Education, Canada. Available at: www.cahperd.ca/e/qsh/promote.htm

Canadian Association for School Health (CASH). 2003. Consensus Statement on School Health. Health Canada. Ottawa: Health Canada. Available at: www.hc-sc.gc.ca/hppb/voluntarysector/publications/2D/intro.html

Center for Health and Health Care in Schools (CHHCS). 2004. Historical content. *School health: A bridge between public health and health care*. Washington, DC: The George Washington University School of Public Health and Health Services. Available at: www.healthinschools.org/sh/pn1.asp

Canadian Home Economics Association (CHEA). 2002. Information. *Canadian Home Economics Journal* 51(2):56.

Cunningham, M., E. Meriorg, and L. Tryssenaar. 2003. *Parenting in Canada: Human growth and development*. Toronto: Nelson Publishing.

Deluca, S. 2000. Finding meaning places for healing: Toward a vigilant subjectivity in the practice of a nurse educator. Ph.D. diss., University of Toronto.

Dewey, J. 1897. *My pedagogical creed*. New York: University Press of America.

Dryden, A. 2002. *Introduction to course prerequisites: J/I program requirements*. London, ON: Faculty of Education, University of Western Ontario. Available at: http://publish.edu.uwo.ca/annabelle.dryden/prerequisites.html

Gidney, R. D. 1999. *From Hope to Harris: The reshaping of Ontario Schools*. Toronto: University of Toronto Press.

Health Canada. 2002. *Comprehensive school health*. Ottawa: Government of Canada. Available at: www.hc-sc.gc.ca/dca-dea/7-18yrs-ans/comphealth_e.html

Heyman, R. D., R. F. Lawson, and R. M. Stamp. 1972. *Studies in educational change*. Toronto: Holt, Rinehart and Winston of Canada, Limited.

Holloway, M., G. Holloway, J. Witte, and M. A. Zuker. 2003. *Individuals and families in a diverse society*. Toronto: McGraw-Hill Ryerson Limited.

Holloway, M., and E. Meriorg. 2001. *Individual and family living in Canada*. Toronto: Irwin Publishing.

Majhanovich, S. 2002. Change in public education. Globalization in action? The case of Ontario, Canada. *Planning and Changing: An Educational Leadership and Policy Journal* 33:53–76.

Noon, S., and M. Arcus. 2002. Student perceptions of their experience in sexuality education. *Canadian Home Economics Journal* 51:15–20.

Ontario Ministry of Education. 1972. *Family Studies: Intermediate Division*. Toronto: Ontario Ministry of Education.

———. 1987. *Curriculum Guideline, Family Studies: Intermediate and Senior Divisions and OAC*. Toronto: The Queen's Printer.

Ontario Ministry of Education and Training. 1998. *The Ontario Curriculum: Health and Physical Education, Grades 1 to 8*. Toronto: The Queen's Printer.

———. 1999a. *The Ontario Curriculum: Health and Physical Education, Grades 9 and 10*. Toronto: The Queen's Printer.

———. 1999b. *The Ontario Curriculum: Social Sciences and the Humanities, Grades 9 and 10*. Toronto: The Queen's Printer.

Ontario Ministry of Education. 2000a. *The Ontario Curriculum: Health and Physical Education, Grades 11 and 12*. Toronto: The Queen's Printer.

———. 2000b. *The Ontario Curriculum: Social Sciences and the Humanities, Grades 11 and 12*. Toronto: The Queen's Printer.

Peterat, L., and M. L. DeZwart, eds. 1995. *An education for women: The founding of home economics education in Canadian public schools*. Charlottetown, PEI: Home Economics Publishing Collective University of Prince Edward Island.

Rowles, E. C. 1964. *Home Economics in Canada*. Saskatoon, SK: University of Saskatchewan.

Safe Healthy Schools. 2003. *Background information on comprehensive school health*. Shannon & McCall Consulting Ltd. [cited 8 April 2004]. Available at: www.safehealthyschools.org/csh.htm

Skrypnek, B. J. 2002. Parent education in Canada: Yesterday, today, and tomorrow. *Canadian Home Economics Journal* 51:5–9.

Stamp, R. M. 1982. *The schools of Ontario, 1876-1976*. Toronto: University of Toronto Press.

Tryssenaar, L. 1993. Changing the subject: From home economics to family studies. Master's thesis, The University of Western Ontario.

Tryssenaar, L. 2004. The teacher-curriculum relationship: A theory grounded in teacher perceptions of writing a reform-driven curriculum. Ph.D. diss., The University of Western Ontario.

WHO Director-General. 2000. *About school health and youth health promotion.* United Nations, World Health Organization. Available at: www.who.int/school_youth_health/en/

Witte, J., L. O'Leary-Reesor, H. Miller, and Z. Bersenas-Cers. 2003. *Food for today: First Canadian Edition.* Toronto: McGraw-Hill Ryerson.

Chapter Seven

# *Researching Perceptions of Physical Education Classes*

## Joanne Y. Pelletier

According to the literature, high school physical education is not necessarily valued by all students (Siedentop 1992) and can lack personal
meaning (Carlson 1995). There may be a variety of reasons for why some
students do not like physical education. Activity preferences differ markedly as a function of sex and age (CFLRI 1996). Stereotyping leads students to believe that certain physical activities are more appropriately
"male" or "female" (CFLRI 1996). Different patterns of socialization can
limit physical activity opportunities for females (Allison and Adlaf 1997;
Tappe, Duda, and Ehrnwald 1989). Teachers, also, often pursue a traditional, male-dominated model that emphasizes team sports and competition (Lock 1992). Both boys and girls can feel alienated by such physical
education classes (Carlson 1995). It is important, therefore, to ensure that
the physical education curriculum addresses the needs and interests of all
students engaged in these classes.

An inclusive physical education teaching practice consists of creating a learning climate that attempts to address the diversity of students
within the class. It can consist of taking a differentiated approach to both
the development and the delivery of the physical education curriculum.
For example, current physical education teachers' perceptions of teaching
in inclusive settings support a need to build a generally more inclusive
teaching practice (Lloyd, Pelletier, and Brown 2002; Pelletier, Lloyd, and
Brown 2002). There are many ways to investigate this question. One is to

examine what students in physical education classes have to say. In this chapter, we will examine student perceptions of physical education classes.

These perceptions not only can provide a student perspective of physical education classes but also are a relevant source of information for teachers who wish to build an inclusive teaching practice. As depicted in the model below, inclusive teaching consists of constructing beliefs, knowledge, and skills which promote a more equitable learning environment in physical education. An inclusive model is based on the belief that teachers should go beyond the traditional sports model to promote a physical education that can benefit everyone. A model based on an inclusive philosophy can help preservice teachers gain an understanding of student perceptions of physical education classes, gender equity, culturally relevant pedagogy, the disability experience, relationships across difference, and physical education and body image and sexuality. Inclusive knowledge is pedagogical knowledge about teachers, students, content, and the context that can help teachers make thoughtful decisions about what students should be experiencing. Inclusive teaching skills are the skills teachers develop through research, planning, reflective thinking, and critical thinking that enable them to create changes they feel are necessary to address a diversity of interests, readiness and learning profiles. Student perceptions can help teachers to comprehend the complexity of teaching and to construct a philosophy that guides them toward a more inclusive teaching practice.

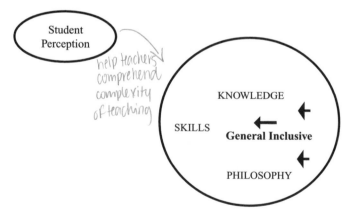

*Figure 1:* Inclusive Teaching

This chapter discusses action research conducted by preservice and in-service teachers who wanted to take action to improve the learning

context of their students. Action researchers "look at what they themselves are or should be doing" (Sagor 1992, 7). Doing action research with
physical education students can help preservice and in-service teachers develop an inclusive teaching practice in physical education. Action research
initiates action by gathering information on student perceptions of physical
education classes. This first step informs the researchers about what they
can do to develop or to improve an inclusive teaching practice within their
physical education classes. In a second step, teachers use the knowledge
they have gained to develop and implement inclusive teaching strategies
that are tailored to the diversity of students within a physical education
class.

This chapter will describe how student perceptions

◈ inform teachers about students' experience in physical education classes;
◈ are a relevant source of information for constructing inclusive
teaching philosophy, knowledge, and skills;
◈ provide relevant feedback for secondary-school teachers; and
◈ offer a context for authentic preservice teacher projects.

## Student Perceptions: A Relevant Source of Information for Physical Education Teachers

Student perceptions are a relevant source of information for teachers who pursue an inclusive philosophy. For example, research on student
perceptions in physical education unequivocally states that students are
aware of differential treatment by the teacher (Martinek 1988; Morency
1990; Mros 1990; Gagnon et al. 2000). Students identify many teaching
behaviours indicating to them that some students are preferred over others
(Martel et al. 1999). When students perceive unfavourable teaching behaviours that indicate to them they are unappreciated by their teacher, un-
satisfactory relationships result (Gagnon et al. 2000). The literature also
indicates that the experiences of students greatly influence their conduct
(Dyson 1995). It seems important, therefore, to consider students' perspectives when making decisions related to one's practice. Student perceptions
also provide information about how they view the learning climate. Students not only question unfavourable teaching behaviours, they also perceive that it is not possible to change them (Gagnon et al. 2000). This
knowledge can assist teachers to make thoughtful decisions about the types

of experiences students should have in their physical education classes. It is thus necessary to provide an avenue for students to voice their thoughts; beyond that, they should feel they can make a difference within their learning environment.

## Research on Student Perceptions in Secondary Schools

Student perceptions can be relevant clues as to what students experience in secondary schools. A teacher coaching in a Canadian high school conducted a project to investigate female soccer players' perceptions (Pelletier and Bower 2002). The coach in this study felt it was important to model his expectations and his inclusive philosophy. However, he was unsure what his players were really experiencing within the setting he provided. At the beginning of the school year, the coach invited his senior high school players to respond to two questionnaires dealing with their perceptions of his expectations. He emphasized that a student athlete's perspective on his coaching was important to him. Their participation in the study would help him improve his coaching. Each participant was randomly assigned a number by the team trainer for the duration of the study. The players were told that if they chose to fill out one or both of the questionnaires, they should place them in a drop box located in the school. Most of the female students perceived positive experiences related to the learning environment that the coach provided. However, a number of the younger student athletes on the team were dissatisfied with certain behaviours. These players explained that these behaviours had significant negative effects on them. Specifically, they perceived a need to make adjustments to playing time and to how athletes received feedback. Athlete responses during interviews with the university researcher corroborated the coach's findings. These female athletes' experiences were similar to those described by male college athletes in a comparable study (Gagnon 1990). From the description of the coach's philosophy (Pelletier and Bower 2002), it seems clear that he valued student athletes and their perceptions of the coaching environment he provided. His project on student athlete perceptions provided him with relevant information to go beyond modelling his philosophy and to seek a coaching climate more beneficial to all. The student athlete perceptions informed him that teachers and coaches may not perceive to the same degree as students a need for change to the learning climate. The coaching behaviours described by the students provided insight into practitioner skills that this coach now felt more compelled to develop and use.

## Research on a Preservice Teacher Project on Student Perceptions of Physical Education Classes

Student perceptions can provide a context for authentic preservice teacher projects. As a teacher educator, my role is to facilitate the development of authentic projects that support the construction of inclusive teaching practices with my preservice physical education students. The current literature on student-teacher research indicates that this type of authentic project can be useful in developing knowledge, a philosophy, and skills for an inclusive physical education practice. In doing this I am utilizing a constructivist approach (Feiman-Nemser et al. 1989; Hollingsworth 1989; McDiarmid 1990; Prawat 1992; Thornton 1992). Klein (1996) explains that "constructivists believe that learners build knowledge from experiences under the influence of their previous beliefs and that this often involves problem solving or reflection" (361). There has been much discussion regarding the beliefs teachers and preservice teachers have about teaching knowledge (Brookhart and Freeman 1992; Calderhead 1996; Kagan 1992a, 1992b; Pajares 1992). Fishbein and Ajzen (1975) have defined belief as a "person's understanding of himself and his environment" (131).

I am also an action researcher within my teacher education classes. My roles are to facilitate the development and implementation of preservice projects and to collect data on the knowledge, skills, and understanding the preservice teachers gain from conducting a project with physical education students. In this chapter, I am reporting on a case study in which a group of three preservice teachers engaged in a project that sought out a first-hand perspective of high school physical education classes from actual participants. The case study described in this chapter was a pilot study for a more extensive student-teacher project. This larger project focused on the effectiveness of engaging students in research projects within Bachelor of Education programs. It is the purpose of physical education methods courses to provide a learning environment in which students may develop authentic projects which permit them to reflect on their teaching philosophies. They are encouraged to construct knowledge relevant to their teaching practices and to develop teaching skills based on the knowledge they have gained from engaging in projects. Students were placed in small groups and asked to select a topic they felt was relevant to them, such as gender equity, learned helplessness, inclusion, and cultural diversity. Students were required to (a) read physical education research literature during a process called problem formulation; (b) develop an authentic project based on issues emerging from the problem formation; and, (c) create teaching and lesson plan units based on the knowledge gained from engaging in their projects. The student teachers could experiment with their lessons during micro-teaching exercises or in other more authentic teaching environments.

This project on student perceptions was designed and implemented within an advanced curriculum and instruction methods course for undergraduate preservice students in physical education within the School of Education at Acadia University. Three students were enrolled in the course. Since then, the class size has grown, and projects have been carried out, with the help of the instructor, by small groups within classes of twenty students on topics such as student motivation, student alienation, ALT-PE (Academic Learning Time–Physical Education), and student participation and physical education advocacy. This pilot project on student perceptions of physical education classes was one of many studies conducted within a teacher education action research program on inclusive physical education. Research projects on student perceptions of physical education (Gagnon et al. 2000; Martel et al. 1999; Martel, Pelletier-Murphy, and Gagnon 1999; Pelletier and Bower 2002) and on teaching inclusive physical education (Lloyd 2000; Lloyd, Pelletier, and Brown 2002; Pelletier and Brown 2002; Pelletier, Brown, and Lloyd 2000a, 2000b; Pelletier, Lloyd, and Brown 2002) have led to a more in-depth understanding of inclusive physical education and to the design and implementation of four research-based physical education methods courses at Acadia. Project-based courses within the action research program at Acadia have also led to the investigation of teaching strategies for an inclusive physical education teaching practice (MacKinnon, Pelletier, and Brown 2002; Pelletier, Brown, and MacKinnon 2002; Pelletier and Langille 2003; Pelletier 2003, 2004; Pineo 2004). A preservice research group called S.T.R.I.P.E. (Student Teachers Researching in Inclusive Physical Education) has emerged from these projects.

## *The Preservice Project on Student Perceptions of Physical Education Classes*

All three preservice teachers involved in this project (2 males and 1 female) were physical education students enrolled in a two-year Bachelor of Education Secondary Program within the School of Education. Each had previously completed a four-year physical education/kinesiology degree. The first student became interested in the teacher education program when he entered the undergraduate kinesiology program at Acadia and joined the intercollegiate hockey team. The second student was a retired Canadian Air Force pilot who had completed his physical education degree many years before. The third student was a Nova Scotia resident who applied to the School of Education after recently graduating from a kinesiology program at another university.

As the three students planned and conducted their class-based research, I began to think about three questions as part of the initiation of my own action research project. What kind of developmental changes occurred as these preservice teachers conducted this project on students' perceptions? Specifically, what knowledge did they construct—how did their philosophies change? What impact did this project have on the way they prepared for teaching students in physical education classes?

In the planning stages of the project, the preservice teachers engaged in a problem-formulation process on gender equity in high school physical education. This began with the viewing of a video produced for CAHPERD (Canadian Association for Health, Physical Education, Recreation and Dance) entitled *Girls in Action: Speaking Out* (1998). The preservice teacher researchers then gathered relevant information for their project from a study conducted by Gibbons et al. (1999). Because the student teachers wanted to find out more about their schools and students, they generated (with the help of the instructor) a questionnaire (see Appendix) and distributed it to the students. An analysis of the questions was conducted by the student teacher researchers. The joint report they wrote was submitted to the instructor prior to their developing their final unit plans.

My reporting of this case study about the research project on student perceptions of physical education classes is based on class discussions, student journals, the research report, and final unit plans. Interviews also took place with the student teachers during the following semester. These interviews were conducted in an attempt to triangulate the data collected during the methods course. Interview questions were designed to follow qualitative research guidelines (Patton 1990). After every phase of the research project, including the interviews, students were asked what they learned, what impact, if any, this project was having on their teaching philosophy, and what skills they wished to develop. Data analysis was conducted using Sagor's (1992) action research matrix. It consisted of identifying themes that cut across sources of data and identifying particularly noteworthy information. The reporting of the results was prepared by two of the three student teachers, who met with the instructor more than once to discuss the content of the case study and how it would be reported. The preservice teachers prepared the draft of this case study.

## Preservice Teacher Problem Formulation

In an initial phase of the project, the preservice teacher researchers participated in a process of identifying a problem related to gender they felt was relevant to them. They were invited by their professor to view the video *Girls in Action: Speaking Out* (1998), in which several grade 9 girls provided a synopsis of issues they were experiencing in physical education. The research group felt that the students alluded to three main issues: boredom, inappropriate forms of evaluation, and marginalization in physical education. The students were tired of participating in the same competition-driven sports activities year after year. These girls preferred more leisure-oriented physical activity pursuits instead of traditional sports. The female students also commented about the manner in which they were evaluated in physical education class. They felt the emphasis on skill testing and criterion-referenced fitness tests should be removed and the importance of maintaining a healthy, physically active lifestyle should be stressed more. The female students also addressed the issue of feeling alienated or marginalized within their physical education class. For example, several of the girls discussed how teams were generally formed, with some students always being picked last. The preservice teacher researchers felt the female students were referring to having little choice in and input into the sports and other activities in which they were required to participate.

One of the preservice teacher researchers' primary goals was to acknowledge student diversity and attempt to provide for a wider range of needs. Their objective was to identify which issues outlined in the video they would attempt to address in the creation of their teaching units. Over the course of several discussions supported by further research in the literature, they reached a consensus: they decided their focus would be on curriculum content with an emphasis on variety and more novel activities. Their reading and discussions also led them to conclude that negative factors affected not only just the girls.

> We agreed as a group that by offering more variety and choice in curriculum, we might successfully reduce the boredom expressed by the girls and increase their enjoyment. By doing so

 *3 main issues?*

we also hoped to counteract the marginalisation experienced by many girls in a traditional sports setting. We became convinced that if we could address some of the girls' issues then we would likely be improving the situation for everyone. One might assume that these factors affect only female physical education students. However, many less kinesthetically skilled males are also probably being similarly marginalised in existing traditional classrooms. (Andrew)

## The Preservice Teacher Data Collection

The preservice teacher researchers next gathered diverse information to broaden their knowledge base and identify teaching skills they felt were worth investigating for teaching in a more inclusive manner. Specifically, they reviewed selected readings from existing research in the area of physical education. The article by Gibbons et al. (1999) was of particular interest to them. The Gibbons group of researchers conducted focus groups with female students in grades 10 and 11 to investigate their perceptions of physical activity and physical education. The study included both girls enrolled in physical education classes and those who had chosen not to enrol. The purpose of their study was to gain information directly from female students. Their paper highlighted several themes that recurred frequently in the focus groups. The three major themes the research group discussed were curriculum change, student choice and control, and participation versus skill in physical education. During the reading of students' responses from the focus groups, the researchers discovered that female students favoured an academic challenge in physical education, wanted a more diverse curriculum, and felt a need to de-emphasize competition. The female students wanted input into the high school curriculum content, preferred a student-centered program versus teacher-driven activities, and felt it was important to evaluate fairly because some students have less opportunity to practise skills than athletes who are also participating on sport teams.

The preservice teachers explain how the Gibbons et al. (1999) article and the discussion it generated were helpful to them. The article added to their knowledge by prompting them to fully discuss issues of student choice and control and the merits of promoting participation over skill.

At this point we decided to develop units which would provide choice, introduce more non-traditional activities and employ multi-faceted assessments. Our unit outlines were revisited and revised after every meeting as our understanding and ability to provide better and wider options grew. Again, we felt that many of the issues and problems raised in the Gibbons et al. (1999) article were not isolated to the girls alone. They are also not gender-specific. They are prevalent in the female student population but are by no means restricted to that group. (Jennifer)

The university student research group constructed a questionnaire to collect perceptions from high school students of their physical education class experiences. They did this to obtain a first-hand understanding of how high school students perceive the learning conditions the students felt they were experiencing in physical education classes. Specifically, the researchers created questions which they then used in gathering information based upon the issues they wished to investigate more fully. The student responses to the questionnaire were to be used solely to assist the student researchers with writing their units. Having obtained permission, the researchers distributed the questionnaires to all grade 9 physical education students at a high school that had agreed to take part in the project. The preservice teachers explain why they chose to target this grade.

We chose grade nine because of our interest in adolescent perceptions and because physical education is no longer compulsory in most provinces after grade nine. We felt that gaining more knowledge of the perceptions of a group of adolescent students might help us to improve what we hoped would be inclusive teaching units. (Adam)

The questions to which the grade 9 physical education students were invited to respond included one on expectations. What did they expect from their physical education classes? The physical education students responded by indicating a need for novel, interesting activities and to feel that they were respected by their teacher. They wanted "to learn new things...rather than old activities" not to "be bored by what the teacher is doing" and "to have fun and be very tired at the end." They also did not like it when "guys are playing against girls." They did not want "to be forced but to also have a choice in what the class is doing." According to them, it is important to "get everyone involved in the games because with bigger teams, [fewer] people participate." They felt that if the physical education teacher "gives respect...then...he/she will get it back."

expectations of students (9)

## Preservice Teacher Philosophy

An inclusive philosophy implies going beyond the lifetime sports model to make physical education work for everyone. At first, the preservice teachers did not think the responses to the questionnaires would substantially affect their teaching philosophies, but the student responses affected them much more than they anticipated.

> We were surprised how much the student perceptions from the questionnaires significantly affected us. The most considerable thing we learned was to listen to our students and to allow them to help us with our pedagogical decision making. Only they can describe what they are experiencing. Gaining an understanding of student perceptions is essential at every stage in the process from unit development to assessment. (Adam)

## Understanding Inclusive Teaching Knowledge

Inclusive teaching knowledge can help teachers to make thoughtful decisions about their students' learning climate and about the types of learning experiences the students should have. Reading students' handwritten responses to questions asked by the preservice teacher researchers made the problems being addressed more personal to the research group. The preservice teachers indicate what they learned:

> Our goal was to include more students in their classes. We discovered what our students wanted, resulting in a shift toward more novel and non-traditional activities and assessment strategies. We became convinced that students are best placed to help us decide how we should go about making changes to our teaching. We were unprepared for the powerful effect of hearing student voices first hand. This turn of events was a little ironic given that a week before distributing the questionnaires we had become concerned that we would only receive a few responses. We had already decided that the results would likely have little if any effect on our units anyway. By the end of that week, a significant number of questionnaires were completed. In the end, the responses to the questionnaires told us what to pay attention to while developing our units. (Andrew)

## Action on Inclusive Teaching Skills

Inclusive teaching skills enable teachers to make the changes they feel are necessary to their professional practice to address a diversity of interests, levels of readiness, and learning profiles. This project informed the research group about what students wanted, helping them to take action on the changes they felt were needed to address the needs of students within their physical education classrooms. The preservice teachers explain what impact the project had on their teaching units:

> The power of the direct communication to us by students was evident. We responded by immediately revisiting intentions for the planned teaching units. While many of the responses we felt were initially a little discouraging, the student perceptions ultimately gave us more confidence as we constructed our units. Consulting our students lent more validity to the process and because much of what we were hoping to achieve was based upon giving students greater autonomy, choice, and voice in the education process, we really felt that we were beginning from a more honest position. We realised that we all underestimated the importance of novelty to this age group. The subtle differences in student responses from the literature emphasized actual student concerns within their learning environment. They had an immediate effect on us and our teaching units. (Andrew)

## Preservice Teachers' Closing Remarks

Inclusive physical education implies providing an enjoyable learning climate and content that is meaningful to everyone. The preservice teacher researchers concluded that it is possible to address a wide range of needs by differentiating instruction, offering choice, and by giving students a voice. The students collectively described how they changed as a result of engaging in such projects within physical education methods courses.

> It became clear to us that virtually every marginalised student in physical education classes can describe very similar types of dissatisfactions. We have come to the conclusion that general inclusive strategies to improve the experiences of a particular group or an individual will often also help address the needs of

other students within that same classroom. This makes us optimistic that providing for the needs of very diverse groups of students is achievable and less daunting than it first appears. Inclusive classrooms while requiring more preparation can be easier to manage as more students find meaning in the tasks, are engaged in activities and stay on task. (Andrew, Adam, and Jennifer)

At the end of this research process, the research group pointed out that the project they conducted was certainly meaningful to them and would, they hoped, have meaning for their future students. The preservice teachers also clearly indicated that this project had provided them with the opportunity to voice their own thoughts on issues related to teaching high school physical education. As to student teachers' developing research projects within their Bachelor of Education courses, it appears essential to investigate the developmental changes, if any, that occur within the actual teaching practice of preservice teachers.

## *Discussion of the Preservice Teacher Research Project*

The results from this preliminary study on a research project conducted by three preservice physical education student researchers suggest that this project enabled these students to construct a philosophy and gain knowledge and skills promoting the development of an inclusive teaching practice. The research project was devised to encourage student teachers to inquire more deeply into pedagogical issues potentially affecting their future students. Thus, students were required to (a) read physical education research literature during a process called problem formulation; (b) develop an authentic project based on issues emerging from the problem formulation; (c) create units and lesson plans based on the knowledge gained from engaging in their projects; and, (d) reflect upon their experiences with journal entries. Responses within this case study indicate that, although the preservice teachers did not expect that this project would have an impact on their philosophies, they were surprised by how much the student perceptions affected them. The most significant thing they learned was the importance of considering students' perceptions. Specifically, reading student responses to the questionnaires the student teachers developed made the problems they were addressing more personal to them. As described in the case study, by finding out what their future students needed, the student teachers learned they may need to emphasize activities different from those they first expected to teach. They responded by making changes they felt were necessary to the teaching units they were developing. For example, they developed themes for their units, provided choice in physical activities, and organized multi-faceted assessments.

From my perspective as an action researcher investigating how student research projects can facilitate learning, I believe future investigation into these theories can help physical education teacher educators understand how preservice teachers actually construct their teaching knowledge and philosophy and consequently develop teaching skills for teaching in today's physical education classes. In the literature on teachers' conceptions of teaching, researchers and reviewers have made the distinction between teacher knowledge and teacher beliefs (Calderhead 1996; Fenstermacher 1994; Richardson 1996; Thompson 1992).

## Conclusion

As I describe my findings concerning this case study on student teachers doing research in their preservice program, I am reminded of the critical review of research on the teaching beliefs and practices of university academics conducted by Kane, Sandretto, and Heath (2002). Their review revealed that the "espoused theories of action of academics have not been distinguished from their theories-in-use" in some studies (177). The article indicates a number of questions to be addressed, including how student teachers' beliefs and conceptions of teaching influence the development of university academics as teachers, and how university teachers' beliefs and conceptions of teaching relate to teaching practice at the university level. This article thus inspired me to ask myself what I learned from the research project my students conducted on student perceptions of physical education classes.

Foremost, I learned that high school students can provide a relevant source of information for teacher educators who wish to help preservice teachers build an inclusive teaching practice. The project on high school student perceptions of physical education classes conducted by preservice students enabled these researchers to develop a project focused on issues and facts relevant to their teaching. As a result, they revisited their unit plans to create teaching units that were more diverse in nature and which catered to different interests and addressed various learning styles.

It is clear to me that preservice teachers can benefit greatly when they are encouraged to construct their own teaching philosophies, knowl-

edge, and skills through research into their own teaching practices. It also
is clear to me that it is important to consider the perspectives of student
teachers in my decision-making process when I am planning for research
and teaching within Bachelor of Education programs. Based on my experiences with these student teachers within this project, I feel committed to
continue developing teacher educator skills, thus enabling me to facilitate
the development of preservice teacher projects within physical education
methods courses. These projects will promote the development of an inclusive teaching practice and links among preservice teacher researchers,
in-service teachers, and students in physical education classes. Thank you
Adam, Andrew, and Jen![1]

## Note

1.  The preservice teacher researchers involved in this project were student
    teachers enrolled in the Bachelor of Education program in the School of Edu-
    cation at Acadia University at the time of the project. Adam Michael
    Armstrong was the leader of the research group, particularly in the research
    phase of the project. Andrew P. Graham instigated the research project and
    was the principal preservice teacher author of the case study. Jennifer
    Patriquin's contribution ensured a high-quality project. She also encouraged
    other members of the group to engage in the writing of this book chapter.
    Mathew MacGillivray was a student in the School of Education at the time of
    the dissemination of this project. He is responsible for coming up with the offi-
    cial acronym for S.T.R.I.P.E. (Student Teachers Researching in Inclusive
    Physical Education).

# Appendix

## Advanced Curriculum and Instruction
## Physical Education Survey

This is an informal questionnaire designed by three students from the School of Education at Acadia University. We are interested in your thoughts about your physical education class. Your comments are very much appreciated and will be kept
confidential.

Thank you for your participation in our questionnaire.

1. What do you expect from physical education class?

2. What activities are you interested in?

3. What type of physical activities do you like to do?

4. What type of physical activities do you dislike doing?

5. What would you keep the same/change about physical education?

6. Do you intend to take physical education in high school? Why/Why not?

## References

Allison, K. R., and E. M. Adlaf. 1997. Age and sex differences in physical inactivity among Ontario teenagers. *Canadian Journal of Public Health* 88(3):177–80.

Brookhart, S. M., and D. J. Freeman. 1992. Characteristics of entering teacher candidates. *Review of Educational Research* 62:37–60.

Calderhead, J. 1996. Teachers: Beliefs and knowledge. In *Handbook of Educational Psychology*, ed. D. C. Berliner and R. C. Calfee, 709–725. New York: Macmillan.

Canadian Fitness and Lifestyle Research Institute (CFLRI). 1996. How active are Canadians? *Progress in Prevention Institute*: Bulletin No. 1.

Carlson, T. B. 1995. We hate gym: Student alienation from physical education. *Journal of Teaching in Physical Education* 14:467–77.

Dyson, B. P. 1995. Students' voices in alternative elementary physical education programs. *Journal of Teaching in Physical Education* 14:394–407.

Feiman-Nemser, S., G. W. McDiarmid, S. L. Melnick, and M. Parker. 1989. *Changing beginning teachers' conceptions: A description of an introductory teacher education course*. Research Report 89–1 East Lansing, MI: National Center for Research on Teacher Learning.

Fenstermacher, G. D. 1994. The knower and the known: The nature of knowledge in research on teaching. In *Review of Research in Education*, ed. L. Darling-Hammond, 20(5):3–56. Washington, DC: American Educational Research Association.

Fishbein, M., and I. Ajzen. 1975. *Belief, attitude, intention and behavior*. Reading, MA: Addison-Wesley.

Gagnon, J. 1990. L'effet Pygmalion dans une équipe sportive de niveau collégial. Ph.D. diss., Université Laval, Sainte-Foy, Québec.

Gagnon, J., D. Martel, S. Dumont, J. Grenier, and J. Pelletier-Murphy. 2000. Student's power on teacher's behaviour: Establishing the powerlessness. *AVANTE* 6:34–47.

Gibbons, S., J. Higgins, C. Gaul, and G. Van Gyn. 1999. Listening to female students in high school physical education. *AVANTE* 5:1–20.

Hollingsworth, S. 1989. Prior beliefs and cognitive change in learning to teach. *American Educational Research Journal* 26:160–89.

Humbert, M. L. and Blacklock, F. (1998). *Girls in Action: Speaking Out*. Video. Ottawa: CAHPERD.

Kagan, D. M. 1992a. Implications of research on teacher beliefs. *Educational Psychologist* 27:65–90.

———. 1992b. Professional growth among preservice and beginning teachers. *Review of Educational Research* 62:129–69.

Kane, R., S. Sandretto, and C. Heath. 2002. Telling half the story: A critical review of research on the teaching beliefs and practices of university academics. *Review of Educational Research* 72(2):177–228.

Klein, D. P. 1996. Preservice teachers' beliefs about learning and knowledge. *The Alberta Journal of Educational Research* 32(4):361–77.

Lloyd, M. 2000. *Strategies in inclusive physical education with children with language and communication disorders as perceived by physical education teachers*. Honours thesis, Acadia University, Wolfville, Nova Scotia.

Lloyd, M., J. Pelletier, and M. Brown. 2002. A study of teaching practices in inclusive physical education settings: What is needed to survive? 6th North American Federation of Adapted Physical Activity (NAFAPA) Symposium, Oregon State University, Corvallis, Oregon.

Lock, L. F. 1992. Changing secondary school physical education. *Quest* 44:361–72.

MacKinnon, G., J. Pelletier, and M. Brown. 2002. Coding electronic discussion to promote critical thinking: A cross-curricular teacher education approach. Society for Information Technology and Teacher Education Conference Proceedings, 1372–74.

McDiarmid, G. W. 1990. Challenging prospective teachers' beliefs during early field experience: A quixotic undertaking? *Journal of Teacher Education* 41:12–20.

Martel, D., J. Pelletier-Murphy, and J. Gagnon. 1999. Perceptions d'élèves sur la façon dont ils sont traités en éducation physique. *AIESEP*, Besançon, France.

Martel, D., J. Gagnon, J. Pelletier-Murphy, and J. Grenier. 1999. Pygmalion en éducation physique: Un mythe bien réel. *Revue canadienne de l'éducation* 24:42–56.

Martinek, T. J. 1988. Confirmation of a teacher expectancy model: Student perceptions and causal attributions of teaching behaviors. *Research Quarterly for Exercise and Sport* 59:118–26.

Morency, L. 1990. Les conditions d'apprentissage sont-elles les mêmes pour tous les élèves? *Revue des sciences de l'éducation* 14:43–53.

Mros, M. 1990. A description of the causal attribution made to perceived teaching behaviours across three elementary physical education contexts. *Dissertation Abstracts International* 51(9):3012.

Pajares, M. F. 1992. Teachers' beliefs and educational research: Cleaning up a messy construct. *Review of Educational Research* 62:307–32.

Patton, M. Q. 1990. *Qualitative evaluation and research methods*. Newbury Park, CA: Sage.

Pelletier, J. 2003. Case studies on inclusive physical education. Unpublished paper presented at the Council of University Researchers and Professors Research Forum, MPETA/CAHPERD Conference, Winnipeg, Manitoba.

———. Developing web-based focus groups for constructing preservice general inclusive physical education teaching knowledge. In *Proceedings of the Society for Information Technology and Teacher Education*, ed. D. Willis, R. Carlson, N. Davis, J. Price, and R. Weber, 2531–35.

Pelletier, J., and G. Bower. 2002. Athlete's perceptions of coach's expectations. *AVANTE* 8:1–11.

Pelletier, J., and M. Brown. 2002. Growth model for teaching in inclusive physical education settings. Unpublished paper presented at the meeting of the Atlantic Educators, Fredericton, New Brunswick.

Pelletier, J., M. Brown, and G. MacKinnon. 2002. Critical thinking and electronic discussion. Society for Information Technology and Teacher Education Conference Proceedings, 80–84.

Pelletier, J., M. Brown, and M. C. Lloyd. 2000a. Inclusive practice in physical education classes with children with language and communication disorders as perceived by physical education specialists. Unpublished paper presented at the Council of University Researchers and Professors Forum, OPHEA, CAHPERD Conference, Banff, Alberta.

———. 2000b. A survey of physical education teacher specialists in inclusive schools: Accommodating students with communication and language disorders. Paper presented at the meeting of the Atlantic Educators, Charlottetown, Prince Edward Island.

Pelletier, J., and L. Langille. 2003. Collaborative electronic discussion groups: Using cognotes to create accountability. Society for Information Technology and Teacher Education Conference Proceedings, 2463–66.

Pelletier, J., M. C. Lloyd, and M. A. Brown. 2002. A study investigating inclusive teaching strategies: What do physical education teachers mean by inclusive teaching strategies? Unpublished paper presented at the North American Federation of Adapted Physical Activity (NAFAPA), Corvallis, Oregon.

Pineo, E. 2004. Knowledge, skills and philosophy of future teachers on inclusive physical education. Honours thesis, Acadia University, Wolfville, Nova Scotia.

Prawat, R. S. 1992. Teachers' beliefs about teaching about learning: A constructivist perspective. *American Journal of Education* 100(3):354–95.

Richardson, V. 1996. The role of attitudes and beliefs in learning to teach. In *Handbook of Research on Teacher Education*, ed. J. Sikula, 102–19. New York: Simon & Schuster.

Sagor, R. 1992. *How to conduct collaborative action research.* Alexandria, VA: Association for Supervision and Curriculum Development.

Siedentop, D. 1992. Thinking differently about secondary physical education. *Journal of Physical Education, Recreation and Dance* 63:69–72, 77.

Tappe, M., J. Duda, and P. Ehrnwald. 1989. Perceived barriers to exercise among adolescents. *Journal of School Health* 59(4):153–55.

Thompson, A. G. 1992. Teachers' beliefs and conceptions: A synthesis of the research. In *Handbook of Research on Mathematics Teaching and Learning*, ed. D. A. Grouws, 127–46. New York: Macmillan.

Thornton, S. J. 1992. How do elementary teachers decide what to teach in social studies? In *Teacher personal theorizing: Connecting Curriculum Practice, Theory, and Research*, ed. E. W. Ross, J. W. Cornett, and G. McCutcheon, 83–95. Albany, NY: SUNY Press.

Chapter Eight

# "Look at That Cow Over There":

## Sexual Harassment and Shaming of Adolescent Girls in High School Physical Education

Helen Jefferson Lenskyj and
Cheryl van Daalen

Despite the gains of the last three decades for Canadian girls and women in sport, with affirmative action legislation, policies, and programs contributing to increased opportunities and participation rates, adolescent girls remain an "at risk" group because of their low physical activity levels. In the high school context, their reluctance to engage in sport and physical activity is reflected in the pattern of dropping physical education as soon as the required credits are completed.

Physical educators and health professionals often express concern over the threat that inactivity poses to adolescent females' immediate and long-term health—greater risk of heart disease, high blood pressure, certain types of cancer, and diabetes, for example—and the potential drain on scarce health care dollars (Ganley and Sherman 2000; Kroll 2002; Summerfield 1990). Arguments based on human rights and equity—that is, the position that adolescent girls have a right to access and enjoy school-based sport and physical activity geared to their interests and abilities—appear to carry less weight. We will argue that it is not some deficiency on the part of adolescent girls, but rather the emphasis on competition and the unwelcoming climate in many school physical education programs, that leads to a high dropout rate among this group.

In a pilot study conducted by one of the co-authors (van Daalen) in 1996, three Ontario high school students shared their thoughts about and experiences of physical education. One of the young women, Gurpreet, aged 19, is South Asian, whereas the other two—Maggie, 17, and Ashley, 15—are Caucasian; Maggie is lesbian, Gurpreet and Ashley are heterosexual.[1] First, they were asked to write a story about physical education experiences; next, they were invited to observe a grade 9 girls' physical education class and to record their memories of their own experiences at this age; finally, they participated in a one-to-one interview. The interview questions were generated from the students' own stories. Some questions explored their childhood and adolescent experiences and memories. Other questions investigated the impact of sociocultural factors and the influence of family members and peers. Finally, some questions explored the students' thoughts on the "ideal" physical education program and teacher, and on the girls' decision to drop physical education. Data from the study will be integrated into the following discussion to illustrate adolescent girls' activity patterns and practices, and the barriers to their continued involvement. As it was organized in these girls' public elementary, middle, and high schools in a southern Ontario city in the 1990s, physical education served to glorify the "winners" and shame the "losers" in a very public way. Coeducational classes exacerbated the problems for these girls, and issues of physicality and sexuality—body size and shape, heterosexual attractiveness, and athletic competence—produced feelings of profound inadequacy.

## The More Things Change...

Despite the popularity of notions like "post-feminism" and "Third Wave Feminism," the basic struggles for gender equality and equity are not things of the past, the current generation of Canadian girls has not grown up in a discrimination-free society, and the need to increase female participation in physical education and sport remains pressing. On the issue of declining female participation rates in physical education, sport, and physical activity, recent Canadian surveys (CFLRI 1999; Deacon 2001; Sport Participation in Canada 1998) show a decline of about 11 percent among young people aged 15 and older between 1992–98, with the gender gap widening by 3 percent; although 38 percent of all females reported involvement in sport in 1992, this dropped to 26 percent in 1998 compared to 43 percent of males. Furthermore, female involvement in regular physical activity was lower than male involvement in every age category; in the 15–18 age group, 80 percent of males and only 55 percent of females were physically active. As well, only 39 percent of girls, compared to 52 percent of boys, were active enough for optimal health benefits; among girls aged 13–17, only 32 percent were at this level. Sixty-one percent of boys aged 5–14 years, but only 48 percent of girls in that age group, reported regular sport participation. CAHPERD's Quality Daily Physical Education, introduced in the 1980s and requiring thirty minutes of physical education daily, is followed in only about 10 percent of Canadian schools. In British Columbia, enrolment in year 11 and year 12 physical education courses has steadily declined for both girls and boys since 1992, and the gender gap has grown, with only about 10 percent female enrolment in 1999–2000. Finally, only 17 percent of children aged 6–17 have physical education every day; moreover, the rates declined between 2000 and 2002, resulting in a gender gap of about 8 percent among high school students.

## Body Issues for Adolescent Girls

Physiological changes during adolescence, particularly weight gain and the development of breasts and hips, produce a mature body that is, for many girls, a source of embarrassment and shame—a body that no longer serves them well on the playing field or in the gym, where the Olympic-generated "faster, higher, stronger" model defines sporting achievement. For many girls, trying, failing, "looking dumb," and losing confidence are their most salient memories of physical education classes. Canadian surveys have found a decline in girls' self-image and confidence during adolescence (Canadian Teachers' Federation 1990; Holmes and Silverman 1992), and a corresponding drop in their physical activity levels (CFLRI 1988). Maggie explained her reasoning for dropping physical education after grade 9:

> I just decided that it was too much of a hassle, that I was tired of having to put up with the other kids and not being as good as some of them, and being made fun of for it and feeling stupid in front of everybody...everyone would stand around and watch and if you missed it [shooting a basketball into the net] everybody laughed. I was afraid of looking dumb.

Ashley had similar negative experiences in coeducational physical education, with its emphasis on competitive team sports, even though she did not lack athletic ability:

I didn't like competitive sports at all, they were coed and the guys would always laugh if you couldn't do something right or didn't kick the ball properly or couldn't get it in the net, so I wouldn't try, and then I'd make myself look stupid because I wouldn't try. In grade 8, it got a little better because I found something I was good at—which was running. That is where my confidence was—running. In grade 9, because I didn't try all the other years, I got in the habit of not trying. So I didn't have very much experience in any of the sports because I would always be sitting back. Phys. ed. was sport based....When they'd blow the whistle, I'd get so nervous because they'd say that we'd have to do the volleyball tournaments with the other classes. That just made me sick. My stomach would go crazy because I knew I wasn't very good.

For many boys, the developmental changes of puberty, particularly muscular development, are an asset in mainstream sport and physical education, whereas, for many adolescent girls, the changing body is a liability. Of course, if flexibility, balance, coordination, and kinesthetic merit were values that animated school physical education programs, girls' experiences would be significantly more positive.

## The "Femininity" Requirement

Most adolescent girls are influenced by pressures from family, peers, the mass media, and the teen fashion industry to establish their heterosexual credentials at a young age. In the face of these powerful ideological messages about hegemonic femininity, non-conforming girls risk being labelled lesbian and being targeted for homophobic harassment. As well as the obvious threat to the safety and wellbeing of the estimated 10 percent of female adolescents who *are* lesbian, there is also a chilling effect on heterosexual girls, who may feel compelled to give up so-called "unfeminine" sports rather than experience this kind of stigmatization (Morrow and Gill 2003).

Adolescent girls in two British studies reported that many of their female peers sacrificed their sporting participation in order to "get" and "have" a boyfriend. Exemplifying yet another aspect of the sexual double standard, girls were expected to give up their own leisure interests and to adopt those of their boyfriends. The boys initiated most of the couples' shared activities and ignored their girlfriends' attempts to influence what they did in their free time (Biscomb et al. 2000; Coakley and White 1992).

To be perceived as "feminine" in Western societies, girls and young women are expected to restrict themselves to gender-appropriate sports that showcase their heterosexual attractiveness, while posing no threat to the myth of male athletic superiority (Lenskyj 2003). Traditional definitions of gender-appropriate sports have been modified somewhat in the last three decades, largely as a result of women's successful lobbying for legislative and policy changes that have expanded female sporting opportunities to include, for example, international soccer and ice hockey. Nonetheless, the societal expectation that sportswomen should meet some arbitrary "femininity quotient" remains.

Thinness is a key component of heterosexual femininity in North America; blond hair and white skin are also desirable attributes. Exercise is a popular weight-maintenance and weight-loss strategy, but the myth that females will develop unattractive muscles through physical activity serves as a powerful deterrent. So-called masculine muscles are a concern not only among adolescent girls; even adult women in high-performance sport express ambivalence about visible indicators of strength. For example, a member of a national rowing team claimed in a personal communication that she and her teammates, having developed a more "masculine" form (large muscles and low body fat), put considerable effort into presenting a feminine image, with long hair and earrings, to ensure that people would, in her words, "get their gender correct."

In the same "apologetic" vein, a recent motivational event sponsored by a Toronto hospital featured five sportswomen, including boxer Wendy Broad, who was described in the promotional material as "a very feminine and focused woman who lives to 'fight'." The accompanying photograph showed, predictably, a woman with long hair (Breakfast with Champions 2004).[2] Popular women's magazines reassure the reader that "you don't look like Arnold Schwarzenegger" when you do weight training (Van Buuren 2000). And female bodybuilders who resort to breast implants as "femininity" markers in bodies dominated by (probably steroid-fuelled) muscles send out conflicting messages about what a strong female body should look like.

At the practical level, physical education presents time-management problems for girls whose "beauty" routines demand the styling of hair and the applying of makeup. As Gurpreet acknowledged,

It takes me, say, twenty minutes to half an hour to get dressed....I hate changing. If we had gym last period, that would be better, because you don't have to get changed, and you could go straight home and shower there.

On this issue, Ashley recommended that physical education teachers "should give [more] time to get ready. I know a lot more girls would take gym if they had a longer time to get back into...what they looked like before."

Buying into the "beauty myth," a free physical activity kit called "Vibrant Faces," funded by Tampax and Always and approved by various physical education professors and professional associations, devoted a full paragraph in its teachers' and leaders' guide to the differences between hairspray, gel, mousse, and spritz (*Vibrant Faces* 1994, 31). Admittedly, understanding what girls perceive as obstacles to physical education is important, but, on the topic of "change room problems," shame and embarrassment associated with public nudity are much more salient than hairstyling (Humbert 1996; Scraton 1992), and redesigning change rooms would arguably be more effective than offering beauty tips.

## The Chilly Climate

The concept of *chilly climate*—an unwelcome, unsafe, or threatening social environment —is recognized in Canadian legal contexts as a form of harassment, and it is the responsibility of the employers (in this case, boards of education) to ensure a harassment-free climate. However, existing complaint-driven procedures are not the most effective or efficient means of transforming the climate of physical education classes. Rather, it is the responsibility of teachers and administrators to provide a physical education program that is welcoming and rewarding for students of all backgrounds and ability levels, and to intervene whenever any form of harassment takes place.

Research on these issues since the 1980s has documented a number of systemic barriers, including rigid definitions of heterosexual femininity and the chilly climate created by sexual and homophobic harassment, that constrain adolescent females' full participation in school-based physical education and sport programs (see Brackenridge 2001; Derry 2002; Griffin 1998; Humbert 1996; Lenskyj 1992, 2003; Morrow and Gill 2003; Portman 2003; Scraton 1992). Girls in high school physical education classes often experience a chilly climate as a result of verbal or physical harassment, as well as nonverbal behaviour such as leering. The perpetrators are usually male peers and, sometimes, male physical education teachers and coaches. Coeducational physical education in the higher grades exacerbates the problems for many girls.

> *Gurpreet:*   I was a bit embarrassed because that is when I started putting on weight and I was a bit embarrassed to wear my shorts in front of the guys. I guess I didn't feel comfortable...and I had a male gym teacher... [who told] sexist jokes with girls and he always favoured the guys over the girls....

> *Ashley:*   I think in junior high was when it started getting worse because the teachers were all male, and they were really pushy and they'd really push the girls. They'd always be picking on the girls or say[ing] things like "getting off your butt and trying at least." So I didn't like those classes at all. I faked being sick....

Two recent American studies provide further evidence of these problems. Julie Derry (2002) interviewed seventy-three girls aged 12 to 15 years, and found a clear preference for single-sex physical education. The girls reported that it suited their learning styles and needs and alleviated the problem of boys' harassing behaviour. Similarly, in her study of twenty-five grade 9 girls, Penelope Portman (2003) found that the lesser-skilled group resented coeducational physical education because of the harassment and criticism they received from classmates, especially from the boys. As one girl explained,

> When you play with the boys, they criticize you and everything. If you can't run, they say you are too fat and if you can't play volleyball, they laugh at you. Boys are terrible. (156)

In contrast, one highly skilled girl in Portman's study stated that she enjoyed competing against, and beating, the boys. Gurpreet expressed similar sentiments: "I was in a basketball tournament like last year, the first time, my guy friends were like 'Wow, Gurpreet, you're so wicked! I can't believe you can play.'" For most girls, however, comparisons with boys' performance were demoralizing. Male physical education teachers' stereotypical expectations of girls were also discouraging. As Gurpreet expressed it, "I hate sitting there proving to the teachers that are guys: 'so what if I'm a woman, I can do things that you can do.' I hate that."

Other forms of prejudice are also played out in physical education settings. Ethnic minority students, those who are overweight, uncoordinated or disabled, and gay, lesbian, and bisexual youth may experience marginalization, bullying, and harassment at the hands of other students from the dominant group. Homophobic harassment, based on prejudice against lesbians, gays, and bisexuals, or against individuals assumed to be members of these sexual minorities, may take a verbal form—name-calling, slurs, offensive jokes, and stereotyping—or it may escalate to involve physical threats, intimidation, and acts of physical or sexual violence. Some school board and university harassment policies specifically identify and prohibit homophobic harassment, but many fail to provide any protection or recourse for victims. "Zero tolerance" and anti-bullying programs and policies tend to operate on a narrow definition of bullying (in physical terms), and to overlook verbal harassment and verbal violence. If the target of verbal taunts eventually responds to her or his attacker with physical force, it is likely to be the victim of the bullying, rather than the perpetrator, who is punished with a suspension.

As researchers like Sheila Scraton (1992) in the UK and Louise Humbert (1996) in Canada discovered, adolescent girls' self-consciousness about changing clothes and showering in front of peers and physical education teachers was often exacerbated by homophobic fears. Maggie explained how these attitudes affected her as a young lesbian:

> ...it's hard when you're a different sexuality than other people, because you're always afraid that if they find out then they'll say stupid things like "Oh, I don't want to change in front of her because she's always looking at me." I'm afraid of that in my phys. ed. class now, I don't want people to know, because if they do then I'll be singled out for sure.

As adolescents, girls who excel at a particular sport *because* of their large size and musculature—regardless of their sexual orientation—are likely to be labelled "fat dykes." And, whether or not they are athletic, overweight adolescent girls are much more likely than their male counterparts to be the targets of harmful weight-based teasing. A Minnesota-based research study (Eisenberg et al. 2002) reported the disturbing statistic that about 30 percent of overweight girls were teased by both their peers and *family members*, and that about one in four reported having attempted suicide. Teasing was consistently associated with lower body satisfaction and self-esteem, depressive symptoms, and thoughts about suicide.

> Ashley: ...a lot of the heavier girls won't take it [physical education]—a lot of my heavier friends, because they get hot faster and they can't keep up to the rest of them, and they're embarrassed because everyone is like, "Oh, your face is so red," and "Why are you so out of breath?"...And competition...they don't like to compete in things that they aren't good at.

She went on to explain the situation in grade 9:

> ...I was the girl who people hated ..."the fat girl." "Look at that cow over there."...Guys who'd go to the school used to make a lot of fun and fat jokes about me. I used to go to the guidance counsellor every second day.

Significant numbers of Canadian girls and women, even those of average or below-average weight at the outset, use exercise, including fitness classes and jogging, as well as dieting to lose weight (CFLRI 1988). Although maintenance of healthy weight through regular physical activity is a worthwhile goal for women and men of all ages, self-starvation and excessive exercise are a potentially fatal combination (Lenskyj 1993; Davis 1999).

## Different Interests, Different Activities

Gendered preferences for activities need to be considered. The 1999 Canadian Fitness and Lifestyle Research Institute report (CFLRI 1999) found that adolescent girls were more likely than their male peers to list physical activities that were outside mainstream competitive sport, including walking, social dancing, ballet, and exercise and dance classes. Canadian surveys of exercise frequency showed that females aged 12 years and older reported much higher participation rates in the categories of walking for exercise, home exercise, and aerobics or fitness classes than males, and slightly higher rates for swimming (Sport Canada 1994). A later survey (Sport Canada 1998) showed that women's activity preferences were swimming, baseball, and volleyball, whereas men preferred ice hockey, golf, baseball, and basketball. These findings suggest that many girls who drop school physical education continue to play sport or engage in other physical activities at home, commercial gyms, or community recreation centres. Although these trends may allay some concerns among physical educators and health professionals, human rights and equity issues remain: Why should publicly funded sport and physical education programs in high schools serve the male student population first and foremost?

Current trends reflect the need to introduce girls to regular, enjoyable physical activity from a young age. Children, particularly girls, benefit from developing a solid foundation of physical competence and confidence so that they can look forward to enjoying lifelong physical activity. Research evidence supports this emphasis on *enjoyment* and its particular significance for girls. Independent of physical fitness levels, a recent research study (Motl et al. 2001) showed that, for adolescent girls, there was a strong correlation among enjoyment, physical activity, and sport involvement. Whereas much of the research, particularly in the health field, has focused on *extrinsic* factors such as positive health outcomes of physical activity, this study demonstrated the significance of enjoyment both as an immediate *intrinsic* reward and as an important factor in the maintenance of physical activity. In other words, although health messages might prompt girls to begin being active, enjoyment is the key to their continued engagement. Regardless of skill level, both boys and girls in Portman's study (2003) agreed that when they were not successful, the activity in which they were involved was not fun and should be dropped from the physical education curriculum.

Socio-cultural factors also play an important part in shaping girls' and boys' attitudes toward sport in general, and to competitiveness as a value. In families that uphold traditional gender expectations, parents may discourage girls from extracurricular sport or community recreation programs (Borowy and Little 1991; Vertinsky, Batth, and Naidu 1996). Nevertheless, they may allow their daughters to pursue cultural activities such as dance from their homelands, and these preferences are recognized and incorporated into some school-based physical education programs. Children with physically active parents and higher family incomes have significantly greater sport participation rates than those with inactive parents and lower incomes (Children's participation 2000; Morrow, Jackson, and Payne 1999). Given the low-paying jobs that many immigrant parents hold, often as a result of discriminatory hiring practices, girls in these families face yet another barrier to involvement in sport and physical education.

## Competitiveness or Friendship?

Research on gender-related differences in interests and priorities in sport and physical activity has shown that girls and women tend to rank the social aspects of both—fun and friendship—more highly than boys and men, who are likely to put winning and improving their personal performance at the top of their lists. This is not to suggest that females do not want to win, or that males do not want to enjoy themselves. The difference lies in the relative importance each gender group assigns to these goals, largely as a result of lessons learned at a young age concerning the value of relationality versus autonomy. Girls tend to see themselves in relation to others, whereas boys strive to develop a separate, independent self. Although most males tend to experience structured, rule-bound sporting competition as a safe mode of interpersonal connection, many females view beating one's opponent as a threat to bonds of friendship. In other words, many girls and women have mixed feelings about competitiveness in sport, as well as in other spheres of life (Gilligan 1982; Lenskyj 1994).

The priority that girls place on friendships has mixed implications for their participation in sport and physical activity. On one hand, girls value the opportunities for fun and social interaction that these activities offer. On the other hand, they are likely to follow friends who make alternative non-active leisure choices if they perceive that to reject these choices in favour of a sporting activity would jeopardize their friendships (Biscomb et al. 2000). Gurpreet and Ashley both emphasized the importance of fun over competition:

Gurpreet:  I don't want to go through competition against my friends. I hate competing with my friends because we end up getting in fights....If I were a gym teacher, I wouldn't judge or mark or test any woman's ability in athletics....I think phys. ed. should be fun, and that is, no competition. No gold medals just because you ran faster than that girl did.

Ashley:  [If I were a gym teacher] I just wouldn't be so competitive. I wouldn't make the girls compete so much. I think then you'd enjoy it more. The aerobics classes, I loved them, because everyone was having fun joking around, like no one was competing against each other. A lot of the girls loved that.

For these three girls, many memories of their physical education classes were associated with pain, not pleasure. When asked about her experiences of physical education in middle school, Maggie replied,

> some of it was awful, like when we did Canada Fitness, that was awful because all the guys, most of the guys, can do way better than the girls, no matter what it is, and the girls are always competing with each other, and if you can't get a bronze or if you can't get a gold, then it is like "Oh well, I got a gold, I'm better than you....I can do this many more push-ups than you can, so you suck." Like I used to hate that, girls were so competitive with each other.

Gurpreet's negative experiences began at a younger age. Up until grade 5, she recalled, "I couldn't wait for gym class," but when more competitive activities were introduced in later grades, she began to dread physical education:

> Canada Fitness, I guess it started from then, when they had to test you...your athletic ability and I ranked really low...my self-esteem went really down because I wasn't like my best friend who was getting golds....I had always felt gym was fun, gym was where you didn't have to prove to anyone that you need a gold medal to be the best....That is why I hated grade 9 when [the teachers] started marking you....The marks were posted.

When asked about her reflections while watching the grade 9 physical education class, Gurpreet replied,

> Competition getting between each other—I saw a lot in that class. I saw some girls who were isolated and I kind of remember that kind of reminded me of me. Then there [were] other girls who were so perky and so happy—that kind of reminded me of other girls who I was very intimidated by. I remember it was purely intimidation, and never being picked on a team.

## Conclusion

These girls' generally negative physical education experiences were a source of profound embarrassment and a well-founded fear of further humiliation and failure. Although they had some positive experiences in the lower grades, and were not without athletic ability, all three decided to drop physical education after the required Grade 9 course. The human agents implicated in these girls' experiences included parents, male and female teachers, and male and female peers. Portman's advice bears repeating:

> If our intent as physical educators is to encourage students to participate in an active lifestyle in the future, evidence suggests we are not meeting our goals. Changing the curriculum, increasing opportunities to participate, mixing teams by ability and gender, and eradicating criticism and harassment by higher skilled students might encourage some of the non-active students to become active. (Portman 2003, 159)

An innovative pilot program in several schools in the United States as part of a four-year study (2002–06) has the potential to motivate adolescent girls to begin, and to continue, enjoying physical activity. The girls-only program, called TAAG (Trial of Activity for Adolescent Girls), offers kick-boxing, hip-hop aerobics, boxing (for self-defence), jazzercise and African-Caribbean dance, as well as traditional activities like basketball and a walking/jogging program that culminates in a 5-km race. As one physical educator pointed out, "For 50 years, we've been doing football, basketball and volleyball. Why not aerobics and hip-hop?...physical activity is more than just sports" (Kroll 2002, 3–4). Positive outcomes of the TAAG program clearly demonstrated how alternatives to traditional sports were more attractive to many adolescent girls.

On the related issue of the adolescent female body, Canadian educators Carla Rice and Vanessa Russell (1995a, 1995b, 2003) have developed an invaluable guide for educators and service providers. Based on the successful *body equity* workshops that the authors conducted with Toronto Board of Education students in the 1990s, the manual entitled *EmBodying Equity: Body Image as an Equity Issue* encompasses issues of body image (how others see us, how we see ourselves), media portrayals, body-based prejudice, eating and activity, violence and harassment, menstruation, sexual pleasure, and body appreciation. This holistic approach has much more to offer than one-dimensional initiatives that attempt to motivate girls to be physically active for health reasons alone, while failing to acknowledge the very real barriers posed by the chilly climate in school physical education programs.

## Notes

1. To protect the privacy of participants, all names used are pseudonyms.
2. Organizers changed the wording of their promotional messages and dropped the references to "feminine" following a complaint by one of the co-authors.

## References

Biscomb, K., H. Matheson, N. Beckerman, M. Tungatt, and H. Jarret. 2000. Staying active while still being you: Addressing the loss of interest in sport amongst adolescent girls. *Women in Sport and Physical Activity Journal* 9(2):79–92.

Brackenridge, C. 2001. *Spoilsports: Understanding and preventing sexual exploitation in sport.* London: Routledge.

Breakfast with champions. 2004. *S&W News* 6(4):1.

Borowy, J., and M. Little. 1991. *A time and space just for us.* Toronto: Central Neighbourhood House.

Canadian Teachers' Federation. 1990. *A Capella: A report on the realities, concerns, expectations and barriers experienced by adolescent women in Canada.* Ottawa: The Author.

Children's participation in sport. 2000. *Canadian Social Trends* (Autumn). Available at: www.statcan.ca/Daily/English/000912/d000912a.htm

Coakley, J., and A. White. 1992. Making decisions: Gender and sport participation among British Adolescents. *Sociology of Sport Journal* 9(1):20–35.

CFLRI. 1988. Campbell Survey on Well-Being in Canada. Available at: www.cflri.ca/cflri/pa/surveys/88survey/html

———. 1999. 1999 Physical Activity Monitor. Available at: www.cflri.ca/cflir/pa/surveys/99survey/99survey.html

Davis, C. 1999. Eating disorders, physical activity, and sport: biological, psychological, and sociological factors. In *Sport and gender in Canada*, ed. P. White and K. Young, 85–106. Don Mills, ON: Oxford University Press.

Deacon, B. 2001, November. Physical Education Curriculum Review Report. British Columbia Ministry of Education, Curriculum Branch. Available at: www.bced.gov.bc.ca/irp/reports/pereport.pdf

Derry, J. 2002. Single-sex and coeducation physical education: Perspectives of adolescent girls and female physical education teachers. *Melpomene Journal* 21(3):12–14.

Eisenberg, M., D. Newmark-Ztainer, and M. Story. 2002. Association of weight-based teasing and emotional well-being among adolescents. *Journal of Adolescent Health* 32(2):121.

Ganley, T., and C. Sherman. 2000. Exercise and children's health. *Physician and Sportsmedicine* 28 (Feb.):2. Available at: www.physicianandsportsmedicine.com

Gilligan, C. 1982. *In a different voice.* Cambridge: Harvard University Press.

Griffin, P. 1998. *Strong women, deep closets: Lesbians and homophobia in sport.* Champaign, IL: Human Kinetics.

Holmes, J., and E. Silverman. 1992. *We're here, listen to us.* Ottawa: Canadian Advisory Council on the Status of Women.

Humbert, L. 1996. Nowhere to hide. *Women's Education* 12(3):20–25.

Kroll, K. 2002. TAAG—not a game: A study to increase activity by adolescent girls. *Melpomene Journal* 21(3):21–28.

Lenskyj, H. 1992. Sexual harassment: Female athletes' experiences and coaches' responsibilities. *Sports Science Periodical on Research and Technology in Sport* 12(6):1–6.

———. 1993. Running risks: Compulsive exercise and eating disorders. In *Consuming passions: Feminist counselling approaches to weight preoccupation and eating disorders,* ed. C. Brown and K. Jasper, 91–108. Toronto: Second Story Press.

———. 1994. Girl friendly sport and female values. *Women in Sport and Physical Activity Journal* 3(1):35–46.

———. 2003. *Out on the field: Gender, sport and sexualities.* Toronto: Women's Press.

Morrow, R., and D. Gill. 2003. Perceptions of homophobia and heterosexism in physical education. *Research Quarterly* 74(2):205–14.

Motl, R., R. Dishman, R. Saunders, M. Dowda, G. Felton, and R. Pate. 2001. Measuring enjoyment of physical activity in adolescent girls. *American Journal of Preventive Medicine* 21(2):110–17.

Morrow, J., A. Jackson, and V. Payne. 1999. Physical activity promotion and school physical education. *Research Digest* 3 (Sept.):7. Available at: www.fitness.gov

Portman, P. 2003. Are physical education classes encouraging students to be physically active? Experiences of ninth graders in their last semester of required physical education. *Physical Educator* 60(3):150–60.

Rice, C., and V. Russell. 1995a. EmBodying equity, Part I. *Our Schools/Our Selves.* September: 14–36.

———. 1995b. EmBodying equity, Part II. *Our Schools/Our Selves.* December: 32–54.

———. 2003. *EmBodying equity: Body image as an equity issue.* Toronto: Green Dragon Press.

Scraton, S. 1992. *Shaping up to womanhood.* Buckingham, UK: Open University.

Sport Canada. 1994. *Sport Participation in Canada—1992 Report.* Report prepared by Statistics Canada for Sport Canada. Ottawa: Minister of Public Works and Government Services Canada.

Sport Canada. 1998. *Sport Participation in Canada—1998 Report.* Report prepared by Statistics Canada for Sport Canada. Ottawa: Minister of Public Works and Government Services Canada. Available at: www.pch.gc.ca

Summerfield, L. 1998. Promoting physical activity and exercise among children. *ERIC Digest*, ERIC Number 416204. Available at www.eric.ed.gov

van Daalen, C. 1996. Are you goin' to gym? Unpublished paper, Ontario Institute for Studies in Education, University of Toronto, Toronto, Ontario.

Van Buuren, Y. 2000. 15 smart moves to get fit. *Canadian Living* (October), 97–99.

Vertinsky, P., I. Batth, and M. Naidu. 1996. Racism in motion: Physical activity and the Indo-Canadian female. *AVANTE* 2(3):1–23.

*Vibrant Faces Teacher/Leader Event Guide*. 1994. Vibrant Faces Resource Kit. Ontario Physical and Health Education Association, Canadian Association for Health, Physical Education, Recreation and Dance.

Chapter Nine

# Developing a White Race-Consciousness:

## A Foundation for Culturally Relevant Physical Education for Aboriginal Youth

## Joannie Halas

### Introduction

In mainstream society there are a number of barriers that we are really just beginning to understand. Many of those issues... [have] to do with race, class, gender and what not, and we need to understand those issues fully in order to create a system where Aboriginal peoples both in the mainstream and non-mainstream are accepted as athletes, period.

Janice Forsyth[1]

The term "culturally relevant physical education" is used to define those physical education programs that are meaningful and relevant to students across a wide range of cultural, socio-economic class, gender, ability, and age differences. Drawing from the work of Gloria Ladson-Billings (1994), culturally relevant teacher practices in the gym evolve from the development of warm and caring relationships with students, where teachers respect young people and make efforts to understand the cultural landscape of their students' day-to-day lives (Halas 2003). Teachers demonstrate a connectedness with all students as they endeavour to develop a community of learners, where students are encouraged to learn collaboratively and to be responsible to one another (Ladson-Billings 1995). Using examples from a research project that investigated the quality of physical education for aboriginal youth (Champagne and Halas 2003; van Ingen and Halas 2003), this chapter addresses a key component of culturally relevant physical education: the teacher-student relationship.[2]

Over the course of three years, my colleagues and I carried out a series of research studies that involved talking to and interacting with aboriginal youth (Halas, Forsyth, and Shultz 2005).[3] We began the overall investigation by asking over seventy university and high school aboriginal students to reflect upon their experiences in physical education, including their likes and dislikes, their relationships with their teachers, and their personal involvement with physical activity. Analyses of these conversations were used to inform the second phase of our research program, in which we conducted four in-depth case studies of physical education programs offered in different geographic and socio-cultural settings. The four study sites included both all-aboriginal and cross-cultural urban and rural schools.

Methodologically, we used an interpretive approach (Ellis 1998) and incorporated "bricolage" (Denzin and Lincoln 1994), which refers to a pieced-together set of diverse research practices that emerge as the study unfolds. Consequently, we incorporated interviews with students, teachers, and administrators; field observations of physical education and school activities; and a collection of school documents, to construct an in-depth analysis of the quality and cultural relevance of the teachers' practices, the curriculum of activities, and the learning environments at each school.

In the final phase of the project, we invited students from two urban schools to take part in a participatory action research project. For this study, undergraduate students (three aboriginal and one Asian) from the Faculty of Physical Education and Recreation Studies at the University of Manitoba worked as mentors in a leadership training program. The goal of this school-based project was for aboriginal youth to shape their own physical activity program as an extension of their physical education program, with support from university mentors. This approach fostered a reciprocal learning environment, in which university students gained hands-on experience working with and learning from aboriginal youth.

Overall, these three phases of research activity provided a rich background for exploring the design and delivery of more effective physical activity experiences for aboriginal youth. In particular, it allowed us, as a team of co-researchers, to begin to identify the barriers that aboriginal youth face when attempting to integrate into mainstream physical education programs. In tune with Janice Forsyth's observations about the need to understand the influences of race, class, and gender, we incorporated aspects of critical race theory as a means to draw lessons from the experiences of aboriginal youth and the unequal relations of power that shape their lives in physical education, school, and the broader community. The ongoing analysis of our data prompted us to ask a number of questions about how Canada's mainstream sport and physical education programs are organized and delivered.

Why is it, for example, that despite the existence of many determined, enthusiastic, highly skilled, and athletic First Nations, Inuit, and Métis young people (e.g., the North American Indigenous Games), there are so few aboriginal students playing on high school sports teams? Why is it, as one group of "smokers" told me, that aboriginal students who would rather be playing in the gymnasium between classes than smoking out by the "smokers' doors," do not feel welcome in their school gymnasiums? The answers to these questions are not immediately evident, and require, as Dei (1998) suggests, that anti-racist educators critically theorize about personal and collective, and historical and contemporary, experiences to devise a method for social change.

The challenge for teachers is to develop an understanding of the complex factors that contribute to how a student performs in the gymnasium and at school. Teachers must develop relationships with these young people in ways that acknowledge the systemic barriers aboriginal youth may face outside the walls of the gymnasium. We must move beyond colour-blindness which seeks to treat all students equally in ways that ignore how advantages and disadvantages are differentially associated with different race, class, or gender markers. To do so, as Burden et al. (2004) suggest, physical education teacher education programs must also move beyond colour-blind policies and practices that discount the importance of race in sustaining inequities.

Set within the context of culturally relevant teacher practices in the gymnasium, and incorporating key elements of our research results, this chapter addresses some of the challenges of racism (which intersects with sexism, classism, ageism, ableism, and heterosexism) that have a negative impact on aboriginal students' experiences of high school physical education. As a strategy for physical educators to more fully engage students from diverse cultural backgrounds and abilities, the process of building

cross-cultural relationships between teachers and students will be discussed. I focus on the concept of white racial identity and how whiteness is
used as a cultural norm from which Whites in Canada define themselves as
a positive opposite to other racial minorities, including aboriginal peoples.[4]

Why is this important? Currently, the physical education profession represents a white, middle-class hegemony: there are few physical education teachers of colour (including aboriginal teachers), fewer physical
education professors of colour, and little to no evidence of an effort by faculties of physical education to diversify the make-up of their student bodies.
Ignoring the problem that this lack of diversity presents in building a more
equitable society that reflects the Canadian cultural mosaic, physical educators (both current and future) who develop activity programs based on
"white, middle-class values" (McLaughlin and Heath 1993, as cited in
Martinek and Hellison 1997) will experience difficulty when trying to connect with an increasingly diverse high school student population. Unless
middle-class white educators see themselves as *allies* (Bishop 1994) and begin to use their privilege to create more opportunity for under-represented
groups to succeed in physical education, high schools will fail at promoting
active, healthy lifestyles for all students.[5]

Presently, there appears to be a disconnect between many
well-meaning whitestream[6] teachers who would like to see their aboriginal
students more engaged, and the many students who opt out of physical education, all the while wanting to be more active. There are also some successful teachers providing excellent programs. And, there are other teachers who are resistant to any self-reflection about their own practice, and
how their actions may adversely affect student participation. This diversity
amongst and between teachers and students is what makes the struggle for
social justice in physical education so very challenging.

And so, one goal of this chapter is to challenge a mediocre status
quo by broadening intellectual perspectives about race and theorizing a
need for physical educators to develop a white race-consciousness. By
making visible and naming whiteness as a racial construct, physical educators can commit to generating a more inclusive and affirming learning environment that takes into account the diverse needs, experiences, and
perspectives of an increasingly multicultural student body. It is here that
the discussion begins.

## White Race-Consciousness: What Is Your First Memory?

A few years ago, I met Louise Champagne, a Métis woman who was deeply involved in community economic development in the inner city of Winnipeg. Recognizing that we had a shared belief in the value and intelligence of young people, we arranged to meet for coffee. I was excited (and a bit nervous) about this encounter: being non-aboriginal (my parents, though born in Manitoba, were of white, eastern European heritage), I was only beginning to develop an awareness of the injustices that aboriginal peoples had endured as a result of the colonization of Canada.

My past experiences as a physical education teacher working with aboriginal youth had taught me the often unacknowledged fact that aboriginal people (especially those who "look" aboriginal) can have routinely negative experiences in their day-to-day encounters with the dominant, whitestream majority in Canada. Not knowing Louise, but having witnessed racist acts toward aboriginal peoples throughout my life, I expected that her past relationships with white people might have been negative. Beyond that, my anxiety also centered on how Louise's knowledge of inner-city poverty and inequality would affect how she viewed me and the socio-economic privileges that being white had afforded me.[7]

In Winnipeg, as in Canada as a whole, race and racism are dynamic characteristics of our multi-cultural community.[8] White racism, which Kivel (2002) describes as the uneven and unfair distribution of power, privilege, land, and material goods favouring white people, is a defining characteristic of how Canada has come to be. The racialization of aboriginal peoples, from their first contact with the European colonizers through to the present day, is a story of white domination that, as Haney López (1996) writes, necessitates and perpetuates patterns of superiority and inferiority.[9] In meeting Louise, I very much wanted to convey somehow that I was aware of my own white privilege (McIntosh 1989) and that I recognized the social inequalities in our society. I guess you could say that I really wanted Louise to like me, and was not quite sure how my whiteness and her "otherness" would affect our relationship.

Should I have been worried? At that time, it was not uncommon for the media to report stories of overt racism toward aboriginal peoples. Even today, First Nations, Inuit, and Métis peoples might be called derogatory names as they walk down the street, followed indiscriminately while shopping, stopped by the police for random checks, or refused respectful service in restaurants. Such encounters can be more frequent for young people, because adultism intersects with race: my own research illustrates how young aboriginals can be indiscriminately labeled as "bad" or "lazy" or "troubled" or "poor learners" by their predominantly white teachers (Halas, Forsyth, and Shultz 2005).

## When Aboriginal Youth Encounter Whitestream Canada

One of the many enduring memories of my aboriginal students and their encounters with white society involved two teenaged girls who had just moved from the North to continue their studies at a suburban high school. As is often the case, they were billeted with a family in a neighbourhood close to the school. Coming from a small, remote reserve, the girls found suburbia to be a strange environment. During their first week in Winnipeg, they often took walks in the neighbourhood as one way to explore and learn about their new community.

One evening, as the girls set off for a leisurely stroll, they approached a group of middle-aged white women who were chatting on the boulevard grass ahead of them. As the girls approached, the women's banter and laughter abruptly died down, with one, then the other, turning in response to a third woman's hushed tones and glance in the direction of the two teenaged Ojibway girls. Much to the girls' bewilderment, they watched as the women quickly separated and rushed over to where their garbage cans were sitting on the curb: with determination, the women carried their garbage cans closer to the safe confines of their homes.

Seeing this, the girls quietly giggled at how funny it was to see white-skinned women so concerned about their garbage. Being so new to the community, the girls were mostly confused by the women's actions. Was this an act of racism that the girls were encountering? Race is not only about physical appearance and ancestry; its primary function is to *give meaning* to physical appearance and ancestry (Haney López 1996). Exactly what were these white women communicating to the more darkly skinned girls by pushing their garbage out of the way?

The aboriginal parent who recounted this story to me explained how it was not uncommon for white, middle-class people to treat with suspicion the aboriginal youth who moved in to their neighbourhood. Unfortunately, as Ponting (1998) reports, it is not at all uncommon for the dominant society to hold negative stereotypes of native peoples in Canada. For reasons undoubtedly linked to the racialization process, these women had learned to be afraid of two fifteen-year-old girls who meant them no harm and who, in fact, had never before been down that street in their neighbourhood.

The girls' encounter has remained with me to this day because it speaks to the manner in which white racism in Canada exists on many different levels. Whether subtle or overt, to pre-judge human beings negatively, particularly those of a minority culture, is not only hurtful and damaging, but helps keep social inequity in place. It is difficult enough for high school students to study away from the security of family and home; it is tougher yet for them to succeed within a context of racial discrimination, social isolation, and negative expectation. Do race and class have an impact on aboriginal students' success rates in school and physical education, with a concomitant impact on aboriginal youth's place in the socio-economic hierarchy in Canada? Research would so indicate.[10] In fact, moving from one school to another adds to the turbulence that increases the possibility of school failure (Weiss 2001; Rumberger and Larson 1998).

## Theorizing About Race, Class, and Cultural Identity in Canadian Society

As a university educator who helps prepare future physical education teachers to teach in a variety of school contexts, the story of the two Ojibway girls also reminds me of the importance of using history to give theoretical context to contemporary experience, both personal and collective. Why is it that there are so few aboriginal-operated high schools located on reserves in Canada? Why are there so few teachers of aboriginal heritage, and why are non-aboriginal teachers so poorly prepared to teach aboriginal students (see Brown 1998; Halas 1998). In a description of his own cross-cultural experiences teaching in a native community, Taylor (1995) writes that ninety percent of native children will be taught by non-native teachers. However, teacher preparation programs do little to introduce non-native teachers to the culture of Canada's diverse native communities.

The young girls' experience also prompts me to think continually about the consequences of negative stereotyping (e.g., suspicion that a young person will behave maliciously), particularly when expressed by whitestream teachers toward their aboriginal students. In focus-group interviews with over seventy aboriginal high school and university students, many students told painful stories of how their physical education teachers treated them "differently" because they were aboriginal, and did not see them as "athletic." "They're afraid of us," some boys mentioned, and "blame us" first when there's a problem. Notably, our fieldwork observations and interviews with a number of adult educators confirmed many of the students' perceptions that they were often treated differently than their non-aboriginal peers, both in and out of school.

Given the powerful influence of the "self-fulfilling prophesy" (Tauber 1997), when aboriginal students are expected to perform more poorly than their non-aboriginal peers, exactly what are the messages that aboriginal youth receive about their place in Canadian society? And, from a physical education perspective, what are the effects on aboriginal youths' health and wellbeing? When simply walking down the street might trigger a negative reaction from a stranger, how welcoming is it for aboriginal youth to be "active" outdoors in Canadian society? To go for a run in the neighbourhood after school? To play pick-up hockey at the local outdoor rink? These are the types of questions I was thinking about when Louise and I first met at the café.

As we poured milk into our coffee, Louise looked up, paused, and immediately asked me, "What is your first memory of an aboriginal person?" The question caught me somewhat by surprise, and I hesitated before replying, "I'm not sure." "What was your first experience of a white person?" I asked her in return.

Over the next few hours, we talked about growing up, about our parents and families, who our friends were, what our schools were like, and whether we "hung out" with kids from other cultural backgrounds. Louise told me about a white, European landlord who was very disrespectful toward her parents, which, as a child, she found very painful to watch; I talked about how, as children, my cousins made very derogatory remarks toward Natives, and I wondered how that could have been because we had never met anyone who was native. In fact, most of what I knew about aboriginal peoples came from descriptive representations in whitestream-owned and -operated papers and TV. Most were "crisis" stories in line with what critical race theorists call the reproduction of a "cultural deficit model" that positions problems as inevitabilities without any analysis of how race and racism intersect with societal structures and institutions (Solorzano and Yosso 2002).[11]

The stories I read in the paper or watched on TV never provided a context to help explain how the cultural landscape for many aboriginal peoples had been so adversely affected by Canada's colonial history. Like most non-Aboriginals living in Canada, I knew very little about the shared social history between indigenous peoples and the European colonizers, especially as interpreted through those who were colonized, and less yet about indigenous peoples' history prior to contact with the Europeans.[12] Most of the history texts in high school and university were written by white, European males, and reinforced white, colonial notions of superiority and inferiority (e.g., that the white Europeans brought civilization to the "savage" Indian). As Paraschak (1989, 58) notes in a critique of the native sport history literature, "the true record of the native sport experience is twisted because of the ethnic chauvinism of the chronicler," resulting in a trend of ethnocentric distortion.[13]

Nowhere did my history books mention the long-term, stable, complex, and sophisticated Indigenous cultures and economies that characterized the richly populated Turtle Island (later known as North America) prior to Christopher Columbus's invasion (Kivel 2002). As Sapon-Shevin (1999) illustrates in her resource book for building inclusive classrooms (which includes ideas of how to rethink Columbus), there are multiple perspectives of the "truth" and, as educators, we must encourage ourselves and our students to explore multiple views of historical events. We must learn to theorize (inform ourselves about) our lived experience, both personal and collective. We must also question the relationships between power and knowledge in determining what counts as "truth": beyond the inclusion of multiple voices in the production of knowledge about history, we must recognize how the dominant (white) view has presented itself as speaking for all, thereby excluding the diverse experiences and identities of other racial and cultural groups (Douglas 2005; Dyer 1997). As we read textbooks, we must interrupt the silent, invisible, excluded, and distorted "truths" about our shared histories within Canada.

## Re-Thinking Our Colonial History

For example, it was not until the latter stages of my doctoral education that I began reading aboriginal-authored works of history (e.g., Adams 1989). I learned about the millions of indigenous peoples who were brutally slaughtered or dispossessed by the Europeans after 1492 (Churchill 1998). I had never been taught about the forced relocation of indigenous peoples onto reserves, how whole populations were starved to death by the strategic extermination of the buffalo, how communal band societies that had existed for thousands of years were forced to give up their livelihoods and become dependent on Canada's paternalistic federal government. I was unaware that Canada's legal system forbade indigenous peoples from practising their own cultural and spiritual traditions (e.g., the Sundance and the Potlatch: see Francis 1992; Paraschak 1996) and that the game of lacrosse was appropriated by white Europeans and aboriginal teams were excluded from participation because they were too dominant.

Perhaps most importantly for physical educators, I never once learned about how children were forcibly removed from their families and sent to residential schools miles away or sold to private adoption firms across Canada and the United States. The sometimes irreversible separation from their parents, grandparents, and extended families placed a brutalizing strain on both the children and their families who were left in childless communities.[14] As Chrisjohn, Young, and Mauran (1997) point out, the systematic transfer of children from one group to another was a crime against humanity, under Article 2 (e) of the United Nations Convention on the Prevention and Punishment of the Crime of Genocide (1948).

Although it is beyond the scope of this chapter to provide a socio-historical perspective of aboriginal education and health after the arrival of the Europeans, it is important for all Canadians to understand the pernicious nature and long-term effects of the Residential Schools system (Agnes Grant's 2004 book *Finding My Talk* is a good starting place). This race-based assimilation program effectively ingrained notions of superiority and inferiority about white and aboriginal people, respectively, that endure to this day (see Appendix for a brief overview of the Residential School System). For a more in-depth analysis, preservice physical education students who expect to teach aboriginal students in their future programs are strongly urged to take a native studies course and other cross-cultural education classes as a means to enhance their socio-historical understanding of Canadian education.

History, both personal and collective, matters. Just as it was helpful for Louise and me to exchange childhood stories about our experiences with each other's culture, it is also necessary, particularly for educators, to reflect upon how Canada's racial history has created social and economic privilege for white people, while disadvantaging non-Whites. As physical educators, we must be informed about our collective history, and how our present-day relationships across cultures are influenced by what happened "before" us. To not acknowledge the influence of this history is akin to denying the impact of our own childhood.

As physical educators, sincerely committed to social inclusion and educational equity, we can no longer ignore the historical and contemporary significance of racial identity and the positive privileges associated with being white in Canadian society. To grasp this significance, Haney López suggests that we must first develop a white race-consciousness:

Whiteness, as it is currently constituted, perpetuates injurious racial identities and should be abandoned. Whites need to develop
a race-consciousness that places their racial identity squarely in
view in order to better dissemble the meaning systems of racial
superiority and racial inferiority. A self-deconstructive White
race-consciousness is key to racial justice. (156)

In the next section, I explore what a white race-consciousness might look
like for physical educators.

## Interrupting Privilege—Building Equity: A New Type of Physical Education

There is very little racial diversity within the profession of physical
education. Consequently, as Pearl Rosenberg (1997) notes, this "presence of
an absence" places teachers and students "in the position of having to imagine other voices and circumstances that many of the students can only know
from what they read or see on television or film, or infer from the news media,
in regard to other people's lives" (80). Or, as Delia Douglas (2005) emphasizes, when diverse racial identities are invisible, absent, ignored, silenced, or
distorted, (predominantly white) authors can speak generically about physical education as if all the participants are unmarked by racial identities (and
therefore, by implication, are white). Why, as Rosenberg asks, is it so difficult to explore what it means to be white; to name and claim a white identity by saying, for example, that "I have a white, middle-class background
and this means that..."? Typically, race has been viewed as relevant only
when speaking about non-Whites: by naming and claiming our own white
racial identities, we are interrupting the process by which the domination of
whiteness is reproduced through its invisibility. We need to reveal the
dominance of whiteness in the physical education profession, and how this
dominance is present at all levels, from university professors to undergraduate students.

As current and future physical education professionals, we must
make our whiteness transparent: we must work against the naturalization
of race that continues to promote mythologies of superiority and inferiority.
We must work to expose whiteness and the ways in which white racial identity is reinforced and reproduced both consciously and unconsciously in
ways that ensure white privilege remains intact. As Haney López (1996)
says, it is white people, through choice and struggle, who must work to end

the racial systems of meaning that bind Whites and non-Whites in unequal hierarchies of social worth. For example, we must actively work to recruit more aboriginal peoples (and people of diverse racial backgrounds) into our undergraduate physical education programs, and to create more academic opportunities for racially diverse scholars. It is only through these actions, informed by a racial identity perspective, that the dynamic of white supremacy within the profession of physical education can be addressed.

White people must do this, not out of a sense of guilt or responsibility but to make explicit the inherent inequities of race identities, and how these inequities falsely sustain images of superiority and inferiority (Haney López 1996). Over the years, I have come to believe that any efforts to teach aboriginal youth in the absence of a white race-consciousness will only reproduce inequities that contribute to the supremacy of white people in Canadian society. Rather, we must become allies who actively work to end the oppression of aboriginal youth.

In today's racially divided, class-oriented Canadian society, to deny the unequal relations of power and privilege that affirm some racial groups and marginalize others is to deny the personal and social realities of aboriginal students. In her compelling description of black Canadian high school students' experiences of school, Kelly (1998) writes that Canadian educators tend to deny the influence of a student's race in schooling. For future physical educators, the ability to develop successful relationships that acknowledge how race, gender, class, sexuality, and (dis)ability support and constrain a student's experience of school and physical education is an ethical imperative.

Physical educators can no longer be colour-blind in a misguided desire to treat everyone "equally": poverty, for example, is not an equalizer. Racial discrimination is not an equalizer. Cultural dislocation (economic realities that force aboriginal students across Canada to leave their communities to attend high school) is not an equalizer. Inadequate education (e.g., poorly funded aboriginal schools on reserves) is not an equalizer. Misconceptions shared and promoted by the dominant classes (e.g., that aboriginal peoples receive "free" education) are not equalizers. Systemic inequalities (e.g., undergraduate Bachelor of Physical Education programs that have very few aboriginal or culturally-diverse students, and fewer still aboriginal or culturally-diverse faculty and staff) will never change unless specific action is undertaken to interrupt the conditions that lead to inequity. In the following section, I present a concrete example of how the development of a white race-consciousness might help in understanding the challenges of building cross-cultural relationships with aboriginal youth.

## From Residential Schools to the Present

It is important for physical education teachers to know how the lingering trauma from the residential school experience has the potential to make interpersonal relationships with white teachers difficult for aboriginal students. Having listened to the school experiences of their parents and grandparents, many aboriginal youth may enter schools feeling apprehensive toward their teachers and other authority figures in the school. Furthermore, they may have little tolerance for what they perceive to be unfair treatment (Champagne and Halas 2003). The following is an example of resistance to what the aboriginal student-participant perceived to be inappropriate teacher practices:

*Researcher:*    What do they yell about?

*Participant:*    Like to get you going and drill you to do the warm-ups, stuff that you don't want to do and you shouldn't have to do if you don't want to do it. I remember me and that guy K..., I couldn't run because something was wrong with my leg and he was out of breath and our teacher just came and started yelling at us, so we just left because we were not doing what he wanted us to do. It was either their way or no way. (Champagne and Halas 2003, 88)

A legacy of the residential school experience for this generation of aboriginal students may be a willingness to resist inappropriate teaching practice, no matter what the educational consequence. Although the teacher may have been yelling at all students to get moving in class, the large number of aboriginal students who purposefully drop physical education suggests that aboriginal students in particular are less inclined to engage with teachers who yell, even when this means they will not pass the course. Conversely, non-aboriginal students may be more tolerant of this type of teacher behaviour, choosing to grin and bear it by participating in class, thus achieving the necessary credit toward graduation.

Inadequate educational outcomes from residential schooling made it very difficult for many former students to find jobs or to continue their education off the reserve. This has contributed to the systemic poverty that affects many aboriginal youth across Canada. In our study, some students living in low-income families were not eating well (they therefore lacked the energy required to be physically active in class), were inadequately dressed (and excluded from physical education in programs where changing clothing is mandatory), and, in some cases, their poverty and their race made them stand out from the other students. Income-related barriers produced consequences that, whether subtle or overt, can make the experience of mainstream schooling and physical education even more challenging for some aboriginal youth.

During a month of daily fieldwork at one cross-cultural school, I watched Joseph, a sixteen-year-old northern Cree student living in Winnipeg, walk the hallways alone at noon: every single day, he wore the same shiny red sweatsuit. The first time I saw him, it struck me how well his clothes enabled him to "fit in" with the blend of middle- and upper-class students. Even though he was not enrolled in any physical education classes (he had not signed up because, as he told me in an interview, he "didn't like phys ed"), he did not look out of place wearing a sweatsuit in the hallways. The second day I saw him, he had not changed his clothes from the day before. He still looked like he fit in. Over the next three weeks, he wore the same track suit every day and I slowly came to realize that these were most likely the only clothes he had to wear.

I knew Joseph's family did not have much money and marvelled at how, at the very least, he had bought the right type of clothing to fit the culture of the school. By month's end, my perceptions had changed. I was now watching Joseph in relation to the other students that he passed each day: others were talking on cell phones, wearing designer clothes, and in some cases, pulling out their automatic car starters as they exited the school. How, I wondered, within this environment of overwhelming income disparity, was the boy in the red sweatsuit ever going to survive? For me, this was a vivid example of how poverty, when it intersects with race, makes it very difficult for aboriginal (and other marginalized) youth to succeed in a Western, capitalist society.

A week after I completed my fieldwork observations, the Minister of Education in Manitoba announced a ban on certain types and colours of sweatsuits. The dress code policy was designed with the express purpose of targeting the expression of any possible "criminal gang" affiliation in schools. Joseph was one colour-coded dress policy away from being excluded from school. Apparently the Ministry of Education policy-makers were not "theorizing" about the intersections of race and class when they drafted their school dress code guidelines. The last time I saw Joseph was a year later as he was walking down an inner- city street early one weekday morning. He was not in school. He may have never made it to the gymnasium for physical education, but he was still wearing the red sweatsuit.

Joseph's story reminds me how racism is not only about interpersonal connections; it is also policy-driven and institutionalized. "Personal experiences are lived through social relations of power" (Dei 1998, 309). *Systemic* or *institutionalized racism* describes situations where outcomes of an institution's operations differ systematically for people of different races, regardless of the intentions of those working within the institution (Ponting 1998). According to 1996 census data, only 44.1 percent of aboriginal youth aged 15–24 were attending school either full- or part-time in Manitoba (HRDC and Manitoba 2002). As physical educators, do we need to concern ourselves about those students, like Joseph, who are listed on our school registers but who do not make it to our classes? Do we simply ignore statistics that point to the absence of aboriginal youth in our schools and physical education programs, under the guise that "if they're not in our class, they're not our problem"? Or, do we have a responsibility to ask questions about these absent youth, to develop an understanding of how socio-historical factors, like the discredited residential school system, might contribute to their low participation in school today?

Can we imagine possibilities of how our physical education programs might be used as a means to encourage aboriginal youth to attend school? Can physical education be part of a solution whereby we, as educators, create more meaningful, welcoming, and affirming school environments for aboriginal youth? In the following section, I present some strategies for achieving the goal of engaging aboriginal youth more fully in physical education programs. Although the dynamics of teaching will shift according to the cultural and geographical context of the school (e.g., an urban, cross-cultural school versus a small, community-based all-aboriginal school), the following suggestions may provide some helpful tips for developing a culturally relevant program.

## Building Culturally Relevant Physical Education Programs: What Works?

### Be Aware of Your Own Pre-Conceptions

Our research indicates that physical educators who see themselves as a key determinant of a successful relationship with aboriginal (and other) youth are those who are willing to explore ways to develop their cultural competency and understanding of the ways in which race matters. They are reflective teachers who are aware of how they are privileged by their race, class, gender, ability, age, and other factors. They anticipate potential barriers to participation that their students may face, all the while recognizing the individuality of each student, the diversity of student needs, and the potential for each student to be successful. For example, English may be a second language for many aboriginal youth. In this case, teachers can try to foresee how their students' written and oral communication skills might influence their performance in the gymnasium.

Successful teachers always see their students as intelligent and capable human beings and question their personal assumptions whenever they find themselves holding negative expectations for student behaviour in their classes. They look forward to meeting their aboriginal students, and to disrupting the hierarchical nature of the teacher-student relationship by actively seeking to learn from their students. And, they see themselves as an ally, someone who will support aboriginal youth and work hard to help them succeed in physical education and school.

### First Impressions

Given that many aboriginal youth have to leave their home communities to attend high school, it is quite possible that new students will be quite unfamiliar with the culture of the physical education class and extracurricular programs. Within the mix of students, however, there may be other aboriginal students who have lived in the school's community all of their lives. So, one should expect that each student's experience will be different. Given this dynamic, it is important to make an effort to communicate differently with different students. Teachers may want to provide an orientation for new students, which might include the distribution of an information sheet that outlines program goals and objectives. This should include expectations for student participation in class (e.g., changing for class, being active, what to do if they miss a class or are unable to participate), assessment strategies, and opportunities to take part in intramural and interschool activities (with detailed instructions of how these activities are organized). Other important factors that will help students understand how the program is designed and delivered should be clearly articulated at the beginning of the year. Through the communication of clear expectations for behaviour, students will have a better understanding of what they need to do in order to succeed.

When meeting students for the first time, it is a good practice to take the time to ask them about themselves: What are their interests?

Where is their home community? What do they think of their new school? Students who are very new to the school and community should be allowed time to settle in. If they are not prepared with a change of clothes for class, they should not be forced to sit out. If they are not comfortable changing for physical education, give them options such as wearing loose-fitting clothes to the class. If they appear to be uncomfortable or present themselves as very shy, give them space and let them stand off to the side of the class activities until they feel ready to take part. Encourage them, but do not force them, to participate, and do not worry if it takes more than a few classes for them to step up and actively participate in class. They will know when they feel comfortable, and respecting their judgement about their personal safety in the class will increase the possibilities for student engagement as the program unfolds. Always communicate to individual students that they are welcome in class, that their involvement is important to you, and that they have the skills and abilities to succeed in class.

## Create a Community of Learners

Our interviews with both students and teachers produced a variety of recommendations. Many students appreciate those teachers who present themselves as a "friend" who listens, cares, and is positive and encourages all students in the class to be active. They suggest that teachers need to treat all students with equal consideration while recognizing the individual nature of students, including individual accomplishments. They like it when teachers actively take part with students and remind them of how good it feels to be physically active. When necessary, as one physical educator explained, successful teachers put in that "extra little effort" to go after the quiet, shy students and invite them "in."

One effective strategy for creating supportive learning environments is to encourage students to encourage each other. Ennis (1999) illustrated how the delivery of the *Sport for Peace* program enabled disengaged African-American girls to participate meaningfully with their more skilled male counterparts during an extended unit of basketball. Similarly, teachers can ask students to take responsibility for supporting each others' participation in class. In this way, teachers are recognizing the importance of friends and peer relations and, as a group, students can problem solve and strategize ways in which to motivate the class to be more physically active. Student groups can be mixed up, with certain students asked to take leadership in trying to include the lesser engaged students. If things are not working well in the class, ask the students, "What can we do to improve the class?"

When the group dynamics are negative, teachers must quickly intervene. All forms of negative stereotyping (e.g., based on gender, race, class, sexuality, ability, etc.) need to be immediately interrupted. This requires that teachers not only actively observe student interactions in the class, but also that they listen to how students describe themselves. Negative self-perceptions (e.g., self-identifying as lazy or unskilled) should also be interrupted through positive encouragement by teachers. When students choose to sit out, find out why. Often, there is a good reason for their non-participation, and you may find out what is happening only by asking them. If students are keenly aware that your goal is to provide a non-sexist, non-racist, non-threatening environment, then they will be more open to sharing their concerns about why they may not feel like participating. Whenever things are not working well in the class, ask yourself, "What can I do to improve the class?"

### Provide Meaningful Activity Choices

The more students are provided with a variety of choices that are personally meaningful and socially relevant, the more likely they will actively engage in the class, intramurals, and extracurricular programs. Although some students might enjoy mainstream sports like basketball, volleyball, and hockey, others might prefer more traditional activities like jigging, trapping, fishing, and hunting. Some female students prefer exposure to a wide variety of personal fitness activities such as aerobics, Tae Bo and stability ball workouts, resistance training, and belly dancing, whereas others prefer wrestling (Halas and Orchard 2002). Expect a wide diversity of individual preferences and do not assume that all aboriginal students will have had experience with traditional cultural activities. As one student explained, just because he is native, does not mean that he has an interest in or a talent for archery.

The teacher at our all-aboriginal urban school has created a learning environment that differs from the mainstream model. Rather than creating a program that strongly emphasizes formal skill instruction in a variety of activities, this teacher recognizes the value placed on participation and effort that her aboriginal students embody through their activity choices and social interactions in class. She disrupts traditional pedagogy by providing significant opportunities for students to do what they want to do in terms of activity choices, and she actively pursues the shy and quiet students to encourage their participation. She begins classes with games of low organization, includes fitness units that utilize the weight room, but also offers extended units of popular activities (volleyball was often a favourite). On our many school visits, we rarely observed any students who were not participating.

## Disrupting Mainstream Practices: The "Conversion Experience"

The example above illustrates how this physical education teacher worked outside the norms of mainstream teaching to develop meaningful activity programs. Similarly, teachers at an adolescent treatment centre and school for young people with severe emotional and behavioural challenges believed so much in the value of physical education, that they created opportunities for their students not only to have daily physical education, but also to be physically active for as much as 500 minutes per week (Halas 2002, 2003). The physical education teacher succeeded in creating a program that brought students "running to the gym" by being flexible, incorporating students' ideas, and downplaying the importance of skill instruction and competition. As with my own struggles to teach differently than the way I had been taught (Halas 1998), this teacher purposefully changed her philosophy of teaching (moving from an emphasis on skill instruction toward participation, effort, and fun), and the students reciprocated by getting involved in the class.

This change of attitude is sometimes referred to as the "conversion experience" (Brown 1998). It requires that physical educators move beyond a focus on skill instruction (O'Reilly 1998) to reflect deeply upon how they have been socialized to teach. To be effective, teachers must uncover their own values and attitudes, particularly as they have been shaped in Canadian society. That is where future physical educators can make the biggest difference.

As physical educators, we must make conscious efforts, on a daily basis, to disrupt white privilege as a means to make our gymnasiums and physical education programs more just and affirming for aboriginal students. For example, it might mean adapting our mainstream policies about changing for physical education class in recognition that the change room itself can be a racialized space where white and aboriginal bodies meet in unequal relations of social and economic power (see Champagne and Halas 2003). It may require changing our interschool sports policies so that aboriginal students who travel back and forth to their home communities during the school year are not penalized for "missing" practice. Coaches may have to arrange daycare or purchase infant car seats so that aboriginal parent-athletes can play in away games. It may mean that part of the physical education budget is spent on sweatsuits, t-shirts, and running shoes for students, both aboriginal and non-aboriginal, whose families cannot afford these items. In today's image-conscious Western society, "fitting in" often begins with the brand names of the clothes one is wearing: if all students cannot access the popular brand, exclusion is often unconsciously accepted and consequently students drop out without anyone bothering to find out why.

## Who Will Be the Allies for Aboriginal Youth?

Across North America, mostly white, European undergraduate students in faculties of physical education and education are preparing for careers where they will meet an increasingly diverse student population (Burden et al. 2004). In some parts of Canada (especially the Prairies), the aboriginal youth population is growing faster than any other demographic group. Aboriginal children and youth thirst for success in school and physical education. They are waiting for understanding teachers who will welcome them into their gymnasiums and onto their school teams. They are looking for the opportunity to make positive connections to their schools. They want to be physically active. Their health and wellbeing depend on an education system that will enhance their confidence in holistic ways that nurture their bodies, minds, and spirits. What they need are teachers who will understand them, include them, and work with them to create programs that are responsive to the cultural disconnect that many aboriginal youth experience in their mainstream, cross-cultural schools.

For many aboriginal youth, sport can be the bridge that helps them connect to their new school; physical educators who recognize this, and actively pursue new students as they arrive in the school, can contribute to their successful transition by inviting them into the gym. Aboriginal youth want to be healthy, and they want to take control over their personal health and wellness. What they need are physical education teachers who will communicate in ways that are less ethnocentric and more respectful of different cultures.

Although colonization is thought to have ended with the transfer of land from aboriginal peoples to the European colonizers, many colonial assumptions remain intact. The continued and pervasive belief system arising from colonization teaches both the colonizers and the colonized that the European way of life is superior to the aboriginal way of life. These assumptions need to be understood as limitations to our progress as a cross-cultural society. As Sapon-Shevin (1999) writes, the values we have learned from our families, advertising, the media, and personal experience can be interrupted.

> Happily, however, children are not born with prejudice; they do not come into the world believing that light skin is better than dark skin or that people who are large are self-indulgent and lazy, or that certain food preferences are disgusting and strange. Even young babies notice differences in people, but they do not instinctively attach positive or negative judgements to those differences....The good news then, is that these values are not inherent or inevitable, we can structure our classrooms so they are not learned, or, if necessary, so that they can be unlearned or replaced by different information. (50)

As physical educators, we have choices in how we design programs that will enable aboriginal youth to reach their full potential as active, healthy, human beings.

A few weeks after meeting Louise Champagne that first time for coffee, I met with her again. As we walked down Corydon Avenue in Winnipeg, she made an offhand comment that the only white people she "hung out" with were "revolutionaries," or those with "incredible personal integrity." When you become a physical educator working in schools where tremendous social and economic inequities prevail, which students will hang out with you?

## Notes

1. Janice Forsyth is an aboriginal athlete and scholar. These comments were made in a speech at the North American Indigenous Games Sport Leadership Panel in 2002.
2. Throughout the text of this chapter, I will use the terms *aboriginal* and *native*, depending on how they were first used in the citations being referenced.
3. I am very grateful this research project was funded by grants from the Social Sciences and Humanities Research Council of Canada and the Manitoba Health Research Council.
4. A white-dominated society is one in which cultural and national identities have been racialized and constructed around a white norm (Kelly 1998).
5. An ally is a member of an oppressor group who actively works to end forms of oppression that provide privileges unequally.

6. Claude Denis (1997) adopted the term *whitestream* as a means to convey the notion that Canadian society, though principally structured on the European, white experience, is more than a white society in socio-demographic, cultural and economic terms. Like the word *mainstream*, I find this term useful in that it captures the blended effect of whiteness as a socially constructed category; that is, people of colour can move into and out of the whitestream, dependent on their personal (and social) efforts to assimilate into racialized white culture.

7. For a discussion of the market value of race, see Li 1998.

8. Race can be viewed as the socially and legally constructed meanings applied to groups of people with similar physical appearance and ancestry (Haney López 1996). Racism is the institutionalization of social injustice based on skin colour, other physical characteristics, and cultural and religious difference.

9. Racialization is the process by which physical appearances come to assume certain meanings and expectations for human behaviour.

10. Although school drop-out and retention rates for aboriginal youth vary across Canada (Mackay and Myles 1995), in Manitoba (the province with the highest proportion of aboriginal peoples), non-aboriginal youth, aged 18–24 and living in Winnipeg, are approximately two and one-half times as likely as aboriginal youth to complete high school (Silver et al. 2002).

11. Critical race theory questions the asymmetries of power and privilege based on race.

12. Although all Indigenous peoples have a shared experience of colonization, particular experiences varied from one community to another. Aboriginal peoples are diverse peoples; in Canada, there are over 600 First Nations communities, each having a distinct history and culture. Just as there is no one experience of being white in Canada, the same applies to aboriginal peoples, and future educators need to acknowledge this diversity in their classrooms and schools.

13. Ethnocentrism is a belief in the superiority of one's own cultural group. Paraschak (1989) notes how this distortion, a consequence of Europeans' using their own cultural values to assess the actions of native peoples in mainstream sport, also contributes to the invisibility of native peoples in North American society.

14. As reported in highly personal narratives or journalistic reports (Teichroeb 1997), many former residents turned to alcohol and drugs as a means to erase their anger, pain, and confusion, as they were stuck between two cultures—the aboriginal way of life that they had lost, and the white culture of the conquerors.

# Appendix

## A Brief Overview of Residential Schooling

The residential school system was first introduced during the last quarter of the nineteenth century when representatives of the Dominion government made treaties with Indian chiefs as European settlement moved westward across Canada. To seek access to education for their children, many native bands negotiated with federal government officials for the establishment of schools. Aboriginal leaders had hoped that education would help their children learn new ways to make a living as they adapted to the changing socio-economic and cultural landscape brought on by the arrival of the foreigners (Miller 1996). At the time, they did not know that the residential schools would be designed as an oppressive form of cultural assimilation that merged religion (Christianity) with property value: the European conquerors wanted the land and resources of what is now called Canada.

As a consequence, generations of native children were removed from their families and communities and forced to attend poorly funded schools that were run by inadequately trained officials who imposed a curriculum of manual labour and religious indoctrination (Royal Commission on Aboriginal Peoples 1996; Sterling 1992). These harsh conditions, which were unsupervised by parents, who were not allowed contact with their children, included austere disciplinary regimes that helped create the type of environment that enabled many incidents of emotional, physical, and sexual abuse to occur.

By the 1950s, the federal government had amended the *Indian Act* to provide that children were to be integrated into the public school system. Soon students were given the option to attend the boarding schools as day students, or to be bussed to nearby towns where discrimination and exclusion on the basis of race and class in the white education system were common. To this day, many schools remain entrenched in Eurocentric values that provide poor educational outcomes for aboriginal youth (Silver et al. 2002).

Faced with continuous failure and drop-out rates of more than 90 percent in 1973, the federal government allowed the establishment of native-run, reserve-based schools (see Dyck 1997). Of note, the last government-run residential school was closed in the 1980s, some 100 years after the first such school was built. While culturally based schools exist (see the story of Joe Duquette High School in Haig-Brown et al. 1997), most aboriginal children living in urban centres continue to attend whitestream public schools.

The effects of the residential schools continue to resonate throughout many aboriginal communities. The Royal Commission on Aboriginal Peoples (as cited in Fournier and Crey 1997) summarized the situation for children and youth in the following words:

They are the current generation paying the price for cultural genocide, racism, and poverty, suffering the effects of hundreds of years of colonialist public policies. It's as though an earthquake has ruptured their world from one end to the other, opening a deep rift that separates them from their past, their history and their culture. They have seen parents and peers fall into this chasm, into patterns of despair, listlessness and self-destruction. They fear for themselves and their future as they stand at the edge. Yet Aboriginal youth can see across this great divide. Their concern about the crisis is leavened with a vision of a better tomorrow. (207)

## References

Adams, H. 1989. *Prison of grass: Canada from a Native point of view.* Revised Edition. Saskatoon, SK: Fifth House Publishers.

Bishop, A. 1994. *Becoming an ally. Breaking the cycle of oppression.* Halifax, NS: Fernwood Publishing.

Brown, S. 1998. The bush teacher as cultural thief: The politics of pedagogy in the land of the Indigene. *The Review of Education, Pedagogy & Cultural Studies* 20(2):121–39.

Burden, J., S. Hodge, C. O'Bryant, and L. Harrison, Jr. 2004. From colorblindness to intercultural sensitivity: Infusing diversity training in PETE programs. *Quest* 56(2):173–89.

Champagne, L., and J. Halas. 2003. "I quit!" Aboriginal students negotiate the "contact zone" in physical education. In *North American Indigenous Games Research Symposium Proceedings,* ed. V. Parashak and J. Forsyth, 55–64. Winnipeg, MB: Health, Leisure and Human Performance Research Institute.

Chrisjohn, R., S. Young, and M. Maraun. 1997. *The circle game.* Penticton, BC: Theytus Books.

Churchill, W. 1998. *A little matter of genocide: Holocaust and denial in the Americas 1492 to the present.* Winnipeg, MB: Arbeiter Ring Publishing.

Dei, G. 1998. The politics of educational change: Taking anti-racism education seriously. In *Racism and social inequality in Canada. Concepts, controversies and strategies of resistance,* ed. Vic Satzewich, 299–314. Toronto: Thompson Educational Publishing, Inc.

Denis, C. 1997. *We are not you. First Nations and Canadian modernity.* Peterborough, ON: Broadview Press.

Denzin, N., and Y. Lincoln. 1994. Entering the field of qualitative research. In *Handbook of qualitative research,* ed. Norman K. Denzen and Yvonna S. Liarder, 1–17. Thousand Oaks, CA: Sage Publications.

Douglas, D. 2005. Personal communications.

Dyck, N. 1997. *Differing visions: Administering Indian residential schooling in Prince Albert, 1867-1995.* Halifax, NS: Fernwood Publishing.

Dyer, R. 1997. *White.* London: Routledge.

Ellis, J. 1998. *Teaching from understanding: Teacher as interpretive inquirer.* New York: Garland Publishing.

Ennis, C. 1999. Creating a culturally relevant curriculum for disengaged girls. *Sport, Education and Society* 4(1):31–49.

Fournier, S., and E. Crey. 1997. *Stolen from our embrace.* Vancouver: Douglas & McIntyre.

Francis, D. 1992. *The imaginary Indian: The image of the Indian in Canadian culture.* Vancouver: Arsenal Pulp Press.

Grant, A. 2004. *Finding my talk: How fourteen native women reclaimed their lives after residential school.* Calgary, AB: Fifth House Limited.

Haig-Brown, C., K. Hodgson-Smith, R. Regnier, and J. Archibald, eds. 1997. *Making the spirit dance within: Joe Duquette High School and an aboriginal community.* Toronto: J. Lorimer & Co.

Halas, J. 1998. "Runners in the gym": Tales of resistance and conversion at an adolescent treatment center school. *Canadian Native Education Journal* 22(2):210–22.

————. 2002. Engaging troubled youth in physical education: An alternative program with lessons for the traditional class. *Journal of Teaching in Physical education* 21:267–86.

————. 2003. Culturally relevant physical education for students who have emotional and behavioral difficulties. In *Adapted Physical Activity in Canada,* ed. R. Steadward, G. Wheeler, and E. J. Watkinson, 285–303. Edmonton, AB: The University of Alberta Press and The Steadward Centre.

Halas, J., and T. Orchard. 2002. Culturally relevant physical activity for adolescent mothers: An action research study. *Physical and Health Education Journal* 68(1):42.

Halas, J., J. Forsyth, and G. Shultz. 2005. *Nobody wants to fail: Interrupting patterns that sustain and reproduce educational failure for marginalized children and youth.* Seven Oaks Distinguised Scholar Series, Winnipeg, Manitoba (Jan. 24–27, 2005).

Haney López, I. 1996. *White by law: The legal construction of race.* New York: New York University Press.

HRDC and Manitoba. 2002. *Aboriginal peoples in Manitoba.* Winnipeg, MB: Manitoba Aboriginal Affairs Secretariat.

Kelly, J. 1998. *Under the gaze: Learning to be black in white society.* Halifax, NS: Fernwood Publishing.

Kivel, P. 2002. *Uprooting racism: How white people can work for racial justice.* Gabriola Island, BC: New Society Publishers.

Ladson-Billings, G. 1994. *The Dreamkeepers: Successful teachers of African-American children.* San Francisco: Jossey-Bass Publishers.

———. 1995. Toward a theory of culturally relevant pedagogy. *American Educational Research Journal* 32(3):465–91.

Li, P. 1998. The market value and social value of race. In *Racism and social inequality in Canada: Concepts, controversies and strategies of resistance*, ed. V. Satzewich, 115–30. Toronto: Thompson Educational Publishing, Inc.

Mackay, R., and L. Myles. 1995. A major challenge for the education system: Aboriginal retention and dropout. In *First Nations education in Canada: The circle unfolds*, ed. M. Battiste and J. Barman, 157–78. Vancouver: University of British Columbia Press.

Martinek, T., and D. Hellison. 1997. Fostering resiliency in underserved youth through physical activity. *Quest* 49(1):34–49.

McIntosh, P. 1989, July–August. White privilege: Unpacking the invisible knapsack. *Peace and Freedom*: 10–12.

McLaughlin, M., and S. Heath. 1993. Casting the self: Frames of identity and dilemmas for policy. In *Identity and inner-city youth: Beyond ethnicity and gender*, ed. S. Heath and M. McLaughlin, 210–39. New York: Teachers College Press.

Miller, J. 1996. *Shingwauk's vision. A history of native residential schools*. Toronto: University of Toronto Press Inc.

O'Reilly, E. 1998. "Ooh, this sucks...I'll have to change the drill": Moving beyond technical reflection in physical education teacher education. *AVANTE* 4(1):22–39.

Paraschak, V. 1989. Native sport history: Pitfalls and promise. *Canadian Journal of Sport History* 1:57–66.

———. 1996. Racialized spaces: Cultural regulation, aboriginal agency, and powwows. *AVANTE* 2(1):7–18.

Ponting, J. 1998. Racism and stereotyping of First Nations. In *Racism and social inequality in Canada: Concepts, controversies and strategies of resistance*, ed. V. Satzewich, 269–98. Toronto: Thompson Educational Publishing, Inc.

Rosenberg, P. 1997. Underground discourses: Exploring whiteness in teacher education. In *Off white: Readings on race, power and society*, ed. M. Fine, L. Weis, L. C. Powell, and L. Mun Wong, 79–89. New York: Routledge.

Royal Commission on Aboriginal Peoples. 1996. Volume 4. *Perspectives and Realities*, 147–97. Ottawa, ON: The Commission.

Rumberger, R., and K. Larson. 1998. Student mobility and the increased risk of high school dropout. *American Journal of Education* 107(1):1–35.

Sapon-Shevin, M. 1999. *Because we can change the world: A practical guide to building cooperative, inclusive, classroom communities*. Boston: Allyn and Bacon.

Silver, J., K. Mallett, H. Greene, and F. Simard. 2002. *Aboriginal education in Winnipeg inner city schools*. Winnipeg, MB: Canadian Centre for Policy Alternatives–Manitoba.

Solorzano, D., and T. Yosso. 2002. Critical race methodology: Counter-storytelling as an analytical framework for education research. *Qualitative Inquiry* 8(1):23–44.

Sterling, S. 1992. *My name is Septeeza*. Toronto: Groundwood Books/Douglas & McIntyre.

Tauber, R. 1997. *Self-fulfilling prophesy: A practical guide to its use in education*. Westport, CT: Praeger.

Taylor, J. 1995. Non-native teachers teaching in native communities. In *First Nations education in Canada: The circle unfolds*, ed. M. Battiste and J. Barman, 224–44. Vancouver: University of British Columbia Press.

Teichroeb, R. 1997. *Flowers on my grave: How an Ojibwa boy's death helped break the silence on child abuse*. Toronto: HarperCollins.

UN General Assembly. Convention on the Prevention and Punishment of the Crime of Genocide. Adopted by Resolution 260 (III) A of the UN General Assembly on 9 December 1948.

Van Ingen, C., and J. Halas. 2003. Sites of learning? The challenge of location, racism and quality physical education for aboriginal youth in Manitoba schools. North American Sociology of Sport Society Conference, Montreal, 1 November 2003.

Weiss, C. 2001. Difficult starts: Turbulence in the school year and its impact on urban students' achievement. *American Journal of Education* 109(2):196–227.

**Author's Note:** I would like to acknowledge respectfully and thank all of the aboriginal youth participants, as well as their mostly non-aboriginal teachers, for assisting with the research project. Too, I thank Dr. Delia Douglas, a black Canadian scholar, for her theoretical contributions to this paper in progress. As always, Dr. Douglas's critique was very instructive for my own emerging white race-consciousness.

Chapter Ten

# Through Another Looking Glass:
## Gender, Social Issues, and the Media Impact on Body Image

## Jennifer D. Irwin and Patricia Tucker

### Introduction

Flipping through pages of fashion magazines, walking into popular cloth-ing stores, and looking around high school, college, and university cam-puses, it seems that Canadian youth are wearing less and less clothing. Ironically, this is happening at a time when rates for overweight and obesity are rising dramatically among the nation's youth. In fact, for the first time in history, over-nutrition has become responsible for more deaths than has starvation (Dulloo, Antic, and Montani 2002). Being overweight is associ-ated with numerous health concerns, including, but not limited to, diabe-tes, high blood pressure, heart disease, some cancers, and premature mor-tality (Calle et al. 2003; Freedman et al. 1999; Stevens et al. 1998). Being underweight is also associated with health risks such as dehydration, vita-min and mineral deficiencies, kidney and liver damage, infertility, and pre-mature mortality (Katzmarzyk 2001; Troiano et al. 1996). It is a confusing time; Canadians are encouraged to eat less, eat more, eat differently, and to look "perfect" by the diet industry, the media, the popularity of oversized fast-food portions, and the subtle and not-so-subtle societal demands to at-tain an "appropriate" body weight. It is not surprising that body-image anx-ieties are insidious among Canadians.

Social institutions, including the media, peer groups, and the family, provide numerous messages about the importance of being (ultra-)thin for females and muscular for males. Given that about one-quarter of Canadian adolescents and young adults are either overweight or obese (Tremblay, Katzmarzyk, and Willms 2002), and still more are not overweight but *perceive* themselves to be overweight, it is no surprise that young adults are prone to feelings of low self-esteem and dissatisfaction with their bodies. The feeling of body dissatisfaction is so common that it is considered a normal part of life, especially for females (Ohring, Graber, and Brooks-Gunn 2002). The fear of becoming overweight is so prevalent that young girls have reported that they are more afraid of getting fat than they are of having cancer or losing a parent (Berzins 1997). Nearly three-quarters of 15- and 19-year-old Canadian females have expressed the desire to lose weight (Health and Welfare Canada 1998) and 80 percent of 18-year-olds are afraid of becoming fat (Mellin, Irwin, and Scully 1992). Young adults' relationships with their bodies have become distorted to the point that having a healthy body image is now the exception rather than the rule. This lack of satisfaction leads to obsessive thoughts and behaviours that can result in detrimental outcomes such as eating disorders, social isolation, and participating in abusive relationships. Poor body image is a serious issue with serious ramifications; just because it is typical among the young adult population in Canada does not and should not mean that it is acceptable.

This chapter will explore the concept of body image, the differential experiences of males and females, and the influence of the media and social groups on body image; provide an overview of disordered eating, and suggestions for preventing poor body image and promoting positive body image among young adults; and discuss the influence teachers can have in promoting healthy bodies and minds.

## Body Image

Body image is "the subjective concept of one's physical appearance based on self-observation and the reactions of others" (The American Heritage Dictionary of the English Language 2000). An individual's body image is related to feelings of self-acceptance; self-esteem; social self-confidence; academic interest; assertiveness; athletic ability; self-understanding; and self-respecting behaviours related to drugs, alcohol, and sexual activity (Hesse-Biber, Clayton-Matthews, and Downey 1987; Public Health Agency of Canada 2004). A person's level of body (dis)satisfaction provides an accurate gauge of his or her body image. Adolescence through to young adulthood is marked by increased independence, the onset of romantic relationships, and dramatic changes in young adults' body image. For males, the change is typically more positive than for females. Males experience increased muscle mass and overall size, which more closely resemble the ideal male physique and thus enhance their body satisfaction. The fat that females gain during this time is a key contributor to body dissatisfaction. As the social ideal of thinness remains static, young women see their bodies changing and becoming more curvaceous (Sweeting and West 2002). Identifying, planning for, and making life choices such as academic or career pursuits, are done primarily during adolescence and early adulthood. Many young adults, however, are making these important life decisions against the backdrop of low self-esteem and low confidence. It is no wonder that adolescence is among the most stressful periods in one's life (Williams-Evans and Myers 2004).

## Body Image and Gender

At least half of the females in North America are dissatisfied with their bodies, and some researchers have estimated that almost all females experience body dissatisfaction over the course of their lifetimes (National Eating Disorder Information Centre 1987). Body dissatisfaction often facilitates negative and unhelpful thoughts and behaviours, such as feelings of inadequacy and low self-esteem, excessive calorie restriction, and not engaging in the ordinary activities of life such as wearing shorts or dipping into a pool on a hot summer's day. Researchers have found that females' body dissatisfaction is so powerful that it is often generalized to overall dissatisfaction in their lives, leading them to engage in detrimental behaviours, including disordered eating (discussed later) to choose to delay social activities, and even careers, until they lose what they consider to be a sufficient amount of weight (Cash and Pruzinsky 1990; Thompson 1990). A negative body image can be so powerful that it can paralyze a woman's physical, social, and emotional life. Women are more dissatisfied than men with their bodies, even though women have lower body mass index (BMI, a measure used to estimate body fat composition) levels, a lower incidence of being overweight, and a higher incidence of being underweight (Public Health Agency of Canada 2003). The fact that body dissatisfaction is an issue among Canadian females is undisputed. Unfortunately, this issue is becoming more common with males as well.

The vast majority of body image research has focused on females. Recently, however, increased attention has been paid to the growing problem of poor body image among males (Cohane and Pope 2001). Although studies have revealed consistently that males experience a higher level of body satisfaction than females (Graham et al. 2000; Public Health Agency of Canada 2002), researchers have found that 50–95 percent of males experience some level of body dissatisfaction (McCabe and Ricciardelli 2001). For young men, the physical ideal that seems to be particularly attractive is large muscles, especially in the stomach, chest, and arms (Cohane and Pope 2001; Labre 2002; McCabe and Ricciardelli 2001). Although this quest for larger bodies is the opposite of females' quest to be thin, the preoccupation with body size and shape is similarly damaging in males. For instance, body dysmorphia, a condition in which muscular males perceive themselves to be skinny, has been increasingly diagnosed among men. This inaccurate perception of one's physical appearance is associated with low self-esteem, eating disorders, and the choice to use anabolic steroids (Cohane and Pope 2001; Labre 2002). Men and women come in all different shapes, sizes, heights, and widths; yet many members of both genders seem uncomfortable with their bodies. Extensive societal messages about how they should look encourage both genders to set standards for themselves that are unreasonable and often dangerous to attain.

## Media and Peer Pressure

Socio-cultural influences, especially the media, exert the strongest pressures to be thin among adolescent girls (Tiggemann, Gardiner, and Slater 2000). Canadians spend approximately twenty-two hours each week watching television (Statistics Canada 2001) and still more viewing movies and reading magazines. During this downtime, people passively absorb messages that are anything but passive in their impact. The "ideal" body is pervasive in television shows and commercial advertising, and research has demonstrated that these messages have the power to affect and alter perceptions of the world (Nemeroff et al. 1994). As exposure to media images of thinness increases, people feel less positive about themselves and are more likely to experience an eating disorder (Becker et al. 2002; Groesz, Levin, and Murnen 2002).

The media has been seen as a powerful communicator of socio-cultural ideals and its messages can have a detrimental impact on the adolescent population. The media presents a "constant barrage of idealized images of extremely thin women" (Nemeroff et al. 1994; Xie et al. 2003) and endorses images and standards that are impossible for most women to achieve (Tiggemann, Gardiner, and Slater 2000). The vast majority of women, especially successful women, portrayed in the media are very thin and physically attractive. Watching music videos has been found to have a particularly strong and negative influence on young women's levels of body satisfaction (Tiggeman and Pickering 1996). Tiggemann, Gardiner, and Slater (2000) found adolescent girls' three main reasons for wanting to be thinner were the pressure they experienced from viewing models or other celebrities in the media, their desire to be more attractive, and their wish to receive more attention. The girls in this study frequently described models as "just looking perfect" and they recognized how the bombardment of media images could modify their views of what was "normal" (Tiggemann et al. 2000, 649). Although the body sizes of famous personalities are nowhere close to what is normal in society, the overwhelming number of media images led the girls to believe that the ultra-thin physique was normal and how everyone should look (Tiggemann et al. 2000).

The incessant focus on idealized physical appearance in the media is taking its toll on young people. Increasingly, children and adolescents are attempting to mould their bodies to mimic those of celebrities and media personnel. For instance, a quick search of the Internet will bring up dozens of stories of young women who have undergone surgery for buttock implants, with the desire to look more like the popular singer/dancer/movie star Jennifer Lopez. It is hard to imagine that a warped sense of self-improvement is not being facilitated by the current trend of transformational television shows that turn plain-looking people into glamorous beauties through plastic surgery, dental implants, special make-up, new clothes, etc. The predominant female physical ideal currently promoted by the media is that of an ultra-thin and lean physique. The popularity of physically fit movie stars is increasing, which may promote a more health-oriented physique. However, some researchers suggest that the way exercise is being promoted, particularly in women's magazines, may lead to "compulsive exercise," which, in turn, can lead to problems such as injury, excessive weight loss, and psychological issues that disrupt social competence (Nemeroff et al. 1994). Research studies have found that female adolescents who are exposed to more television have higher levels of disordered eating, and those who already experience body dissatisfaction have an even greater level of body image dissatisfaction when they are exposed to media images of thinness (Littleton and Ollendick 2003). To put the media's ideal female body type into context, the average North American female is 5 ft. 4 in. and 140 lbs. The models who portray the thin ideal weigh 13–19 percent less than the average North American female (Region of Peel).

Researchers argue that both the amount of media images viewed and the content in those images can contribute to body image concerns among young adults. Tiggemann and Pickering (1996) administered a questionnaire to ninety-four adolescent women to assess the amount and types of television programming they viewed in addition to their levels of body dissatisfaction and drive for thinness. Unlike other studies, the results of this study demonstrated that the amount of television watched by participants did not correlate with body dissatisfaction or a drive for thinness. However, the category of show (i.e., sports, soap operas, movies) predicted body dissatisfaction and viewing music videos predicted a drive for thinness. In addition to promoting the ideal appearance, the media often presents other damaging messages, such as "defining self-worth in terms of one's appearance, using non-nutritious foods for coping and the promise of transforming one's self [sic] through use of diet or exercise" (Littleton and Ollendick 2003, 55). For instance, in their assessment of magazine articles, Nemeroff et al. (1994) found that the articles which proclaimed that their content was about "self improvement" were actually about self-beautification and had nothing to do with building confidence or developing identity.

Although the above discussion has addressed primarily the effects of media images on female adolescents, male adolescents also experience body dissatisfaction as a result of the media's influence. Presently, the ideal appearance for the male adolescent is a muscular physique. Consequently, anabolic-androgenic steroid use has increased among men (Leit, Gray, and Pope 2002); in addition, there has been an increasing incidence of muscle dysmorphia (men become obsessed with muscularity and misperceive themselves as too thin). This suggests that the cultural ideal of hyper-mesomorphy may be as dangerous for men as the ultra-skinny ideal is for women (Leit, Gray, and Pope 2002). Leit, Gray, and Pope's results indicate that male adolescents' exposure to muscular male figures in the media produces increased body dissatisfaction in men.

## Peer Influences and Social Comparisons

Pressures provided by the media and peer pressure are leading to adolescents' increase in body dissatisfaction. An essential contributor to body image is social comparison, which is defined as the "cognitive judgments that people make about their own attributes compared to others" (Jones 2002, 646). Both same-sex peers and models/celebrities are subjects for social comparison. Jones's (2002) research suggests that both boys and girls compare their own bodies with those of models and peers, and are often left with severe feelings of body dissatisfaction. Stice, Maxfield, and Wells (2003) assessed 120 young women and found that exposure to social and peer pressures to be thin amplified body dissatisfaction. This increase is disconcerting because body dissatisfaction has been identified as the most potent risk factor for the onset of eating pathologies (Stice, Maxfield, and Wells 2003).

Regardless of a person's body size or shape, being teased about weight can be a powerful weapon against an adolescent or young adult's self-esteem, body satisfaction, and overall feelings about life. The influence of weight-based teasing has been underscored by some researchers who have found that adolescents who experience this type of teasing are significantly more likely to feel depressed and to think about and even attempt suicide (Eisenberg, Neumark-Sztainer, and Story 2003). In a study that helped to provide an understanding of who is most at risk for behaviours related to body dissatisfaction, Littleton and Ollendick (2003) found that dieting behaviours were most likely in girls if they were popular, teased about their weight, pressured to diet by peers, or had friends who engaged in dieting behaviours (56). Therefore peers' teasing and modeling behaviours play a powerful role in the development and maintenance of a negative body image.

## Self-Perception

The way we *think* our bodies look, regardless of our *actual* shape and size, is an important aspect of body image; body *perception* reflects overall satisfaction with, and distress about, our bodies. Historically, poor body image was associated with being too thin—the desirable, plump body was considered representative of family fertility and wealth (Xie et al. 2003). Today, dramatic shifts in body beliefs have occurred in Western cultures and the new ideal of the thin body is leading adolescents to strive for unhealthy standards. The standards are particularly unhealthy because many young adults experience a distorted view of their bodies and therefore do not know when they have reached a healthy-looking body size. Self-perceived weight has been identified as the main source of self-dissatisfaction (Pesa, Syre, and Jones 2000). Many young adults, males and females, have the experience of looking in the mirror and seeing the reflection of a body that is actually quite different from the one that is truly standing there. It is as if the "fun-mirrors" at carnivals provide the only visual feedback of these individuals' appearances.

Young women are more likely than young men to perceive themselves as overweight even when they are of normal weight or even underweight (Parkinson, Tovée, and Cohen-Tovée 1998; Tiggemann and Pennington 1990). The link between depressive feelings and body weight helps to illustrate the powerful influence that self-perceptions and body image have over us. For instance, Pesa, Syre, and Jones (2000) assessed psychological factors and body weight, and found that although overweight female adolescents suffer from low self-esteem, this was actually a result of poor body image and not of the weight itself. This finding is supported by Wadden et al. (1989), whose research revealed that "satisfaction with weight in obese and non-obese adolescent girls suggested that obese subjects were more dissatisfied with weight but not more depressed" (cited in Pesa, Syre, and Jones 2000, 335). This research suggests that without the influence of body image, depression is not a factor in differentiating overweight from non-overweight females (Pesa, Syre, and Jones 2000). Furthermore, the condition of being overweight is inadequate to cause psychological problems; rather, the continuous struggle to lose weight, in an attempt to meet the ideal physique, is the reason for anguish (ibid.). Shockingly, the discrepancy between perceived shape and actual shape has been found in children as young as eight years (Parkinson, Tovée, and Cohen-Tovée 1998). In contrast to young women, young men are more likely to perceive themselves as underweight and more likely to wish that they were more heavy-set than their perceived body shape. Although young men have these body-dysmorphic tendencies, they report consistently greater levels of satisfaction with their perceived bodies than their female counterparts (Public Health Agency of Canada 2002; Xie et al. 2003).

Not only do women tend to have inaccurate perceptions of the size and shape of their bodies, they also tend to have inaccurate perceptions about what the opposite sex finds attractive. Rozin and Fallon (1988) conducted a study in which they gave university students and their parents a continuum of body sizes and shapes. They asked the females (female students and female parents) to identify on this continuum the body shape that best represented their actual shape and size, the body they believed males found most attractive, and the body they would most like to have. They asked the males (male students and male parents) to identify the female body type they found most attractive. Both the female students and the mothers believed that they were heavier than their ideal bodies, and that their male counterparts preferred women thinner than those the men actually preferred. In fact, what men identified as attractive in women was nearly identical to what the women identified as their actual shapes and sizes!  One of the authors of this chapter was so struck by this study that she decided to replicate it in her class of first-year undergraduate students (without including their parents). The results were identical to those found by Rozen and Fallon some fifteen years earlier. Body dissatisfaction is not a phase or trend of the current generation of young adults; it has been around for decades and does not seem to have dissipated.

Distorted body perceptions are rampant in society. These misperceptions, coupled with equally distorted views of what the "ideal" body should look like, contribute to the current epidemic of body dissatisfaction. And, as if feeling bad about oneself because of what a mirror or scale says is not bad enough, these negative feelings can, and unfortunately often do, lead to more anguish through self-abusive behaviours.

## Disordered Eating

High levels of body dissatisfaction and a poor body image can make growing into adulthood an emotionally painful time, causing severe physical ramifications. Perhaps the most profound and best documented result of a poor body image is disordered eating. Disordered eating can be defined as including

> a variety of behaviors: unhealthy dieting, such as severe caloric restriction and use of meal supplements; unhealthy eating, such as consumption of large quantities of high fat foods or skipping meals; and anorexic and bulimic behaviors, such as laxative and diet pill use, cycles of binge eating and dieting, and self-induced vomiting. (Littleton and Ollendick 2003, 52)

In essence, disordered eating comprises severe and polarized deviations from "normal" eating. For example, some people with an eating disorder may not eat at all while others may binge, consuming very large amounts of food with apparently no self-control.

Out-of-control, overeating is associated with excessive body weight. The problem of overweight and obesity in Canada and all developed countries has been receiving a lot of attention in academic research as well as in the media. Currently, more than half of Canadians are either overweight or obese (Tremblay, Katzmarzyk, and Willms 2002). Carrying excessive body fat typically results from taking in more food energy than is put out (through physical activity, for example). Although it can play a role, genetic make-up accounts for very little when it comes to determining why people are overweight or obese (Fabsitz, Sholinsky, and Carmelli 1994; Weinsier 1999). The role of genetics can be understood by appreciating that some people are genetically predisposed to being overweight or obese, but what and how they eat and how they exercise will determine whether they become overweight or obese.

People overeat for a variety of reasons: a maladaptive response to emotional pain; a desire to hide their true self behind physical layers of body tissue; and because they were taught that excessive eating is "normal" by parental and other significant adult models during their formative years. Many overeaters are not conscious of their reasons for their dietary intake behaviours. On the other end of the weight spectrum, disordered eating can also result in excessive and potentially deadly thinness, as is the case with Anorexia Nervosa (AN).

It is extremely difficult to get accurate statistics on the number of people who have eating disorders. Many people with eating disorders are embarrassed to admit it, do not seek help, go undiagnosed by their health care providers, or have disordered behaviours without all of the characteristics required to classify them as having a specific type of eating disorder. Some researchers have estimated that approximately 20 percent of females between the ages of 12 and 30 suffer from a major eating disorder (Gilbert, Shaw, and Notar 2000; Nagel and Jones 1992). It is estimated that up to 4 percent of all females suffer from AN (Deshmukh and Franco 2003), and anywhere from 4–20 percent suffer from Bulimia Nervosa (BN) (Prouty, Protinsky, and Canady 2002; Zuckerman et al. 1986). This means that a large number of Canadian young women struggle with some form of disordered eating.

AN is perhaps the more visually recognized disorder. People with AN have a body weight that is less than 85 percent of their expected body mass index; yet they refuse to maintain weight and have a distorted view of their size. They have an extremely strong desire to lose weight and an intense fear of gaining weight and becoming fat, even though their bodies are much too thin to be healthy. Thinking about food, eating, and their outward appearance predominates in these sufferers' lives and achieving an extremely low weight becomes their perceived link to success and high self-esteem (American Psychiatric Association 2000; Ha, Marsh, and Halse 2003). The quick drop in weight among women typically causes amenorrhea, or cessation of their menstrual cycle for three or more consecutive months (ibid.). Amenorrhea puts women at increased risk for fragile bones and infertility.

Although people tend to think of a person with AN as someone who does not eat and is very skinny, there are actually two types of AN, or two paths that are taken to achieve the potentially deadly weight. The first type of AN is the restricting type, which consists of the individual's drastically minimizing her intake of food. The second type of AN is the binging/purging type, which consists of the individual's engaging in binge-eating followed by purging behaviour (i.e., self-induced vomiting, misusing laxatives, diuretics, or enemas) (American Psychiatric Association 2000). Many sufferers maintain long-term distorted body images and body dissatisfaction, and almost 6 percent of people who suffer from AN die (Sullivan 1995). Sadly, most of the people with the disorder do not appreciate the seriousness of their condition (Ha, Marsh, and Halse 2003). Regardless of the type of AN, the American Psychiatric Association describes four objectives of treatment: return the person to a healthy weight; treat any physical problems; boost motivation to cooperate with treatment; and teach people with AN about healthy nutrition and eating habits. Because AN results from distorted perceptions about the physical self, an additional objective of treatment is to shift destructive thought patterns, attitudes, and feelings. It is essential that the recovering AN sufferer have social support; therefore, soliciting the support of friends and family is key for successful treatment and relapse prevention. Treatment for AN is meeting with better success than ever before. Although it might feel like they are "butting in" or being nosy, it is *critical* for those close to people who are likely suffering from the disorder to summon their courage and to contact a professional for guidance and help.

People with Bulimia Nervosa tend to evaluate themselves based predominantly on their body weight and shape, and this distortion leads to recurrent episodes of binge-eating. During their binges, people will consume much larger quantities of food than what is typical for them in that given time period. For example, rather than eating a sandwich, which might take five or ten minutes, a binge during that period of time may consist of five sandwiches and a tub of ice cream. While binging, the person with BN experiences a lack of control and an inability to stop eating. Attempts to compensate for the influx of food include self-induced vomiting;

misuse of laxatives, diuretics, enemas, or other pharmaceuticals; fasting; or extreme exercise (American Psychiatric Association 2000). People with diagnosed BN typically binge at least twice a week over a period of at least three months.

Because bulimia tends to be thought of as "people eating a lot and throwing-up," it is important to be aware of other behaviours that can help to identify someone who is struggling with this condition. As with AN, there are two types of BN. The individual who regularly engages in self-induced vomiting or the misuse of laxatives, diuretics, or enemas characterizes the purging type of BN. The non-purging type of BN is characterized by the use of other compensatory behaviours, such as extreme exercise or fasting, but without the regular use of laxatives, self-induced vomiting, or purging methods (American Psychiatric Association 2000).

People with BN are typically treated with nutritional counselling and psychotherapy (Hay 2002). Changing destructive thought patterns is essential and sometimes antidepressant medications are required to assist with the psychological turmoil that often accompanies BN (American Psychiatric Association 2000). Little is known about the long-term efficacy of BN treatment, although one study found that 60 percent of people who underwent BN treatment had positive, healthy outcomes (Miller 2000).

Eating disorders are among the most extreme results of having a poor body image. Preventing a poor body image and promoting a positive body image are essential for the emotional, physical, and social health of a person.

## What Can Be Done?

It is imperative that a healthy body image be promoted during adolescence, when body fat increases and girls become concerned about their body weight and appearance. This is when girls typically start to diet and to develop unhealthy weight-reducing behaviours. Boys also experience physical changes during adolescence that can be difficult to manage and that might negatively affect their body image. Like most health-related behaviours, it is much easier to create positive behaviours *before* the negative ones have become established. It is more difficult to change behaviours after they have become normalized. The good news is that researchers have found that interventions can work and have long-lasting effects on the self-esteem and body image of young adults. For example, the "Everybody's Different" program (O'Dea 1995), which is a school-based educational program aimed at building general self-esteem to improve body image, had a positive and meaningful impact on the secondary-school students who received it, and those results lasted for at least one year (O'Dea and Abraham 2000).

Fostering positive self-esteem and a healthy body image does not have to be difficult. For example, promoting participation in daily, non-competitive physical activity is a very useful tool for increasing self-esteem and body image among young adults; the stress relief benefits of exercise, combined with the sense of doing something "kind" for one's body, enhance self-esteem, self-confidence, and body image. Using familial, teacher, and peer influence to make weight prejudice and *fatism* unacceptable is important in the quest for kinder ways to view others and ourselves. Focusing on healthy eating rather than eating for weight loss is also essential in helping young people establish long-term, healthy lifestyles. Given the influence that peer groups have over their members, it would be valuable for young adults to be reminded to spend time with people who make them feel valued and appreciated, and to find hobbies that make them feel good about themselves (Health Canada 2002). Youth and adults of all ages receive more than enough messages about the "value" of being thin. What they need to hear are messages about the "value" of honouring themselves through healthy eating, exercise, and stress management; accepting themselves and whatever package they come in; affecting other people's lives in a kind way; learning to receive compliments; listening and not judging; and celebrating mistakes as keys for learning. Not only are these tips for promoting a healthy body image and preventing disordered eating, they are also tips for fostering healthy self-esteem and overall life satisfaction in young people. Teachers may have the most promising influence on young adults' bodies and minds during adolescence.

## Teachers' Roles in Promoting Healthy Minds and Bodies

Teachers of all disciplines can play a role in the promotion of healthy minds and bodies, by focusing on decreasing "dieting," enhancing healthy eating, and promoting a positive body image. Teachers' integration of body image issues within their curricula would be ideal, and could include gender and media influence on body image; social, cultural, and political influences on body dissatisfaction; anti-discrimination, acceptance, and inclusion sessions; lessons on challenging stereotypes; and the exploration of self-esteem. (Children's Health Development Foundation 2004).

Physical and health education teachers, specifically, can focus their curriculum on providing students with body image knowledge; encouraging self-esteem and self-acceptance, healthy balanced eating, and active and fun lifestyles; and providing physical activity lessons that "cater to all sizes, shapes and skill levels" (ibid.). It is important that physical and health education teachers help to make movement fun and that they never use physical activity as a punishment; making physical activity fun is critical for the maintenance of an active lifestyle. Furthermore, it is essential that they provide an environment that supports all body sizes, shapes, and physical abilities, in addition to promoting the development of a strong sense of self. To promote a healthy body image in physical and health education classes, the Children's Health Development Foundation (2004) suggests that teachers

◈ talk about play and fun, rather than lecturing about the health message;

◈ celebrate the experience of movement;

◈ promote physical activity for enjoyment and as an integral part of everyday life, rather than for weight loss or changing body shape;

◈ create supportive environments that cater to all interests, shapes, sizes, skills, and fitness levels, which may mean gender-specific activities;

◈ believe and promote the message that active and healthy people are a diverse range of body types, shapes, and sizes;

◈ provide students with activities that enable them to feel good about their bodies because the activities are pleasurable and challenging, and develop their capabilities;

◈ avoid health and fitness tests that compare body fat and weight against a norm or against other students;

◈ provide opportunities for both groups and individuals;

◈ encourage and design activities based on fun, action, and cooperation; and

◈ model acceptance and appreciation of one's own body. (27)

Given that boys and girls have differing body image concerns, it seems only appropriate to approach the subject differently with each group. Therefore, physical and health education teachers should consider developing gender-specific lessons which accommodate each gender's issues.

When dealing with individual students who may be suffering from poor body image, it is important to focus on increasing their self-esteem, and on providing them with life and wellness skills (Children's Health Development Foundation 2004). One should also encourage the students (especially females) to not compare themselves to other students, and to have more confidence in their own abilities and achievements.

The Children's Health Development Foundation (2004) has provided several questions (adapted below) that teachers might think about or use in their discussions with students:

1.   What is body image?

2.   What does the word *healthy* mean to you? What types of pictures do you think of when you hear this word?

3.   Why do we associate some looks with being healthy?

4.   How are people of each shape treated in society?

5.   How is body image related to health?

6.   Do you think celebrities always feel good about themselves and think they look good?

7.   Have you seen or read anything in the media that has made you feel good or bad about your body? (114–20)

## Conclusion

Canadian society is filled with messages inviting young adults to feel negatively about themselves and their bodies. Media images of thin females and muscular males represent the current idealized description of physical attractiveness (Jones 2002). All forms of media can and do negatively affect adolescents' body image. Appearance magazines have markedly increased the number of images that have reiterated the importance of the idealized appearance (ibid.), and adolescents have stated that the "idealized body" is everywhere (Tiggemann, Gardiner, and Slater 2000). Young adults are experiencing distorted views of their bodies, going to extreme and often dangerous lengths to achieve the elusive "thin ideal" or "muscular ideal," and are experiencing very high levels of body dissatisfaction and very low self-esteem.

More than half of Canadians are either overweight or obese (Tremblay et al. 2002), and one in ten is underweight (Che 2002). We are dealing with two concurrent epidemics and finding the healthy midpoint feels both fragile and elusive. At one extreme, the country has never experienced such a high incidence of overweight and obesity. At the other extreme, it is a country of people with distorted views of their physical bodies coupled with an unhealthy desire for attaining the promoted physical ideals of ultra-thinness for women and ultra-muscularity for men. Rather than spending so much energy on how we ought to look, we should invest time and energy in how we ought to treat ourselves and others. Through healthy eating, regular physical activity, the practice of condemning any and all kinds of prejudice and teasing, and stress management strategies, the nation's youth and not-so-youthful will have a better chance at experiencing a healthy sense of self and, therefore, a more positive image of their bodies and their lives.

## References

American Heritage Dictionary of the English Language, 4th ed. Boston: Houghton Mifflin Company. Updated in 2003. Available at: www.bartleby.com

American Psychiatric Association. 2000. Practice guideline for the treatment of patients with eating disorders (revision). *American Journal of Psychiatry* 157 (suppl):1–39.

Becker, A. E., R. A. Burwell, S. E. Gilman, D. B. Herzog, and P. Hamburg. 2002. Eating behaviours and attitudes following prolonged exposure to television among ethnic Fijian adolescent girls. *British Journal of Psychiatry* 180:509–14.

Berzins, L. 1997. Dying to be thin: The prevention of eating disorders and the role of federal policy. APA co-sponsored congressional briefing. Available at: www.apa.org/ppo/issues/pbrfweb2.html

Calle, E. E., C. Rodriguez, K. Walker-Thurmond, and M. J. Thun. 2003. Overweight, obesity, and mortality from cancer in a prospectively studied cohort of U.S. adults. *The New England Journal of Medicine* 348:1625–38.

Cash, T. F., and T. Pruzinsky. 1990. *Body images: Development, deviance, and change.* New York: The Guilford Press.

Che, J. 2002. Underweight Canadians. Canadian social trends. Statistics Canada Catalogue No. 11-008. Available at: www.statcan.ca/english/kits/pdf/social/underweight.pdf

Children's Health Development Foundation. 2004. Absolutely every body promoting and developing healthy weight and healthy body image: A health promoting schools approach to managing childhood overweight and obesity. Available at: http://activated.decs.act.gov.au/hps/tl/documents/AbsolutelyEveryBodyResource.pdf

Cohane, G. H., and H. G. Pope. 2001. Body image in boys: A review of the literature. *International Journal of Eating Disorders* 29:373–79.

Deshmukh, R., and K. Franco. 2003, December. *Eating disorders.* The Cleveland Clinic Disease Management Project.

Dulloo, A. G., V. Antic, and J. P. Montani. 2002. Pathogenesis of the worst killers of the 21ˢᵗ century. *International Journal of Obesity* 26 (suppl 2):S1–S2.

Eisenberg, M. E., D. Neumark-Sztainer, and M. Story. 2003. Associations of weight-based teasing and emotional well-being among adolescents. *Archives of Pediatric and Adolescent Medicine* 157:733–38.

Fabsitz, R. R., P. Sholinsky, and D. Carmelli. 1994. Genetic influences on adult weight gain and maximum body mass index in male twins. *American Journal of Epidemiology* 140(8):711–20.

Freedman, D. S., W. H. Dietz, S. R. Srinivasan, and G. S. Berenson. 1999. The relation of overweight to cardiovascular risk factors among children and adolescents: The Bogalusa heart study. *Pediatricas* 103(6):1175–82.

Gilbert, A. A., S. M. Shaw, and M. K. Notar. 2000. The impact of eating disorders on family relationships. *Eating Disorders: The Journal of Treatment and Prevention* 8(4):331–45.

Graham, M. A., C. Eich, B. Kephart, and D. Peterson. 2000. Relationship among body image, sex, and popularity of high school students. *Perceptual and Motor Skills* 90:1187–93.

Groesz, L. M., M. P. Levin, and S. K. Murnen. 2002. The effect of experimental presentation of thin media images on body satisfaction: A meta-analytic review. *International Journal of Eating Disorders* 31:1–16.

Ha, M. T., H. W. Marsh, and C. Halse. 2003. Taking a closer look at adolescent girls with anorexia nervosa: How different are they to non-clinical adolescent girls in terms of self-concept and body image? Unpublished paper presented at the New Zealand Association for Research in Education and Australian Association for Research in Education Conference, Auckland, New Zealand. November 2003.

Hay, P. J. 2002. Integrating treatment in eating disorders. *Psychiatric Times* 19:7.

Health and Welfare Canada. 1998. *Canadian guidelines for healthy weights*. Ottawa: Supply and Services Canada.

Health Canada. 2002. *Boosting self-esteem*. Office of Nutrition Policy and Promotion. Available at: www.hc-sc.gc.ca/hpfb-dgpsa/onpp-bppn/boosting_esteem_e.html

Hesse-Biber, S., A. Clayton-Matthews, and J. Downey. 1987. The differential importance of weight and body image among college men and women. *Genetic, Social and General Psychology Monographs* 113:509–28.

Jones, D. C. 2002. Social comparison and body image: Attractiveness comparisons to models and peers among adolescent girls and boys. *Sex Roles* 45(9/10):645–64.

Katzmarzyk, P. T. 2001. Obesity in Canadian children. *Canadian Medical Association Journal* 164(11):1563.

Labre, M. P. 2002. Adolescent boys and the muscular male body ideal. *Journal of Adolescent Health* 30:233–42.

Leit, R. A., J. J. Gray, and H. G. Pope. 2002. The media's representation of the ideal male body: A cause for muscle dysmorphia? *International Journal of Eating Disorders* 31: 334–38.

Littleton, H. L., and T. Ollendick. 2003. Negative body image and disordered eating behavior in children and adolescents: What places youth at risk and how can these problems be prevented? *Clinical Child and Family Psychology* 6(1):51–66.

McCabe, M. P., and L. A. Ricciardelli. 2001. Body image and body change techniques among young adolescent boys. *European Eating Disorders Review* 9:335–47.

Mellin, L. M., C. E. Irwin, and S. Scully. 1992. Prevalence of disordered eating in girls: A survey of middle-class children. *Journal of the American Dietetic Association* 92: 851–53.

Miller, K. E. 2000. Practice guideline for the treatment of patients with eating disorders (revision). *American Journal of Psychiatry* 157(suppl):1–39.

Nagel, K. L., and K. H. Jones. 1992. Sociological factors in the development of eating disorders. *Adolescence* 27(105):107–14.

National Eating Disorder Information Centre. 1987. Working towards a positive body image. *Body Image and Self Esteem* 2(2):1–4. Available at: www.nedic.ca/newsletters.html

Nemeroff, C. J., R. I. Stein, N. S. Diehl, and K. M. Smilack. 1994. From the Cleavers to the Clintons: Role choices and body orientation as reflected in magazine article content. *International Journal of Eating Disorders* 16(2):167–76.

O'Dea, J. 1995. *Everybody's different: A self-esteem program for young adolescents.* Sydney: University of Sydney Press.

O'Dea, J., and S. Abraham. 2000. Improving the body image, eating attitudes and behaviors of young male and female adolescents: A new educational approach that focuses on self-esteem. *International Journal of Eating Disorders* 28:43–57.

Ohring, R., J. A. Graber, and J. Brooks-Gunn. 2002. Girls' recurrent and concurrent body dissatisfaction: Correlates and consequences over 8 years. *International Journal of Eating Disorders* 31:404–15.

Parkinson, K. M., M. J. Tovée, and E. M. Cohen-Tovée. 1998. Body shape perceptions of preadolescent and young adolescent children. *European Eating Disorder Review* 6:126–35.

Pesa, J. A., T. R. Syre, and E. Jones. 2000. Psychosocial differences associated with body weight among female adolescents: The importance of body image. *Journal of Adolescent Health* 26:330–37.

Prouty, A. M., H. O. Protinsky, and D. Canady. 2002. College women: Eating behaviors and help-seeking preferences. *Adolescence* 37(146):353–63.

Public Health Agency of Canada. 2002. Trends in the health of Canadian youth: health behaviours in school-aged children. Chapter 5 Coping with Life. Available at: www.phac-aspc.gc.ca/dca-dea/publications/hbsc_05_e.html

Public Health Agency of Canada. 2003. Women's Health Surveillance Report Body weight and body image. Available at: www.phac-aspc.gc.ca/publicat/whsr-rssf/chap_4_e.html

Public Health Agency of Canada. 2004. Canadian Health Network. How can I help my daughter have a healthy body image? Available at: www.canadian-health-network.ca/servlet/ContentServer?cid=1076701764838&pagename=CHN-RCS%2FCHNResource%2FFAQCHN ResourceTemplate&c=CHNResource&lang=En

Region of Peel. Body image & the media...What's the connection? Available at: www.region.peel.on.ca/health/commhlth/bodyimg/media.htm

Rozin, P., and A. Fallon. 1988. Body image, attitudes to weight, and misperceptions of figure preferences of the opposite sex: A comparison of men and women in two generations. *Journal of Abnormal Psychology* 97(3):342–45.

Statistics Canada. 2001. The Daily Television Viewing. Available at: www.statcan.ca/Daily/English/010125/d010125a.htm

Stevens, J., J. Cai, E. R. Pamuk, D. F. Williamson, M. J. Thun, and J. L. Wood. 1998. The effect of age on the association between body-mass index and mortality. *New England Journal of Medicine* 338:1–7.

Stice, E., J. Maxfield, and T. Wells. 2003. Adverse effects of social pressure to be thin on young women: An experimental investigation of the effects of "Fat Talk." *International Journal of Eating Disorders* 34:108–17.

Sullivan, P. F. 1995. Mortality in anorexia nervosa. *American Journal of Psychiatry* 152:1073–74.

Sweeting, H., and P. West. 2002. Gender differences in weight related concerns in early to late adolescense. *Journal of Epidemiology and Community Health* 56:700–01.

Thompson, J. K. 1990. *Body-image disturbance: Assessment and treatment.* Elmsford, NY: Pergamon Press.

Tiggemann, M., M. Gardiner, and A. Slater. 2000. "I would rather be size 10 than have straight A's": A focus group study of adolescent girls' wish to be thinner. *Journal of Adolescents* 23:645–59.

Tiggemann, M., and B. Pennington. 1990. The development of gender differences in body-size dissatisfaction. *Australian Psychology* 25(3):306–13.

Tiggemann, M., and A. M. Pickering. 1996. Role of television in adolescent women's body dissatisfaction and drive for thinness. *International Journal of Eating Disorders* 20(2):199–203.

Tremblay, M. S., P. T. Katzmarzyk, and J. D. Willms. 2002. Temporal trends in overweight and obesity in Canada, 1981–1996. *International Journal of Obesity and Related Metabolic Disorders* 26(4):538–43.

Troiano, R. P., E. A. Frongillo, J. Sobal Jr., and D. A. Levitsky. 1996. The relationship between body weight and mortality: A quantitative analysis of combined information from existing studies. *International Journal of Obesity* 20:63–75.

Wadden, T. A., J. A. Sternberg, K. A. Letizia, A. J. Stunkard, and G. D. Foster. 1989. Treatment of obesity by very low calorie diet, behavior therapy, and their combination: A five-year perspective. *International Journal of Obesity* 13(suppl 2):39–46.

Weinsier, R. L. 1999. Genes and Obesity: Is there reason to change our behaviors? *Annals of International Medicine* 130:938–39.

Williams-Evans, S. A., and J. S. Myers. 2004. Adolescent violence. *Association of Black Nursing Faculty Journal* 15(2):31–34.

Xie, B., C. Lui, C. Chou, J. Xia, D. Spruijt-Metz, J. Gong, Y. Li, H. Wang, and C. A. Johnson. 2003. Weight perception and psychological factors in Chinese adolescents. *Journal of Adolescent Health* 33:202–10.

Zuckerman, D. M., A. Colby, N. C. Ware, and J. S. Lazerson. 1986. The prevalence of bulimia among college students. *American Journal of Public Health* 76(9):1135–37.

Chapter Eleven

# *Rural Schools/Rural Communities:*
## *Partnerships Between Physical and Health Educators and Public Health Nurses*

## Aniko Varpalotai and Beverly D. Leipert

### *Introduction*

The purpose of this chapter is to explore the mutual challenges and benefits for physical and health educators and public health nurses as they work in partnership in rural schools and communities. Many rural communities have experienced a decline in accessible health care with the closure of small hospitals, the downsizing of rural health unit staff, and the difficulties of recruiting rural health care providers. Rural communities are also experiencing major demographic changes and continued threats of school closures and amalgamations. Despite these challenges, we propose that rural schools are important and viable sites for accessible and appropriate health education, health promotion, and illness- and injury-prevention activities through the collaboration of educators and public health nurses, together with other health care practitioners who might be available to the community. The late twentieth century saw a convergence of health and educational policies:

> the issue of broader community involvement and the need for greater interdependence between the education and service sectors paralleled the principle of comprehensive school health that called for broad community ownership in planning for a healthy school community. (Mytka 1995, 90)

In addition to being locations for student education, rural schools often serve as community centres, recreation facilities, and providers of adult education programs. The "community school" model can be extended to incorporate health care. Some of the diverse issues which can be addressed through the educator/public health nurse partnership include education and health promotion related to nutrition; weight and body image; gender and sexuality issues; relationships and counselling; teen pregnancies; domestic violence; mental health; and parenting issues. The expertise of the public health nurse, combined with the knowledge of various subject specialists, can offer rural schools services not often available otherwise in rural communities. The public health nurse provides support services for students, teachers, and parents, which fosters success in education, improved community health, and the initiation of a coordinated health service, beginning with early childhood.

Small rural schools present special challenges for the physical and health education specialist. This chapter will examine the significance of these subjects, particularly health, for rural schools, and ways in which teachers can address issues of scarce resources and multigrade classes, as well as other geographic and cultural factors, in partnership with community health care providers, such as public health nurses. Based on research and experience in rural schools and communities in southwestern Ontario, rural Saskatchewan, northern British Columbia, and elsewhere, we will examine issues of particular concern to rural educators and public health nurses and the ways in which teachers and public health nurses can work together to promote relevant and appropriate health education in the most comprehensive way possible.

## Health Education in Rural Schools

According to the Ontario Ministry of Education and Training (1999):

> The health and physical education curriculum...promotes important educational values and goals such as tolerance, understanding, excellence, and good health. These values are reinforced in other curriculum areas, as well as in society itself. Parents, schools, health-care agencies, peers, businesses, government, and the media are all vital partners in helping promote these values to students. Working together, schools and communities can be powerful allies in motivating students to achieve their potential and lead safe, healthy lives. (3)

Our observations arise from our backgrounds: as a teacher educator in the areas of health education, gender issues and educational policies, and as a rural/farm resident; and as a public health nurse/nurse educator/researcher in rural and remote communities in various regions across Canada. Together we bring perspectives from within both the school and the community, from both educators and health care practitioners. In both environments the following holds true:

> wherever a school exists, the professionals who work within it must focus their pedagogical energy on the immediate place inhabited by the school; that is, they must make the word "local" in the phrase "local school" mean something if we are ever to be successful at elevating a sense of community in this society. (Theobald 1997, 1)

All teachers, regardless of location, ought to familiarize themselves with their communities and the availability of resources both within and around their schools, and develop creative and engaging curricula for their students. Rural teachers, however, share some particular concerns which will be addressed in this chapter as they relate specifically to the teaching of physical education and health, and the accessibility of community resources in these areas.

The Rozanski Report (Rozanski 2002) notes that schools often serve as delivery centres for services which complement their educational mission, including health and social services, and that they are often also community hubs where many local activities take place. The Downey Report (Downey 2003) expresses several concerns regarding rural education: multigrade classes; the need for specialist teachers; the lack of specialized teaching spaces such as a gymnasium; and transportation issues, including their impact on extracurricular activities . Downey also recommends that if school consolidation (closure) were being recommended, the recreational and other community contributions of the local school should be recognized and taken into account before any final decisions were made by the local school board (see also Rural school advocates 2003).

Thus, physical and health education in the rural school takes on a broader, community and whole-school perspective, transcending the specifics of the provincially mandated curriculum for physical and health education classes. Set within this larger context of the rural school as the primary provider of much of the physical education, physical activity, and health education and information that is accessible to rural residents both

young and old, the school's physical and health education specialists become even more central figures. They are called upon to educate not only
students, but also other teachers, parents, and sometimes the community as
a whole. They may also be the liaison between the school and community
health care practitioners, including public health nurses, dietitians, and
counsellors.

Although some of the issues discussed below could just as easily apply to urban schools, the concerns and ideas which follow come from case
studies and interviews, observations, and education students' practicum
experiences in rural Ontario schools, specifically those in the agricultural
regions of southwestern Ontario, and from ten years of public health nursing in rural Saskatchewan. Some of the ideas cited come from interviews
carried out with current and retired rural teachers who witnessed and experienced major changes to both education and the broader social landscape
during the past century.

The themes and recurring issues addressed below include the implications of long bus rides to and from school; the size, context, and culture
of the local school and community; facilities, equipment, and other resources that are accessible both within the school and within the broader
surrounding community; teacher expertise; curriculum and extracurricular
or cocurricular activities; possibilities for daily physical education, fitness,
and health breaks; nutrition or breakfast programs; special needs, both individual and collective; primary versus secondary school programs and
needs; multigrade classrooms; and the potential of new information
technologies.

Implicit in the above list is the scope of what is considered to be
within the realm of physical and health education. In Ontario, the elementary health and physical education curriculum is organized into three
strands: healthy living, fundamental movement skills, and active participation. The secondary school health and physical education program, which
may include from one to seven credits (one is mandatory), involves various
levels of healthy active living education, health for life, recreation and fitness leadership, and exercise science (Ontario Ministry of Education and
Training 1999, 2000; OPHEA 2003). Although the mandated curriculum
is clear, all teachers and school administrators have a complementary role
in the general health and well-being of their students. Activities might include before- and after-school programs, as well as the use and development of the school facilities as a community resource for leisure and
recreational opportunities (Saskatchewan Education 1999). The commu-

nity school model provides mutual benefits to all members of the school and the wider community surrounding the school.

## The School Day: General Physical Activity and Health Concerns

On a typical day at a rural school, children arrive in the morning after a long bus ride. Some will have missed breakfast, others will have fallen asleep on the bus, and still others will have been up for several hours assisting with farm chores. It is clear that sleepy, hungry students are not ready to engage in the intellectual tasks facing them in their classrooms. Increasingly, universal breakfast programs are being introduced as a way of ensuring that all children have a nutritious start to the day, regardless of socioeconomic background. Although these programs were initially introduced only for needy students, the stigma attached to them, as well as the realization that other children were arriving at school without a proper breakfast, led to the offering of a universal breakfast program. Often cooperative ventures between parent volunteers, concerned educators, and local businesses, the programs are either free or at minimal cost, and ensure a good start to the day (Morgan 2003). Health educators are in a unique position to advocate for such programs in their schools because nutrition is a significant aspect of health at all levels of the curriculum. In addition to breakfast, some schools also offer snacks and lunches for those in need. Health educators, including public health nurses, also have a role to play by advocating the removal of junk food vending machines from schools and the provision of healthy snacks and wholesome and affordable cafeteria meals.

Some smaller schools are unable to hire or retain subject specialists in all curriculum areas. One small school visited by James Downey, the Ontario government-appointed advisor on small and remote schools, was able to offer a full program by sharing subject specialists in physical education, music, and the library with another small rural school in the district. The local Lions Club created and maintained an ice rink for the school (and community) each winter (Sweaburg school toured by small school advisor 2003). Another rural elementary school was able to provide a first-rate playground through the contributions of the local community. Fundraising was followed by the actual building of the playground; local farmers contributed their equipment and labour to the project. Other community school models use the school gymnasium and outdoor grounds year-round for fitness, sports leagues, seniors' programs, and summer day camps. Both the school and the community benefit from these shared facilities. The problem of multigrade classes is addressed through various professional development resources; some teachers are now choosing to teach two- and even three-grade-level classes because of the opportunities they provide for new learning and teaching initiatives (Saskatchewan Professional Development Unit 1997). With its large number of rural schools, Saskatchewan has become a leader in community education that emphasizes community involvement, the maximum use of resources, integrated services, inclusiveness, and lifelong learning (Saskatchewan 2003).

We encourage physical and health education student teachers, as well as practising teachers, to conduct a "physical activity and health audit" at their schools during their first practicums, or early on in a new teaching assignment. It is helpful to start with the current or most recent physical and health education teacher to find out how much and what types of formal physical and health education are included in the curriculum. Next, one should talk to school administrators, public health nurses, family studies teachers, guidance counsellors, coaches and intramural sport coordinators, and anyone else who engages in implementing broader forms of physical activity and health promotion within the school. This may include the provision of birth control information by a nurse or school counsellor to individual students; school-wide assemblies on substance abuse, safety, or anti-violence initiatives; the visibility of health-promoting posters, pamphlets, and other types of information; before- and after-school or lunchtime activity programs; and relevant school clubs. The point is that there are many opportunities for physical and health education in the school. Neither health nor physical education needs to be confined to the few hours devoted to each of these important subjects in the formal curriculum. Although the physical and health education specialist ought to be central to the development and coordination of such programs, many others may be called upon to assist and support these ventures.

## Health Education

Whereas physical education is confronted by practical challenges of space, equipment, availability of specialist teachers, and differing levels of abilities or skills of students in small or multigrade classes, health education is often challenged by cultural and religious issues and a lack of specialized local health services, particularly related to mental health (Trute et al. 1994). It is imperative for teachers in rural schools who are not familiar with the culture of the community, to become informed about their students' cultural backgrounds. Health issues such as nutrition, hygiene, sex education, and personal relationships, are deeply embedded in cultural assumptions and practices. Although the provincial curriculum appears to be standardized and acultural, it behooves a teacher who is new to a community to become aware of the prevailing religious beliefs, ethnic practices, and even livelihoods of the families within the school. Are there groups of parents who would likely object to any type of sex education on religious or moral grounds? Might there be cases of abuse of women and children? Isolated communities often do not or cannot offer the services (e.g., shelters) or public transportation necessary for women to leave abusive homes (Leipert and Reutter 1998; Leipert and Reutter 2005). Close-knit communities, where many families are related to each other, may make it difficult for discussion about such matters to take place.

If these sensitive issues are raised in the classroom, is the teacher prepared for disclosures that may follow? What kinds of resources *are* available in the community should someone disclose abuse of women or children, concerns about sexual orientation, mental health concerns, or an eating disorder? And, beyond the general curriculum, how should one address the individual needs of sexually active or pregnant teenagers, gay and lesbian or bisexual students, or others with concerns that are not generally discussed openly in their families, churches, or communities? What is the role of the health teacher? Is the school prepared to offer counselling or other services for students in need? Are there experts in the surrounding community who can be called upon to assist? These are all controversial issues that need to be addressed by health teachers and school administrators, thereby creating a climate that fosters further discussion and referral to the necessary support services. Because physical and health educators often become the resource persons in these matters, they must be up-to-date, knowledgeable, approachable, and open to students' and communities' diverse needs.

In the past, rural teachers emerged from the rural communities in which they lived. Today, the recruitment and retention of rural teachers are problems in many areas, particularly where a school board encompasses both rural and urban schools, as is increasingly the situation in Canada because of the amalgamation of rural and urban school boards into very large district school boards. The rapid turnover of teachers in some areas, and the fact that many teachers do not live in the communities in which they teach, mean that school administrators and individual teachers have to do additional work to initiate the new teachers into the school and its community, and that all new teachers must familiarize themselves with the surrounding culture to better inform their work. The following examples illustrate the potential for a collision between health issues and community sensitivities and interests.

◇ Tobacco farming continues to be a major enterprise in south-western Ontario. Not only do many students live on these farms, but even more work on tobacco farms in the summer and early fall (in fact, until recently, schools were allowed to overlook student absenteeism during the tobacco harvest, recognizing the economic necessity of this activity to the community). How does a health teacher follow the curriculum and address the harmful effects of smoking in this community? Despite many Ontario municipalities establishing by-laws banning smoking in public places, the rural counties where tobacco is grown have resisted such measures (No smoking by-law 2003, 5), and "there's a significantly higher percentage of daily smokers in the tobacco belts" (We're fat 2004, 1).

◇ PETA (People for the Ethical Treatment of Animals), the animal rights group, has targeted elementary schools as a part of their campaign against drinking cow's milk and eating meat. Someone dressed like a Holstein cow shows up at the gates of the schoolyard at the end of the day and hands pamphlets to the children discouraging them from drinking milk based on the alleged cruelty the dairy industry inflicts on dairy cows and their offspring, as well as the questionable benefits of cow's milk for humans (*London Free Press* 2001). How is a teacher in a community where dairy farming is a sizable industry to react? A similar campaign was launched in 2003 prior to the Thanksgiving weekend with actress Pamela Anderson's urging Canadians to go vegetarian and to say "No thanks to having a dead bird as a holiday centrepiece" (People for the Ethical Treatment of Animals 2003). Each of these examples highlights the controversy in rural communities where raising animals for food is central to the economy and illustrates health-related concerns when young teens choose to become uninformed vegetarians for ethical reasons. These issues also bring into relief the differences between urban and rural attitudes and realities, and in many parts of the country these two groups are increasingly sharing schools.

❖ Parents have written lengthy letters to the editor of the local weekly paper, objecting to sex education and claiming that it encourages premarital sex and contradicts their religious beliefs, for example by distributing condoms and condoning homosexuality (*Dutton Advance* 2001). How does one teach safer sex and tolerance for sexual diversities in a way that fulfills the curriculum guidelines yet respects community values and beliefs?

Although rural teachers must be sensitive to the local culture, they must also teach a curriculum that will prepare their students to live in the world beyond their immediate families and communities. Parents might deny the sexual activities of their children, but teenage pregnancies, sexually transmitted diseases, and suicides among gay youth, are all significant concerns in both urban and rural communities (Langille and Maritime Centre of Excellence for Women's Health 2000). The health teacher's responsibility is ultimately to the students, though preferably in cooperation and in harmony with the parents, school council, and broader community. Information nights for parents, held with local health care providers such as public health nurses, allow parents to discuss sensitive and controversial issues and to express their fears and concerns, while opening the door to dialogue with teachers and discouraging parents from simply reacting to what their children bring home from school. Such school outreach programs can address parents' sense of loss of control and their antagonism toward the school.

Because of their small size and community base, rural schools can be wonderful, sheltering, and caring places where everyone knows and cares about everyone else (Bonner 1997). Rural schools, however, can also be cruel and exclusive towards students and families who are newcomers or who—as often is the case with single parents, gays and lesbians, visible minorities, rebellious kids with piercings and dyed hair—go against community norms. The school is a place to facilitate acceptance, educate about fairness and equity, and help to build a more tolerant and caring community. The alternative is early drop-outs, with the long-term consequences that this brings for both the individual and the community: run-aways and further youth drain to cities where youth who are "different" can disappear into the relative anonymity of urban culture. Many of the "street kids" and young prostitutes in Toronto and other large cities come from small communities; they are trying to escape intolerable family and community situations, little realizing that they are putting themselves in even greater danger, yet having no other choices presented to them (Morton 2003;

Riordan 1996). One study of gay/lesbian/bi-sexual/transgendered (glbt) youth in rural Ontario recommends more education and awareness through schools to create safer, more supportive environments for these youth. As stated by one young participant in the study, "every glbt youth leaves this area as soon as they can and then there are no adult role models left for the next generation of youth" (Morton 2003, 117).

Comprehensive community health care is not new to rural communities. The Women's Institutes (Ambrose 1996) have been concerned with the health and wellbeing of their communities for more than a century. Rural communities are also developing community health clinics and wellness centres which house a variety of health care workers, including physicians, nurses, dieticians, social workers, and youth workers. These professionals can be resources to schools by providing direct health care (such as care provided by the public health nurse) and teaching resources in the classroom, and by informing students of what is available to them in their communities and through new and emerging information technologies.

The Internet is increasingly bridging rural/urban gaps. The government has made rural Internet access a priority, and many homes, schools, and public libraries in rural and First Nations communities are connected to the World Wide Web. This provides a useful educational resource but also a further challenge for students and teachers alike. Mangiardi (2003) cites a recent Statistics Canada study reporting that "9 out of every 10 individuals aged 15–19 reported using the Net in 2000; the largest proportion of any age group" (12). Another survey found that the Internet was the second major source of information regarding sexuality for 10th graders (their friends were the first) (Sieving, Oliphant, and Blum 2002, cited in Mangiardi 2003). How does one make sense of the multitude of information sources and often contradictory messages about health issues? Students are engaged in virtual relationships with one another, and with total strangers, through their computers. Teachers need to remain current and informed about youth culture and the types of information available on the Internet and include in the curriculum lessons about being critical consumers and about the benefits and dangers of the Internet.

Previously isolated communities suddenly have easy access to pornography, fantasy relationships half-way across the world, mixed messages about sexuality, and other titillating information for young minds. New technologies are ignored at great peril; it is better to harness them in ways that simultaneously will engage students' interest and enable them to make sense of the world around them, make informed decisions about their own health and lifestyle, and learn to seek and manage information sensibly. Teachers can make use of Internet resources for their own professional development and as a teaching tool in the classroom by accessing up-to-date, accurate, and informative websites. Where computer facilities in the school permit, classroom message boards may enable students to ask questions they might be embarrassed to ask aloud in the classroom.

Although small rural schools may be challenged by geography, culture, and a relative lack of resources, an audit of both the school and wider community may reveal opportunities that have yet to be embraced, and issues that need to be addressed. Rural schools need to work more closely with parents, health professionals, and others within their areas to ensure that their students have access to the services available to urban schools and students. Ultimately, creating closer ties between the school and the community will serve to enhance the overall curriculum possibilities for both physical education and health education, and may overcome the perception that rural schools are unable to offer a complete program for their students. One such partnership is with the local public health nurse.

## Partnerships Between Educators and Public Health Nurses

Educators and public health nurses can form important partnerships to advance health in rural communities. To more fully understand this partnership, it is important to appreciate what public health nursing is generally, what public health nursing is in rural communities that include rural schools, and what activities public health nurses, together with educators and others in rural communities, can engage in to promote the health of those communities. This discussion draws on the experience of one of the authors as a public health nurse in rural and urban locations, as well as research conducted on the topics of public health nursing and rural settings.

### What is Public Health Nursing?

The practice of public health nurses is based on health promotion, illness and injury prevention, and primary health care principles (Canadian Public Health Association 1990). Public health nurses assume the roles of service provider, educator, consultant, community developer, facilitator, manager, planner, team member, researcher, and policy formulator (ibid). A broad range of knowledge, skills, attitudes, and personal qualities is required to fulfill public health nursing roles and activities (Leipert 1996; Stewart 2000), especially in geographically isolated settings (Leipert and Reutter 1998). Public health nurses use knowledge from nursing science, public health sciences such as epidemiology, and social sciences such as psychology (American Public Health Association 1997). They must have good listening and communication skills and be open to other people's attitudes and values. As one public health nurse stated,

> You can have your own set of values and attitudes but it is the willingness to accept other people's values and attitudes...to have the attitude of "I want to hear what you say and I may not agree with it but you are allowed to have that viewpoint"[that is critical]. (Leipert 1996, 54)

Public health nurses are concerned with health and its advancement. It is now thought that multiple factors, or *determinants of health*, contribute more to health than improvements in medicine and other health care (Canadian Public Health Association 1997; Health Canada 1996). Determinants of health include social and economic environments, gender, culture, physical environments, health services, biological influences, and health behaviours and skills (Canadian Public Health Association 1997; Health Canada 1996). For example, because public health nurses know that social isolation and poverty have a great impact on people's health, they work to decrease them. One public health nurse noted the diverse factors and their effects on people's health:

> There are all sorts of different things that influence [people's] health and it happens mostly when they're at home and in the community....I think what we do a lot is support people in their roles...and that's really important. (Leipert 1996, 54)

Another elaborated:

> What I like best about [public] health is that you're working with all different ethnic groups and different perspectives on people's beliefs and values and you yourself grow as a person. (Leipert 1996, 53)

### Public Health Nursing in Rural Communities and Rural Schools

Almost 30 percent of Canadians live in rural or remote areas of Canada (Health Canada 2003). Rural communities in Canada have unique health needs. Recent research indicates that people living in rural areas are not as healthy as urban people (Romanow 2002). Rural people have smoking, alcohol, and obesity rates that are above the national average, and their life expectancies are shorter than those for urban people. Teen pregnancy rates are often higher in rural areas. Changing socio-economic circumstances in Canada's rural resource-based communities mean that there are fewer people who live there, and that lower family incomes and poverty are very real concerns for many farm families (Blake and Nurse 2003; Diaz, Jaffe, and Stirling 2003). Women in rural areas often have three or four jobs as they care for their families, assist with farming, work away from the farm, volunteer in the community, and care for older family members (Kubik and Moore 2003). Loss of one's farming livelihood can lead to decreased self-esteem, depression, the need to sell a farm that may have been in the family for generations, and the stress of beginning a new career, perhaps in a new community. Aboriginal people, many of whom live in rural areas, have very high mortality rates due to cancer, circulatory diseases, respiratory diseases, and suicide. Infant mortality is also very high (Diverty and Perez 1998).

Public health nurses have provided health care to rural communities and rural schools in Canada since early in the last century (Mill, Leipert, and Duncan 2002; Ross Kerr 1998). Then, as today, public health nurses were often the only health care providers in rural and remote communities. In the early years, public health nurses engaged in a wide variety of tasks and endeavours, including operating clinics for maternal and child health and welfare; providing education in the community about such topics as tuberculosis, communicable diseases, immunization, and parenting; and providing social welfare services, especially for families new to Canada or who were living in isolated and low-income situations. Nurses "found in most cases...a shortage of food and clothing with the accompanying despondency was at the root of the trouble" (City of Edmonton 1933). School nursing was a significant part of the public health nurse's role at that time, with duties including health education as well as the inspection of children's eyes, ears, and skin for signs of uncleanliness, infection, or disease. The nurses were also concerned with the nutrition of children and families.

Public health nursing practice today is much more circumscribed. In schools, the types of care that public health nurses can provide depend on several factors, such as the interest of teachers in health concerns, the needs of the school, and the time and expertise of the nurse. Nevertheless, public health nurses often provide a variety of health care services in schools.

❖ *Providing direct care to ill and injured students, teachers, and staff.*
This includes administering first aid, diagnosing symptoms, and
making referrals to parents and professionals.  In small rural
areas where there is no physician or where the physician and
hospital are far away, these types of care are especially important.

❖ *Assessing height, weight, hearing, and vision of children; providing*
*immunizations to children; screening for diseases such as measles,*
*colds, and flu and for conditions such as asthma and allergies.*
Teaching students, teachers, and parents about these health
issues and making health recommendations for care and
referrals to other care providers are also important aspects of
these assessments.

❖ *Teaching students and parents about topics such as nutrition, farm*
*safety, healthy lifestyles, and physical and social changes as puberty*
*arrives.*   These activities help support education offered by
teachers, parents, and groups such as 4-H clubs.

❖ *Being a case manager in helping students, teachers, and parents*
*access care for children with disabilities or who are chronically ill.*
This is especially helpful in rural areas where resources are
scarce and distant.  The nurse often has in-depth knowledge
about the location of resources and how to access them.

❖ *Being a consultant to the school about changes in policies and the*
*school environment that will make the school a healthier place.*  Public
health nurses help engage community agencies to support school
health.  In rural communities, public health nurses are often
known to community agencies and their credibility helps them to
secure interest in and support for school activities and needs.  For
example, local women's groups, such as Kinettes and church
groups, may assist with hot lunch programs, clothing exchanges,
and the provision of food baskets for needy families as a result of
an invitation by the public health nurse.

❖ *Being a counsellor to students and teachers.*  Because of the trust
students generally have in public health nurses, they often
consult them about depression, grief, family discord, birth
control, relationships, and many other issues.  Teachers sometimes consult them about similar issues.   The public health

nurse may be the only person with a health background who enters the rural school or the rural community; consequently, the expertise of the nurse is very important in promoting a healthy rural school population and community environment.

◆ *Providing an important link between the school and the parents.* Public health nurses visit homes and can facilitate communication between teachers and parents. They can explain school policies and parents' and families' needs and resources, thereby ultimately helping students to stay healthy and to learn effectively. For example, the public health nurse can help school personnel understand rural family issues regarding poverty, education, and stress which will help teachers work more effectively with families, and families with teachers.

◆ *Adopting the roles of social worker, physician, home care nurse, mental health nurse, psychologist, and other types of care providers.* Because of their rich expertise and knowledge, and their ability to work in and "go-between" homes, schools, and communities, public health nurses are a valuable resource to students and teachers in rural areas.

It is evident that public health nurses are or could be involved in many important activities in rural schools and communities as both generalists and specialists (Bushy 2004; Gillis 2000; Ihlenfeld 2004; Leipert 1999). However, working in rural areas requires that the public health nurse (as well as the rural teacher) be able to face many challenges (Lee 1998; Leipert 1999; Rennie et al. 2000):

(a) geographical and professional isolation
(b) scarcity of community resources
(c) a lack of anonymity, overfamiliarity
(d) challenges that might occur when working with various cultural, linguistic, and religious communities, such as, Hutterite colonies, Mennonite communities, and immigrant populations (Kulig 2000)
(e) stress and burnout issues due to heavy workloads, understaffing, the nursing shortage, fatigue, the challenges of weather and long-distance driving, and lack of resources.

Sometimes schools do not fully understand the comprehensive nature of public health nursing work. As a result, nurses may be expected to provide only first aid or other limited types of care, rather than the full complement of their roles. This limits the care that rural schools receive. In such cases, public health nurses need to explain to teachers, principals, school boards, and others that they are capable of a much broader scope of practice that can only enhance rural health and education.

## Conclusion

Recent restructuring and cutbacks to health services across the country have resulted in the employment of fewer public health nurses by governments and the limiting of public health nursing activities. Consequently, public health nurses are often able to focus on only the physical health aspects of their school programs, to the detriment of their ability to see students for counselling, referral, teaching, and other purposes. Whereas public health nurses might have been able to visit their schools on a weekly basis in the past, they are now often limited to visiting schools on a monthly or as-needed basis. As a result, when teachers and students require teaching, counselling, or other health support, public health nurses are often not available to provide it. Not having a public health nurse on site at rural schools has left students, teachers, parents, and communities in rural areas without essential public health nursing services that they need and have come to rely on. Not being able to meet the needs of rural schools as public health nurses once could has contributed to several negative consequences. Rural health nurses feel stress, demoralization, and burnout as they realize that needs exist that they cannot address. Rural teachers now struggle to include health in their classes without the support of public health nursing expertise, and rural schools have less or none of the wide scope of skills and knowledge that public health nurses bring. As a result, the health and education of rural children are at risk because their families and teachers must struggle virtually alone to address health issues and needs.

It is clear that the health of rural communities is in jeopardy. The reduction of personnel, scope of practice, time, funding, and other resources is compromising the health of rural children and their families and communities. Several recommendations can be made to strengthen rural health, rural schools, and rural public health nursing practice. First, more public health nurses must be immediately employed for dedicated service to rural communities. More public health nurses would mean that the full scope of their practice and services could then be provided in rural schools and communities. Second, public health nurses and teachers need to become partners with rural communities, rural school boards, and other rural education, health, and social services agencies to advocate for more resources (Leipert and Reutter 1998). The Office of Rural Health, which was established by the federal government in 1998, should also be included in this partnership. The Office provides advice on rural health issues, fosters understanding about them, builds consensus on how to address them, and works with others to promote, encourage, or influence the involvement of rural citizens, communities, and health care providers to advance rural health (Health Canada 2003). These partnerships increase the likelihood that the health and educational needs of rural areas will be more readily identified and addressed. Third, public health nurses, educators, and others in rural areas must advocate for the establishment of provincial and national rural health objectives. A yearly report card on the health status of rural residents and communities should be widely disseminated across the country and should form the basis for health care policies and programming in Canada. Having such a report card will help keep the needs of rural health at the forefront of the agendas of governments, policy-makers, and those providing the funding. Finally, it is critical that rural teachers, public health nurses, and other health care practitioners receive professional development opportunities and in-service training which introduce them to the unique needs, challenges, and opportunities in rural schools and communities.

## References

American Public Health Association. 1997. The definition and role of public health nursing: A statement of the APHA pubic health nursing section. *Public Health Nursing* 14:78–80.

Ambrose, L. M. 1996. *For home and country: The centennial history of the Women's Institutes of Ontario*. Federated Women's Institutes of Ontario. Erin, ON: Boston Mills Press.

Blake, R., and A. Nurse. 2003. *The trajectories of rural life: New perspectives on rural Canada*. Regina, SK: University of Regina.

Bonner, K. 1997. *A great place to raise kids: Interpretation, science and the urban-rural debate*. Montreal and Kingston: McGill-Queen's University Press.

Bushy, A. 2004. Community and public health nursing in rural and urban environments. In *Community and public health nursing*. 6th ed., ed. M. Stanhope and J. Lancaster, 374–95. St. Louis, MO: Mosby.

Canadian Public Health Association. 1990. *Community health—Public health nursing in Canada*. Ottawa: The Author.

Canadian Public Health Association. 1997. *Health impacts of social and economic conditions: Implications for public policy.* Ottawa: The Author.

City of Edmonton. 1933. *Health department report.* Edmonton, AB: The Author.

Diaz, H., J. Jaffe, and R. Stirling. 2003. *Farm communities at the crossroads: Challenge and resistance.* Regina, SK: University of Regina.

Diverty, B., and C. Perez. 1998. The health of northern residents: Health reports. *Statistics Canada* 9(4):49–58.

Downey, J. 2003. *Strengthening education in rural and northern Ontario: Report of rural education strategy.* Toronto: Rural Education Strategy. Available at: www.edu.gov.on.ca/eng/document/reports/ruraled/finalreport.pdf.

*Dutton (Ontario) Advance.* 2001. Letters to the Editor, 6 June and 3 October.

Gillis, A. 2000. Adolescent health promotion: An evolving opportunity for community health nurses. In *Community nursing: Promoting Canadians' health.* 2d ed., ed. M. Stewart, 241–61. Toronto: W. B. Saunders.

Health Canada. 1996. *Towards a common understanding: Clarifying the core concepts of population health.* Ottawa: The Author.

Health Canada. 2003. *Rural health.* Available at: http://www.hc-sc.gc.ca/english/ruralhealth

Ihlenfeld, J. 2004. Community-oriented nurse in the schools. In *Community and public health nursing.* 6th ed., ed. M. Stanhope and J. Lancaster, 1042–65. St. Louis, MO: Mosby.

Kubik, W., and R. Moore. 2003. Changing roles of Saskatchewan farm women: Qualitative and quantitative perspectives. In *The trajectories of rural life: New perspectives on rural Canada,* ed. R. Blake and A. Nurse, 25–36. Regina, SK: Saskatchewan Institute of Public Policy.

Kulig, J. 2000. Culturally diverse communities: The impact on the role of community health nurses. In *Community nursing: Promoting Canadians' health.* 2d ed., ed. M. Stewart, 194–210. Toronto: W. B. Saunders.

Langille, D. B., with Maritime Centre of Excellence for Women's Health. 2000. *Adolescent sexual health services and education: Options for Nova Scotia.* Policy Discussion Series, Paper No. 8. Halifax, NS: Dalhousie University.

Lee, H., ed. 1998. *Conceptual basis for rural nursing.* New York: Springer.

Leipert, B. 1996. The value of community health nursing: A phenomenological study of the perceptions of community health nurses. *Public Health Nursing* 13(1):50–57.

Leipert, B. 1999. Women's health and the practice of public health nurses in northern British Columbia. *Public Health Nursing* 16:280–89.

Leipert, B., and L. Reutter. 1998. Women's health and community health nursing practice in geographically isolated settings: A Canadian perspective. *Health Care for Women International* 19(6):575–88.

Leipert, B., and L. Reutter. 2005. Developing resilience: How women maintain their health in northern geographically isolated settings. *Qualitative Health Research* 15(1):49–65.

*London Free Press.* 2001. Letter to the Editor, 3 November.

Mangiardi, R. 2003. Sex education and the benefits of the Internet. Unpublished paper, The University of Western Ontario, London, Ontario.

Mill, J., B. Leipert, and S. Duncan. 2002. A history of public health nursing in Alberta and British Columbia, 1918–39. *The Canadian Nurse* 98(1):18–23.

Morgan, C. 2003. Reading, 'Riting, 'Rithmetic and Nut'rition—Ontario schools add "N" to the 3Rs. *ETFO Voice* (spring) 26–28. Available at: www.etfo.on.ca/attachments/ReadingRitingRithmatic.pdf

Morton, M. 2003. Growing up gay in rural Ontario. *Our Schools/Our Selves* (summer). Toronto: The Canadian Centre for Policy Alternatives.

Mytka, S. 1995. Changing roles of public health nurses: The case of London, 1972–1995. Master's thesis, The University of Western Ontario, London, Ontario.

No smoking bylaw in Elgin County may take some time. 2003. *The Elgin Banner,* 19 November.

Ontario Ministry of Education and Training. 1999. The Ontario Curriculum Grades 9 and 10: Health and Physical Education. Toronto: The Author.

Ontario Ministry of Education. 2000. The Ontario curriculum grades 11 and 12: health and physical education. Toronto: The Author.

OPHEA. 2003, September. OPHEA Health and Physical Education Curriculum Implementation Support. Toronto: The Author.

People for the Ethical Treatment of Animals (PETA). 2003. http://goveg.com, PETA.

Rennie, D., K. Baird-Crooks, G. Remus, and J. Engel. 2000. Rural nursing in Canada. In *Orientation to nursing in the rural community,* ed. A. Bushy, 217–31. London: Sage.

Riordan, M. 1996. *Out our way: Gay and lesbian life in the country.* Toronto: Between the Lines.

Ross Kerr, J. 1998. *Prepared to care: Nurses and nursing in Alberta.* Edmonton: University of Alberta Press.

Rozanski, M. 2002. Investing in public education: Advancing the goal of continuous improvement in student learning and achievement. Report of the Education Equality Task Force. Toronto: Education Equality Task Force.

Rural school advocates say report shows value to community. 2003. *Ontario Farmer,* 23 September.

Saskatchewan. 2003, Spring. *School plus: Well-being & educational success for all children and youth.* Regina, SK.

Saskatchewan Education. 1999, March. *On course: Addressing community needs.*

Saskatchewan Professional Development Unit. 1997. Learning together in multi-level classrooms. Regina, SK: Learning Resources Distribution Centre.

Stewart, M., ed. 2000. *Community nursing: Promoting Canadians' health* (2d ed.). Toronto: W. B. Saunders.

Sweaburg school toured by small school advisor. 2003. *London Free Press,* 7 June.

Theobald, P. 1997. *Teaching the commons: Place, pride, and the renewal of community.* Boulder, CO: Westview Press.

Trute, B., E. Adkins, and G. MacDonald, with K. McCannell and C. Herbert. 1994. *Coordinating child sexual abuse services in rural communities.* Toronto: University of Toronto Press Inc.

We're fat: Increased risk of early death due to heart disease, cancers: Study. 2004. *St. Thomas (Ontario) Times-Journal,* 1 September.

**Authors' Note:** We gratefully acknowledge the support of the Social Sciences and Humanities Research Council of Canada provided through Standard Research Grant No. 410-2000-0357; the support of the Faculty of Education, The University of Western Ontario, Research & Development Grants; and the many rural people whose perspectives and experiences inform this work.

Chapter Twelve

# The Experience of Disability in Physical Education

Donna L. Goodwin, Paul Gustafson, and Brianne N. Hamilton

## Introduction

Inclusive physical education has been interpreted in many ways. It has been discussed as a philosophy (DePauw and Doll-Tepper 2000; Paul and Ward 1996), a placement (Broadhead 1985; Jansma and Decker 1992; Loovis 1986), a process (DePauw 1996), an attitude (Kozub, Sherblom, and Perry 1999), and a lifestyle (Sherrill 2004). Its openness to interpretation and multiple meanings has created many challenges and pitfalls for those directly involved in inclusive practice. In addition, the link between research and practice has been elusive, in part because of the complicated nature of field-based educational research (Broadhead 1986; Reid 2000).

Although adapted physical education researchers have been active since the late 1950s (e.g., Francis and Rarick 1959; Oliver 1958), it was not until the 1960s and 1970s that research on the motor performance and fitness of children with disabilities came into its own (Broadhead and Burton 1996). Since that time, the legacy of adapted physical activity research has provided a knowledge base that has guided practice and enhanced understanding of physical activity for persons with disabilities. The history of research in this area reveals documentary evidence of the evolution of ideas, changing perspectives of disability, challenges faced by professionals in the field, and the multidisciplinary nature of adapted physical activity.

This chapter will explore the historical contribution made by adapted physical education researchers as well as the contemporary trends in best practices for teachers of inclusive physical education. By understanding the foundation upon which our current knowledge and understanding are based, we make our philosophical, historical, and ideological assumptions explicit. We can also celebrate progress and successes while keeping a critical eye on emerging ideas in need of further investigation.

## Definitions of Inclusive Physical Activity

Inclusive physical education has been defined in numerous ways in the literature. Very early on, the importance of physical education for students with disabilities was understood and promoted. The 1952 definition put forward by the American Association of Health, Physical Education, and Recreation (AAHPER) reflects an initial focus on specialized or adapted physical education programs that were separate from general physical education:

> Adapted physical education is a diversified program of developmental activities, games, sport, and rhythms suited to the interests, capabilities, and limitations of students with disabilities who may not safely or successfully engage in unrestricted participation in the vigorous activities of the general physical education programs. (American Association 1952, 15)

In 1971, AAHPER updated the definition to read:

> Adapted physical education should apply to any motor activity or movement program designed for persons who are impaired, disabled, and handicapped in any setting with an educational focus. (American Association 1971, 64)

In time, definitions emerged that reflected the inclusion of students with disabilities in the general physical education program. The term inclusive physical education, rather than adapted physical education, came into use, as outlined by Craft (1994):

> Inclusive physical education refers to the placement of a student with a disability, even a severe disability, into regular physical education classes with typical peers in the neighborhood school not as an occasional visitor, but as a member of the class. (22–23)

Block (1994a) added the recognition that supports were needed to facilitate positive educational experiences for both the student and the teacher:

> Inclusive physical education is a place where individual differences are not hidden or ridiculed but rather shared among students who learn to respect each other's limitations and unique abilities. Supports in the form of adapted equipment, specialized instruction, and personnel are provided to any student who needs them as well as to the regular physical educator. (16)

We offer another definition, one that builds on the principles of previous definitions and emphasizes the goals of the program:

> Inclusive physical education means providing students with activity limitations the opportunity to participate in physical education with their peers with supplementary support as appropriate to their abilities so as to take full advantage of the goals of the program.

Careful reading of the definitions of inclusive physical education will identify the key ideas behind the inclusion of students with disabilities in physical education: participation in the regular physical education program; a willingness for students of all abilities to be actively involved; a sense of social belonging; the need for supports; and the requirement that the outcomes of participation be reflective of the goals of the physical education program.

## Bandwagon Discourse

Discussions around inclusion in physical education have not been without controversy. Block (1994b), a strong advocate of inclusion for all students in physical education, has questioned, over time, the success with which inclusive physical education programs have been implemented. In his article, "Did We Jump on the Wrong Bandwagon? Problems with Inclusion in Physical Education," he suggested that "inclusion zealots," who did not accept anything less than full inclusion of all students with disabilities, may have overlooked the needs of the students in their zest for promoting the philosophy of inclusion (Block 1999, 33). Upon reflection, he suggested that the assumptions held about the regular physical education programs may have been inaccurate, thereby making the implementation of inclusive physical education far more difficult than originally believed. Block indicated that we may have been incorrect in assuming that general physical education is high in quality and individualized in nature. He contended that teachers tend to teach to the middle, or that which the average student is capable of achieving. Students who are more skilled or less skilled than average students may not receive individualized programming. A second assumption Block questioned is whether physical education mirrors the size of the general education classroom. Some schools combine classes for physical education, resulting in double, triple, and even quadruple numbers of students in one class and raising management concerns. The implementation of an inclusive physical education program also assumes that general physical educators are willing to work with students with disabilities. This third assumption may not prove true if teachers do not take responsibility for the participation of all students in their programs. Finally, the assumption that general physical educators would have access to training and adapted physical education specialists is dubious. Block indicated that teachers feel inadequately prepared to teach students with disabilities and often learn as they go. In turn, the adapted physical education specialists do not have training in how to consult with generalist teachers.

Although all of these challenges exist, DePauw and Doll-Tepper (2000) caution against thinking about inclusion as a bandwagon. Inclusion should not be perceived as something that will fade in time with the education of students with disabilities returning to the status quo of dual systems of regular and special education (Stainback and Stainback 1992). "Rather, inclusion should be considered a philosophical approach to implementing social justice in our schools....Successful inclusion requires decision-makers, including individuals, to have choice (informed choice) and to have choices" (DePauw and Doll-Tepper 2000, 139).

Although the ideology of inclusion has been debated, we should not be skeptical about the benefits of inclusive physical education for students with and without disabilities. The benefits are well documented and include decreased isolation, enhanced socialization, a sense of belonging, availability of role models, improved understanding, stimulating instructional environments, and increased teacher expectations (Block 1999; DePauw 2000). We should be thoughtful, however, in our understanding of the complexity of inclusive educational settings and the supports required for these educational settings to be meaningful to students and teachers. Unfortunately much of the work completed on inclusive physical education addresses the elementary school context, as was the case with a study by Vogler et al. (1990). In an effort to investigate the impact of the presence of students with disabilities on effective teaching in physical education, these authors described the percentage of time devoted to instruction, rates of on-task behaviour, and the emotional climate of thirty inclusive classrooms. They concluded that the presence of students with disabilities was not detrimental to overall class processes (time spent in transition, managing behaviour, instruction, practising skills, or playing games). The time devoted to waiting, managerial activities, receiving information, and non-motor activity was comparable to that in non-inclusive physical education programs. One shortcoming was that more general than specific feedback was provided in inclusive than in non-inclusive programs, although no differences were noted in the amount of negative or skill-related feedback in the two settings. Overall, the authors concluded that, compared to other physical education programs, an inclusive physical education context was an effective teaching context. Studies such as this one need to be completed in middle and high school settings to determine whether the same positive findings hold true.

## Comparative versus Ethical Paradigms

According to Paul and Ward (1996), two broad paradigms have guided our understanding of inclusion: a *comparison paradigm* and an *ethical paradigm*. A paradigm, in this instance, refers to the social responses we display toward persons with disabilities that are often driven by philosophy and personal conviction rather than scientific discovery (Polloway et al. 1996). Much of the early adapted physical education research reflected the *comparative paradigm*. Children with disabilities were compared to children without disabilities on various anthropometric and performance measures (Pyfer 1986). Variables such as body composition (Parizkova et al. 1971), reaction time (Baumeister and Kellas 1968; Wade, Newell, and Wallace 1978), fitness (Rarick, Widdop, and Broadhead 1970; Stein 1963), growth measures including stature and sitting height (Rarick and Seefeldt 1974), motor performance (Malpass 1960; Smith 1972), and motor skill development (Auxter 1971; Howe 1959) were measured and reported. This line of research, although extremely valuable in increasing our understanding of growth and development and motor skill acquisition of children with disabilities, also documented and highlighted the differences between groups of children who were given labels—often by the medical profession. Research within the comparative paradigm that highlighted differences tended to support the question, "Can students with disabilities be accommodated in physical education?" (Kozub, Sherblom, and Perry 1999). Considerable research attention was focused on comparing the attitude, experience, and performance of teachers and students in "segregated" and "integrated settings." This was an attempt to demonstrate that the conditions in one setting (e.g., teacher attitude, student ability, peer acceptance, curriculum) were more beneficial than the conditions in another (Kozub et al. 1999). This research resulted in cautious claims about the benefits of inclusion (Paul and Ward 1996). A drawback of focusing on how one type of learner affected other learners, the quality of the program, or the attitudes of those teaching the programs was less research attention being given to how to *support* students with disabilities in physical education programs.

In time, with increased understanding of the abilities of children with disabilities and the ideology of inclusive education resonating through the school systems, a new line of inquiry emerged. In addition to a continued interest in evaluating the performance of students with disabilities, there was a trend towards advancing knowledge about how to program effectively for students with disabilities in mainstream or typical classrooms (Broadhead and Burton 1996).

The question, *"Can* students be accommodated in physical education?" was in contrast to the question, *"How* can students with disabilities be accommodated in physical education?" The *"how"* question reflects the ethical paradigm. The ethical paradigm provides a conceptual framework from which to generate research questions that look at instructional models and strategies that support inclusive learning environments (instructional assistants, peer tutoring, team- teaching), facilitate the interpretation of the curriculum, alleviate real and perceived barriers to inclusion, and increase our understanding of the complex reciprocal interactions among the student, the teacher, the environment, and the instructional program (Kozub, Sherblom, and Perry 1999). Hutzler (2003) sums up the ethical paradigm this way:

> For some authors, inclusion is viewed as a moral imperative (Bricker 1995; Rogers 1993; Stainback and Stainback 1996) consisting of a noncategorical, almost limitless inclusion of children of all abilities. With this in mind, inclusion becomes more than simply placing children with and without disabilities together. It means allocating services, changing attitudes, and

developing a sense of responsibility, suggesting that instead of getting a child with a disability ready for the regular class, the regular class gets ready for the child. (348)

Research under the ethical paradigm has looked at such important issues as effective use of instructional assistants (Block 1994a); peer tutoring (Block 1995a; Houston-Wilson et al. 1997); understanding the experiences of children with and without disabilities (Blinde and McCallister 1998; Goodwin 2001; Goodwin and Watkinson 2000; Hutzler et al. 2002; Place and Hodge 2001; Slininger, Sherrill, and Jankowski 2000; Taub and Greer 2000), and finding meaning in the curriculum for all learners (DePauw and Doll-Tepper 2000).

In addition to the needs of the students, the needs of teachers must also be placed in the equation of inclusive education. Teachers' changing attitudes and experiences (Kowalski and Rizzo 1996), together with their needs pertaining to preservice professional preparation, instructional support, and equipment have not kept pace with the rate at which students with disabilities are being included in general physical education programs (LaMaster et al. 1998; Lienert, Sherrill, and Myers 2001; Potter Chandler and Greene 1995). The complex interactions that occur in an instructional context among teachers, instructional assistants, and students require further consideration if the needs of each are to be fully understood.

## Finding Meaning in the Curriculum

Stein (1987) wrote about the myth of the adapted physical education curriculum. The comparative paradigm of the 1960s and 1970s resulted in curriculum guides, assessment devices, books, and articles advocating corrective, therapeutic, or remedial physical education programs that were to be implemented by teachers with specialized skills. This left teachers unsure of their own skills and the appropriateness of participation by students with disabilities in the regular physical education programs. Concerns about professional preparation, safety, and curriculum suitability were legitimately raised by practising teachers (Watkinson and Bentz 1986). Stein (1987) challenged the adapted physical activity community to set aside its preoccupation with physical activities that were categorically determined by the nature of a student's activity limitation (e.g., bowling and darts for students who used wheelchairs) and "influenced by perceptions of what could not be done, and offered little challenge and motivation to participants" (35). He reminded the physical education community that the accommodations needed to include students with disabilities in their instructional programs involved accommodations in instructional methods and adaptive devices, not in the curriculum or in the activities themselves. He asked, "Have you ever seen adapted physical education activities that are different from activities found in good, appropriate, individualized, and developmental physical education programs?" (34).

What was occurring in physical education was not unique to the overall philosophy of education for students with disabilities. At the same time that Stein (1987) was putting forth his view, the efficacy of a dual system of education (i.e., regular education and special education) was being challenged on ethical grounds around equality, the benefits to students without disabilities in building tolerance and understanding, and avoiding the ill effects of segregation (Stainback and Stainback 1984, 1992).

A residual effect of the early focus on corrective, therapeutic, and remedial adapted physical education was uncertainty about the role of physical therapy programs within the school setting. There is evidence to suggest physical therapy programs have been viewed as an appropriate substitute for physical education (Connor-Kuntz, Dummer, and Paciorek 1995). The goals of physical education and physical therapy are complementary: development and maintenance of movement are at the core of both of these disciplines. One is not a suitable replacement for the other, however, as the underlying assumptions and models guiding the two disciplines are fundamentally different. Physical education is grounded in an educational or learning theory model, whereas physical therapy is grounded in the medical model of illness and rehabilitation (Stein 1987). The knowledge, experiential, and social components of the goals of physical education make them distinct and unique from those of physical therapy (Goodwin, Watkinson, and Fitzpatrick 2003).

According to Davis (1989) and Sherrill and Montelione (1990), the acquisition and improvement of motor skills and the improvement of physical fitness are of primary importance for students with disabilities. Equally important are a solid base of knowledge about how the body moves and the application of movement skills to physical activity that support a physically active lifestyle across one's lifespan. In a study completed by Potter Chandler and Greene (1995) that included 148 regular physical education teachers (98 elementary school, 31 middle school, and 19 high school), an average of 46 percent of the instructional time was spent in traditional games and sports, with this content being as high as 90 percent in some instances. Traditional games are perceived to be difficult to adapt for students with disabilities and may be contributing to teachers' reluctance to include students with disabilities.

> In order for inclusion to be successful, traditional curricula need to be examined to ensure that the needs of the entire school population are being met. Shifting emphasis away from traditional games and sports skills instruction may in fact allow all students access to knowledge and leisure skills that will result in a healthier and more profitable use of leisure time across the lifespan. (ibid., 272)

Although social skills are a very significant part of physical education, they should not become the main focus of the class. Social skills can be taught across the educational curriculum; however, physical education is the only class during the school day in which students can learn about and benefit from participation in physical activity. If a lesson does not include a physical component, such as motor skill development or fitness, can it really be called physical education (Davis 1989)? In many respects, secondary school teachers are better prepared to implement an inclusive physical education program than their elementary school counterparts because their solid background in the activities of the curriculum make a skill and fitness focus of the physical education program very feasible.

Think about your own physical education experiences, or think forward to the instructional program you would like to create for students with disabilities. How would you answer the following questions?

- ◈ Do the activities presented include motor skill development or fitness components?
- ◈ Are there parallel opportunities for participation in the community?
- ◈ Is the activity socially valued among students of this age group?
- ◈ Is this an activity students can continue to participate in throughout their lifespans?
- ◈ Is there support for your instructional program available in the community?
- ◈ Are the students interested in the activity?
- ◈ Have the students been provided with the opportunity to make choices?
- ◈ Does the activity promote frequent and positive social interactions?

◈ Does the activity promote equal status relationships among the students?

◈ Have you made the best use of the instructional supports available to you?

◈ Does your program have a skill-enhancement or -application and fitness focus?

After you have finished reading this chapter, return to these questions and answer them again. Compare your two sets of answers.

## Disability Experiences in Physical Education

### Instructional Assistants

Instructional assistants (also referred to as teacher aides and paraprofessionals) have been utilized as key supports in the implementation of inclusive physical education programs (Horton 2001). Recent literature suggests, however, that instructional assistants are persistently underappreciated, undercompensated, lacking in role clarification, and increasingly asked to take on instructional responsibilities (Giangreco, Edelman, and Broer 2003). There is also strong evidence to suggest that physical educators themselves do not have the information needed to best utilize the support of instructional assistants in physical education (Horton 2001). The lack of direction by teachers and the resultant uncertainty experienced by instructional assistants can lead to confusion and frustration by both parties, with the experience of the students being potentially compromised.

It has been demonstrated that teachers' engagement with students with disabilities is greater when they use a program-based instructional assistant model rather than a one-on-one model (Giangreco, Edelman, and Broer 2001). In a one-on-one model, the instructional assistant is assigned to the student(s) with activity limitations, whereas in the program-based model the instructional assistant supports the delivery of the program for all students. In a program-based model, teachers take more ownership and are more engaged in the education of students with disabilities because the instructional assistants are not always available to work with the student(s) with activity limitations. Being more engaged in the education of students with disabilities translated into the teacher's being more knowledgeable about the functioning level and learning abilities of the students; collaborating more closely with the instructional assistant, parents, and other members of the education team; retaining instructional decision making; communicating more directly with students with disabilities; providing mentorship and direction to the instructional assistant; and fading out instructional supports as student independence increased. In one-on-one models of instructional assistant support, students reported feelings of isolation, experienced insular relationships, and were subject to stigma (Giangreco, Edelman, and Broer 2001).

Additional insights into the roles and responsibilities of teachers and instructional assistants in inclusive education settings were provided by Giangreco (2003) through a multiyear research program. The research program resulted in the development, implementation, and evaluation of a Guide to Schoolwide Planning for Paraeducator Supports (Giangreco, Edelman, and Broer 2001). Some highlights of the self-assessment component of the guide are provided below.[1]

### Acknowledging Instructional Assistants

◆ Consider instructional assistants as part of the educational team that includes such people as parents, special educators, rehabilitation professionals, and bus drivers.

◆ Acknowledge that their services are important to student learning, social development, and often crucial to the success of the inclusion process.

◆ Recognize their work, unique competencies, and contributions to the program.

### Orienting Instructional Assistants

◆ Provide orientation to the student, class, and school. Instructional assistants should be informed about the educational needs of the student, classroom practices, and school policies.

◆ An accurate written job description should be agreed upon and its contents should be known to the supervising teacher.

◆ Identify roles and responsibilities (e.g., a written outline of the nature and extent of support needed referenced to the needs of the student and the class as a whole).

◆ Provide on-the-job training in light of assigned responsibilities.

◆ Instructional assistants should have access to ongoing learning opportunities (e.g., workshops, Internet courses that promote their skill development).

◆ Constructive interpersonal skills with students and other team members are expected (e.g., all communication is respectful, confidentiality is maintained, dignity of all involved is upheld).

◈ Work habits should encourage student independence, foster appropriate interdependence, promote peer interactions, enhance student self-image, and prevent the negative effects of hovering.

### Roles and Responsibilities

◈ Instructional assistants function as vital support to students under the direction and leadership of the teacher.
◈ Instructions provided by the teacher and other team members (e.g., special educators) are carried out by the instructional assistant.
◈ Opportunities for input into educational programs, instructional plans, and activities discussed by the educational team should be provided to the instructional assistant, but should not be the assistant's sole responsibility.
◈ Some of the duties may include implementing the instructional program, facilitating participation in learning activities, collecting student data, and assisting in preplanning activities (e.g., contacting sport organizations for support with equipment).
◈ Times and mechanisms (e.g., weekly scheduled meetings, daily journals) should be in place to facilitate communication of teacher plans to instructional assistants, and reporting of student progress.

### Supervising and Evaluating Instructional Assistants

◈ Ongoing supervision should be provided by the classroom teacher.
◈ Regular performance evaluations should be conducted based on the job description using clearly defined processes and procedures.
◈ Teachers should be provided with preservice or in-service training, or both, on effective supervisory practices.
◈ An evaluation plan for fading instructional support to natural supports (e.g., peers or classroom teacher) with increased student independence should be in place.

## Experiences of Teachers

The attitudes and attributes of teachers associated with inclusive physical education programs have received considerable research attention. The relationship between attitudes of teachers toward students with disabilities and such variables as years of teaching, university course work, nature of practicum experiences, gender of teachers, nature of disabilities, and perceived competence have been investigated (e.g., Block and Rizzo 1995; Folsom-Meek et al. 1999; Hodge and Jansma 1998; Rizzo and Vispoel 1991). The findings of this research have been somewhat conflicting. A review by Hutzler (2003) of the literature on attitude toward students with disabilities summarized the outcomes of the research.

◈ Previous contact with children with disabilities has resulted in controversial findings as to its importance in attitude development.

◈ Course preparation seems to be a significant factor in the development of positive attitudes. Teachers reported a deficiency in their course preparation.

◈ Teachers' perceived competence is a significant predictor of positive attitudes.

◈ Attitudes towards students based on the nature of their disabilities (e.g., learning disabilities, physical disabilities, intellectual impairments) is nonconclusive. (355–56)

Taking an undergraduate course in adapted physical activity has had mixed effects on the resulting attitudes of preservice teachers toward teaching students with disabilities. Whereas Hodge and Jansma (1998, 1999) and Patrick (1987) reported more favourable attitudes toward teaching students with disabilities following an adapted physical education course, no pre-test/post-test differences were reported in a later study (Hodge, Murata, and Kozub 2002).

A consistent message coming forward, however, is that teachers' perceived competence is a strong indicator of a positive attitude toward including students with disabilities in physical education (Block and Rizzo 1995; Kowalski and Rizzo 1996; Rizzo and Kirkendall 1995). This research suggests that the more confident teachers felt in their ability to provide a physical education program (possessed the knowledge base and instructional skills) for students with a wide range of abilities, the better their attitudes were toward inclusive physical education settings. Perceived competence appears to be linked to the opportunity to participate in hands-on experiences with persons with disabilities during undergraduate courses (Folsom-Meek et al. 1999; Hodge, Murata, and Kozub 2002; Kowalski and Rizzo 1996). But greater teacher experience or expertise does not necessarily result in better inclusion outcomes. In other words, "less experienced and nonexpert teachers have the capacity to be as effective as the experienced and expert ones" (Vogler et al. 1992).

Beyond the attitudes of teachers, relatively little work has been completed on the experiences of practising teachers in inclusive physical education settings. The completed research focuses primarily on the elementary school experience (e.g., Heikinaro-Johansson et al. 1995; LaMaster et al. 1998; Lienert, Sherrill, and Myers 2001) or early education programs (Vogler, Koranda, and Romance 2000). The paucity of research addressing the experiences of teachers of secondary school requires us to extrapolate from the experiences of elementary school teachers of physical education to increase our understanding. The experiences of secondary school teachers may or may not be reflected in those of their elementary counterparts given the increased focus on motor skill application at the secondary level, the specialist physical education role, and the lack of opportunity to see students outside of the physical education setting. An understanding of the needs and concerns, as well as the successes and celebrations, of secondary teachers is direly needed.

Teachers' perceptions of barriers to their success in inclusive physical education have been documented. A study of 148 physical education teachers who had students with visual impairments in their classes reported that the most prevalent barriers to their success were professional preparation, equipment, programming, and time (Lieberman et al. 2002). Many of the participants in the study indicated that they did not know what to do with children with disabilities, particularly children with visual impairments, because of their lack of adequate professional preparation. Specialized equipment was the second most identified barrier. The teachers did not have easy access to equipment that possessed tactile properties (e.g., changes in surface texture to demarcate boundaries), auditory properties (e.g., balls with electronic sounding devices), guide wires (e.g., guide ropes strung along the running track), or visually contrasting equipment (e.g., balls or other equipment in bright colours). It was also clear that the teachers did not know how to interpret the curriculum to best meet the needs of students with visual impairments. Group activities such as football, basketball, and volleyball dominated the instructional time even though they are less well suited to students with visual impairments than activities such as swimming, curling, track and field, and many fitness activities. Lack of time for programming, for preparing peer tutors, and for creating a more individualized instructional setting was presented as a prevalent barrier to successfully including students with visual impairments in physical education.

Concern over lack of adequate professional preparation has been reinforced in other studies, as have issues of management (LaMaster et al. 1998). Lack of administrative support in the provision of instructional support resources, decision making, (e.g., resource allocations, staffing, information flow, operating procedures) and collaboration among school personnel has been identified as a frustration by practising teachers. The need to rely on goodwill and a shared commitment to inclusion can result in resentment about workload and inequity between physical educators and classroom teachers (LaMaster et al. 1998; Praisner 2003). These very real and heartfelt concerns should not be ignored. It takes a sensitive administration, self-assured teachers, and an emotionally healthy school climate to address the diverse issues that are concomitant with inclusive education settings. A whole-school approach, which embraces the need for a common aim of welcoming all students into their community school, home-school liaison, planning and meeting requirements, and teacher equity, is considered key to the successful implementation of inclusive education (Utley, Whitelaw, and Hills 2001).

## Experiences of Students

Many scholars purport the need for contact between individuals with differences to bring about changes in attitude. Contact theory (Allport 1954) supports one of the often cited variables in success for inclusive physical education that bring about positive social-attitudinal changes in students without disabilities (Slininger et al. 2000). The direction of the change, positive or negative, depends upon the conditions associated with the contact between groups. Attitudes will shift depending upon such variables as whether contact is of equal status or produces competition between groups; whether the social climate is rewarding and pleasant or unpleasant, involuntary, or tension-laden; and whether the contact is intimate and involves common goals that are higher ranking than the group goals, or whether the groups differ overall on moral or ethical standards that are objectionable to each group (Tripp, French, and Sherrill 1995; Tripp and Sherrill 1991; Slininger et al. 2000).

The term *segregated inclusion* has been used to describe the infrequent social interaction that can occur between students with and without disabilities in physical education (Place and Hodge 2001). In a study of eighth grade students of mixed genders, social talk time occurred between three girls with physical disabilities and their nineteen classmates only 2 percent of the time. Positive social interaction does not necessarily occur spontaneously when students with diverse abilities are placed in close proximity to each other (Goodwin and Watkinson 2000). Students with disabilities have been viewed as objects of curiosity by their classmates, ignored altogether due to perceptions of inability, or outwardly rejected through the words or actions of classmates (Goodwin and Watkinson 2000; Place and Hodge 2001). Social isolation can result (Verderber, Rizzo, and Sherrill 2003; Vogler, Koranda, and Romance 2000). It has been suggested that girls have more positive attitudes toward their peers with disabilities than do boys (Tripp, French, and Sherrill 1995; Slininger et al. 2000) and previous experience with someone with a disability, such as a family member or a classmate in an earlier grade, also appears to influence attitudes positively (Block 1995b; Block and Zeman 1996). Although more information is needed on social climates within inclusive physical education classes, there is also evidence to suggest that peers without disabilities can be accepting of students with disabilities when their interactions are positive (i.e., respectful, supportive, non-threatening), frequent, meaningful, and encourage equal status relationships (Goodwin 2001; Sherrill, Heikinaro-Johansson, and Slininger 1994).

A study by Murata, Hodge, and Little (2000) investigated the attitudes, experiences, and perspectives of high school students toward classmates with disabilities four years after they had been in the same class. The results clustered around three themes: initial skepticism, direct interaction, and appreciable differences. Over time the students lost their initial feelings of discomfort and uneasiness. Although the students had classes together during other parts of their school day, there was little need or opportunity for interaction. During these initial encounters the students came to realize that their classmates with disabilities were able to do many of the same things as they. During this early period of coming to know each other, some students expressed concern, however, at being asked to take regular responsibilities for being a helping peer. With ongoing direct interaction, the students came to see past the disabilities and to experience fun and positive contact with their classmates. The third theme reflected the emergence of an open-mindedness about their classmates with disabilities, and an appreciation of the differences between themselves and others. Supportive interactions may need to be systematically encouraged and monitored. More research on how to provide positive, frequent, meaningful, and equal-status relationships within the physical education context is certainly needed. Simply putting children in proximity to each other does not necessarily result in attitudinal change or positive social interactions. Bringing students with and without disabilities together in physical education requires that the following variables related to interpersonal contact be considered (Slininger et al. 2000, 179):

- ❖ The frequency and duration of, the number of persons involved in, and variety in the nature of the contact
- ❖ The status established through contact (i.e., inferior, equal, superior)
- ❖ Roles within the contact (i.e., cooperative or competitive)
- ❖ Social atmosphere surrounding the contact (i.e., real or artificial, voluntary or involuntary)
- ❖ Personalities and prejudices held by those brought in contact with each other.

Students with disabilities have been described as having significantly less positive attitudes toward high school physical education than their peers without disabilities (Toon and Gench 1990). This finding has also been supported across elementary and middle school years (Goodwin 2001; Goodwin and Watkinson 2000; Hutzler et al. 2002). Interactions with peers in physical education can have dual meanings. Students of upper elementary school age experienced good and bad days in physical education. Good days were characterized by opportunities to feel a sense of belonging, demonstrate skilful participation, and experience the benefits of the program. Bad days were defined by feelings of social isolation, restricted participation, and having their competence questioned (Goodwin and Watkinson 2000).

Support in physical education from peers can also have dual meanings. Help from peers was supporting if it was instrumental in facilitating participation and caring in nature, but it could also be threatening if the help provided resulted in loss of independence or restricted opportunities for participation (Goodwin 2001). Experiences of this nature, accumulated over time, may help to explain why students come to the high school program with negative attitudes about physical education. This information brings cause for reflection on the use of peer tutors in inclusive physical education settings. Providing students with opportunities to demonstrate skill competence and to be active participants in the program should not be thwarted by peers who are overzealous in their help by assuming that the student is not capable of participating independently.  An educational stance taken by students and teachers which sees students with disabilities as *needed* members of the group rather than *needy* members of the group may create an instructional climate worth adopting and promoting.  Using the peer group to "expand...experience repertoire[s] and to creatively suggest solutions to potentially stressful events" (Hutzler et al. 2002, 310) may build relationships that are empowering and built on mutual respect.  Peers can provide effective and meaningful instructional support when given specific instructional and feedback information (Houston-Wilson et al. 1997).

## Creating a Positive Learning Environment

To foster positive outcomes for inclusive physical education programs, there is a need to reflect carefully upon the appropriate application of curriculum adaptations, instructional modifications, and the experience of the students.  The following suggestions highlight ways to think about your program from the perspective of students with activity limitations (Murate et al. 2000; Place and Hodge 2001; Potter Chandler and Greene 1995):

### Curriculum Balance

◈ Bring a lifestyle approach to selective activities.
◈ Search out certain individual and team activities that bring unique opportunities for participation for students with disabilities.
◈ Include activities that showcase a student's accomplishments (sledging during skating, sit-skiing during a skiing unit, swimming prowess during an aquatics unit, wheelchair curling during curling).

### Curriculum Adaptations

◈ Provide flexibility in skill forms used to meet activity goals.
◈ Modify rules.
◈ Provide equipment choices.
◈ Emphasize lifelong activity participation.

### Instructional Modifications

◈ Be sensitive when grouping students.
◈ Share instructional assistant support amongst all students.

◈ Provide choice in how activities are completed.
◈ Encourage equal status relationships in peer tutoring.
◈ Provide instrumental support only when needed to facilitate participation.
◈ Encourage independence whenever possible.

*Informed Decision Making*

◈ Share participation responsibility with the students (e.g., ideas for rule changes, equipment options).
◈ Ask students with activity limitations for input on how activities could be organized to foster participation by everyone.
◈ Gather information from previous teachers and instructional assistants.

*Tuned into Student Experiences*

◈ Listen for and intervene in incidents of negative language, inappropriate comments, or barbs directed at individual students.
◈ Watch for behavioural indicators of social isolation, such as, moving to the periphery of instructional spaces, groups of students with disabilities working together, or a lack of personal interaction during classes.

It is very easy to create the list of items you just read. It is quite another thing to take the information and apply it to a particular group of students, within a curriculum unit, and with a specific teacher's skill set. It takes pedagogical thoughtfulness. Pedagogically tactful teachers are those who do not believe their own education to be completed, who know why they are doing what they are doing, who have developed a sensitivity to what is best for the student, and who can breathe life into their subject area (van Manen 2002). It takes time to become a master teacher. Not all instructional units will be successful and there will always be room for improvement. Reflecting upon what worked, what was less successful, and what could be changed will permit you to build depth in your instructional experiences and result in pedagogical tactfulness in your teaching.

## A Framework for Planning, Instructing, and Evaluating

Motor skill acquisition is one of the primary goals of physical education (Davis 1989). To facilitate the learning of motor skills, teachers are increasingly taking an ecological approach to their instruction. By looking at the interaction of the motor task, the environment, and the capabilities of the student, the teacher can plan and implement lessons that take advantage of the opportunities presented to the learner while minimizing the constraints. In an ecological approach, curriculum activities are categorized by function and intention (e.g., send an object such as a curling rock and place it in the house). Achieving the intention of the motor task or activity (placing the rock in the house) takes precedence over achieving the "correct" movement form of delivering a curling rock (Davis and Burton 1991). Students, with the support of the teacher, identify the movement form that best meets the desired intention or outcome. Movement solutions are often determined through exploration and self-discovery by the student and direct instruction from the teacher (Balan and Davis 1993). (A sample of an ecological approach to curling is presented in Appendix B.)[2] An ecological approach to instruction removes the onus of having to know, or presuming to know, the best movement form for all students and all activity limitations. It is designed to provide strategies for individualizing instruction, providing student choices, and enhancing collaborative decision making. Hence, this approach is well suited for inclusive physical education programs (Balan and Davis 1993).

There are four steps involved in ecological task analysis. The first is to identify the task in terms of function (e.g., moving from one place to another, sending an object, receiving an object, or changing the position of the body or an object). The second step grants the learner choices in the determination of skills, which when carried out will achieve the task. The third step involves the identification and manipulation of relevant task variables to determine the optimal skill choice and movement form in relation to the performer. Finally, the instructor further manipulates the task variables, such as equipment or rules, thereby varying the complexity of the task to continually challenge the learner (Davis and Burton 1991). For an ecological approach to be embraced by teachers and students there must be a willingness to interpret the curriculum from the perspective of the students' interests and abilities, create a learning environment where students can succeed, and create opportunities for choice in the manner in which motor tasks are achieved.

## Creating Choice for Students

An ecological approach to teaching inclusive physical education means creating choice in movement solutions, thereby matching student abilities to the desired movement outcome (e.g., score a goal, hit the target, move the ball forward, put the ball in play). This is achieved by maximizing the interaction of the environment (e.g., playing surface, equipment, student and teacher attitudes), the task (the outcome desired rather than the mechanism for achieving the outcome), and the students (their skills, interests, and abilities). Curling, for example, is a Canadian passion in many parts of the country. It is socially valued in many communities, participated in by people of all ages, and even the smallest of communities seem able and willing to sustain curling facilities. Unfortunately, some people may not consider curling possible for students with reduced mobility or who use a wheelchair. However, with minor adaptations, curling can be made accessible to diverse learners.

The first step is to identify the task in terms of function (e.g., send a curling rock down the ice toward the house). The second step provides choice in skills that can be used to achieve the release and sending of the curling rock down the ice. The task of delivering the curling rock to the house can be accomplished by throwing, sliding, or pushing the rock. The third step involves the identification and manipulation of relevant task variables in relation to the performer to determine the most appropriate skill movement form of the selected skill. In the case of curling, performers can be standing or sitting, or using a delivery stick, depending upon their balance, strength, and mobility. Finally, the instructor can manipulate other performance variables, such as the use of a junior-weight curling rock and a delivery point forward of the hack (Davis and Burton 1991). Rather than staying back at the school or watching their classmates through the glass, students with disabilities can actively participate at ice level and curl with family and friends outside of school hours for years to come.

By utilizing an ecological approach to instruction, teachers assist students with disabilities to be involved actively and meaningfully in much of the physical education curriculum. An ecological approach may help you find more meaning in the curriculum as it applies to students with disabilities. Your interpretation of participation and success may expand. There is no right way and no wrong way to complete the activity. Instructional efforts are directed toward finding the best way to complete the activity goal. How the student gets there is specific to the child and often independent of the traditional skill form.

## Conclusion

Teaching an inclusive physical education class can be a professionally rewarding experience if it is approached with a willingness to celebrate student diversity and a recognition of the importance of a physically active lifestyle to all students' health and enjoyment of life. Successes will be found in daily accomplishments. Flexibility in program planning, curriculum implementation, skill performance requirements, rule adaptations, and student expectations will contribute positively to your experience as a teacher and the experiences of your students. A physical education program that promotes personal achievement, fosters relationships of equality among students, monitors the use of peer and adult help to students, respects the abilities of all students, and creates an environment of growth and personal challenge is one where self-determination is possible. Active and shared decision making with and among your students will create opportunities for you and your students to learn together and share in the joy of each other's accomplishments. Celebrate your successes and greet the challenge of including meaningfully all of the students in your programs as an opportunity to grow in your professionalism. You and your students will share the rewards.

### Notes

1. Refer to the full guide for more complete information. It can be downloaded in its entirety from the University of Vermont website at: www.uvm.edu/~cdci/parasupport

2. Materials are available through Curl BC and Curl Ontario (www.curlbc.bc.ca and www.curlontario.com). Curling manuals are also available from Curl BC for students who have visual impairments and for those who are eligible for the Special Olympics.

# Appendix A

## Tips for Successful Inclusion

*Celebrate Your Successes*

    Tell someone, take photographs, share with parents

*Avoid Looking for "Issues"*

    Identify what worked well and apply what you learned to other activities

    Ignore "perceived" barriers and eliminate "real" barriers where possible

*Involve the Students*

    Ask the student how he or she would like to be involved

    Share problem solving with members of the class

*Provide Opportunities for Students to Shine*

    Permit students to demonstrate accomplishments such as proficiency in wheelchair basketball or swimming

*Use Instructional Support*

    Facilitate your instruction by involving support personnel in planning and implementation

*Foster Equal Relationships*

    Use a *needed* rather than *needy* framework for establishing social and instructional relationships among students

# *Appendix B*

## Wheelchair Curling

*Activity Goal*

1) Intention:
   a) To send an object.
   b) To deliver a curling rock down the ice.

2) Purpose:
   a) To learn the skills involved in curling—delivery, rules, and strategies.

3) Meaning:
   a) The student can meaningfully and skillfully participate with classmates.
   b) The student will have an opportunity to participate with family and friends in the game of curling.

*Preparation*

1) There must be wheelchair access to the curling rink and ice surface.

2) Participants should dress in layers. People in wheelchairs can become cold quickly due to poor circulation.

3) Good wheelchair brakes are important for rock delivery.

4) A wheelchair seatbelt is recommended to prevent falling out of the wheelchair.

5) Bring clean towels to clean wheelchair tires before accessing ice surface to prevent damage to the surface.

6) Upon entering the ice surface area, allow time for the wheelchair tires to "cool down" so that marks are not left on the ice surface.

7) If a wheelchair tire becomes flat, do not roll the wheelchair because this will seriously damage the ice surface. The wheelchair must be tilted and rolled on the remaining good tires.

*Skill Choices*

To send the curling rock down the ice:
   a) Throw the rock down the ice (traditional delivery).
   b) Slide the rock down the ice.
   c) Push the rock down the ice.

*Movement Forms Available*

1)  Throw the rock down the ice from a sitting position:
    a) The student must have adequate strength and mobility to perform this task.
    b) Bend over the side of the wheelchair and throw the rock down the ice.

2)  Push the rock down the ice from a sitting position using a delivery stick.
    a) Side delivery:
        i) Use one hand on the delivery stick beside the wheelchair.
        ii) Rotate your wrist either to the "palm up" (in turn) or "palm down" (out turn) position near the end of the push to apply curl to the rock.

    b) Front delivery:
        i) Use two hands on the delivery stick in front of the wheelchair.
            A. This works well with manual or electric wheelchairs.
            B. Physical strength and mobility are not necessary.
            C. Use the rubber grip attached to the delivery stick to increase the friction on the handle.
            D. Modify the delivery stick as necessary to facilitate the student's arm movement.

    c) Electric wheelchair delivery:
        i) Secure the delivery stick (with hockey tape, tensor bandages, velcro tape, etc.) to the student wheelchair if the student is using an electric wheelchair.
        ii) Drive the wheelchair down the ice pushing the rock with the delivery stick to the release point. Stop the wheelchair at the release point thereby sending the rock down the ice.

*Manipulate Task Variables*

1)  Position of the wheelchair:
    a)  Place one of the back wheels in the hack for stability, or
    b)  Position the wheelchair just behind the hog line to decrease the distance of the throw.
        i) If a participant is using an electric wheelchair to push the rock, he or she should allow enough distance before the hog line to do this.

2)  Stabilizing the wheelchair:
    a)  The wheelchair must be stabilized to prevent it from rolling or sliding backwards during delivery. There are three main methods to stabilize the wheelchair:
        i) Good brakes keep the wheelchair from sliding or rolling backwards during delivery.
        ii) The "buddy system" works well alone or in conjunction with good

wheelchair brakes. A curler holds the back wheels of the sender's wheelchair. This significantly increases safety and stability.
  iii) A stabilizing bar or curling rocks can be used.
        A. Curling rocks can also be placed behind the sender's back wheels to stabilize the wheelchair. This is a simple and effective technique that increases student confidence.

3) Size and weight of the curling rock:
   Junior rocks are lighter and easier to send down the ice.

4) Shorten the target distance:
   A shorter distance will be easier to reach and requires less strength.

## References

Allport, G. W. 1954. *The nature of prejudice*. Cambridge, MA: Addison-Wesley.

American Association for Health, Physical Education, and Recreation. 1952. Building principles of adapted physical education. *Journal of Health, Physical Education & Recreation* 23(15):28.

American Association for Health, Physical Education, and Recreation. 1971. Programs for the handicapped: A clarification of terms. *Journal of Health, Physical Education & Recreation* 41(7):63–66, 68.

Auxter, D. 1971. Motor-skill development in the profoundly retarded. *Training School Bulletin* 68:5–9.

Balan, C. M., and W. E. Davis. 1993. Ecological task analysis: An approach to teaching physical education. *Journal of Physical Education, Recreation, and Dance* 64(9):54–61.

Baumeister, A. A., and G. Kellas. 1968. Distribution of reaction times of retardates and normals. *Journal of Mental Deficiency* 72:715–18.

Blinde, E. M., and S. G. McCallister. 1998. Listening to the voices of students with physical disabilities. *Journal of Physical Education, Recreation, and Dance* 69(6):64–68.

Block, M. E. 1994a. *A teacher's guide to including students with disabilities in regular physical education*. Baltimore, MD: Paul H. Brookes.

———. 1994b. Why all students with disabilities should be included in regular physical education. *Palaestra* 10:17–24.

———. 1995a. Use peer tutors and task sheets. *Strategies* 8(7):9–11, 13–14.

———. 1995b. Development and validation of the children's attitudes toward integrated physical education—revised (CAIPE-R) inventory. *Adapted Physical Activity Quarterly* 12:60–77.

———. 1999. Did we jump on the wrong bandwagon? Problems with inclusion in physical education. *Palaestra* 15(3):30–36, 55–56.

Block, M. E., and T. L. Rizzo. 1995. Attitudes and attributes of physical educators associated with teaching individuals with severe and profound disabilities. *Journal of the Association for Persons with Severe Disabilities* 20(1):80–87.

Block, M. E., and R. Zeman. 1996. Including students with disabilities in regular physical education: Effects on nondisabled children. *Adapted Physical Activity Quarterly* 13:38–49.

Bricker, D. 1995. The challenge of inclusion. *Journal of Early Intervention* 19:179–94.

Broadhead, G. D. 1985. Placement of mildly handicapped children in mainstream physical education. *Adapted Physical Activity Quarterly* 2:307–13.

———. 1986. Adapted physical education research trends: 1970–1990. *Adapted Physical Activity Quarterly* 3(3):104–11.

Broadhead, G. D., and A. W. Burton. 1996. The legacy of adapted physical activity research. *Adapted Physical Activity Quarterly* 13:116–26.

Connor-Kuntz, F. J., G. M. Dummer, and M. J. Paciorek. 1995. Physical education and sport participation of children and youth with spina bifida myelomeningocele. *Adapted Physical Activity Quarterly* 12:228–38.

Craft, D. 1994. Inclusion: Physical education for all. *Journal of Physical Education, Recreation & Dance* 65(1):22–23.

Davis, W. E. 1989. Utilizing goals in adapted physical education. *Adapted Physical Activity Quarterly* 6:205–16.

Davis, W. E., and A. W. Burton. 1991. Ecological task analysis: Translating movement behaviour theory into practice. *Adapted Physical Activity Quarterly* 8:154–77.

DePauw, K. P. 1996. Students with disabilities in physical education. In *Student learning in physical education: Applying research to enhance instruction*, ed. S. J. Silverman and C. D. Ennis, 101–24. Champaign, IL: Human Kinetics Publishers.

DePauw, K. 2000. Social-cultural context of disability: Implications for scientific inquiry and professional preparation. *Quest* 52:358–68.

DePauw, K., and G. Doll-Tepper. 2000. Toward progressive inclusion and acceptance: Myth or reality? The inclusion debate and bandwagon discourse. *Adapted Physical Activity Quarterly* 17:135–43.

Folsom-Meek, S. L., R. J. Nearing, W. Groteluschen, and H. Krampf. 1999. Effects of academic major, gender, and hands-on experience on attitudes of preservice professionals. *Adapted Physical Activity Quarterly* 16:389–402.

Francis, R. J., and G. L. Rarick. 1959. Motor characteristics of the mentally retarded. *American Journal of Mental Deficiency* 63:792–811.

Giangreco, M. F. 2003. *Final report: Paraprofessional support of students with disabilities in general education*. Available at the University of Vermont website: www.uvm.edu/~cdci/parasupport

Giangreco, M. F., S. W. Edelman, and S. M Broer. 2001. *A guide to schoolwide planning for paraeducator supports*. Available at the University of Vermont website: www.uvm.edu/~cdci/parasupport

————. 2003. Schoolwide planning to improve paraeducator supports. *Council for Exceptional Children* 70(1):63–79.

Goodwin, D. L. 2001. The meaning of help in PE: Perceptions of students with physical disabilities. *Adapted Physical Activity Quarterly* 18(3):289–303.

Goodwin, D. L., and E. J. Watkinson. 2000. Inclusive physical education from the perspective of students with physical disabilities. *Adapted Physical Activity Quarterly* 17(2):144–60.

Goodwin, D. L., E. J. Watkinson, and D. A. Fitzpatrick. 2003. Inclusive physical education: A conceptual framework. In *Adapted Physical Activity*, ed. R. D. Steadward, G. D. Wheeler, and E. J. Watkinson, 189–212. Edmonton: University of Alberta Press.

Heikinaro-Johansson, P., C. Sherrill, R. French, and H. Huuhka. 1995. Adapted physical education consultant service model to facilitate integration. *Adapted Physical Activity Quarterly* 12:12–33.

Hodge, S. R., and P. Jansma. 1998. Attitude change of physical education majors toward teaching students with varied disability types. *Clinical Kinesiology* 51(4):72–79.

————. 1999. Effects of contact time and location of practicum experiences on attitudes of physical education majors. *Adapted Physical Activity Quarterly* 16:48–63.

Hodge, S. R., N. M. Murata, and F. M. Kozub. 2002. Physical educators' judgements about inclusion: A new instrument for preservice teachers. *Adapted Physical Activity Quarterly* 19:435–54.

Horton, M. L. 2001. Utilizing paraprofessionals in the general physical education setting. *Teaching Physical Education* 12(6):22–25.

Houston-Wilson, C., J. M. Dunn, H. van der Mars, and J. McCubbin. 1997. The effect of peer tutors on motor performance in integrated physical education classes. *Adapted Physical Activity Quarterly* 14(4):298–313.

Howe, C. E. 1959. A comparison of motor skills of mentally retarded and normal children. *Exceptional Children* 25:352–54.

Hutzler, Y. 2003. Attitudes toward the participation of individuals with disabilities in physical activity: A review. *Quest* 55:347–73.

Hutzler, Y., O. Fliess, A. Chacham, and Y. Van den Auweele. 2002. Perspectives of children with physical disabilities on inclusion and empowerment: Supporting and limiting factors. *Adapted Physical Activity Quarterly* 19(3):300–17.

Jansma, P., and J. T. Decker. 1992. An analysis of least restrictive environment placement variables in physical education. *Research Quarterly for Exercise and Sport* 63:171–78.

Kowalski, E. M., and T. L. Rizzo. 1996. Factors influencing preservice student attitudes toward individuals with disabilities. *Adapted Physical Activity Quarterly* 13:180–96.

Kozub, F. M., P. R. Sherblom, and T. L. Perry. 1999. Inclusion paradigms and perspectives: A stepping stone to accepting learner diversity in physical education. *Quest* 51:346–54.

LaMaster, K., K. Gall, G. Kinchin, and D. Siedentop. 1998. Inclusion practices of effective elementary specialists. *Adapted Physical Activity Quarterly* 15(1):64–81.

Lieberman, L. J., D. Houston-Wilson, and F. M. Kozub. 2002. Perceived barriers to including students with visual impairments in general physical education. *Adapted Physical Activity Quarterly* 19:364–77.

Lienert, C., C. Sherrill, and B. Myers. 2001. Physical educators' concerns about integrating children with disabilities: A cross-cultural comparison. *Adapted Physical Activity Quarterly* 18:1–17.

Loovis, E. M. 1986. Placement of handicapped students: The perpetual dilemma. *Adapted Physical Activity Quarterly* 3:193–98.

Malpass, L. F. 1960. Motor proficiency in institutionalized and noninstitutionalized retarded children and normal children. *American Journal of Mental Deficiency* 64:1012–25.

Murata, N. M., S. R. Hodge, and J. R. Little. 2000. Students' attitudes, experiences, and perspectives on their peers with disabilities. *Clinical Kinesiology* 54(3):59–66.

Oliver, J. N. 1958. The effect of physical conditioning exercises and activities on the mental characteristics of educationally subnormal boys. *British Journal of Educational Psychology* 28:155–65.

Parizkova, J., M. Vaneckova, S. Sprynarova, and M. Vamberova. 1971. Body composition and fitness in obese children after special treatment. *Acta Paediatricia Scandinavica* 217:80–85.

Patrick, G. D. 1987. Improving attitudes toward disabled persons. *Adapted Physical Activity Quarterly* 4:316–25.

Paul, P. V., and M. E. Ward. 1996. Inclusion paradigms in conflict. *Theory into Practice* 35:4–11.

Place, K., and S. R. Hodge. 2001. Social inclusion of students with disabilities in general physical education: A behavioral analysis. *Adapted Physical Activity Quarterly* 18:389–404.

Polloway, E. A., J. D. Smith, J. R. Patton, and T. E. C. Smith. 1996. Historic changes in mental retardation and developmental disabilities. *Education and Training in Mental Retardation and Developmental Disabilities* 31:3–12.

Potter Chandler, J., and J. L. Greene. 1995. A statewide survey of adapted physical education service delivery and teacher in-service training. *Adapted Physical Activity Quarterly* 12:262–74.

Praisner, C. L. 2003. Attitudes of elementary school principals toward the inclusion of students with disabilities. *Exceptional Children* 69(2):135–46.

Pyfer, J. 1986. Early research concerns in adapted physical education. *Adapted Physical Activity Quarterly* 3:95–103.

Rarick, G. L., and V. Seefeldt. 1974. Observations from longitudinal data on growth in stature and sitting height of children with Down Syndrome. *Journal of Mental Deficiency Research* 18:63–78.

Rarick, G. L., J. H. Widdop, and G. D. Broadhead. 1970. The physical fitness and motor performance of educable mentally retarded children. *Exceptional Children* 36:509–19.

Reid, G. 2000. Future directions of inquiry in adapted physical activity. *Quest* 52:369–81.

Rizzo, T. L., and D. R. Kirkendall. 1995. Teaching students with mild disabilities: What affects attitudes of future physical educators? *Adapted Physical Activity Quarterly* 12:205–16.

Rizzo, T. L., and W. P. Vispoel. 1991. Physical educators' attributes and attitudes toward teaching students with handicaps. *Adapted Physical Activity Quarterly* 8:4–11.

Rogers, J. 1993. The inclusion revolution. *Phi Delta Kappa Research Bulletin* 11(4):1–6.

Sherrill, C. 2004. Inclusion: In search of self and social justice amidst diversity, complexity, and fantasy. Unpublished paper presented at Inclusion or Illusion? Inclusion Through Work, Play, and Learning Conference, Edmonton, Alberta, April 29–May 1, 2004.

Sherrill, C., P. Heikinaro-Johansson, and D. Slininger. 1994. Equal-status relationships in the gym. *Journal of Physical Education, Recreation, and Dance* 65(1):27–31, 56.

Sherrill, C., and T. Montelione. 1990. Priorizing adapted physical education goals: A pilot study. *Adapted Physical Activity Quarterly* 7:355–69.

Slininger, D., C. Sherrill, and C. M. Jankowski. 2000. Children's attitudes toward peers with severe disabilities: Revisiting contact theory. *Adapted Physical Activity Quarterly* 17(2):176–96.

Smith, P. B. 1972. Acquisition of motor performance of the young TMR. *Mental Retardation* 10(5):46–49.

Stainback, S., and W. Stainback. 1984. A rationale for the merger of special and regular education. *Exceptional Children* 51(2):102–11.

———. 1992. Schools as inclusive communities. In *Controversial issues confronting special education: Divergent perspectives*, ed. W. Stainback and S. Stainback, 29–43. Needham Heights, MA: Allyn and Bacon.

———. 1996. *Inclusion: A guide for educators*. Baltimore, MD: Paul H. Brookes.

Stein, J. U. 1963. Motor function and physical fitness of the mentally retarded: A critical review. *Rehabilitation Literature* 24:230–42, 263.

Stein, J. 1987. The myth of the adapted physical education curriculum. *Palaestra* 4(1):34–37.

Taub, D. E., and K. R. Greer. 2000. Physical activity as a normalizing experience for school-age children with physical disabilities. *Journal of Sport and Social Issues* 24(4):395–414.

Toon, C. J., and B. E. Gench. 1990. Attitudes of handicapped and nonhandicapped high school students toward physical education. *Perceptual and Motor Skills* 70:1328–30.

Tripp, A., R. French, and C. Sherrill. 1995. Contact theory and attitudes of children in physical education programs toward peers with disabilities. *Adapted Physical Activity Quarterly* 12:323–32.

Tripp, A., and C. Sherrill. 1991. Attitude theories of relevance to adapted physical education. *Adapted Physical Activity Quarterly* 8(1):12–27.

Utley, A., S. Whitelaw, and L. Hills. 2001. Equality, differentiation, support and a whole school approach. *British Journal of Teaching Physical Education* 32(3):37–41.

van Manen, M. 2002. *The tone of teaching.* London, ON: The Althouse Press.

Verderber, J., T. L. Rizzo, and C. Sherrill. 2003. Assessing student intention to participate in inclusive physical education. *Adapted Physical Activity Quarterly* 20:26–45.

Vogler, E. W., P. Koranda, and T. Romance. 2000. Including a child with severe cerebral palsy in physical education: A case study. *Adapted Physical Activity Quarterly* 17:161–75.

Vogler, E. W., H. van der Mars, B. E. Cusimano, and P. Darst. 1992. Experience, expertise, and teaching effectiveness with mainstreamed and nondisabled children in physical education. *Adapted Physical Activity Quarterly* 9:316–29.

Vogler, E. W., H. van der Mars, P. Darst, and B. E. Cusimano. 1990. Relationship of presage, context, and process variables to ALT-PE of elementary level mainstreamed students. *Adapted Physical Activity Quarterly* 7:298–313.

Wade, M. G., K. M. Newell, and S. A. Wallace. 1978. Decision time and movement time as a function of response complexity in retarded persons. *American Journal of Mental Deficiency* 83:135–44.

Watkinson, E. J., and L. Bentz. 1986. *Cross Canada survey on mainstreaming students with physical disabilities into physical education in elementary and secondary schools.* Gloucester, ON: CAHPERD.

Chapter Thirteen

# Masculinity in Physical Education:

## Socialization of New Recruits

# Tim Hopper and Kathy Sanford

## Introduction

Recent concerns in Western society regarding the health and inactivity of children have provoked an examination of physical education programs in schools and efforts to provide more effective physical education for all students. Curriculum documents have broadened the scope of physical education, encompassing the areas of active living, movement, personal and social responsibility, and leadership and community involvement. These identified learning outcomes, however, do not always appear in physical education programs offered in schools. Rather, traditional masculine sports-focused programs persist, dominating physical education from elementary school through to post-secondary education. It is the purpose of this chapter to examine (a) How physical education teachers develop their understanding about what teaching physical education entails; (b) How gender issues affect the socialization of physical educators, and, (c) How social constraints limit changes to traditional physical education programs and activities. We will be considering how preservice teachers who specialize in physical education have been influenced by their former teachers and coaches, and the role of gender as a social construction in forming these relationships and perpetuating traditional values and practices in physical education.

## Background

   As a social construction, gender has had a powerful impact on the way that physical education in schools has evolved, and it continues to shape the way physical education is offered in schools today (Braham 2003; Brown and Evans 2004; Curtner-Smith 1999; Flintoff and Scraton 2001; Gilbert and Gilbert 1998; Rich 2001). Constructions of masculinity dictate, in large measure, the types of activities that are considered desirable in physical education programs and the types of students who will be successful in these activities (Lesko 2000; MacDonald 1997). Western societies continue to draw on the Olympic model of physical education and sport that began in the seventh century B.C. and was revived over a century ago, one that celebrated male athletic prowess. The events celebrated in the Olympics were highly nationalistic, engaged in by men, and viewed largely by men. Single women were relegated to the role of spectator, and married women were banned from the events altogether. Another significant influence on the development of physical education has been the military model, with its emphasis on battle, winning, strategizing, and physical strength. The values of the military can be seen in the language used to describe game play, such as, "strike," "power play," "long bomb," "offence," and "defence," and the pervasiveness of words such as "penetration" suggests how male-dominated sports are seen as the core of the traditional physical education curriculum and how they support the hegemonic masculinity that permeates the profession (Evans, Davies, and Penney 1996).

   Several authors have problematized this notion of hegemonic masculinity in physical education (Braham 2003; Brown 1999; Flintoff and Scraton 2001; MacDonald 1997; Rich 2001). The gender order in physical education is such that girls are generally marginalized and absent, whereas boys are at its centre. Sports, and games in particular, celebrate male space, male physicality, and male dominance. As Flintoff and Scraton (2001) note, physical education did not "help...[girls] develop physical identities as other than antithesis [sic] of men—less able, less strong and less competitive" (8). Indeed, Brown (1999) argues that novice physical education teachers,

> to accommodate the social expectations placed upon them... draw upon their background experience and in so doing shift their teaching identities towards a complicit masculine teaching identity. Although unintentional this situation represents a dilemma that serves to perpetuate a link between generations of

physical education discourse and practice, helping to reproduce and legitimize hegemonic masculinity and the gender order in physical education. (143)

These unexamined notions of physical education imply a sense of embodied power and a sense of competence exercised over others that generate status, pride, and identity at the expense of others. In other words, the very success that motivates students to become physical education teachers may be the factor that leads them to perpetuate the boys' physical culture and the subsequent gender order.

Gender influences physical education in many ways, from the types of activities that are valued and supported in Western society, to the types of students who are encouraged to participate, and the types of teachers who are attracted to the physical education teaching profession (Brown 1999; Lawson 1988). Most often, prospective teachers are drawn to the profession because of their own personal experiences in school—in the case of secondary school teachers, as a result of their experiences in particular subject areas (Lortie 1975; Van Maanan c1976). Many physical education teachers were students who succeeded in team sports both in school and in the broader community, and most had positive relationships with physical education teachers and coaches. Lawson (1988) defined this occupational socialization as "all kinds of socialization that initially influence persons to enter the field of physical education and later are responsible for their perceptions and actions as teacher educators and teachers" (107).

As noted by Lawson (1983a, 1983b) and applied in detailed case studies by several authors (Brown 1999; M. Curtner-Smith 2001; Curtner-Smith 1999; O'Bryant, O'Sullivan, and Raudensky 2000), prospective physical education teachers seem to be attracted to and socialized into the physical education profession by either a coaching orientation or a teaching orientation. The coaching orientation embodies masculine attributes of competitiveness, strength, and power. Lawson (1988) suggests that the coaching orientation tends to be more attractive to male teachers who see instructional physical education as secondary in their careers, with interscholastic sport being the focus for their success and an experience they wish to create for students like themselves. The teaching orientation attracts prospective teachers who emphasize student learning, with participation and improvement in physical ability as focuses for success. Lawson suggests that this orientation tends to be more attractive to female teachers, though not exclusively, who see coaching as incidental to being a physical education teacher. The participants in this research, however, reflected almost exclusively the coaching mindset, although there were glimmers of a more inclusive teaching orientation. These glimmers, which offer suggestions for working differently with prospective teachers, will be discussed in the conclusion.

Lawson's work suggests that physical education teachers' emphasis on creating good-quality physical education programs is often connected to their positive instructional experiences as students in such programs. Like Brown and Evans (2004), we do not see teachers' engagement with others in their profession as the only experience that shapes their orientation toward physical education, but we believe that these experiences—interacting with gender constructions in families, peer-groups, and socio-cultural communities—will offer insights into the perpetuation of a hierarchical and competitively oriented physical education curriculum focused on boys' physical culture.

The socialization research has mapped the connection of physical education teachers' perception of physical education, linking their enculturation into a career as a physical education teacher to their time as students in school (Curtner-Smith 2001; Lawson 1983a, 1983b; O'Bryant, O'Sullivan, and Raudensky 2000; Schempp and Graber 1992; Stroot 1993). The socialization literature has identified the need to address this pre-socialization in teacher education programs as a way of enabling prospective teachers to understand and broaden their frames of reference for teaching physical education (Lawson 1988). Differences between teaching physical education and coaching a sport are not explicitly recognized or addressed in physical education teacher education programs and hence the approaches used for elite players are often imported and applied to physical education programs. The distinctions between the two types of experiences are not clearly distinguished; teachers, coaches, and the general populace do not recognize the differences between a physical education class and an extracurricular sports team. The coaching mindset is based on a patriarchal understanding of the world that values competition, physical prowess, endurance, and individuality, and includes many of the sports that are given prominence in school, such as basketball, football, soccer, and volleyball. These activities have a limited lifespan—once students have completed high school, there is little opportunity for those who have been able to play these sports to continue playing them. The activities are nevertheless valued and perpetuated by male coaches who themselves participated in this world, or by female coaches who succeeded in the male world of sport. A teaching mindset for physical education should be based on an inclusive and balanced approach to active living, movement, personal behaviours, safety practices, leadership, and community involvement, as identified in the curriculum. However, often the distinction between the coaching mindset and the teaching mindset is blurred and traditional sport values dominate physical education classes as well as team practices. The teaching orientation should be focused on redefining the physical education program to develop ongoing activities (e.g., hiking and other outdoor pursuits, yoga, racquet sports, golfing) that are inclusive and communal, and that value shared experiences, and in which it is acceptable to pursue the activity without competition—without pitting one person against another.

## Methodology

The insights presented in this chapter are drawn from themes generated from a qualitative, semi-autobiographical study. The participants in the study were sixteen preservice teachers (eight female and eight male) completing their final curriculum and instruction course for secondary school physical education at a major Canadian university. The participants were generally from white, middle-class communities with rural and urban backgrounds. The participants reflected the typical age range (22–25) for students enrolled in a five-year Bachelor of Education degree program. Their schooling experiences included private and public schooling. Their sport backgrounds were varied, with all having played for some type of representational team in sports such as rugby, soccer, volleyball, and basketball. They were all quite able players in a range of sports and believed that the goal of physical education is to offer a diverse set of activities to encourage all children to pursue an active lifestyle.

Similar to life story research by Brown and Evans (2004), Curtner-Smith (2001), and Sparkes and Thomas (1992), insights from the preservice teachers in our study were limited to a focused analysis of their storied memories of past teachers and coaches. The repertory grid technique from George Kelly's (1955) personal construct psychology (PCP) was used to elicit the memories (see Hopper 1999 for a detailed description of the use of the repertory grid). In the repertory grid process, the grid drew from the sixteen physical education teacher education students' data on how gender constructions influenced their socialization into physical education. The repertory grid evoked participants' memories as students in school physical education and explored the relationships they had with teachers and coaches in their schooling, and the influence these experiences had on their perceptions of effective teaching in physical education. The participants were asked to select from junior and senior high school physical education teachers and coaches from their past. Each participant generated approximately ten teachers' names, which were written onto cards. Using a triad process, the participants dealt three cards and compared how two teachers/coaches were similar to and different from the third teacher/coach (see Figure 1). The descriptions generated a bipolar construct as shown in Figure 1 (i.e. "Kids improved—Not a lot of learning").

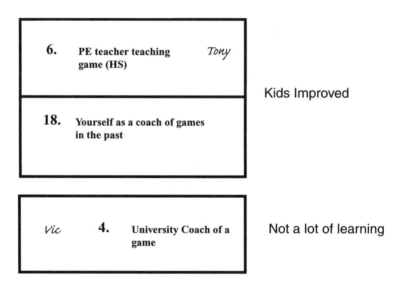

*Figure 1:* Triad process to elicit a bi-polar construct.

Participants repeated this process, changing the cards, as they felt appropriate, to generate eight to ten bipolar constructs. They then used the bipolar constructs to rate each of their teachers/coaches using a one to five ordinal scale ("one" = very positive pole, "three" = neutral, "five" = very negative pole). The computer software program Rep-Grid 2 (Shaw 1991) was used to create a cluster analysis of the number patterns generated for each teacher/coach role and for each bipolar construct. Figure 2 shows a typical repertory grid with the closeness of the number patterns shown by the connection from one teacher/coach or bipolar construct to another. These clusters became the focus of the interview with each of the participants.

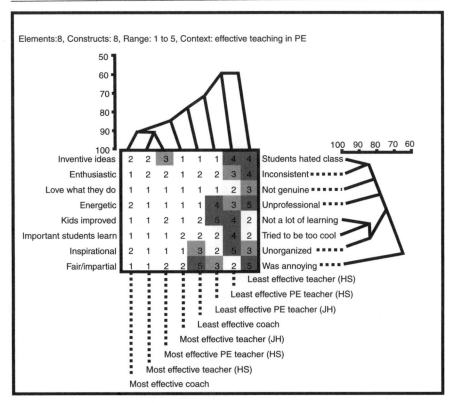

*Figure 2:* An example repertory grid produced by the RepGrid 2 software program.

In a conversational style, the interviewer asked the participants to explain why certain teachers/coaches generated similar number patterns. Participants often told stories involving the teachers/coaches. The clusters for the bipolar constructs encouraged participants to generate explanations for why certain descriptors for teaching seemed to be associated with each other on their grids. The repertory grid process was used in the course to help preservice teachers understand the idea of becoming reflective practitioners by examining the effective and ineffective teachers who framed their understanding of teaching physical education. All interviews were transcribed and coded using qualitative NUD*IST Vivo (Bazeley and Richards 2000) and paper-and-pencil memos.

The sixteen physical education teacher education students' interviews enabled an examination of how gender constructions influenced their socialization into physical education. The repertory grid evoked participants' memories of physical education and teaching that explored the influence of the relationships they had with teachers/coaches in their schooling, particularly the influence the relationships had on their perceptions of effective teaching in physical education.

## Findings

Analysis of the data provided by the sixteen participants generated three major themes: (a) dominance of male role models; (b) personal "special" involvement in physical education teacher education students' lives; and (c) gendered valuing of coach/teacher characteristics. These themes provide insights into how preservice teachers specializing in physical education have been influenced by their former teachers and coaches. The participants' privacy has been protected by the use of pseudonyms in the discussion that follows.

### Dominance of Male Role Models

We do not wish to suggest that gender and biological sex imply a deterministic sense of attributes, but we will suggest that certain "male" traits are more prevalent in male teachers than female teachers and that these "male" traits are dominant in prospective teachers specializing in physical education. As summarized in table 1, male role models dominated the physical education teacher education students' memories of both effective and ineffective teachers, with the vast majority of role models being coaches or physical education teachers. Though more female students selected female role models (33.33 percent of females compared to 11.39 percent of males), male role models still featured prominently in the female students' memories of teaching. When consideration was given to the gender of the coaches experienced by the students it was noted that no male student selected any female coaches, whereas the female students selected five male coaches and three female coaches. This data may not be surprising, but considering that when these students were going through the provincial school system (from the early to the late 1990s) approximately 60 percent of teachers were female (BCED 2004), one could expect more female representation. However, as students advance through the education system 60 percent of their secondary school teachers are male (BCED 2004), and, for physical education teachers, the ratio of males to females becomes almost two to one. This male representation in the upper levels of the school system may encourage the traditional gender positions with a focus on male physical culture in physical education. A "demanding" teacher/coach, a performance orientation, "high expectations," and a high level of physical stamina represent this culture. The implicit and explicit expectations communicated by the teacher/coach may also be a factor in maintaining hegemonic masculinity in physical education and coaching in schools (Braham 2003; Brown and Evans 2004; Gilbert and Gilbert 1998). These criteria became the standards by which the participants in the study measured the effectiveness of the teachers. The dominance of male role models influenced these prospective physical education teachers' notions of effective teaching by giving them a construction of "effective" that is highly gendered and virtually unexamined.

| | Female effective selected | Female ineffective selected | Male effective selected | Male ineffective selected | Total teachers selected |
|---|---|---|---|---|---|
| Eight Female Students | 20 | 7 | 29 | 25 | 81 |
| Female % by type | 24.69% | 8.64% | 35.80% | 30.86% | |
| Female % by gender | 33.33% | | 66.66% | | |
| | | | | | |
| Eight Male Students | 6 | 3 | 39 | 31 | 79 |
| Male % by type | 7.59% | 3.80% | 49.37% | 39.24% | |
| Male % by gender | 11.39% | | 88.61% | | |
| | | | | | |
| Totals | 26 | 10 | 68 | 56 | 160 |
| Total % by type | 16.25% | 6.25% | 42.5% | 35% | |
| Total % by gender | 22.50% | | 77.50% | | |

*Table 1:* Summary of effective and ineffective teachers selected by the eight female and eight male physical education teacher education students.

## Personal Involvement in the Lives of Physical Education Teacher Education Students

Another mark of the effectiveness of teachers/coaches was the ability to connect personally with the participants. A recurring notion throughout all sixteen interviews was the sense of personal connection with effective teachers. This was normally associated with teachers involved in a sport that the physical education teacher education students played. What made the teacher effective was the relationship that extended beyond the school. For example, Charlie stated, "I think looking back it was probably more than just what is going on in the class, they [effective teachers] have an understanding as to what is going on in the students' lives." Deanne supported this notion but also included teachers who did not coach a sport: "Most effective teachers...they put in that little extra effort, like, to know your name or to find out an interest of yours and to, you know, give out nicknames or to joke around."

However, for most physical education teacher education students it was the individual attention they received that made a teacher effective, made the student feel that the teacher was his or her friend. As Rick explained,

> Yeah, we got along really well and we are still good friends today. I have coached with him at the racquet club out here. A fairly high level of bantam, and midget AAA....I actually do the UVic hockey school with him....Very relaxed, [I've] only seen him get mad a couple of times, and I think even that was an act, just to get people going.

As suggested by other authors (Braham 2003; Brown 1999; Brown and Evans 2004; Rich 2001), this personal acknowledgement and invitation into the physical education fold represent a key process in attracting fledgling sport players into the physical education profession. Some physical education teacher education students experienced many benefits, such as a sense of importance and a sense of being given special treatment when they were high school athletes. For example, Judy commented in relation to a provincial exam, "I wrote it early because it was the last opportunity I had to coach a bunch of kids and the exam was on the same day so she [the teacher] was willing to let me write it a little bit early."

In high school all the physical education teacher education students were encouraged to take on coaching roles and to run teams of younger players. These coaching experiences were very positive and often shaped the students' desire to enter the teaching profession. As Joan explained,

> I always enjoyed coaching because it is a different sort of experience with the kids, you get to know them on a different sort of level; the kids want to be there...so in that way I tend to have a little bit more fun with them than I do with the classes that I am

teaching because I get a little tenser with the other classes, because they are "I don't want to do this" and complaining.

For Joan, who had taught physical education in only a few trial experiences, coaching was the enjoyable part of teaching. Because "kids want to be there when you are coaching, that really gives you enthusiasm and makes it fun for you...[and provides the] opportunity to be buddies." The challenges of teaching a physical education class, in Joan's view, would be balanced by the energizing fun of coaching a small, select group of children. As O'Connor and Macdonald (2002) comment, these coaching and teaching roles do not necessarily produce conflict in teachers' lives, but the emphasis on coaching as the joy of being a physical education teacher may channel efforts away from the demanding role of teaching large classes of students with diverse physical abilities and indifferent attitudes. The coaching role may also orient a physical education teacher toward the traditional activities and sports in school cultures, and away from the lifelong activities offered in society at large. The successes experienced by the physical education teacher education students as sports figures offered them no insights into the lives or realities of their peers who were not selected for the elite group. Their lack of awareness of this differential treatment for a select few did not prepare them to teach diverse groups of physical education students; those physical education students who did not meet the high expectations of teachers/coaches were at risk of being seen as a "joke" or "remedial" physical education students by the elite, sports-playing prospective teachers.

## Gendered Valuing of the Characteristics of Coaches and Teachers

### High Expectations

The sixteen participants consistently referred to coaches who showed the students how to pursue a sport to a high level, to achieve success and accomplishment. As Anne explained about two coaches who were also teachers, "They were both really demanding, and they expected a lot from us, they weren't really willing to accept a half-assed job or whatever, they wanted us to try our best and do our best. So they had high expectations and they wanted us to meet those expectations." She had internalized their ideals:

> Well you have to be, in order to be demanding and have high
> expectations of your students or athletes, you have to be confi-
> dent, you have to know what you are expecting of them, other-
> wise they will just think you are a joke. They won't take you
> seriously.

Being female and living in a rural area gave Anne increased access to elite
sports teams: "We lived in a small community so there weren't very many
girls, so if you were athletic and female you could play on all the sports
teams, because there was so few." Her achievements and successes as a university student seemed intertwined with the high expectations of her male
coaches.

This sense of high expectation seemed very much a part of the students' identities; they had succeeded in reaching the high levels demanded
by their effective male teachers. As Laura said, "Yeah, the teachers aca-
demically that had high expectations of you really drew a lot out of you.
More so than the ones that didn't have high expectations, like they challenged you individually." As with Anne, Laura's high expectations were
embedded in her understanding of coaching:

> I am a bit of a perfectionist and so I want it done a certain way
> and that doesn't always come across as kind and compassionate
> and laid back or something like that. You know this is how I
> want it done, and you have to keep working until we get it done.
> And the most effective coach that I had was very much like
> that. Perfectionist, he wanted it done just right and you worked
> to that level.

The sense that effective teachers drive for achievement was also
represented in the male physical education teacher education students'
role models but it was most evident in the female students' models. High
expectations were effective, however, only if the teachers knew the students personally and connected with them as persons. Joan commented,
"my coach who was unfriendly was just, you know, we would be playing the
game and he would be screaming at the top of his lungs at us...he could not
be bothered with us outside of the game."

### Easygoing
Although high standards were a dominant notion voiced by the
male physical education teacher education students, they also focused on

the importance of the coach's being "easygoing." Rick talked about a teacher: "I think I kind of liked him because he was my basketball coach as well. Basically the same, easygoing, you know, joked around with the kids." Rick saw this teacher as creating a kind of "boys' sport club" in the school. He said, "It was a mixed class but there was only a couple of girls. It was grade 11 or 12 so there wasn't many girls partaking." For this physical education teacher education student and many others, this "boys' sport club" was the experience of grade 11 and 12 physical education, a place to connect with (predominately male) high-level, able sport players, including the teacher. This perception reflects what Brown (1999) describes as the inner sanctum of the physically able and keen young male athletes.

## The "Naturalness and Practiced Performance" of Effective Male Physical Education Teachers

The male physical education teacher education students aspired as teachers to what Brown and Evans (2004) refer to as the "naturalness and practiced performance" (59) of their effective male teachers. These physical education teacher education students spoke of "active and energetic," "fun but in control," teachers who "joked around...[were] laid back" but always "respected...a model." These qualities existed in all their physical education role models. As Tom stated, they were "laid back but because the respect...[was] there [he didn't]...have to worry about getting the kids to toe the line."

For the female physical education teacher education students, the effective male teachers were "tough but fair." They "gave confidence"— "they forced the confidence on [them, saying], 'nope you are not backing down.'" As well, effective male teachers seemed to focus on a sense of connection and sharing. As Dawn said, these effective teachers "let us have our own ideas...[but they] shared their own experience in humorous stories." These teachers were also sympathetic: "He knew that something else was going on in our lives so he would just leave us alone."

## Caring for Students' Learning

Outside of the dominant coaching theme, the participants also displayed a common desire to care for students, to reach out to students who were not considered to be talented sport players. Although this characteristic was recognized and valued by the participants, they did not see it as particularly relating to them, but rather to the students who were less capable and successful. Physical education teacher education students universally expressed a desire to model how effective teachers cared about all of their students, regardless of ability. Anne described her female physical education teacher:

> So we didn't actually go in depth because most of the girls in my PE class probably wouldn't be able to understand what she was trying to teach us. But she made it really relevant to them and she encouraged them to be active and encouraged them to participate in grade eleven PE and to think about why it is important to stay active and stuff.

O'Connor and Macdonald (2002) discuss physical education teachers' attempts to negotiate the role conflict between teaching and coaching suggested by the socialization literature (Lawson 1988; Templin et al. 1994). Indeed, Anne was able to offer a contrast to her "high expectations" of the coaching world, drawing from teaching models that "encourage the students to apply learning to their life, that is making it relevant and authentic." In a sense, Anne saw this as adapting the physical education curriculum to meet the needs of the less-capable students. Similarly, Joan felt that her female physical education teacher created the attitude of participating at one's own level. "Otherwise," Joan confided, "I don't think I would ever have gotten into PE." For Joan, this teacher also modelled what she preached: "She meant it about physical activity, like she believed it, and I ended up going out for cross country and, like, she ran with us and she was, like, 45 and she kicked our butts, and it was just really cool." This teacher modelled achievement but adapted it to the needs of her students. Joan explained,

> I didn't really like physical activity when I got into grade 8, and she just totally brought us along at our own level within the PE class. I didn't run or anything and I started running on my own time because she made it fun, because we could be terrible at it and it didn't matter. And I was dreading PE, like I didn't think I would ever be a PE person, and my most effective teacher was really good but it wasn't the same thing as wanting me...making me want to do it outside of class type of thing.

This "female" sense of an effective teacher's being caring was also evident among the male participants, but never in relation to themselves, rather in relation to other students. They made observations, such as, "she took extra time," "tried to make connections to kids' lives," and "students knew she was there for them." The majority of male physical education teacher education students, however, did not bond with their female teachers, and they did not exhibit a sense of an effective female coach or physical education teacher.

## Same-Gender Criticisms of Physical Education Teachers

According to the male physical education teacher education students, ineffective male teachers were lazy—as Tom said, "too laid back." Andrew stated, "I mean there is always a necessity to be able to work on your feet and ad lib but he would come to every class with nothing prepared and just kind of set up a floor hockey game and let us play."

Similarly, the female physical education teacher education students criticized ineffective female teachers for being unprepared but also for lacking control. Judy commented, "She had absolutely no control over her class. I can't really remember any routines or doing anything in class except running around like idiots." Being seen as limited in one's teaching approaches and understanding also generated criticism by the females. Laura said, "In our field hockey she was an excellent teacher, but it was just that she limited...like she limited the fun, she made it so structured that it took the enjoyment out of the play of it."

## Different-Gender Criticisms of Physical Education Teachers

The female participants' ineffective male teachers seemed hostile and even intimidating. Alice commented, "He looked me straight in the eye and said, 'Do you really think this is where you should be?'" Dawn recounted a similar experience: "There was a math teacher in college and he used to tell us, we would walk in there and he used to say that we were all stupid." And other male teachers were seen as just "full of themselves," "stuck in [their] own ways." As Joan stated about several ineffective male teachers, "They just talked about their credentials, and all of the things that they ha[d] done and why they were so great." Rather than demonstrating their effectiveness, these male teachers attempted to impose their authority on their students, by virtue of their position rather than of their effectiveness.

During their grid selections and subsequent discussions, the male respondents largely ignored ineffective female teachers. However, Rick referred to a female teacher who was very confrontational: "We butted heads sometimes, you know if somebody said something that she didn't agree with or didn't know." Two of the male physical education teacher education students corroborated Rick's view that ineffective female teachers were not knowledgeable: "She did not know any more than we did." In a traditionally male-dominated domain such as physical education, women teachers/coaches must struggle to be seen as competent sports players; otherwise they become unnoticed, virtually invisible to their peers and colleagues. However, if they try to impose alternative views, they are described as strident and hostile (Lesko 2000; MacDonald 1997). Female students in coeducational physical education classes are relegated to the same roles, either being pushed to the sidelines as little more than spectators, or becoming aggressive and masculinized.

## Conclusion

Physical education is necessary more than ever in our isolated and sedentary lives. We need to be aware, therefore, of how we are socializing new teachers into physical education and who is being attracted to the profession. As described by the participants in the study, and as in previous decades, physical education roles continue generally to be filled by a small group of successful sports figures. Those who enter the profession to replicate their own positive experiences in physical education and on sports teams have a difficult time conceptualizing a balanced curriculum that is not focused on team sport and envisioning students whose interests and needs lie beyond the scope of elite sports activities. They draw predominantly from an exclusive coaching orientation rather than from a more inclusive teaching orientation, usually not by choice but because of a lack of awareness of alternatives.

The ongoing hegemonic masculinity that shapes sport perpetuates competition, elitism, physical prowess, and narrow focus, while excluding balance, inclusion, cooperation, and lifelong involvement. Rather than continuing to support physical education programs that emphasize terminal activities that often end when participants leave formal schooling, physical education teachers need to offer programs providing a wide range of lifelong activities. What the participants in the study do not recognize is the number of girls and boys who miss opportunities to participate in physical education activities, and who are ignored and overlooked by teacher/ coaches preoccupied with skilled and athletic sports players—students like themselves who are destined to become the next generation of physical education teachers. It is also hard to see how these physical education teacher education students might get the opportunity to consider the needs of different cultural groups or how socio-economic status affects students' capacity to become physically active.

The continuation of existing physical education/coaching programs is highly problematic for a number of reasons. Participation in elite athletics is not a healthy and balanced way to live; it negatively affects physical and emotional health in many ways. Physical education programs that focus on elite sport teams restrict access for many students, all of whom need and are entitled to daily physical activity. Such elite physical education programs are very costly, funneling money needed to fund a range of programs for all students into exclusive competitive programs.

Physical education is vital for all children, adolescents, and adults; it is necessary to maintain lifelong physical and mental activities. It should include coherent programs that begin in elementary school and continue through secondary school. Such programs should adopt pedagogical approaches that encourage students to make appropriate choices, adapt situations to enable physical engagement, offer a variety of physical activities that students can access outside of school, and develop skills for building a physical lifestyle beyond school. As Flintoff and Scraton (2001) noted, female students in schools want a more diverse curriculum focused on the health benefits of exercise. Moreover, male students are constrained by traditionally masculine sports that do not transfer into an active lifestyle (Braham 2003). The next generation of physical education teachers need to renew their curricula as they establish the value of physical education within the evolving school curriculum as a whole.

Studies such as the one we conducted are important because they reveal the attitudes of potential change agents—schoolteachers who can encourage activity for all children. The participants' own growing awareness of a more inclusive attitude was evident. However, physical education teacher education students have limited opportunities to identify with the needs of a diverse student population. They need to engage in reflective assignments that help them understand how their past experiences frame their present understandings of physical education. The repertory grid process caused some students to look critically at themselves. For example, Charlie, who had the opportunity to reflect during his post-practicum interview, commented about his model teacher:

> This teacher was also my basketball coach in high school so I had a really tight relationship with this person, so I may have had a sort of bias of him as a teacher because I knew him out of the school confines. So maybe when I first graded this person...I

was looking at [him as] the entire person and not just as the teacher in the classroom. Because he was definitely a different person in the classroom than he was coaching basketball. So maybe I was just biased in the fact that I knew this person quite well out[side the classroom], and I thought of course they are entertaining because they are such an engaging person as a coach....[A]s a teacher...though, they may not have been quite so good.

The capacity to "see differently" after using the repertory grid process in the physical education context has been well documented (Hopper 1999, 2001; Rossi 1997; Rossi and Hopper 2001) and is a recognized feature of autobiographical research (Sparkes and Thomas 1992). What is needed in physical education teacher education and in teacher education across all subject areas (for some ideas, see Bullough and Gitlin 2001) is a commitment of time and space for undergraduates to examine the assumptions shaping their notions of practice. We need to create time and safe spaces to enable prospective and practising teachers to engage in professional development activities to counteract the still-prevalent hegemonic forms of masculinity in schools today (Connell 1989, 1995; Gilbert and Gilbert 1998; Martino and Meyenn 2001). Our study adds to research that links the social and cultural inertia in gender relations in physical education to prospective physical education teachers' school-based apprenticeship in sport and physical education (Brown 1999; Brown and Evans 2004; Curtner-Smith 1999; Curtner-Smith 2001; Rich 2001).

This research highlights what a group of graduating physical education teacher education students drew on to construct their notions of effective teaching in physical education. How these students were able to develop their practice within the field as they established the confidence to manage and teach classes of children was not within the scope of this study, but is a needed line of inquiry. Physical education teacher education programs need to work with schools to address hegemonic forms of masculinity that undermine physical education that benefits everyone for a lifetime. Only through a supportive and continued dialogue between those committed to the education of all students can issues of inequality and contradictions between intent and action be addressed and new alternatives developed. Our work with school-integrated teacher education (Hopper and Sanford 2004), where portions of university courses are taught in local schools, has offered us hope that universities can partner with schools to promote more effective education, both at the university and in the schools. The shape of this effective education is open to debate, but the insights provided by principals, teachers, student teachers, and parents indicate its potential. In physical education we can only speculate about the extent to which a teacher education program can enable prospective physical education teachers to counteract the discourse of hegemonic forms of masculinity. Research needs to examine how those entering the profession find a "position" in this dominant discourse where they are change agents creating more inclusive discourses. In the present political climate, physical education in schools is underfunded and marginalized. In the school district adjacent to our university, recent restructuring to a middle-school system resulted in the loss of physical education specialists from grades 6, 7, and 8. It is critical to show that physical education is vital for the education of all children, especially before high school, otherwise it will continue to be only for the elite few, and continue to embody the "boys' physical" culture of the high school.

## References

BCED. 2004. *British Columbia education report. K-12 data reports.* Available at: www.bced.gov.bc.ca/k12datareports/qual_reports.htm [This site is no longer active; however, one is redirected to www.bced.gov.ca/reporting/enrol].

Braham, P. 2003. Boys, masculinities and PE. *Sport, Education and Society* 8(1):57–71.

Brown, D. 1999. Complicity and reproduction in teaching physical education. *Sport, Education and Society* 4(2):143–60.

Brown, D., and J. Evans. 2004. Reproducing gender? Intergenerational links and the male PE teacher as a cultural conduit in teaching physical education. *Journal of Teaching in Physical Education* 23:48–70.

Bullough, R., and A. Gitlin. 2001. *Becoming a student: Linking knowledge production and practice of teaching.* 2d. ed. New York: Routledge Falmer.

Connell, R. W. 1989. Cool guys, swats and wimps: The interplay of masculinity and education. Oxford Review of Education 15(3):291–303.

———. 1995. *Masculinities.* Cambridge, MA: Polity Press.

Curtner-Smith, M. 1999. The more things change the more they stay the same: Factors influencing teachers' interpretations and delivery of national curriculum physical education. *Sport, Education and Society* 4(1):75–97.

———. 2001. The occupational socialization of a first-year physical education teacher with a teaching orientation. *Sport, Education and Society* 6(1):81–105.

Evans, J., B. Davies, and D. Penney. 1996. Teachers, teaching and the social construction of gender relations. *Sport, Education and Society* 1(2):165–83.

Flintoff, A., and S. Scraton. 2001. Stepping into active leisure? Young women's perceptions of active lifestyles and their experiences of school physical education. *Sport, Education and Society* 6(1):5–21.

Gilbert, R., and P. Gilbert. 1998. *Masculinity goes to school.* London: Routledge.

Hopper, T. 1999. The grid: Reflecting from pre-service teachers' past experiences of being taught. *JOPERD* 70(7):53–59.

———. 2001. Personal construct psychology as a reflective method in learning to teach: A story of de-centering "self" as PE teacher. *AVANTE* 6(3):46–57.

Hopper, T., and K. Sanford. 2004. Representing multiple perspectives of self-as-teacher: Integrated teacher education course and self-study. *Teacher Education Quarterly* 31(2):57–74.

Kelly, G. 1955. *The psychology of personal constructs.* Vol. 1. New York: W. W. Norton and Co., Inc.

Lawson, H. 1983a. Toward a model of teacher socialization in physical education: The subjective warrant, recruitment and teacher education. *Journal of Teaching in Physical Education* 2(3):3–16.

———. 1983b. Towards a model of teacher socialization in physical education: Entry into schools, teacher's role orientations, and longevity in teaching (Pt. 2). *Journal of Teaching in Physical Education* 3(1):3–15.

———. 1988. Occupational socialization, cultural studies, and the physical education curriculum. *Journal of Teaching in Physical Education* 7:265–88.

Lesko, N. 2000. Preparing to coach: Tracking the gendered relations of dominance on and off the football field. In *Masculinities at school,* ed. N. Lesko. London: Sage.

Lortie, D. 1975. *Schoolteacher: A sociological study.* Chicago: University of Chicago Press.

MacDonald, D. 1997. The feminisms of gender equity in physical education. *CAHPERD Journal* 63(1):4–8.

Martino, W., and B. Meyenn, eds. 2001. *What about the boys? Issues of masculinity in schools.* Buckingham, UK: Open University Press.

O'Bryant, C., M. O'Sullivan, and J. Raudensky. 2000. Socialization of prospective physical education teachers: The story of new blood. *Sport, Education and Society* 5(2):177–93.

O'Connor, A., and D. Macdonald. 2002. Up close and personal on physical education teachers' identity: Is conflict an issue? *Sport, Education and Society* 7(1):37–54.

Rich, E. 2001. Gender positioning in teacher education in England: New rhetoric, old realities. *International Studies in Sociology of Education* 11(2):131–55.

Rossi, T. 1997. Seeing it differently: Physical education, teacher education and the possibilities of personal construct psychology. *Sport, Education and Society* 2(2):205–21.

Rossi, T., and T. F. Hopper. 2001. Using personal construct theory and narrative methods to facilitate reflexive constructions of teaching physical education. *Australian Education Researcher* 28(3):87–116.

Schempp, P. G., and K. C. Graber. 1992. Teacher socialization from a dialectical perspective: Pretraining through induction. *Journal of Teaching in Physical Education* 11(4):329–48.

Shaw, M. 1991. RepGrid 2 (Version 2.1b) [Windows]. Calgary, AB: Centre for Person-Computer Studies.

Sparkes, A., and J. Thomas. 1992. Life histories and physical education teachers. In *Research in physical education and sport: Exploring alternative visions*, ed. A. Sparkes, 118–145. London and Washington, DC: The Falmer Press.

Stroot, S. A., ed. 1993. Socialization into physical education. *Journal of Teaching in Physical Education* 12(4):337–469.

Templin, T., A. Sparkes, B. Grant, and P. Schempp. 1994. Matching the self: The paradoxical case and life history of a late career teacher/coach. *Journal of Teaching in Physical Education* 13:274–94.

Van Maanan, J., ed. c1976. *Organizational careers: Some new perspectives*. New York: Wiley.

Chapter Fourteen

# *Teaching Within the Law:*
## *Liability for Physical Harm and the Need for Proper Risk Management*

## Gregory M. Dickinson

### INTRODUCTION TO
### CHAPTERS FOURTEEN AND FIFTEEN

Although, from time to time, each of us is cynical about the law and its purposes, practices, and effects, one thing is clear: entanglement with the law is generally not a pleasant and fulfilling experience. Teachers can find themselves affected by many laws, some possessing sharp teeth. Those who are the targets of allegations of wrongdoing may face an array of legal actions and implications, depending on the nature of the situation. In general, these include (a) possible criminal sanctions under the *Criminal Code* for assault or criminal negligence, to cite just two examples; (b) civil liability for damages for an intentional tort, such as assault, or for negligence; (c) disciplinary action by their school boards, including reprimand, suspension, and dismissal; (d) a complaint lodged with a human rights commission[1] or under the *Canadian Charter of Rights and Freedoms* (hereafter the "*Charter*")[2] concerning discriminatory treatment of a student or group of students; and (e) professional discipline by a college of teachers, teachers' federation, or ministry of education, that could result in the suspension or revocation of their professional certification.

It is indisputable that understanding one's legal obligations and potential liability is critical for teachers' self-preservation. However, my experience has shown me time and time again that practising and aspiring teachers are among the most altruistic and self-sacrificing of professionals and that their motivation is very often much more about the interests of the children they teach or will teach than their own. On one hand, that can be dangerous for the teacher who may risk her personal legal welfare to satisfy what she feels needs to be done educationally, socially, or morally on behalf of a child. On the other hand, given that our laws are also fundamentally concerned with the best interests of children and other vulnerable persons, "teaching within the law" should serve the dual purposes of teacher self-preservation and the best interests of children. To take a simple example, practising reasonable risk management in outdoor education activities insulates teachers against tort liability because, in legal terms, they exercised a "reasonable standard of care" and, in practical terms, the likelihood of something bad befalling the students in the activity will have been dramatically reduced.

There is no point trying to cover adequately in one chapter all the areas of legal concern outlined above. Instead, in Chapter Fourteen I will examine tort, and even criminal, liability for accidents and the need for appropriate risk management that mirrors the legal principles of negligence.[3] Chapter Fifteen will consider some human rights dimensions of teaching physical and health education, including the accommodation of students with disabilities; the accommodation of students whose religious beliefs and practices may collide with curricular content and clothing requirements; the need to provide a tolerant and harassment-free learning environment; and, the attendant question of a health education teacher's right to disclose and speak affirmatively about his or her sexual orientation.

## LIABILITY FOR PHYSICAL HARM AND
## THE NEED FOR PROPER RISK MANAGEMENT

### A Dearth of Information

It is important to understand, as trite as it may seem, that risk has two dimensions: the relative chances of something bad occurring, and the chances that this misfortune will be serious. Anyone who has studied school accident cases in any depth will agree that the areas of seemingly greatest risk—in both senses described above—are athletics and physical education. Not only do injuries occur there frequently, but they also tend to be serious enough to evoke lawsuits. It would be nice to be able to provide definitive statistics supporting the assumption that physical education and sports produce the greatest number of school-based accidents and the most serious injuries related thereto, but there appears to be a dearth of data permitting such a conclusion. Even in the United States where one might have expected to find such data, given Americans' appetite for litigation, it is apparently either non-existent, or so well-hidden as to be useless.[4] In fact, the Centers for Disease Control ("CDC") state that "[t]here is no national reporting system for school-associated injuries or violence, and only a handful of states have voluntary or mandatory reporting systems" (Centers for Disease Control 2004). However, based on a conglomeration of sporadic data, the CDC concluded that

- ◈ injury is the most common condition treated by school health personnel
- ◈ about four million children and adolescents are injured at school each year
- ◈ most injuries are unintentional
- ◈ the most frequent causes of injuries requiring hospitalization are falls (43 percent), sports (34 percent) and assaults (10 percent).

A search of the literature and the Internet yielded very little data for Canada on the incidence and type of school injuries. Although it is not an unreasonable assumption that such information is squirreled away in the files of school board insurance companies and exchanges, and of the boards themselves, it does not appear to be easily accessible. Having such data and the ability to analyze it would shed light on the management of risk and assist in drawing sensible conclusions about where to focus policies and practices.

## Tort Law

Accidents are the business of the law of torts—an area of law largely defined and carried out under the common law, that is, according to judge-made case law. Tort is defined as a civil wrong a person commits against another. The term "civil" connotes that the wrong is actionable through a claim in damages, although the very same conduct could also lead to criminal liability. The two types of liability are not mutually exclusive. Hence, a punch in the mouth is both the intentional tort of battery (leading to an award of compensatory damages) and the crime of assault (leading to criminal sanctions, such as a fine or imprisonment). Since we are justified in concluding that very few teachers go around punching their students, whereas far more fail to supervise them properly, it is appropriate that we focus on the *unintentional* tort of negligence.

## Negligence and Its Elements

The legal definition of negligence is comparatively straightforward: it is the failure to take reasonable care to avoid foreseeable harm that results from that failure. An action framed in negligence has the following elements:

- ❖ a legal duty of care
- ❖ breach of a recognized standard of care
- ❖ a causal link between the breach and injury (MacKay and Dickinson 1998, 3)

### Duty of Care

Although it is possible to identify, in any number of school acts and their regulations, duties imposed on teachers concerning student safety, the notion of duty of care in negligence law arises under the common law, that is, as a result of case law. There is no civil liability in damages for simply failing to do one's statutory duty unless the statute specifically states such a remedy exists, and I am unaware of that being the case in the education legislation of any province. There has been no doubt for more than a century, however, that teachers owe a legal duty of care to their students to keep them safe from physical harm. A succession of cases since the benchmark English case of *Williams v. Eady* (1894) has cemented this principle into Canadian law.

### Standard of Care

The general standard of care in negligence law historically has been the conduct one might expect of a "reasonable person" acting under like circumstances (Fleming 1987, 97). For over two centuries the British common-law doctrine of *in loco parentis* defined the legal relationship between children and persons who, for various reasons, were standing in for their parents. Hence it was hardly astounding when the standard of care expected of the teacher in *Williams v. Eady*—a case involving mischievous adolescents who took phosphorus from a locked cupboard and burned themselves—was held to be that of the careful or prudent parent. The careful-parent test has remained the quintessential standard of care expected of teachers ever since, despite some reservations having been expressed about its appropriateness.[5] It seems an unlikely model in situations where special experience, training, and expertise are required of a supervisor because of the nature of the activity. This seems particularly true in situations involving coaching and instruction in physical education, especially gymnastics or other demanding, high-risk activities.

Although the courts have recognized this anomaly, and suggested that a test based on the notion of the "competent instructor" might well apply (e.g., *McKay v. Board of Govan* 1968; *Thomas v. Board of Education* 1994), they have been averse to relying on it, choosing most of the time to fall back on the careful-parent model. In practical terms, however, in cases involving gymnastics or football accidents the evidence of expert professionals has often been a critical determinant of the outcome (e.g., *Thomas v. Board of Education* 1994; *Myers v. Peel County* 1981). In any event, there is every reason to believe that this touchstone used by the courts to define the standard of care is not what is most important: after all, who would recognize the quintessential "careful parent" on the street? Such a person is clearly a legal fiction. Of far more importance and interest are the particular facts of negligence cases that courts analyze within several areas of inquiry to determine whether there was a breach of the duty of care.

## The Determinants of Breach of the Standard of Care

Judicial analysis of the facts in negligence cases has become almost formulaic; several factors are routinely examined to determine whether a breach of the duty of care occurred, including:

◆ the overall foreseeability of harm
◆ the nature of the activity
◆ the student's attributes (age, intelligence, experience, strength, coordination etc.)
◆ previous instruction received by the student and his or her knowledge of the risks
◆ whether similar accidents had occurred previously
◆ whether approved general practice was followed. (Thomas 1976, 42)

Liability for negligence is not based on a standard of perfection or one that is tantamount to insuring student safety. The general concept framing most of the factors determining breach of duty is reasonable foreseeability. In its most basic form, the question is: Would the careful parent (or competent instructor should the court entertain the model) have foreseen risk leading to injury? Note that the question does not ask whether the teacher *actually* foresaw the risk. It is not a subjective, but rather an objective, inquiry. Indeed, if a teacher foresaw and recklessly ignored a risk, and injury ensued, it might be a matter for the police and criminal courts, as well as the civil courts. Section 219 of the *Criminal Code* (1985) establishes the offence of criminal negligence where a person "shows wanton and reckless disregard for the lives or safety of other persons" in doing or failing to carry out a duty imposed by law. Although few teachers have faced such a charge, it remains a possibility for those who, for example, subscribe too wholeheartedly to the "sink or swim" model of teaching, without careful appraisal of whether the students are prepared and able to undertake the particularly risky tasks set for them.

An interesting but worrisome dichotomy pits the teaching of self-reliance, responsibility, and self-confidence against protecting students from harm. Proponents of the former view decry what they see as the coddling of students by a paternalistic approach fostered by a tort system all too inclined to lay responsibility at the feet of teachers rather than the students themselves. Such views, while not entirely without appeal, can lead to dangerous absurdities, such as the refusal to place matting underneath climbers because it gives the students "a false sense of security" (van Holst and Dickinson 1988). Such a stance also fails to take into consideration that part of students' education and personal development is to teach them that judgment is formed rationally through assessing risk and planning how to avoid or reduce it, not through the "school of hard knocks" experienced during trial and error. In many places in the school setting, the "errors" can have tragic consequences.

Foreseeabilty is logically affected by many of the factors outlined above. The type of activity, especially coupled with the attributes of the would-be participants, is suggestive of risk, not only of something bad happening but also of the seriousness of any injury that were to occur. The calculus involves a careful matching of student attributes to the nature of the activity. This is of particular relevance given the wide spectrum of student abilities and exceptionalities—physical, intellectual, and behavioural—that one routinely finds in classes today. As sympathetic as we may be to the plight of teachers who face large and diverse classes, it is no excuse in law to say, "How can I be expected to know *all* my students and their strengths, weaknesses, and exceptionalities?" The Supreme Court of Canada ruled in *Myers v. Peel County* (1981) that a teacher who had let an unsupervised student work on the rings in a part of the gym where he could not be seen should have anticipated that he would not follow directions about spotting because of "the proclivity of young boys of high school age to act recklessly in disregard, if not in actual defiance, of authority" (282). Unfortunately, the student, who had continued to practise a reverse-straddle dismount after his spotter had left, fell and broke his neck. Understanding one's students and their abilities and proclivities is even more pertinent in the case of students with disabilities. It is clear that the courts will expect a higher standard of care in the supervision of such students, as discussed below. Hence, their inclusion in one's class is an important factor to be taken into consideration in risk-management planning.

The amount of prior instruction given to students is another factor the courts consider. It is related to foreseeability as well as to ensuring a proper match between ability and the task to be performed. Prior instruction not only provides information to the students about risk, allowing them to assess for themselves their ability to perform the task or to follow measures to avoid harm, but when the instruction is "progressive" it also enables both teacher and student to assess the student's readiness to attempt increasingly risky actions.

The courts will expect teachers to follow practices generally approved in the field, such as progressive instruction, deployment of matting appropriate to the activity, the teaching of proper techniques for landing, falling, and tackling, and the proper use of safety equipment—along with the supervision and enforcement of such practices! Simply following such practices, however, is not a guarantee of exoneration from liability because the courts will not delegate their responsibility for determining negligence, which necessarily has to be done on a case-by-case basis. Moreover, the very fact that such practices are called "general" practices indicates that they may not be deemed appropriate for all students in all circumstances. Nevertheless adherence to approved practice is usually strong evidence of compliance with the standard of care.

The factor perhaps most closely connected to foreseeability is the occurrence of previous accidents under similar circumstances. Prior occurrences are warnings that teachers ignore only at great risk—to their students, in terms of injury, and to themselves, in terms of legal liability. In *Thornton v. Board of School Trustees* (1978) the teacher, who took no steps to find out why a student had fallen awkwardly during a makeshift vaulting activity, was found liable when another student subsequently overshot the foam matting and broke his neck. Not only had he not investigated why the first accident had occurred and whether the students were competent enough to perform the stunts safely, the steps he had taken after the prior occurrence did not amount to reasonable care because the hard add-a-mats that he deployed were entirely unsuited to absorbing a fall such as that experienced by the student-victim.

### Duty of Care to Students with Disabilities: More Than Semantics

The general principle that requires attention be paid to student attributes—both in a general and specific sense—has been extended by the courts to effectively ratchet up the standard of care where pupils with disabilities are involved. The first indication of this was *Dziwenka v. Regina* (1972), a case in which a student with a hearing disability was injured while operating shop equipment. The Supreme Court of Canada pointed out that a higher duty was owed such a student because he was unable to be verbally warned on the spot if danger arose suddenly (MacKay and Dickinson 1998). In a later case, *F.C. (Litigation Guardian of) v. 511825 Ontario Ltd.* (2003), a developmentally challenged twenty-one-year-old student wandered away from his school and was missing for four days during which he suffered severe frostbite requiring the amputation of his legs. The Ontario Court of Appeal refused to set a higher standard of care *per se* in the case of pupils with disabilities but held that an exceptionality[6]—its nature and extent—was simply an important component of the student-victim's attributes, which the courts have routinely considered as bearing on the issue of whether the standard of care was met. So the issue was not whether a different legal characterization of the standard of care is necessary or whether the standard of care applied to students with disabilities was "higher" than that applied to other students; rather, "the important questions...[were] how the standard is to be applied in this case, given F.C.'s particular circumstances, and whether the Board exercised the care that would be expected of a reasonably prudent parent in like circumstances" (para. 50).

Two points are worth noting: first, the court reaffirmed the importance of paying particular attention to an individual student's characteristics in determining negligence, and, second, it displayed the usual judicial reluctance to deviate from use of the careful-parent test. Whether one can say that there is a higher standard of care in the case of a student with a disability, or that one simply needs to be scrupulously careful about weighing such a student's special characteristics in determining proper supervision, seems little more than semantics. In practical, if not in juridical terms, a higher standard of care toward students with disabilities will be expected.

Indeed, in a recent comment on this case, the author observes that while the court refused to adopt a new standard of care, it clearly was applying a test based on the standard of "the reasonably prudent parent of a vulnerable student" (Court of Appeal confirms 2004, 4). When supervising exceptional students, therefore, teachers are well advised to assume that their actions will be scrutinized on the basis that their degree of care is expected to rise in accordance with the extent and nature of any exceptionalities that render the students more vulnerable. This returns us one more time to the exhortation: "know thy students!"

## Defences to Negligence Based on Student Responsibility: Passing the Risk?

A fair question to ask, especially given the tension between student-self-actualization and an alleged overprotective legal model of negligence, is whether students are ever responsible for their own injuries. The question is likely of even greater interest to physical education teachers and coaches because one might argue that there is somewhat more opportunity for students to exercise choice and judgement in the course of these activities. In general, plaintiffs in negligence actions can be held fully or partially responsible for their own injuries in two ways: through the voluntary assumption of risk and by contributing to their injuries through their own negligence. The application of these defences does not necessarily mean that no one else was careless or negligent but rather that, as a matter of law, recovery of damages will be denied altogether in some cases or reduced in others.

### Voluntary Assumption of Risk

The legal doctrine of voluntary assumption of risk operates in cases where it can be shown that the plaintiff voluntarily assumed the risk that caused his or her injuries. Successful application of this defence completely bars recovery of any damages. Because of its winner-take-all (or more rightly loser-lose-all) character, the defence is not particularly popular with courts and judicial rules have developed that limit its chances of success. All we need to know here is that in the case of students, who are usually minors (under the age of eighteen in most provinces), the defence is even more problematic.

First, one must convince the court that the activity or the student's actions giving rise to the injury were "voluntary—a simple enough word in ordinary usage but one fraught with difficulty in this context. It is more than conceivable that a student's desire to impress his teacher or his peers, or to obtain a higher grade, might push him to attempt something he should not. The pressure of grades has been recognized as an influence on students' actions (see, for example, *Myers v. Peel County* 1981[7]) and peer pressure, especially in sports, is also a familiar reality. Furthermore, it is unlikely that students themselves should be expected to know and appreciate the nature and extent of the risks involved in all their activities. There is an obvious linkage to the expectation, discussed above, that prior and progressive instruction, including warnings about risk, will be provided to students. The fact remains, however, that it is the teacher who is expected to understand risks and to communicate them fully and clearly to students.

Second, it is not enough that the *physical* risks of the activity be understood and voluntarily assumed; assumption of risk in law also includes the assumption of the *legal* risks. This means that quite apart from consenting to participate in a risky activity in the full understanding of its risk of physical harm, the student must also understand that, in doing so, he or she is assuming all the legal responsibility and agreeing that the teacher and school board will not be responsible for damages, even if there is negligence. Whether students understand this to be the case will obviously vary according to their ages and relative sophistication and knowledge, but it is probably fair to say that not many young people think about, let alone weigh, the legal niceties of liability before engaging in athletics or other physical activities. Lastly, there is always the problem of proving all of these components of consent.

One way to attempt to obviate the problems of proof is to provide students with consent or waiver forms that must be signed by them and/or their parents before they are permitted to participate in an activity. The use of such forms makes little sense in most curriculum-related activities because it is contradictory to request evidence of consent to something that presumably in most instances is required in the curriculum. Moreover, the issues raised above about teacher and peer pressure need to be taken into account.

Consent and waiver forms are much more legally viable when the activities are voluntary in nature, especially participation on sports teams and in non-mandatory out-of-school excursions and trips. Once again, though, based on the emphasis placed on the academic, social, and health benefits of co-curricular activities and athletics, one might question whether such participation is truly "voluntary." More difficult legal problems exist, however. First, it is fairly well accepted under the common law that minors cannot contractually waive their right to sue someone for negligence that might cause them harm (MacKay and Dickinson 1998). Second, case law also suggests that parents cannot waive their children's independent right to sue.[8] Quite apart from whether such waivers are valid in law, is the question of whether it is ethical for schools to attempt to shift onto students and parents the legal and economic risk of activities they sponsor and recommend.[9] Nonetheless, permission forms remain a valuable, and likely indispensable, tool of communication, especially for field trips, as discussed below under Risk Management. Henderson (1991 as cited by Shackelton-Verbuyst 1999, 123–124) suggests that the following information should be obtained and provided in a release and permission form for participation in athletics:

❖ parental permission for the student's participation
❖ a physician's statement (if applicable) verifying the student's physical ability to participate
❖ parental permission to transport the student to and from off-school sites
❖ medical information about the students that the staff should know
❖ any other information that the parents consider important under the circumstances
❖ the extent to which the medical and personal information should remain confidential[10]
❖ parental and student acknowledgment that the student will abide by all safety rules and instructions regarding the activity and that failure to do so could exclude the student from participation
❖ a statement that all athletics involve an element of risk and that the school will provide due care to each participant but cannot insure that he or she will not suffer injury.[11]

It is critical that all types of consents or permissions be "informed." Therefore, especially in high-risk activities, the use of permission forms should be supplemented by information sessions that provide teachers or coaches with the opportunity to meet parents and to provide information and answer any questions they may have regarding the proposed activities and their risks. If nothing else, parental permission given in the full knowledge of the proposed activities can only reinforce a teacher's claim, should it become necessary, that he or she acted as a prudent parent.

*Contributory Negligence*

Lest we leave this part of the discussion believing that students are rarely held responsible for their own actions and injuries, it should be noted that courts frequently apply the doctrine of contributory negligence to that end. This doctrine rests on the theory that, because there can be numerous parties responsible for causing an injury, including the plaintiff himself or herself, formal and meaningful apportionment of fault should occur. Accordingly, courts will determine the degree of fault of various parties and apportion responsibility for the damages on that basis.[12] Hence, a student found to have been contributorily negligent by failing to act as a reasonable person of like age, intelligence, and experience would have acted, will have her award of damages reduced in proportion to the degree of her own fault. In *Myers* (1981), for example, a fifteen-year-old gym student performed a dangerous dismount from the rings without a spotter, in violation of the instructions given to him. Although the court refused to accept the defence of voluntary assumption of risk, it did find young Myers contributorily negligent and 20 percent responsible for his injury.

## Managing Risk

The concept of risk management is inherent in many spheres of human endeavour, from dangerous physical activities, to politics and warfare, to business affairs and investment strategies. Despite the variability of the enterprises, the nature and purpose of risk management remain the same, as captured in the following definition:

> *Risk management* is a coordinated effort to protect an organization's human, physical, and financial assets. The first step is systematic *identification of risks* to which a district may be exposed and *analysis of their probable frequency and severity*. Then loss control measures are implemented to reduce or eliminate risks. [Emphasis in original] (Gaustad 2004, 2)

In the broadest sense the management of risk comprises two tasks: managing physical risk and managing legal risk. In many respects, the former can be seen as looking after the latter as the proper fulfillment of one's duty to reasonably reduce physical risk should in most instances obviate legal liability. Although there are ways of managing or avoiding legal risk that involve underwriting risk through insurance, attempting to shift the risk by requiring parents and students to carry their own insurance, or attempting to have the province enact liability-limiting provisions in their school legislation,[13] these system-wide policy issues need not concern us here. Instead, our attention needs to be focused on the local management of physical risk of accident and injury.

## Some General Considerations

Proper risk management requires the careful melding of the legal concepts and principles outlined above with the best practices in one's specialty. Although those practices will vary, common principles can be identified to guide sound risk management. The first is *planning*. Despite how experienced and talented a teacher might be, no one can practise proper risk management "on the spot." The components of reasonable foreseeability—knowledge of the inherent risk of the activity and of the characteristics of the participants, and the need to match tasks with participants and to ensure that each participant is given progressive instruction where applicable and warnings about risks—all suggest a considerable investment of time and effort in the planning phase. This is clearly not the place to make up the rules as one goes along or to "fly by the seat of one's pants," as the popular saying goes.

Most risk-management models begin with the identification of the possible risks of the proposed activity. Identifying the risk should come easily to someone with proper training, education, and experience in the activity. If it does not, the first question to be raised is whether he or she is suited to be a leader for the activity. There are ways of obtaining information about the risks inherent in certain activities, including consulting colleagues and other professionals in the field, journals and professional publications,[14] school records regarding adverse events related to such activities, and information provided by private insurers and school insurance collectives who are in the business of assessing risk. Beyond these, one can also scout out the proposed sites for activities or excursions, as well as getting to know the characteristics of the student-participants that might increase the risk of certain activities. Student records can be consulted and personal interviews of students and parents conducted.

Risk has two dimensions: the *chance* of injury and the *severity* of injury. While one might consider factoring the two to arrive at a risk index, the assumption that both elements are of equal weight is dangerous. Given the dire consequences of severe injury or death, in both human and economic terms, severity should always be given more weight than frequency in quantifying risk. Risk elimination or reduction is the second part of the management model. One foolproof tactic, it must be said, is the elimination of the activity. Indeed that should be considered if the activity's curricular or co-curricular merits are non-existent or marginal, or if the risks are such that they cannot be eliminated or brought within a reasonable sphere of risk tolerance. In general terms, risk reduction can be accomplished in the following ways:

◆ providing additional supervisory personnel
◆ obtaining advice from specialists or people with local knowledge (for excursions)
◆ providing additional training and preparation of supervisors
◆ ensuring the availability of first-aid equipment and that supervisors have up-to-date first-aid and CPR qualifications
◆ obtaining additional or better equipment, and maintaining and repairing existing equipment
◆ training and preparing the student-participants
◆ making changes to activity sites, if possible, to make them safer
◆ establishing rules targeting the dangerous aspects of the activity
◆ communicating with students and parents about special medical needs or health problems
◆ acting consistently in policy implementation and enforcement
◆ having contingency plans based on foreseeable risks.

Many of these general risk-reduction tactics have financial implications. The unavailability of funds is certainly a rational reason—though often an unpalatable one for students and parents—for cancelling an activity, but it will never be seen by the courts as a viable excuse for failure to meet a reasonable standard of care if the activity does go ahead and injury occurs because of failure to spend what was necessary to provide sufficient supervision or proper equipment (Roher and Hepburn 2004).

To help give context to the general risk management model outlined above, it is useful to turn to case law and post-tragedy inquiries, for some "tragic lessons."

## Tragic Lessons

### Lessons from the Bench

Although countless school negligence cases exist in the jurisprudence of Canada, the United States, and the United Kingdom, it is possible to synthesize several general principles related to managing risk. I shall provide ten—though there are doubtless more—with very brief exemplary case descriptions.

1. *The degree of supervision required rises and falls in accordance with the degree of danger or risk of an activity:*

   ◈ In *Thornton* (1978), a teacher's casual supervision of gymnastics using an inherently dangerous configuration of equipment was held negligent;
   ◈ In *Myers* (1981), a teacher's failure to provide on-the-spot supervision for inherently dangerous rings exercises was found negligent;
   ◈ In *Board of Education for the City of Toronto* (1959), the Supreme Court of Canada held that it was not a teacher's duty to keep all students under minute-to-minute observation during general playground supervision.

2. *Teachers cannot rely on warnings, rules, or directions alone to escape liability, and must expect students to act recklessly and possibly even defiantly:*

   ◈ In *Myers* (1981), the Court stated that the teacher should have expected careless action by the plaintiff because adolescent boys have a "proclivity" for reckless and even defiant behavior;
   ◈ In *Kowalchuk* (1991), the failure to remove matting on which students were playing a dangerous game, despite being ordered to stay off the mats, resulted in liability for negligence.

3. *Prior mishaps must be treated as warning signs that raise the foreseeability of another accident or injury and hence are ignored at great risk:*

   ◈ In *Thornton* (1978), the teacher's failure to recognize that a previous accident involving a boy's failure to land on the foam chunk matting was the result of the students' basic ineptitude in the manoeuvres they were attempting, to put a stop to the activity, and to provide a wider landing area of foam were central reasons for a finding of negligence.

4. *Care must be taken to properly match activities with student abilities, sizes, strength, coordination, and other physical and behavioural exceptionalities:*

   ◈ In *Boese* (1979), the court held that a prudent parent would not have required an obese thirteen-year-old boy to complete a seven-foot vertical jump, especially as he had expressed anxiety about doing it;

◈ In *Thornton* (1978), the court found the teacher negligent for permitting students to participate in an activity they had designed that involved using a springboard to propel themselves over a box-horse; the activity exceeded their gymnastic abilities, resulting in many students' landing awkwardly and dangerously out of control.

5.  *Students must be properly instructed and warned of the risks of activities prior to their engaging in them—even those with relatively low risk:*

◈ In *McKay* (1968), a student's lack of experience and training on the parallel bars led to a finding of negligence;

◈ In *Petersen* (1991), a teacher was found negligent for failing to warn students of the danger of being hit by a bat and the need to pay attention to the batter during a game of rag-ball.

6.  *Because of their special legal relationship with students, teachers are under a duty to provide emergency first-aid assistance at a level expected of a reasonable provider of first-aid:*

◈ In *Board of Education for the City of Toronto* (1959), a teacher ignored a student's complaints of an injured hip after he had fallen on the ice and forced him to march in line into school, thus aggravating the injury;

◈ In *Poulton* (1975), a school's hockey coach was found liable for refusing a player's request to see a doctor for an infection and hip injury;

◈ In *Mogabgab* (1970), two football coaches were found negligent and liable for the death of a student player suffering from heatstroke whom they had wrapped in a blanket while they consulted first-aid manuals.

7.  *Deviation from plans or protocols, especially regarding field trips, can lead to liability because of the impact on planned risk-reduction measures:*

◈ In *Moddejonge* (1972), during a field trip, students persuaded an outdoor education teacher, who was unable to swim, to allow an unplanned excursion to an unguarded swimming beach; the teacher was found liable after two of the students drowned;

- ◈ In *Bain* (1993), a teacher was found liable after a student fell off a steep cliff and suffered serious brain injury after he and other students on a forestry field trip had convinced the teacher to permit them to climb a mountain rather than going to a movie as planned.

8. *Equipment must not only be provided and maintained in proper condition, but must also be appropriate for the activity and not be permitted to be used in an unusual manner that renders it dangerous:*

- ◈ In *Thornton* (1978) and *Myers* (1981), the teachers were found negligent for providing matting that was insufficient for the activities;
- ◈ In *Everett* (1978), negligence was found because a hockey helmet supplied by the coach of a school team was found unsafe after a puck came through a gap and struck the player's head;
- ◈ In *Thornton* (1978), the court observed that the vaulting equipment used by students was safe and in good condition but that its unintended use in a "dangerous configuration" posed an inherently dangerous risk.

9. *Teachers who permit students to participate in games or athletic activities without proper clothing or equipment run a high risk of liability should injury result:*

- ◈ In *Brod* (1976), a teacher was found negligent for permitting a student who had left his gym shoes at home to go barefoot during a ball game in the gym; the student lost his balance when his foot stuck to the floor causing him to strike his head against the concrete wall;
- ◈ In *Berman* (1983), a student was awarded more than $80,000 in damages for dental injuries suffered after he was struck in the face during a floor-hockey game for which no protective equipment had been supplied due to the administration's failure to purchase it despite the teacher's request.

10. *The common-law doctrine of vicarious liability, and hence the insurance of the school board, will indemnify teachers found liable for damages for negligence only if the conduct of the teachers occurred within the ordinary scope of their duties; although courts are averse to ruling against the doctrine's application for obvious practical reasons, it is*

*nevertheless still important that teachers not engage in activities pro-
hibited by board rules or by their principal:*

◈ In *Beauparlant* (1955), a board was held not vicariously liable
for a teacher's negligence when the teacher had given his class a
half-day holiday and packed them into the back of a truck, from
which some of them had tumbled during a trip to a neigh-
bouring town. Although the result in this case is unclear, the
implication is that the teacher would have been held solely
liable and responsible for the damages awarded to the victims.

### Lessons from Inquiries and Inquests

Unfortunately, the seriousness of some school accidents has far
surpassed the broken bones or teeth, or dislocations or bruises that most often result from such mishaps. Indeed, there have been cases in which several students have lost their lives—often on school outdoor education
excursions—necessitating both judicial and independent inquiries to investigate what went wrong and how to avoid a recurrence of the tragic
events. Therefore, these inquiries are excellent vehicles for learning more
about managing risk, especially related to the activities in question, but also
in general. Two such inquiries are discussed below.

### The Tobermory "True North II" Inquest[15]

In June of 2000, thirteen grade 7 students set out on a camping trip
to Flowerpot Island in Georgian Bay off Tobermory, Ontario. They were to
travel to and from the island on a tour boat named the *True North II*. When
the time came to leave the island, the lake was rough and a small-craft
warning had been issued. No arrangements had been made for communicating with the campers if the weather were too foul to pick them up. The
tour-boat master set out despite the rough seas. During the return trip the
boat began to take on water and sank quickly, so quickly that there was insufficient time to hand out life jackets. Two students drowned. At the conclusion of a coroner's inquest in July 2001 the coroner's jury issued several
recommendations.

The jury's recommendations were aimed at various parties involved
in the accident. The recommendations provided below are paraphrased and
edited excerpts of those directed specifically at the school board.

◈ Students should be briefed fully in advance of the field trip
regarding the use of safety gear and emergency procedures

◈ There should be contingency plans for each aspect of an excursion and they should be communicated to parents, students, and anyone providing transportation
◈ A Safety Management Plan should be developed and filed, containing the following components:

1. The trip's educational rationale
2. Specific details about the activity
3. Emergency contact numbers
4. A proposed itinerary, with anticipated risks and countermeasures
5. A route map and escape plans
6. A health information summary
7. An expense summary
8. A list of participants and their supplies and equipment
9. A list of all modes of transportation

◈ The board should hold a parent information meeting to explain risks and answer questions
◈ A mandatory buddy system should be established to determine student numbers quickly in an emergency

As Warner (2001) emphasizes, the coroner's jury did not opt for the "foolproof" risk-avoidance measure I mentioned above—the elimination of this type of excursion—but recommended that outdoor education trips be continued as "an important educational tool."

*The Strathcona-Tweedsmuir School Avalanche Disaster Review*
Strathcona-Tweedsmuir School in Alberta has operated outdoor education excursions for more than twenty-seven years with a "very good safety record" (Cloutier 2003, 10). Unfortunately, an extremely serious occurrence during a 2003 skiing excursion badly marred that record. In February 2003, fourteen fifteen-year-old grade 10 students from the elite academic private school that also specializes in outdoor education, participated in a course-required back-country ski trip to Rogers Pass in the Rockies, an area with a known propensity for avalanches. On the day in question the avalanche risk posted by the Glacier National Park staff was "considerable" but "moderate" below the treeline where the skiers intended to ski. However, some risk associated with unstable early winter snowfalls had been noted (Na 2003, 9–10). Seven students were asphyxiated when an avalanche slid off Cheops Mountain and buried the group. This tragedy

prompted a review of the school's outdoor education program and policies, in general, and of the Rogers Pass trip, in particular. The review was conducted by Ross Cloutier, Chair of the Adventure Programs Department of The University College of the Cariboo. His report (Cloutier 2003) listed thirty-two recommendations, the most pertinent of which I have summarized and adapted as follows:

◆ There should be a *rationalization and articulation of the written goals and objectives* for the outdoor-education program as well as each individual course and trip, within the context of the program's overall philosophy, educational benefit, and the school's tolerance for risk.

◆ The school should *provide staff with direction regarding the tolerance for risk*; it should not be left to the staff to determine on behalf of the school and parents.

◆ A *disclosure policy enabling parents to assess levels of risk* for each trip should be implemented.

◆ *The impact of grade effect, curricular requirements, peer and teacher pressure, commercial influences*, etc. on program structure and activity locations should be considered.

◆ *The communication process should ensure adequate information* about a trip is given to parents.

◆ Receiving and tracking mechanisms should be checked to *ensure that all consent forms are collected* and accounted for before each trip.

◆ The format for disclosure should *assume that parents do not understand outdoor-education* terminology and concepts.

◆ *The form and content of information should motivate parents* to read and understand it.

◆ *Reviews of trip leader qualification requirements* should be conducted and the levels of qualification acceptable for staff, assistant leaders, and volunteers should be determined, including drawing a distinction between trip leaders playing the role of chaperones and those playing leadership or instructional roles.

◆ *The location of trips and the level of activities should be adjusted* to correspond to the qualifications and abilities of activity leaders.

◆ *Local leadership knowledge should be tapped*, including adding locally based leaders where the level of risk suggests it.

◆ *An adequate ratio of qualified leaders to students* should be ensured.

- ◈ A *standard-of-care policy recognizing the difference between school and commercially operated outdoor activities* related to operating standards, staff qualifications, and the acceptability of activities should be developed.
- ◈ Consideration should be given to *whether the program should be reactive to student demand* or enrolment should be limited.
- ◈ An *intentional, consistent, and documented trip-planning process* should be implemented.
- ◈ A *formal decision-making model* that documents decision-making points, and that is subject to administrative controls, should be implemented.
- ◈ *Group sizes should be reviewed* so as to be in line with norms regarding the activity in question.
- ◈ A *rule-based hazard criteria system* should be used to set objective limits to determine when outdoor activities will not be conducted, such as weather conditions, water levels and conditions, etc.
- ◈ *Specific policies and procedures should be developed for outdoor education activities that have high risk*, such as horseback riding, whitewater canoeing, kayaking, backcountry skiing, scuba diving, mountaineering, and rock climbing.[16]

**Summary**

Looking at all of the above messages about risk management permits several general conclusions. First, risk for all activities must be assessed and measured. Second, a suitable level of "risk tolerance" must be determined by the school or, more likely, school board policy. Third, consideration must be given to the practical solutions available to eliminate or reduce the risks in a given activity. Fourth, the nature of the activity and its risk must be clearly and transparently communicated to students and parents in order for them to provide informed consent. Lastly, there should be a proper fit between the proposed activity, on one hand, and program philosophy, curricular goals, and general academic worth, on the other.

## Conclusion

As Thomas (1976) correctly observed, "accidents will happen." Although the law of torts does not expect physical education teachers to guarantee the safety of students under their care, liability will be imposed where negligence can be proven. Negligence involves the breach of the teacher's legal duty of care through acts or omissions that fail to meet the standard of care expected of a prudent parent (or in some cases, a reasonable instructor of physical education) and that result in injury. Such injuries are compensated through monetary awards called damages. Although damages can be substantial, especially where injuries are serious and permanent, so long as the negligence occurred in the ordinary course of the teacher's employment, the doctrine of vicarious liability will apply and the school board's insurance will satisfy the award of damages.

Negligence is an objective concept. It is therefore determined according to whether a prudent parent (or competent instructor as the case may be) would have reasonably foreseen the risk of accident and injury and what steps one would reasonably expect to have been taken to avoid that risk. Key analytical criteria include the victim's attributes, the degree of risk inherent in the activity, the degree of prior instruction and preparation given the student, adherence to general practice, and attention paid to prior occurrences.

Students can be held responsible for their own injuries through the legal principles of voluntary assumption of risk and contributory negligence. The former involves showing that a student accepted both the physical and legal risks associated with an activity. A complete defence to a negligence claim, voluntary assumption of risk is not commonly accepted by the courts in cases involving child plaintiffs. Contributory negligence is based on the court's determination that the plaintiff bore a measure of responsibility for his or her own injury as the result of the failure to live up to the standard of care reasonably expected of someone of like age, intelligence, and experience. Damages are reduced *pro rata* with the degree of the plaintiff's fault.

Risk management represents the praxis of tort theory and educational practice. The two dimensions of risk—physical and legal—can be controlled through proper risk management strategies. Planning is crucial. Risk identification helps teachers establish and practise safety measures specifically targeted at reducing the risks, or eliminating them where possible. Responsible physical educators learn and practise effective risk management. By so doing they not only avoid the financial and human costs of litigation but, more important, the human tragedy associated with loss of life or serious injury.

## Notes

1. All provinces and territories have human rights acts or codes, most of which apply to educational services.

2. Part of the federal Constitution, the *Charter* applies to all laws and governmental actions in Canada, including those at the provincial level. Though not yet definitively decided by the Supreme Court of Canada, it is well accepted that the actions of school boards and their employees comprise governmental actions to which the *Charter* applies.

3. For a more comprehensive consideration of this area, including an activity-by-activity examination of cases, see Shackelton-Verbuyst (1999).

4. When my research assistant queried one U.S. expert about finding such data, he simply responded, "I wish there were such a source, but I don't believe there is."

5. It has been suggested that because teachers supervise far more children than do parents, and usually in activities of more complexity and risk, the test is inapposite: see, e.g., Hoyano (1984) and MacKay and Dickinson (1998). Others, however, argue that "'there could not be a better definition'" of the standard of care than Lord Esher's classic test: see Metcalfe (2003–04).

6. The court used the term "exceptionality" because Ontario's *Education Act* (1990) employs that nomenclature to describe students who are entitled to receive special education services.

7. In *Myers* (1981), the Supreme Court stated, "The manoeuvre attempted by the appellant is admittedly one of some danger. He had not been told not to try it. In fact, he had been virtually invited to do so, since higher marks could be obtained by the performance of Level 2 exercises" (para. 18).

8. For a more detailed explanation of this complex area, see MacKay and Dickinson (1998), 69–71.

9. While it extends beyond our immediate concern, the question of shifting or spreading risk is nevertheless an important one for school boards, for whom potential liability for student injury remains financially onerous, and suggestions have been made how this might be solved through no-fault insurance or hybrid tort-insurance schemes: see Brown (2002–03).

10. Medical and other personal information is subject to provincial privacy laws, typically under both school acts and privacy legislation (in Ontario, for example, the *Education Act*, 1990 and the *Municipal Freedom of Information and Protection of Privacy Act*), and must not be disclosed without the express consent of a parent or the student, where he or she is an adult.

11. The Ontario School Boards' Insurance Exchange (OSBIE) provides a sample permission/acknowledgment form online at: www.osbie.on.ca/english/rma%2FP%2D1print%2Ecfm

12. In some provinces such apportionment is affected by statutory provisions.

13. See, e.g., the Saskatchewan *Education Act*, 1995, section 232, and Brown (2002–03).

14. For example, the Ontario Physical and Health Education Association (OPHEA) provides Ontario Safety Guidelines for Physical Education (Secondary Curriculum), accessible online at: www.ophea.net/upload/6930_1.pdf
15. The information about this tragedy and the inquest recommendations are taken from Warner (2001).
16. OSBIE has set out risk categories for school activities. Included in its list of high-risk field trips are "extreme" sports activities (skydiving, skateboarding, downhill mountain biking, snowboarding); whitewater rafting, cliff rapelling; rock climbing; firing ranges; paintball games; and wilderness or winter camping. Also included as high-risk under the category of "travel" are excursions to natural disaster areas, war zones, or places with political instability and the threat of terrorism: Ontario School Boards' Insurance Exchange (2003). For a good discussion of travel-related risk management, see Shariff (2004).

## References

### Statutes

*Canadian Charter of Rights and Freedoms*, Part 1 of the *Constitution Act, 1982*, being Schedule B of the *Constitution Act, 1982* (U.K.), c. 11.

*Criminal Code*, R.S.C. 1985, c. C-46.

*Education Act* (Ontario), R.S.O. 1990, c. E.2.

*Education Act* (Saskatchewan), S.S. 1995, c. E-0.2.

*Municipal Freedom of Information and Protection of Privacy Act*, R.S.O. 1990, c. M.56.

### Cases

*Bain* v. *Calgary Board of Education* (1993), 14 Alta. L.R. (3d) 319 (Alta. Q.B.).

*Beauparlant* v. *Board of Trustees of Separate School Section No. 1 of Appleby*, [1955] 4 D.L.R. 558 (Ont. H.C.J.).

*Berman* v. *Philadelphia Board of Education*, 456 A.2d 545 (1983 Pa.).

*Board of Education for the City of Toronto and Hunt* v. *Higgs* (1959), 22 D.L.R. (2d) 49 (S.C.C.).

*Boese* v. *St. Paul's Roman Catholic School District No. 20* (1979), 97 D.L.R. (3d) 643 (Sask. Q.B.).

*Brod* v. *Central School District No. 1*, 386 N.Y.S. 2d 125 (1976 N.Y.).

*Dziwenka* v. *Regina*, [1972] S.C.R. 419 (S.C.C.).

*Everett* v. *Bucky Warren, Inc.*, 380 N.E. 2d 653 (1978 Mass.).

*F.C.* (*Litigation Guardian of*) v. *511825 Ontario Ltd.* (2003), 171 O.A.C. 119 (Ont. C.A.).

*Kowalchuk* v. *Middlesex County Board of Education* (1991). Unreported. Action No. 10064F. Ontario Court of Justice - General Division (Gautreau J.), London, Ontario, June 14, 1991.

*McKay v. Board of Govan School Unit No. 29 Saskatchewan* (1968), 64 W.W.R. 301 (S.C.C.).
*Moddejonge v. Huron County Board of Education* (1972), 25 D.L.R. (3d) 661 (Ont. H.C.J.).
*Mogabgab v. Orleans Parish School Board,* 239 So. 2d 456 (La. C.A. 1970).
*Myers v. Peel County* (1981), 17 C.C.L.T. 269 (S.C.C.).
*Petersen v. Board of School Trustees of Surrey* (1991), 89 D.L.R. (4th) 517 (B.C.S.C.).
*Poulton v. Notre Dame College* (1975), 60 D.L.R. (3d) 501 (Sask. Q.B.).
*Thomas v. Board of Education of the City of Hamilton* (1994), 20 O.R. (3d) 598 (Ont. C.A.).
*Thornton v. Board of School Trustees* (1978), 83 D.L.R. (3d) 480 (S.C.C.).
*Williams v. Eady* (1894), 10 T.L.R. 41 (C.A.).

## Secondary Literature
Brown, C. 2002–03. School board liability, the insurance crisis and accident compensation. *Education & Law Journal* 12:273–91.
Centers for Disease Control. 2004. Healthy youth. Health topics: Injury and violence: Slide presentation. Available at: www.cdc.gov/HealthyYouth/injury/slides/slides11.htm [This site is no longer active.].
Cloutier, R. 2003. Review of the Strathcona-Tweedsmuir School outdoor education program. June, 23, 2003. Bhudak Consultants Ltd. Available at: www.sts.ab.ca/sts_OE.asp [This site is no longer available.].
Court of Appeal confirms standard of care for special-needs students. 2004. *Edu-Law Newsletter* 2, no. 1:3–4. Available from Keel Cottrelle LLP, Mississauga, Ontario.
Fleming, J. 1987. *The law of torts.* 7th ed. Agincourt, ON: Carswell.
Gaustad, J. 2004. Risk management. ERIC Digest 86–February 1994. Clearinghouse on Educational Policy Management. Available at: http://eric.uoregon.edu/publications/digest086.html
Hoyano, L. 1984. The prudent parent: The elusive standard of care. *University of British Columbia Law Review* 18:1–34.
MacKay, A. W., and G. Dickinson. 1998. *Beyond the "careful parent": Tort liability in education.* Toronto: Emond Montgomery.
Metcalfe, J. 2003–04. "[T]here could not be a better definition": A defence of the careful or prudent parent standard. *Education & Law Journal* 13:257–76.
Na, G. 2003. Adventure guide: Managing the risks of outdoor school excursions. *Education Law News* (Fall): 9–13. Available from Borden Ladner Gervais LLP, Toronto, Ontario.
Ontario School Boards' Insurance Exchange. 2003. Risk management at a glance. Guelph, ON: The Author.
Roher E., and T. Hepburn. 2004. Legal liability in an era of budget cutbacks. *Capsle Comments* 13(3): 1, 3–5.

Shackelton-Verbuyst, B. G. 1999. Negligence: A study of the potential liability of physical education teachers and coaches for student injury. Unpublished Master's of Education Directed Research Project, The University of Western Ontario, London, Ontario.

Shariff, S. (2004). Travel and terror: Re-allocating, minimizing and managing risks on foreign excursions and outdoor education field trips. *Education & Law Journal* 14:137–65.

Van Holst, A., and G. Dickinson. 1988. Present practices regarding the use of protective floor covering for climbing apparatus. *Canadian Association for Health, Physical Education and Recreation Journal* (Sept./Oct.): 7–10.

Warner, M. 2001. Tobermory boating accident: A lesson in excursion safety. *Education Law News* (Fall): 1–6. Available from Borden Ladner Gervais LLP, Toronto, Ontario.

## Chapter Fifteen

# *Teaching Within the Law:*

## *The Human Rights Context of Physical and Health Education*

## Gregory M. Dickinson

### Introduction

The diversity of students today carries the corollary of an ever-expanding envelope of human rights that must be respected and modelled in school. Physical, emotional, intellectual, and other exceptionalities must be accommodated according to most provincial education acts (Smith and Foster 2003–04). Failure to do so can evoke not only appeals under such legislation but also complaints to human rights commissions and even to courts under the *Canadian Charter of Rights and Freedoms*. Moreover, rules and practices, and even curricula, that are insensitive to ethnic and religious diversity not only provoke political strife within a school community but can also be the subject of human rights litigation claiming discrimination and a failure to accommodate. Similarly, issues relating to sexuality and sexual orientation are often catalysts for conflict in schools, sometimes in health education, and can lead to involvement by human rights tribunals and the courts.[1]

### *The Duty to Accommodate Students with Disabilities*

The legal rights of students with disabilities in Canada have been the subject of many books and articles.[2] The general principles discussed here, however, should help place in a legal context the other chapters in this book that deal with the educational and practical implications of diversity in the gym and the classroom. As stated above, provincial legislation typically provides for the accommodation of students with disabilities who are formally identified as such. It is not the case, though, that the law requires such accommodation necessarily to occur in a regular classroom setting. For example, although Ontario's special education policies promote an inclusive philosophy, the law contains no such requirement.

The leading Canadian case on inclusion rights for students with disabilities is *Eaton v. Brant County Board of Education* (1995, 1997). In this case, the parents of Emily Eaton, a twelve-year-old student with profound multiple disabilities caused by cerebral palsy, brought a complaint under the *Charter* against the Brant County Board of Education when it refused to keep Emily in an integrated classroom setting at her neighbourhood school. The Board, and ultimately the Special Education Tribunal to which the parents appealed, concluded that Emily's needs were best met in a segregated special education class at a different school. The parents applied for judicial review of the tribunal's decision, arguing a violation of Emily's equality rights under section 15(1) of the *Charter*, which states:

> 15. (1) Every individual is equal before and under the law and has the right to the equal protection and equal benefit of the law without discrimination and, in particular, without discrimination based on race, national or ethnic origin, colour, religion, sex, age or mental or physical disability.

Although the Ontario Court of Appeal agreed with the parents (*Eaton* 1995) and "amended" the Ontario *Education Act* (1990) by inserting a constitutionally based presumption that exceptional students must be integrated into a regular classroom unless overridden by parental wishes, the Supreme Court of Canada (*Eaton* 1997) reversed this ruling. The Supreme Court held that, in every case, a decision whether to place a student in an integrated or segregated setting should not be based on a presumption that equality would be served only by inclusion but on the assessment of the student's bests interests under the particular circumstances. This decision gave considerable power to school personnel to determine placements based on the "best interest" principle.

Best interests are not always easy to determine, especially in the case of children whose disabilities preclude their ever achieving knowledge, skills, or abilities anywhere near those expected of their non-disabled classmates. In such cases, though, "best interests" should still include the student's *dignitary* interests and the refusal to revisit the days when children with disabilities were segregated or even kept out of sight simply because they were "different." The landmark equality rights decision of the Supreme Court of Canada, *Law v. Canada* (1999), established the general principle that discrimination occurs when differential treatment on a prohibited ground, such as disability, is based on stereotypical assumptions about a person's abilities or worth and does not afford the person the human dignity and equal care and concern to which he or she is entitled as a citizen of Canada.

The failure of teachers, schools, and boards to provide students with the means of access, equipment, resources, personnel, or modified teaching methods, learning or performance expectations and testing procedures necessary to accommodate their disabilities, can also result in claims under provincial human rights legislation that equal treatment in the provision of services or facilities is being denied.[3] Despite the fact that a student with a disability may be incapable of actually exercising the rights that he or she seeks, for example, by not being able to participate in a certain physical or sporting activity as staged, in general there is an obligation on the school to reasonably accommodate the student's disability up to the point of undue hardship, taking into consideration "cost, outside funding, if any, and health and safety requirements" (Ontario *Human Rights Code* 1990, section 17, which is typical of such provincial legislation). Hence, if an assistive device or human aide would help a student with a disability participate in an activity, the school would be obligated to provide either, considering the factors outlined above. Human rights boards of inquiry and courts have served notice that they put a very high price on human rights and will not accept financial excuses easily. On a broader scale, a school board's failure to have in place opportunities for athletes with disabilities to compete or participate in intramural or possibly even inter-school sporting activities, could amount to systemic or "constructive" discrimination.[4] If so, a duty to reasonably accommodate exists, qualified by the same criteria outlined above.

## Accommodating Religious and Cultural Diversity

Freedom of religion is explicitly protected in Canada under section 2 (a) of the *Charter*. It is also protected indirectly under equality rights provisions in the *Charter* (section 15) and in provincial human rights codes that prohibit discrimination on the basis of religion, creed, and national and ethnic origin. Flashpoints for such issues exist where classroom, gymnasium, and playing-field activities clash with the religious or cultural norms of some students. For instance, certain sports may require protective gear that is incompatible with religious apparel worn by the members of certain faiths. The uniform usually worn in gym—shorts and tee shirts—may violate the principles of modesty adhered to by certain faith groups.[5] This collision of norms may be compounded where coeducational activities are involved. Moreover, a health curriculum that openly discusses sex outside of marriage, homosexuality, and bisexuality as normal expressions of one's sexuality, and that promotes respect and equal rights for gay, lesbian, and transgendered persons is almost guaranteed to be unacceptable to a number of students and their parents. This can pose a difficult problem, especially where such classes comprise a mandatory part of the program.

Proving how central religious freedom is to our democracy, the Supreme Court of Canada was called upon very early in the *Charter*'s history to interpret the meaning of "freedom of religion." In a unanimous ruling in *R. v. Big M Drug Mart* (1985) Justice Dickson stated:

> The essence of the concept of freedom of religion is the right to entertain such religious beliefs as a person chooses, the right to declare religious beliefs openly and without fear of hindrance or reprisal, and the right to manifest belief by worship and practice or by teaching and dissemination.
>
> ...
>
> Freedom means that, subject to such limitations as are necessary to protect public safety, order, health, or morals or the fundamental rights and freedoms of others, no one is to be forced to act in a way contrary to his [or her] beliefs or his [or her] conscience. (353, 354)

Freedom of religion includes, therefore, both the *positive* right to manifest religious belief or non-belief and the *negative* right to not be forced to conform to the beliefs of anyone else (Smith and Foster 2000–01, 25). Hence, subject to the limitations within Justice Dickson's definition, especially public safety and health, school activities and curriculum content could be considered to violate the *Charter* if they amounted to a restriction on the right to manifest religious belief or coercion to reject one's own religious principles or to accept those of another religion or secular philosophy. Certainly arguments might be mounted that safety issues are involved where protective headgear is not worn or other apparel is worn that poses a safety risk (depending on the actual circumstances); that general health concerns are implicated in a curriculum that discusses the need for safer sex; or that concern for the freedom of expression and association and equality rights of others is served by a curriculum that teaches respect and support for gay rights. The real question, however, is not whether to shut down such activities and curricula because they are inconsistent with some students' and parents' beliefs and practices, but rather how they can be accommodated within them. Options exist, from creative reassignment to other activities or single-sex venues, to the provision of exemptions for those who choose to opt out of some activities or classes for religious reasons.

Equality rights under the *Charter* are also implicated because the state must not treat individuals or groups differently on the basis of prohibited grounds such as religion, race, or ethnic or national origin in a way that denies them human dignity and the equal concern and respect they deserve as members of Canadian society (*Law v. Canada* 1999). Differential treatment is possible, of course, if it benefits individuals or groups and is seen that way by them.

The right to equality is also provided under human rights codes. The kinds of examples of cultural clashes we have been discussing—for example, physical education clothing requirements' inconsistency with the apparel of some minority faith groups—generally are considered "constructive discrimination." The rules and requirements are *not intended* to discriminate and appear not to implicate religion but do so in their *effect* on some individuals or groups. The rule requiring the wearing of shorts and t-shirts is facially neutral but it has a discriminatory impact on certain groups because of their religious values. The rule in question may not be discriminatory, however, if it is a reasonable and *bona fide* qualification. The law will not consider a rule to be a reasonable and *bona fide* qualification unless the school has made reasonable attempts to accommodate the needs of affected students up to the point of undue hardship, taking into account financial cost, the availability of funds, and health and safety considerations.

Difficulties arise when the limiting factors mentioned both by Justice Dickson in *R. v. Big M.* (1985) and within the qualifying words of the duty to accommodate in human rights codes, come into play. This has been especially the case with safety. Few cases exist in this area; the most instructive is *Pandori v. Peel Board of Education* (1990), where a Khalsa Sikh student and teacher were forbidden to wear their kirpans at school.[6]  A kirpan is a ceremonial dagger the Sikh religion requires all Sikh males to carry at all times.  Like practically every school district in North America, the Peel board had a regulation forbidding the bringing of knives onto school property.[7]  Because the rule was not aimed intentionally at Sikhs but rather at the general preservation of safety, it was viewed as a form of constructive discrimination.  The mandatory nature of his religion's requirement led the student complainant to argue that the board's regulation denied him equal educational opportunity.  After hearing lengthy testimony about the board's safety concerns, the nature of Sikhism and the significance of the kirpan—which has been transformed over the years from a weapon to a symbol of power, order, and dignity—and that the use of the dagger in anger as a weapon was punishable conduct that could lead to excommunication, the human rights board of inquiry ruled in favour of the complainants.  The board of inquiry held that the school board had not shown any evidence of a kirpan's use as a weapon on school property anywhere in Canada or that it was an unacceptable safety risk amounting to undue hardship.  This ruling was upheld on appeal to the courts.[8]

The kirpan cases are admittedly different from the kinds of situations we are discussing because they involved safety issues related to the threat of school violence.  However, the fact that religious accommodation was judicially required in the face of such serious safety concerns suggests that a very heavy onus is faced by those who would attempt to rely on undue hardship as an exemption from the human rights requirement to accommodate religious diversity in the schools under *any* circumstances.

Clashes over curriculum content, such as those envisioned above regarding sex education, that pit religious and secular norms against one another, can pose serious concerns for schools.  Not only do they raise thorny questions about the place of religion in general—let alone anyone's particular religion—in guiding educational policy, they also raise the prospect that everyone's educational experiences could be modified because of the dissonant views of one or more minority groups.  It must be understood as a backdrop to the following discussion that in the public schools of most provinces (excluding Catholic schools in Ontario and elsewhere where they are publicly funded) religious instruction in a "confessional" or "devotional" sense has been eliminated from the curriculum.  For example, in Ontario, it is widely accepted that the Court of Appeal's rulings in *Zylberberg v. Sudbury Board of Education* (1988)—regarding religious opening exercises—and *C.C.L.A. v. Ontario* (1990)— regarding indoctrinating religious instruction—have judicially rendered schools secular institutions (Dickinson and Dolmage 1996).  So the curriculum-content cases that concern us in the present context are not in the nature of complaints about the schools' teaching of Christian beliefs and practices to the exclusion of other believers and non-believers, but rather the contrary: complaints that the "secular humanist" curriculum attempts to inculcate values that are inconsistent with those of many different faith groups, including conservative Christians.

In British Columbia, a school board reacted to complaints raised by religious ratepayers by banning the use of primary school learning resources that depicted stories of children with same-sex parents. In this case, the British Columbia Supreme Court quashed the board's resolution banning the books on the grounds that the board was significantly influenced by religious considerations in violation of a section of the British Columbia *Education Act* (1996). The Court of Appeal reversed this finding and the case ended up at the Supreme Court of Canada, which allowed the appeal (*Chamberlain v. Surrey School District No. 36* 2002). The Supreme Court held that the board was required to act in a way that promoted respect and tolerance for all the diverse groups that it represented. Its actions had been wrongly based on an exclusionary philosophy because of the concerns of certain parents about the morality of same-sex relationships and had ignored the interests of same-sex families and their right to receive equal respect and concern in the education system. Also crucial was the curricular goal that all children should be able to discuss openly their family models and should be taught about the diverse models of family relationships in Canadian society. The main lesson learned from the Surrey decision is that the Supreme Court determined that a school board should not permit religious objection to trump the central goals of the provincial curriculum, presumably so long as those central goals complied with *Charter* principles of equality.

It is certainly in everyone's best interest to avoid reaching the point where issues such as those discussed above require determination by human rights boards of inquiry or the courts. The best solution probably lies in the negotiation of a sensible political arrangement with the involved students and parents, so long as fundamental goals and values—such as safety, respect and tolerance—and core curricular requirements are not compromised.

## A Respectful and Harassment-Free Learning Environment

Physical and health education classes, especially in sex education, are probably more conducive than most others to behaviour and comments with sexual content or overtones. Physical contact is more likely and comments concerning sexuality are expected. They are teaching venues, therefore, in which considerable care must be exercised to ensure that students' rights are respected and an appropriate learning environment is maintained.

One of the most basic human rights afforded students under Canadian law is the right to a learning environment free from discrimination. In *Ross v. New Brunswick School Board District No. 15* (1996) the Supreme Court of Canada held that a teacher's anti-Semitic writings outside of class so poisoned the learning environment in school for Jewish students that a human rights board of inquiry was correct in ordering the school board to remove him from the classroom. Although the Court acknowledged that such a ruling violated the teacher's freedom of expression, the removal order constituted a reasonable and justifiable limit on his rights because his behaviour conflicted so fundamentally with the education system's mission to teach and model *Charter* values, including equality. Moreover, Jewish students could hardly be expected to have faith in the teacher's ability to treat them fairly. Similarly, in *Kempling v. British Columbia College of Teachers* (2004, 2005), a teacher was disciplined by the B.C. College of Teachers for publicly condemning homosexuality and gay rights. The teacher's conduct ran contrary to the core values of the education system and justified discipline. The offensive conduct and its potential harm were compounded by the fact that the teacher was also a counsellor and the College found it reasonable to infer that gay students would be reluctant to go to him for counselling. Hence his ability to carry out his role and public faith in the system he represented were compromised. The College's imposition of a one-month suspension of the teacher's certificate of qualification was upheld by both the B.C. Supreme Court and Court of Appeal.

Conduct that constitutes sexual harassment violates not only *Charter* values but also provincial human rights legislation, school board policies, and professional norms established by virtually every college of teachers or teacher's federation in the country. Some forms of harassment, involving threats, stalking, harassing phone calls or sexual assault, also constitute criminal offences under the *Criminal Code* (1990).[9] Although there can be subtle differences among definitions of sexual harassment, in general it is conduct—including words—of a sexual nature or based on gender stereotyping or hatred that is unwelcome or that the person doing the acts or making the comments ought reasonably to know is unwelcome. The Canadian Association for the Advancement of Women and Sport and Physical Activity (1994) elaborates on the concept of sexual harassment:

> Sexual harassment can be defined as unwelcome sexual advances, requests for favours, or other verbal or physical conduct of a sexual nature when:
>
> ◆ submitting to or rejecting this conduct is used as the basis for making decisions which affect the individual; or
> ◆ such conduct has the purpose or effect of interfering with an individual's performance; or
> ◆ such conduct creates an intimidating, hostile, or offensive environment.

Types of behaviour that constitute harassment include but are not limited to:

> ◆ written or verbal abuse or threats;
> ◆ the display of visual material which is offensive or which one ought to know is offensive;
> ◆ unwelcome remarks, jokes, comments, innuendo, or taunting about a person's looks, body attire...gender, or sexual orientation;
> ◆ leering or other suggestive or obscene gestures;
> ◆ condescending, paternalistic, or patronizing behaviour which undermines self-esteem, diminishes performance, or adversely affects working conditions;
> ◆ practical jokes which cause awkwardness or embarrassment, endanger a person's safety, or negatively affect performance;
> ◆ unwanted physical contact including touching, petting, pinching, or kissing;
> ◆ unwelcome sexual flirtations, advances, requests, or invitations; or
> ◆ physical or sexual assault. (8–9)

Similar kinds of behaviour that target persons because of their sexual orientation can also constitute harassment (*Jubran v. Board of Trustees* 2002).[10] Although harassment implies repeated conduct, human rights boards of inquiry have decided that a single act, if serious enough, can constitute harassment.

It is the duty of teachers not only to refrain from comments and behaviours that are discriminatory or harassing and that poison the learning environment, but as persons in positions of authority they are also expected to ensure that the students they supervise do not act that way. A teacher's failure to curb sexual discrimination or harassment or homophobic behaviour by students, thereby abetting the creation of a poisoned environment, amounts to a separate violation of human rights legislation, and no doubt professional rules of conduct and school board policies.

Sensitive to both the responsibility and vulnerability of coaches and athletic instructors concerning sexual harassment, the National Association for Sport and Physical Education (NASPE) offers the following advice aimed at providing not only a safe and harassment-free environment for students/athletes, but also protection for teachers and coaches against allegations of harassment or abuse.

◈ Use discretion when alone with an athlete, and when coaching students, try to have another coach or supervisor present.
◈ Don't touch an athlete outside of necessary touch [sic] to teach a skill.
◈ Don't drive alone with an athlete.
◈ Stay in separate sleeping quarters when travelling for athletic events.
◈ Educate your athletes about sexual harassment and encourage them to talk to you if anyone makes them uncomfortable.
◈ Document any behaviour by students directed toward you which is sexual in nature. Include witnesses, how you dealt with the situation, and who [sic] you talked to about the situation.
◈ Tell your athletic director or school principal about any accusations.
◈ Educate students/players about what sexual harassment is, providing quality examples, and about who the...person is that they should contact in such case [sic]. (National Association for Sport and Physical Education 2000, 3)[11]

Teachers of the sexuality components of health education can also face possible legal implications related to their disclosure of not only their personal views about sexuality but also their own sexual orientations. Teachers who discuss their own sexuality, or go beyond the normal bounds

of teaching and enter the realm of counselling students about personal—especially sexual—problems, run the risk of having their motivation misinterpreted. In light of the all-too-frequent reports of sexual abuse
of students, teachers are well advised to steer away from classroom discussions that disclose personal, especially sexual, information, and from engaging in counselling students about their sexual and personal problems,
unless of course they are trained and hired for that purpose. In an advisory
released in 2002 concerning sexual misconduct, the Ontario College of
Teachers offered its members the following wise counsel:

> Using good judgment
> Members understand that students depend on teachers to in-
> terpret what is right and wrong. This judgment can be difficult
> when certain acts seem innocent, but may be considered later
> as a prelude to sexual abuse or sexual misconduct. (Ontario
> College of Teachers 2002, in Allison and Mangan 2004, 246)

Members are advised by the College to consider the extent to
which their actions and words might be interpreted as an attempt "to promote or facilitate an inappropriate relationship with a student" (ibid.). In
particular, they should avoid exchanging personal notes, comments, or
emails with students, involving themselves in students' personal affairs, and
sharing personal information about themselves (ibid.). Regardless that a
teacher's real motive in discussing his or her own sexuality or in counselling
and befriending a student might have been in that student's best emotional
and educational interests, the unfortunate teacher will find that once a
complaint is lodged, perhaps years later, "reality" is what is reconstructed
through the recollections and perceptions of the complainant and other
witnesses. Thus it is important to avoid behaviour that is consistent with
the reconstruction of an evil motive.

But what if a personal disclosure by a teacher is related to curricular
objectives and overall human rights values, and is potentially protected
freedom of expression? Such a scenario can arise regarding a teacher's decision to disclose his or her own sexual orientation. MacDougall (1998) is
harshly critical of the judiciary's failure to protect homosexual expression
and visibility in education.[12] He argues in favour of the right of teachers to
identify their sexual orientation as part of a general need for increased expression in schools regarding homosexuality:

> Schools...need expression regarding homosexuality reflected in
> the teaching and materials used. They also need these materi-

als to be presented by comfortably-homosexual-identified
teachers, students and staff. The presence of positive expression about homosexuality will help counter the overwhelming
negativity that is associated with the prevailing speech regarding homosexuality, for the most part, name calling on the playground, in locker rooms, and in school board meetings.
(80–81)

It seems the only Canadian case that has dealt with the issue of a
teacher's legal right to disclose her sexual orientation to her students is *Assiniboine South Teachers' Assn. of the Manitoba Teachers' Society v. Assiniboine South School Division No. 3* (1997, 2000). In that case the school
board turned down the grade 7 and 8 teacher's request to disclose to her
students that she was lesbian. Although the case raised important *Charter*
issues of freedom of expression and equality rights, unfortunately the Arbitration Board decided that the issue was really a question of management
rights and therefore that it had no jurisdiction to hear the grievance, so the
merits were never considered in the arbitration award given by the majority
of the board. The board's decision was upheld by the Manitoba Court of
Appeal. It is worth noting that the dissenting member of the Arbitration
Board—although it is probably fair to assume that she was the grievor's
nominee—would have upheld the grievance on the basis that the em-
ployer's actions were discriminatory and unjustified by any legitimate
interest.

Given the Supreme Court's stance toward gay rights in a series of
recent cases, it is reasonable to conclude that the denial of a right to disclose one's sexual identity could well be viewed as a violation of equality
rights and that the onus then would fall to the board to show that its limitation on such disclosure was reasonable and justified. Though there appears
to be no Canadian case directly on point, such a disclosure might even be
protected expression under section 2 (b) of the *Charter* in the nature of "academic freedom." Based on United States constitutional jurisprudence,
Clarke (1998–99) argues that teachers might well enjoy freedom of expression in the classroom so long as it complies with the "legitimate pedagogical
concerns" principle, which the American courts have found to be com-
posed of several critical concerns: the "'fair and objective presentation of
materials'"; the "'appropriateness of the materials'"; the "'general control of
the curriculum'"; and, whether there is "'material and substantial disrup-
tion'" (356–357). In his view, such criteria would play an important role in
determining whether an interference with freedom of expression was reasonable and justified under the test for applying section 1 of the *Charter*.[13]

It is significant that a teacher's disclosure of his or her sexual orientation becomes a relevant ethical and legal point of contention only when the teacher is gay or lesbian. Disclosure of one's heterosexuality generally is ethically and legally unremarkable, thus setting up a classic double standard. Moreover, a teacher's heterosexuality routinely is implicitly disclosed and validated in a school's culture through the sharing of family photographs, wedding announcements, bridal and baby showers and so on.

In summary, it seems unlikely that disclosure of sexual orientation alone would provide grounds for any disciplinary action, unless done for improper motives unconnected to the curriculum, and unless followed up by conduct that breached the boundaries of teacher-student relationships governing all teachers' conduct, as discussed above.

## Conclusion

Over the past forty years human rights have become increasingly prominent in Canadian society. Part of the explanation for this lies in the growing diversity of the population and resulting demands that cultural, linguistic, religious, and gender differences be recognized and respected. The enactment of provincial human rights codes beginning in the 1960s, and especially the arrival of the federal *Canadian Charter of Rights and Freedoms* in 1982, helped create a "group rights" consciousness that forms a strong part of the Canadian identity.

The impact of human rights has been felt in schools as elsewhere. This chapter has discussed several human rights implications affecting physical and health education teachers. Although human rights issues concern all teachers, some have particular application for physical and health education. Some students reject the clothing requirements normally associated with certain physical education activities because of their impact on the norms of decency adhered to by the students' religions or cultures. Human rights laws forbid the unequal treatment of persons based on their religion, creed, or ethnicity and require that they be reasonably accommodated, including at school, up to the point of "undue hardship." Creative solutions are required to accommodate diversity while, at the same time, ensuring that important curricular objectives and safety concerns are met.

Heightened awareness of human rights has also resulted in the increasing inclusion of students with special needs within regular classroom settings. Students with disabilities are protected against discrimination on the basis of their disabilities under both human rights codes and section 15 of the *Charter*. Although the general expectation is that students' disabilities must be accommodated, the Supreme Court of Canada has held that "the best interests of the child" principle is the paramount concern, displacing any presumed legal requirement that children with disabilities must always be placed in a regular classroom setting or treated precisely as their school mates without disabilities. Indeed, equal educational opportunity may sometimes require that children with disabilities be treated differently from their classmates. Physical educators, assisted by technology, have creatively derived ways of ensuring that the educational and safety needs of students with disabilities are met, while enhancing their human dignity—the core of true equality—through their meaningful inclusion in physical education and sporting activities. This is the essence of the legal obligation to accommodate.

Health educators face particular human rights challenges related to the curriculum they are mandated to teach. The contents of curriculum units on family life and sexuality are sometimes offensive to students and their families because of the dissonance between the implicit, if not explicit, moral stances in the curriculum and the students' and families' religious beliefs. Teachers can find themselves dealt a seemingly impossible task—mediating a collision between the beliefs of a particular religious group and the general secular values of equality, tolerance, and respect found in the *Charter*, which the Supreme Court of Canada has said form the core values of the education system. The dissonant views of some cannot be allowed to call the educational tune for all and, sometimes, where freedom of religion is truly at stake, the only answer may be an exemption from attending the classes or studying the material found to be offensive.

Lastly, educators play an important role in fostering human rights and equal educational opportunity by ensuring that the educational environment is not poisoned by harassment based on gender or sexual orientation. Physical and health education classes sometimes provide fertile ground for harassment, given the politics of competition and athleticism, the apparel and physical actions associated with gym class and athletics, and the sexual nature of some of the content in the health education curriculum. Teachers have a professional and legal obligation not only to refrain from actions and words that comprise sexual harassment but also to deal effectively with such conduct by their students.

Physical and health education teachers and coaches are often more vulnerable to accusations of improper touching or personal relationships with students by virtue of the physical skills they teach, the subjects they discuss, and the opportunities for mistaken perceptions by students and others. It is important that physical education and health teachers and coaches heed suggestions, like those provided in this chapter, for safeguarding themselves against false allegations of sexual harassment or abuse.

Human rights are a fundamental part of Canadian democracy and belong to us all. They should not be viewed as posing problems, but rather as offering solutions and opportunities. Accommodation of diversity leads to richer, more inclusive educational experiences for the broadest possible array of students. Although safety and individual students' best interests must always be borne in mind, administrative inconvenience and financial costs are poor excuses for denying students respect for their fundamental human dignity.

## CONCLUSION TO CHAPTERS FOURTEEN AND FIFTEEN

I shall end where I began: by exhorting you to "teach within the law." There are considerable legal incentives for doing so, including avoiding liability for damages for negligence, and professional and employment discipline for human rights complaints. But even more compelling is the thought, rightly held, that teaching within the law is the best way to ensure a safe, welcoming, and productive learning environment—something that ought to be the mission of all educators.

By no means have these two chapters provided an exhaustive look at all areas of the law that may be implicated in the day-to-day lives of teachers of physical and health education. Moreover, law is a dynamic social force. It is constantly changing, we hope for the better. My final words, then, are to urge you, as part of your professional development, to remain up-to-date about your legal responsibilities. You owe it to yourselves, but, most of all, you owe it to your students.

### Notes

1.  I must emphasize, however, that the comments I make below regarding accommodation of religious diversity and sexual orientation appertain mostly to non-Roman Catholic public schools. At the risk of over-generalization, Catholic schools and private schools usually are able to avail themselves of constitutionally entrenched denominational educational rights (in the case of Catholic schools in some provinces), and *bona fide* and reasonable qualification provisions in provincial human rights codes (in the case of both types of schools),

in order to exempt themselves from the legal obligation to treat people equally. However, in claiming such exemption the onus is on Catholic and private schools to show that the particular reason they excluded or preferred a person on what otherwise would be a prohibited ground—sexual orientation, for example—was truly a matter of denominational rights or a *bona fide* qualification based on the nature of their organization. This is a complicated area of human rights law that cannot and need not be explored any further in a chapter of this scope. Readers wishing to do so, however, should see Smith and Foster (1999–2000; 2000–01a; 2000–01b).

2.   For a detailed discussion of such rights see, e.g., Williams and Macmillan (1999–2000; 2002–03). For a comprehensive explanation of the legal issues involved in Ontario's special education system, see Bowlby et al. (2001).

3.   See, e.g., Ontario's *Human Rights Code* (1990), section 1.

4.   Constructive discrimination occurs where a facially neutral requirement, rule, or other factor has the effect of excluding a person on the basis of a prohibited ground. So, although an intramural sports league probably would not have a rule barring students with disabilities, the nature of the sport itself and its general rules of play may have that very effect.

5.   See, e.g., Yazdani (2004).

6.   For a detailed discussion of this case, see Brown and Zuker (2002), 224–249.

7.   Indeed, possession of a "weapon" is grounds for mandatory expulsion under Ontario's safe schools reforms enacted in 2000: see *Education Act* (1990), section 309.

8.   A similar ruling occurred in Alberta in *Tuli v. St. Albert (Protestant Board of Education)* (1985), but different conclusions were reached in Manitoba in *Hothi v. R.* (1985) (regarding the wearing of a kirpan in a courtroom) and in Quebec in *Quebec (Commission scolaire Marguerite-Bourgeois v. Multani* (2004). For a critical comment on the *Multani* decision, see Smith (2004).

9.   See sections 151 (sexual interference), 152 (invitation to sexual touching), 153 (sexual exploitation), 153.1 (sexual exploitation of a person with a disability), 271 (sexual assault), 264 (criminal harassment), and 372(3) (harassing telephone calls).

10.  In this case, however, the decision of the human rights tribunal was overturned based on the court's view that there had been no harassment on the basis of sexual orientation because the boy subjected to homophobic comments was in fact heterosexual: *North Vancouver School District No. 44 v. Jubran* (2003). I have criticized this decision (see Dickinson 2003–04) and it has been reversed on appeal: *North Vancouver School District No. 44 v. Jubram* (2005).

11.  The Women's Sports Foundation offers a coach's self-assessment for determining whether one is crossing the line with an athlete. Though aimed at coaches, the questions and analysis also apply broadly to others, including teachers who

work closely with vulnerable populations and for whom crossing boundaries is a critical concern. Available at: www.womenssportsfoundation.org/cgi-bin/iowa/issues/coach/article.html?record=27

12. MacDougall's criticism is based largely on the Alberta Court of Appeal's ruling in *Vriend v. Alberta* (1996) upholding a religion-based college's termination of a gay teacher for failure to comply with its rules prohibiting homosexuality. However, the Supreme Court of Canada reversed the ruling, implying sexual orientation as a prohibited ground of discrimination in the Alberta *Individual's Rights Protection Act* (1980): *Vriend v. Alberta* (1998).

13. The "*Oakes* test" involves asking: (1) Is the governmental purpose in limiting the right in question sufficiently important, disclosing a pressing and substantial concern? (2) Is there a rational connection between the purpose and the law or rule that seeks to achieve it? (3) Is there a proper proportionality between the importance of the governmental purpose and the seriousness of the rights violation—could the purpose be achieved by a means that violated rights less? See *R. v. Oakes* (1986).

# References

## Statutes

*Canadian Charter of Rights and Freedoms*, Part I of the *Constitution Act, 1982*, being ScheduleB of the *Constitution Act, 1982* (U.K.), c. 11.
*Education Act* (Ontario), R.S.O. 1990, c. E.2.
*Human Rights Code* (Ontario), R.S.O. 1990, c. H.19.
*Individual's Rights Protection Act* (Alberta), R.S.A. 1980, c. I-2.
*School Act* (British Columbia), R.S.B.C. 1996, c. 412.

## Cases

*Assiniboine South Teachers' Assn. of the Manitoba Teachers' Society v. Assiniboine South School Division No. 3* (1997), 64 L.A.C. (4th) 155.
*Assiniboine South Teachers' Assn. of the Manitoba Teachers' Society v. Assiniboine South School Division No. 3* (2000), 187 D.L.R. (4th) 169 (Man. C.A.).
*Chamberlain v. Surrey School District No. 36* (2002), 221 D.L.R. (4th) 156 (S.C.C.).
*Commission scolaire Marguerite-Bourgeois v. Multani* (2004). Unreported. Montreal 500-09-012386-025, March 4, 2004 (Que. C. A.).
*Eaton v. Brant County Board of Education* (1995), 22 D.L.R. (3d) 1 (Ont. C.A.).
*Eaton v. Brant County*, [1997] 1 S.C.R. 241 (S.C.C.).
*Hothi v. R.* (1985), 33 Man. R. (2d) 180 (Man. Q.B.).
*Jubran v. Board of Trustees* (2002). Unreported. British Columbia Human Rights Tribunal (C. Roberts), April 8, 2002.
*Kempling v. British Columbia College of Teachers* (2004), 27 B.C.L.R. (4th) 139 (B.C.S.C.).

*Kempling v. British Columbia College of Teachers* (2005), 255 D.L.R. (4th) 169 (B.C.C.A.).

*Law v. Canada*, [1999] 1 S.C.R. 497 (S.C.C.).

*North Vancouver School District No. 44 v. Jubran* (2003), 9 B.C.L.R. (4th) 338 (B.C.S.C.).

*North Vancouver School District No. 44 v. Jubran* (2005), 39 B.C.L.R. (4th) 153 (B.C.C.A.).

*Pandori v. Peel Board of Education* (1990), 12 C.H.R.R. D/364 (Ont. H.R. Comm.).

*R. v. Big M Drug Mart*, [1985] 1 S.C.R. 295 (S.C.C.).

*R. v. Oakes*, [1986] 1 S.C.R. 103 (S.C.C.).

*Ross v. New Brunswick School District No. 15*, [1996] 1 S.C.R. 825 (S.C.C.).

*Tuli v. St. Albert (Protestant Board of Education)* (1985), 8 C.H.R.R. D/3736 (H. R. Bd. of Inq.).

*Vriend v. Alberta* (1996), 141 D.L.R. (4th) 44 (Alta. C.A.).

*Vriend v. Alberta*, [1998] 4 S.C.R. 493 (S.C.C.).

*Zylberberg v. Sudbury Board of Education* (1988), 65 O.R. (2d) 641 (Ont. C.A.).

**Secondary Literature**

Bowlby, B., C. Peters, and M. Mackinnon. 2001. *An educator's guide to special education law*. Toronto: Canada Law Book

Brown, A., and M. Zuker, 2002. *Education law*. 3rd ed. Toronto: Carswell.

Canadian Association for the Advancement of Women and Sport and Physical Activity. 1994. *Harassment in sport: A guide to policies, procedures and resources*. Gloucester, ON: The Author.

Clarke, P. 1998–99. Canadian public school teachers and free speech: Part III–A constitutional law analysis. *Education & Law Journal* 9:315–82.

Dickinson, G. 2003-04. Homophobic harassment of heterosexual victim not proscribed under Human Rights Code. *Education & Law Journal* 13:127–29.

Dickinson, G., and W. R. Dolmage. 1996. Education, religion and the courts in Ontario. *Canadian Journal of Education* 21:363–83.

MacDougall, B. 1998. Silence in the classroom: Limits on homosexual expression and visibility in education and the privileging of homophobic religious ideology. *Saskatchewan Law Review* 61:41–86.

National Association for Sport and Physical Education. 2000. Sexual harassment in athletic settings: A statement from the National Association for Sports and Physical Education (NASPE). Available at: www.aahperd.org/naspe/pdf_files/pos_papers/sex-harr.pdf

Ontario College of Teachers. 2002. Professional advisory: Professional misconduct related to sexual abuse and sexual misconduct. In *Legal digest for Ontario educators 2004-2005*, ed. D. Allison and J. Mangan, London, ON: The Althouse Press.

Smith, W. 2004. Balancing security and human rights: Quebec schools between past and future. *Education & Law Journal* 14:99–136.

Smith, W., and W. Foster. 2003–04. Equal opportunity and the school house: Part 1—Exploring the contours of equality rights. *Education & Law Journal* 13:1–75.

———. 1999–2000. Part I—Religion and education in Canada: The traditional framework. *Education & Law Journal* 10:393–447.

———. 2000–01a. Religion and education in Canada: Part II—An alternative framework for the debate. *Education & Law Journal* 11:1–67.

———. 2000–01b. Religion and education in Canada: Part III—An analysis of provincial legislation. *Education & Law Journal* 11:203–261.

Williams, M., and R. Macmillan. 1999–2000. Part I—Litigation in special education (1978-1995): From access to inclusion. *Education & Law Journal* 10:349–69.

———. 2002–2003. Litigation in special education between 1996–1998: The quest for equality. *Education & Law Journal* 12:293–317.

Yazdani, A. 2004. Muslim women find fitness. *The London Free Press*, 27 September, A9.

# Contributors

**Andy Anderson,** Ph.D., has been an Associate Professor at the Ontario Insitute for Studies in Education at the University of Toronto for the last ten years and has been dedicated to research addressing the question, "How can schools and districts be transformed through health promotion initiatives into organizations that have the capacity to continuously improve their practices?" Projects currently underway in the Caribbean and El Salvador continue to inform his work in Canada and around the world that health is much more than the absences of disease—it is about the dignity of human life. Literacy for and through health reflects this fundamental human effort and forms the basis for his activities as a teacher educator, consultant, and speaker.

**David Booth** is Professor Emeritus at the Ontario Institute for Studies in Education of the University of Toronto where he is the Scholar in Residence in the Department of Curriculum, Teaching and Learning. For over thirty years, Professor Booth has been involved in education, as a classroom teacher, language arts consultant, professor, speaker, and author. During his academic career, he has written widely on language and the arts in education, and has won several awards for his classroom teaching, for his contributions to the teaching of reading, and for his books for young people.

**Gregory M. Dickinson,** B.A. (Hon.), LL.B., Ed.D., of the Bar of Ontario is a Professor in the Faculty of Education at The University of Western Ontario, where he has taught Education Law and Social Foundations of Education since 1983. Professor Dickinson has also been a faculty member in the Faculty of Law at Western, where he was Director of the Clinical Legal Education Program and The London Legal Clinic. The co-author and co-editor of several books on education and the law, including *Understanding the Law* (1989, 1996), *Rights, Freedoms, and the Education System in Canada*

Stones in the Sneaker

(1989), and *Beyond the "Careful Parent": Tort Liability in Education* (1998), he is also the founding Editor in Chief of the *Education & Law Journal* published three times a year by Thomson Carswell Canada since 1988.

**Donna L. Goodwin** is an Associate Professor in the College of Kinesiology at the University of Saskatchewan. She teaches in the area of adapted physical activity. Professor Goodwin is particularly interested in qualitative inquiry and its methodological significance for understanding the subjective experience of physical activity by persons with disabilities. She is currently completing a series of studies focusing on the messages received by youth with physical disabilities about what their bodies can do, how the messages are interpreted by the youth, and the significance of the messages for their understanding of physical potential.

**Paul Gustafson** is a graduate student at the University of Saskatchewan in the College of Kinesiology. His research interests are in the area of physical activity and persons with spinal cord injuries. He is currently researching the meaning young adults with spinal cord injuries give to physical activity opportunities during the transition from rehabilitation back to their home communities.

**Joannie Halas,** Ph.D., is an Associate Professor in the Faculty of Physical Education and Recreation Studies at the University of Manitoba. As a research affiliate in the faculty's Health, Leisure and Human Performance Research Institute, Professor Halas's research program investigates the quality and cultural relevance of physical education for marginalized youth. She incorporates culturally relevant pedagogy, critical race theories, case study, and participatory action research as a means to inform her teaching, research, and community service. As a personal commitment to social and economic justice, she actively works to enhance access to post secondary education for under-represented groups in physical education.

**Brianne N. Hamilton** is a graduate student at the University of Saskatchewan in the College of Kinesiology. Her research interests are in the area of sport biomechanics for persons with disabilities. She is currently researching the biomechanics for the free throw in wheelchair basketball.

**Tim Hopper,** Ph.D., is currently an Assistant Professor at the University of Victoria in the School of Physical Education. Formerly, he was a secondary physical educator in the United Kingdom. His research interests include: examining the links between student teachers' prior experiences of being taught and their forming practices of teaching; school-integrated teacher education focused on situated learning and communties of practice; and, teaching games for understanding. His related publications include The Grid: Reflecting from Pre-Service Teachers' Past Experiences of Being Taught, *JOPERD* (1999) and Personal Construct Psychology as a Reflective Method in Learning to Teach: A Story of De-Centering 'Self' as a PE Teacher, *AVANTE* (2001).

**M. Louise Humbert** is an Associate Professor in the College of Kinesiology at the University of Saskatchewan. She previously spent ten years teaching physical education and health to high school students. Her research interests are focused on the integral role that schools can play in offering children and youth the knowledge, skills, and opportunities to be physically active. She is also interested in the health and physical activity patterns of girls and young women, and conducts research in this area using an array of research methods.

**Jennifer D. Irwin,** Ph.D., C.P.C.C., is an Assistant Professor in Health Sciences at The University of Western Ontario. Formally trained as a health behaviourist and life coach, her current areas of research include three streams: childhood and youth obesity; physical activity and university students; and, life coaching and health-related behaviours.

**Beverly D. Leipert,** Ph.D., R.N., holds the first and only Chair in North America in Rural Women's Health Research. Her research program focuses on rural women's health from social determinants and empowerment perspectives. Dr. Leipert has published widely and presented at many national and international conferences on the topics of rural women's health and community health nursing.

**Helen Jefferson Lenskyj** is a recreational athlete, and a Professor at the Ontario Institute for Studies in Education at the University of Toronto. She has written seven books, as well as numerous articles and book chapters, on women, sport, and sexuality; Olympic industry critiques; feminist pedagogy; and, physical and health education. Her most recent book is entitled *A Lot to Learn: Girls, Women and Education in the 20th Century* (2005).

**Chunlei Lu,** Ph.D., is currently an Assistant Professor at the School of Human Kinetics, Faculty of Health Sciences, University of Ottawa. He obtained a B.Ed. and a M.Ed. in China, a M.Sc. in the United States, and a Ph.D. in Canada. He has rich lived experiences in teaching and research in the East and the West. He has authored a textbook, three refereed book chapters, and twenty refereed papers. He has strong research interests in the inter-related areas of physical education pedagogy, holistic health, and cross-cultural studies. He takes a comprehensive approach to the understanding of physical activity and health from the perspectives of both Eastern (e.g., Buddhism, Confucianism, Daoism, Eastern martial arts and meditation) and Western discourses (e.g., postmodernism, postcolonialism, poststructuralism, hermeneutics, and somatics).

**Nancy Melnychuk,** Ph.D., is an Associate Professor in the Faculty of Education at the University of Alberta. As Coordinator of Secondary School Physical Education, her research program focuses on teacher education and physical education; bridging the gap between theory and practice while involving schools, inservice and preservice teachers; and, students as research partners. She continues to mentor many graduate students from different parts of the world and enjoys an active lifestyle with her husband and daughter.

**Joanne Y. Pelletier,** Ph.D., was an Assistant Professor in the School of Education at Acadia University at the time she wrote her chapter for this book. Her research focuses on teaching inclusive physical education. She is the facilitator of the pre-service, teacher-generated group called S.T.R.I.P.E. (Student Teachers Researching in Inclusive Physical Education) and is currently working on a government project in the province of Nova Scotia.

**Marnie Rutledge** teaches part-time at the University of Alberta in the Faculty of Education and the Faculty of Physical Education and Recreation, primarily in pedagogy and dance. She holds a Ph.D. from the University of Alberta. Her doctoral work, "Dance as Research: The Experience of Surrender," used intrinsic dance, or improvisational movement to explore participant experiences of surrender. She has always been interested in the role of the body in knowing, and how we might understand through dance. Her areas of interest include: rhythm and movement, popular dancing, artistic sport, arts-based research, and alternate forms of representing research. Dr. Rutledge is a former chair of the Dance Committee of CAHPERD, and has been involved in Synchro Canada. She continues to be involved in issues surrounding physical education—particularly dance education—through local, provincial, national, and international associations.

**Kathy Sanford,** Ed.D., is currently an Associate Professor at the University of Victoria in the Department of Curriculm and Instruction. Formerly, she was an elementary and junior high school teacher in Alberta with a focus on Langage Arts curriculum. Her research interests include: feminist teacher education; school-integrated teacher education; student assessment and evaluation; and, gender and literacy. Dr. Sanford's recent publications include Morphing Literacy: Boys Reshaping Their School-Based Literacy Practices (with H. Blair), *Language Arts* (2004), and Teachers as Products of Their Schooling: Disrupting Gendered Positions, *NCTE Journal* (2002).

**Ellen Singleton,** Ph.D., is currently Chair of Preservice Education in the Faculty of Education at The University of Western Ontario. She teaches pedagogy classes to undergraduate students majoring in high school physical education and with her colleague, Aniko Varpalotai, teaches classes in research methods to graduate students. Dr. Singleton's research interests focus on how issues of gender, sexuality, competition, and moral decision making influence the work of female physical educators. Also, she is interested in exploring how cultural conceptions of female participation in sport and physical activity have been shaped by depictions of girls and women in juvenile series books and other literature for children from the previous century.

**Laura Tryssenaar,** P.H.Ec., B.A.Sc., B.Ed., M.Ed., Ph.D., is a professional home economist and recently retired secondary school teacher of family studies. Dr. Tryssenaar has written family studies curriculum at the board, region, and ministry levels, collaborated on a Healthy Active Living course integrating family studies and health education, and co-authored *Parenting* *in Canada: Human Growth and Development.* Her passion for curriculum led her to complete her M.Ed. and Ph.D. in Education at The University of Western Ontario where she has served as a preservice instructor in both health and family studies.

**Patricia Tucker** is a Master of Arts candidate (2005) at The University of Western Ontario, with a focus on health promotion. Her current areas of research include childhood and youth obesity, and physical activity and university students. She intends to continue with these streams of research for her Ph.D. dissertation.

**Cheryl van Daalen,** R.N., B.Sc.N., M.A., Ph.D., is an Assistant Professor in the School of Nursing, York University. Dr. van Daalen is Special Advisor on Child and Youth Health for the Canadian Coalition for the Rights of Children. Her research interests include: child rights, women's health, girls and sport, ecofeminism, oppression and mental health. Her doctoral dissertation is entitled "Living as a Chameleon: A Feminist Analysis of Young Women's Lived Experience of Anger."

**Aniko Varpalotai,** B.A./B.P.H.E., M.A., Ph.D., is an Associate Professor at the Faculty of Education, The University of Western Ontario. She teaches in the areas of education policies, research methods, gender issues in education, and health education. Her research interests include equity issues and rural education. She lives on a farm and raises goats in rural Ontario.